CSR and Management Accounting Challenges in a Time of Global Crises

Ionica Oncioiu
Titu Maiorescu University, Romania

IGI Global
PUBLISHER of TIMELY KNOWLEDGE

A volume in the Advances in Finance, Accounting, and Economics (AFAE) Book Series

Published in the United States of America by
IGI Global
Business Science Reference (an imprint of IGI Global)
701 E. Chocolate Avenue
Hershey PA, USA 17033
Tel: 717-533-8845
Fax: 717-533-8661
E-mail: cust@igi-global.com
Web site: http://www.igi-global.com

Library of Congress Cataloging-in-Publication Data

Names: Oncioiu, Ionica, 1972- editor.
Title: CSR and management accounting challenges in a time of global crises / Ionica Oncioiu, editor.
Description: Hershey, PA : Business Science Reference, [2021] | Includes bibliographical references and index. | Summary: "This book presents an interdisciplinary perspective of the various theoretical and practical approaches of management accounting and its impact in the 21st century on different areas of activity, including sustainable performance faced by the current business environment, and in particular management corporations"-- Provided by publisher.
Identifiers: LCCN 2021021760 (print) | LCCN 2021021761 (ebook) | ISBN 9781799880691 (hardcover) | ISBN 9781799880707 (paperback) | ISBN 9781799880714 (ebook)
Subjects: LCSH: Managerial accounting. | Social responsibility of business.
Classification: LCC HF5657.4 .C795 2021 (print) | LCC HF5657.4 (ebook) | DDC 658.15/11--dc23
LC record available at https://lccn.loc.gov/2021021760
LC ebook record available at https://lccn.loc.gov/2021021761

This book is published in the IGI Global book series Advances in Finance, Accounting, and Economics (AFAE) (ISSN: 2327-5677; eISSN: 2327-5685)

British Cataloguing in Publication Data
A Cataloguing in Publication record for this book is available from the British Library.

Advances in Finance, Accounting, and Economics (AFAE) Book Series

Ahmed Driouchi
Al Akhawayn University, Morocco

ISSN:2327-5677
EISSN:2327-5685

Mission

In our changing economic and business environment, it is important to consider the financial changes occurring internationally as well as within individual organizations and business environments. Understanding these changes as well as the factors that influence them is crucial in preparing for our financial future and ensuring economic sustainability and growth.

The **Advances in Finance, Accounting, and Economics (AFAE)** book series aims to publish comprehensive and informative titles in all areas of economics and economic theory, finance, and accounting to assist in advancing the available knowledge and providing for further research development in these dynamic fields.

Coverage

- E-Accounting
- Field Research
- Finance
- Economics of Intellectual Property Rights
- Fiscal Policy
- Auditing
- Entrepreneurship in Accounting and Finance
- Economic Theory
- Economics of Migration and Spatial Mobility
- Macroeconomics

IGI Global is currently accepting manuscripts for publication within this series. To submit a proposal for a volume in this series, please contact our Acquisition Editors at Acquisitions@igi-global.com or visit: http://www.igi-global.com/publish/.

The Advances in Finance, Accounting, and Economics (AFAE) Book Series (ISSN 2327-5677) is published by IGI Global, 701 E. Chocolate Avenue, Hershey, PA 17033-1240, USA, www.igi-global.com. This series is composed of titles available for purchase individually; each title is edited to be contextually exclusive from any other title within the series. For pricing and ordering information please visit http://www.igi-global.com/book-series/advances-finance-accounting-economics/73685. Postmaster: Send all address changes to above address.

Titles in this Series

For a list of additional titles in this series, please visit:
http://www.igi-global.com/book-series/advances-finance-accounting-economics/73685

Handbook of Research on Developing Circular, Digital, and Green Economies in Asia
Patricia Ordóñez de Pablos (The University of Oviedo, Spain)
Business Science Reference • ©2022 • 400pp • H/C (ISBN: 9781799886785) • US $225.00

Handbook of Research on Climate Change and the Sustainable Financial Sector
Odunayo Magret Olarewaju (Durban University of Technology, South Africa) and Idris Olayiwola Ganiyu (University of KwaZulu-Natal, South Africa)
Business Science Reference • ©2021 • 573pp • H/C (ISBN: 9781799879671) • US $295.00

Impact of Global Issues on International Trade
Ahu Coşkun Özer (Marmara University, Turkey)
Business Science Reference • ©2021 • 325pp • H/C (ISBN: 9781799883142) • US $215.00

Handbook of Research on the Empirical Aspects of Strategic Trade Negotiations and Management
Nuno Crespo (ISCTE – Instituto Universitário de Lisboa, Portugal) and Nadia Simoes (ISCTE – Instituto Universitário de Lisboa, Portugal)
Business Science Reference • ©2021 • 446pp • H/C (ISBN: 9781799875680) • US $265.00

Handbook of Research on Financial Management During Economic Downturn and Recovery
Nuno Miguel Teixeira (Center for Research in Business and Administration, School of Business Sciences, Polytechnic Institute of Setúbal, Portugal) and Inês Lisboa (CARME, School of Management and Technology, Polytechnic of Leiria, Portugal)
Business Science Reference • ©2021 • 566pp • H/C (ISBN: 9781799866435) • US $295.00

Understanding the Active Economy and Emerging Research on the Value of Sports, Recreation, and Wellness
David J. Finch (Mount Royal University, Canada) and David Legg (Mount Royal University, Canada)
Business Science Reference • ©2021 • 312pp • H/C (ISBN: 9781799879398) • US $225.00

Applied Doughnut Economics and Neuroeconomic Psychology for Business and Politics
Torben Larsen (DEALs Online Collaborative Platform, Denmark)
Business Science Reference • ©2021 • 257pp • H/C (ISBN: 9781799864240) • US $195.00

IGI Global
PUBLISHER of TIMELY KNOWLEDGE

701 East Chocolate Avenue, Hershey, PA 17033, USA
Tel: 717-533-8845 x100 • Fax: 717-533-8661
E-Mail: cust@igi-global.com • www.igi-global.com

Editorial Advisory Board

Table of Contents

Preface xv

Acknowledgment xx

Chapter 1
Ensuring the Quality of Information by Creating a Sustainable Framework in the Context of CSR Reporting 1
Nicoleta Farcane, West University of Timisoara, Romania
Ovidiu Constantin Bunget, West University of Timisoara, Romania
Rodica Blidisel, West University of Timisoara, Romania
Alin Constantin Dumitrescu, West University of Timisoara, Romania
Delia Deliu, West University of Timisoara, Romania
Oana Bogdan, West University of Timisoara, Romania
Valentin Burca, West University of Timisoara, Romania

Chapter 2
E-Accounting: Future Challenges and Perspectives 35
Dan Ioan Topor, 1 Decembrie 1918 University, Romania
Umair Akram, Jiangsu University, China
Melinda Timea Fülop, Babes-Bolyai University, Romania
Sorinel Căpușneanu, 1 Decembrie 1918 University, Romania
Constantin Aurelian Ionescu, Hyperion University of Bucharest, Romania

Chapter 3
Reviving Green With Accounting in the Era of Sustainability 53
Mansi Shah, Amity University, Jharkhand, India

Chapter 4
Using Digital Programs and Technologies to Simulate Business Development 71
Ionica Oncioiu, Titu Maiorescu University, Romania
Mihaela Mirela Dogaru, Titu Maiorescu University, Romania
Manoela Popescu, Independent Researcher, Belgium

Chapter 5
CSR and Greenwashing in Finland: Analysis About the Public Discussions of Greenwashing.......... 88
Rauno Rusko, University of Lapland, Finland

Chapter 6
CSR in the Tourism Industry 103
Andreea Marin-Pantelescu, Bucharest University of Economic Studies, Romania

Chapter 7
Flexible Budget: Management Method for Cost Control and Monitoring the Performance of Economic Entities 128
Mariana Zamfir, Valahia University of Targoviste, Romania
Constantin Aurelian Ionescu, Hyperion University of Bucharest, Romania
Nicoleta Luminita Gudanescu Nicolau, Romanian Academy, Romania
Sorina Geanina Stanescu, Valahia University of Targoviste, Romania
Liliana Paschia, Hyperion University of Bucharest, Romania
Mihaela Denisa Coman, Valahia University of Targoviste, Romania
Alexandra Delia Bugnariu, 1 Decembrie 1918 University, Romania

Chapter 8
Business Model in a Time of Global Crises 156
Ionica Oncioiu, Titu Maiorescu University, Romania
Mihaela Mirela Dogaru, Titu Maiorescu University, Romania
Manoela Popescu, Independent Researcher, Belgium

Chapter 9
Top Seven Trends in Management Accounting 173
Gary Cokins, Analytics-Based Performance Management LLC, USA

Chapter 10
A Qualitative Research on Sectoral Problems and Expectations... 189
Fahri Özsungur, Mersin University, Turkey
Himmet Karadal, Bolu Abant İzzet Baysal University, Turkey

Chapter 11
A Vision Regarding the Role of Financial-Accounting Practices in Tourism 208
Traian Ovidiu Calotă, Titu Maiorescu University, Romania

Chapter 12
The Budget: The Basic Element of Management Accounting... 219
Alin Eliodor Tănase, Titu Maiorescu University, Romania

Chapter 13
Managerial Accounting: An Integral Part of the Decision-Making Process 233
Traian Ovidiu Calotă, Titu Maiorescu University, Romania

Compilation of References 247

About the Contributors 270

Index 276

Detailed Table of Contents

Preface xv

Acknowledgment xx

Chapter 1
Ensuring the Quality of Information by Creating a Sustainable Framework in the Context of CSR Reporting 1
Nicoleta Farcane, West University of Timisoara, Romania
Ovidiu Constantin Bunget, West University of Timisoara, Romania
Rodica Blidisel, West University of Timisoara, Romania
Alin Constantin Dumitrescu, West University of Timisoara, Romania
Delia Deliu, West University of Timisoara, Romania
Oana Bogdan, West University of Timisoara, Romania
Valentin Burca, West University of Timisoara, Romania

This chapter aims to identify basic pillars around which issues related to non-financial reporting are going to be outlined by testing the quality of information presented by the top 50 largest listed companies according to non-financial reporting criteria, considering the environment, human and social resources, human rights, and the fight against corruption. By highlighting the diversity of information disclosed by the corporations (i.e., the economic, social, and environmental impact caused by the daily activities carried out), common benchmarks that determine the quality assurance are ascertained. Research methods include quantitative analysis of the sustainability reports, along with the authors' observation regarding the existing frame of reference. Findings show that there is significant diversity in how non-financial information regarding CSR is disclosed. Modeling a unitary reporting framework could be the keystone to which companies could relate in ensuring a good correlation with users' need for accurate, reliable, and relevant information.

Chapter 2
E-Accounting: Future Challenges and Perspectives 35
Dan Ioan Topor, 1 Decembrie 1918 University, Romania
Umair Akram, Jiangsu University, China
Melinda Timea Fülop, Babes-Bolyai University, Romania
Sorinel Căpuşneanu, 1 Decembrie 1918 University, Romania
Constantin Aurelian Ionescu, Hyperion University of Bucharest, Romania

This chapter addresses the main challenges of current e-accounting systems and also some future perspectives. The main objectives of this chapter are to present the conceptual approaches to e-accounting and ICT, their role and the determinants underlying the implementation of e-accounting systems in the business environment, the principles of security and processing of accounting information, and the impact of implementation and the advantages and limitations of e-accounting. Based on the literature, the authors present the interpretations brought by specialists to the concept of e-accounting, analyze their roles in terms of ICT and the factors that determine the acceptance of the concept in the implementation of various organizations. The chapter ends with the general conclusions of the authors related to the challenges brought by e-accounting systems in managerial accounting and CSR in the conditions of current crises.

Chapter 3
Reviving Green With Accounting in the Era of Sustainability... 53
Mansi Shah, Amity University, Jharkhand, India

In the era of 'Reviving Green', sustainability is no longer a luxury; it has become a global necessity. The late 1990s saw the evolving concept of triple bottom line. The growing importance of the environmental agenda that 'sustainability' had been mainly focused upon to that point led to the inclusion of the environment as one of the defining factors of 'sustainability'. The new paradigm in the third millennium puts business in the driving seat. Consequently, their role and responsibility towards the environment is manifold. The tradeoff between economic growth and the environmental costs has become one of the major challenges for businesses. This chapter examines the traditional accounting practiced by organizations. The premise of internalizing environmental costs in the investment decision making is highlighted. The costs and benefits that arise through the environment protection and depletion of the existing capital have been held forth.

Chapter 4
Using Digital Programs and Technologies to Simulate Business Development 71
Ionica Oncioiu, Titu Maiorescu University, Romania
Mihaela Mirela Dogaru, Titu Maiorescu University, Romania
Manoela Popescu, Independent Researcher, Belgium

The priorities of business people in the digital age are human capital and innovation. As the changes are fast, in the digital age, the decision maker will not look for the optimal solution, but will stop at the first solution that he considers satisfactory and will put it into practice as soon as possible, given the fact that there is a high probability that the opportunity or the conditions for materializing the decision must change, even before the implementation of the decision. The use of digital programs and technologies to simulate the company's development decisions can circumvent these shortcomings, at least for a short period of time. This chapter shows that, in an increasingly digitized world, there is widespread recognition that a strong organizational goal is essential for any company, as well as an awareness that trust is becoming increasingly difficult to gain. Also, the proper management of the growing expectations of stakeholders contributes to building the confidence needed for an organization to survive and thrive.

Chapter 5
CSR and Greenwashing in Finland: Analysis About the Public Discussions of Greenwashing........... 88
Rauno Rusko, University of Lapland, Finland

Due to the general tendency to express environmental protection, environmentalism, and the actions to slow down the greenhouse effect in the world, the enterprises have noticed the importance of environmental values in their public announcements, documents, and homepages. In other words, corporate social responsibility (CSR) is a very important and topical theme of the firms. The popularity of environmentalism tempts the firms to follow the direction of public opinion even though the actual environmental activities might be minor or even absent. This kind of quasi-environmentalism is called as greenwashing. This chapter focuses on greenwashing and CSR in the Finnish context via public discussions about greenwashing. This chapter is emphasizing the understandings and the sense-makings in the concepts of greenwashing and CSR and their numerous connotations basing on the results of the textual analysis. The outcomes are completed and compared with the international contexts, and, therefore, they are also internationally robust.

Chapter 6
CSR in the Tourism Industry 103
Andreea Marin-Pantelescu, Bucharest University of Economic Studies, Romania

CSR in the tourism industry aims to bring to the fore social responsibility initiatives. The decline in the first 10 months of the year 2020 represents 900 million fewer international tourist arrivals compared to the same period of the year 2019, and translates into a loss of US$ 935 billion in export revenues from international tourism. According to the World Tourism Organization, international arrivals will drop by 75% in 2020. This would mean that international tourism has returned to the levels of 30 years ago. In order to restore tourism, extensive social responsibility campaigns involving stakeholders should be launched. The main stakeholders in the tourism industry carry out social responsibility campaigns that take into account employees, guests, the environment, and the local communities. Environmental protection, fair working conditions for employees, and contributing to the welfare of local communities are key issues in the strategies of international tourism corporations and will be explored in the chapter on CSR in the tourism industry.

Chapter 7
Flexible Budget: Management Method for Cost Control and Monitoring the Performance of Economic Entities 128
Mariana Zamfir, Valahia University of Targoviste, Romania
Constantin Aurelian Ionescu, Hyperion University of Bucharest, Romania
Nicoleta Luminita Gudanescu Nicolau, Romanian Academy, Romania
Sorina Geanina Stanescu, Valahia University of Targoviste, Romania
Liliana Paschia, Hyperion University of Bucharest, Romania
Mihaela Denisa Coman, Valahia University of Targoviste, Romania
Alexandra Delia Bugnariu, 1 Decembrie 1918 University, Romania

The ever-changing business environment and the shorter product life cycle impose the need to develop new forecasting models and replace static budgets with flexible budgets. Thus, the analysis of deviations from budgeted costs becomes a desideratum of any entity. Flexible budgeting is based on the analysis of expenditure behavior and involves setting budgeted expenditure levels for different activity levels to monitor activity. The chapter highlights the importance of flexible budgeting of expenditures. It presents a comparison between static budgets and flexible budgets, the methodology for preparing flexible budgets, exemplifying how to prepare them for more predictable levels of activity, and budgetary control based on flexible budgets. The research is addressed to the academic environment and the practitioners concerned with the enterprise's management through the budget system, having as motivation the desire to satisfy the need for information both in higher economic education and in economic practice.

Chapter 8
Business Model in a Time of Global Crises 156
Ionica Oncioiu, Titu Maiorescu University, Romania
Mihaela Mirela Dogaru, Titu Maiorescu University, Romania
Manoela Popescu, Independent Researcher, Belgium

Globalization has created complex production chains, in which many countries contribute to the creation of added value. Globalization influences almost all aspects of life, but the way this evolution is felt differs from one country to another, from one region to another, from one individual to another. Globalization is an objective process that is taking place with astonishing speed, covering all the states of the world. It was determined and favored by the ultra-fast advances of technology, especially information technology, but also by the manifestations of the digital economy or information economy. Digitization has fundamentally changed the way companies operate while providing new entities with opportunities for survival and development. Websites have become powerful advertising and commercial tools, being used in all areas of activity. The technologies used to create and develop websites have diversified and become increasingly complex.

Chapter 9
Top Seven Trends in Management Accounting 173
Gary Cokins, Analytics-Based Performance Management LLC, USA

Ultimately, costing principles, such as the causality principle, must be converted into practical practices with supporting tools. This chapter describes how cost modeling has evolved over the last century. It describes the trends and obstacles that have helped or delayed developments. These evolving areas and trends include (1) the expansion from product costing to include channel and customer profitability reporting and analysis, (2) the integration of managerial accounting with other enterprise and corporate performance management (EPM/CPM) methods, (3) the shift from historical reporting to predictive accounting (e.g., marginal/incremental costing, (4) driver-based budgeting and rolling financial forecasts, (5) customer lifetime value (CLV), (6) imbedding analytics into managerial accounting (e.g., correlation and regression analysis), (7) acceptance of two or more co-existing managerial accounting methods, and (8) chargebacks to internal users and service-level agreements of information technology (IT) and shared services.

Chapter 10
A Qualitative Research on Sectoral Problems and Expectations.. 189
Fahri Özsungur, Mersin University, Turkey
Himmet Karadal, Bolu Abant İzzet Baysal University, Turkey

This research aims to investigate the sectoral market share of the professional committees, their current status, and expectations in the context of employment. It was determined that the market share of the sectors of 58.55% of the participants decreased in 2019. 46.71% of participants had the prediction that there would be no change in their market share in 2020. 45.39% of the participants anticipated a decrease in employment in 2019, and 58.55% anticipated that there would be no change in employment in 2020. 69.74% of the members of the professional committees participating in the research stated that there was a qualified employee shortage in the sector. The agriculture sector comes to the fore in the required employment areas. Participants stated that qualified employees trained according to the sector should be increased. According to the results, it was determined that there was a need for employment in agricultural products sales, textile, medical equipment, restaurants and cafes, insurance, private health services, advertising and media, paper, and packaging sectors.

Chapter 11
A Vision Regarding the Role of Financial-Accounting Practices in Tourism 208
Traian Ovidiu Calotă, Titu Maiorescu University, Romania

The primary role of general management's professionalism depends, to a large extent, on the correct assessment of the value of using the accounting information provided by the accounting management and, respectively, the efficient use in the decision-making process. What is extremely important is the fact that this process must be seen as in a continuously dynamic, as well as the fact that the options used must be in line with the permanent flow of opportunities that must be notified in time and exploited in the interest of economic entities. In the author's opinion, this aspect is predilection specific to tourism activities, with an important impact on success in this type of business. Thus, the opportunities are manifested and often start from them, from the start-up phase of a business, when the capital contribution will be made according to the perspectives opened by these opportunities, and then the construction of the tourist entity itself (including the system information-accounting) will be influenced by this.

Chapter 12
The Budget: The Basic Element of Management Accounting... 219
Alin Eliodor Tănase, Titu Maiorescu University, Romania

Knowing precisely the costs by sectors, products, activities, and functions helps locate in time and space the sub-units contributing to the improvement or, on the contrary, the depreciation of the results obtained by the company. Breaking down the costs by each function is another way to acquire knowledge about the internal accounting management conditions. A comparative analysis of expenditure by functions related to certain forecasts is the main way of identifying performance, efficient responsibility centers, as well as those whose functioning is deficient. On the other hand, the budget may be seen as a correlation and streamlining instrument for the relation between expenditures and income. Budgeting can also be seen as a systematic economic practice involving a formal process of allocating financial resources to achieve the objectives set for the following period of time. The revenue and cost budget are the objects of managerial accounting and the instruments to control the costs and the income by comparing the forecasts with the achievements.

Chapter 13
Managerial Accounting: An Integral Part of the Decision-Making Process 233
Traian Ovidiu Calotă, Titu Maiorescu University, Romania

The role of managerial accounting consists in detailing, analyzing, and interpreting the information provided by the general accounting, presenting it in a form that is accessible to the company management. Financial information is confidential, addressed to the internal environment of the company and presented as no standardized periodical reports adapted to the internal management needs. Costs play a determinant role in substantiating the decisions regarding the optimum production system and its adjustment in any competitive economic environment, as a special instrument determining the management of the company both as a whole and for each internal subdivision. But cost will only be able to play its true role if determined in a realistic and pertinent way. Consequently, the final objective of management from the point of view of forecasting, rational organization, information, analysis, prompt decision, and constant control is to obtain production at minimum cost.

Compilation of References 247

About the Contributors 270

Index 276

Preface

Modern companies are subject to increasing pressures in conducting their business in an environmentally responsible manner due to social and environmental problems. Management of sustainable performance is one of the phenomena faced by the current business environment and, in particular, management corporations. The focus of management on profitability remains the main objective of any company, but it must also take into account the sustainability of social, economic, and environmental aspects. Under these circumstances, managerial decisions need to be adjusted and strongly substantiated, considering the information required by internal and external stakeholders, including financial reporting. The information requirements of customers and other stakeholders are steadily increasing, and some companies face certain problems in implementing the concept of sustainability and environmental reporting. Eco-performance indicators present information in a focused and accurate manner on the entity's environmental activity segment. An entity can use several categories of indicators: operational, environmental status, management, economic.

On the other hand, the merging of aspects such as sustainability and corporate governance, the increasingly insistent demands of information users to have access to information other than financial results, resulting from the activity of companies, the need to look at the company as a living organism in the ecosystem of the current economy – they have all contributed to the development of non-traditional methodologies that allow counterbalancing the strengths of finance and accounting with the integration of non-traditional information in the annual financial statements. On top of that, management accounting reflects the comprehensive vision of financial performance that professionals in the field must adopt in order to evolve in an increasingly complex business environment. However, companies recognize that such commitments are aimed at strengthening their corporate image, rather than fundamental sustainability goals.

The book *CSR and Management Accounting Challenges in a Time of Global Crises* is a comprehensive reference source that explores various theoretical and practical approaches of management accounting and its impact in the 21st century and investigates new accounting and financial approaches where economic and social aspects become mutually supportive to enhance their impact on community development. Covering topics such as CSR reporting, sustainability and greenwashing, this book is an essential resource for academicians, specialty organizations, chief financial officers (CFOs), financial controllers, business analysts, financial planning and analysis (FP&A) analysts, budgeting managers, students, researchers, and business environment managers and specialists.

The authors Nicoleta Farcane, Ovidiu Constantin Bunget, Rodica Blidisel, Alin Constantin Dumitrescu, Delia Deliu, Oana Bogdan and Valentin Burca of the first chapter, "Ensuring the Quality of Information by Creating a Sustainable Framework in the Context of CSR Reporting," identify basic pillars around which issues related to non-financial reporting are going to be outlined by testing the quality of information presented by the top 50 largest listed companies according to non-financial reporting criteria, considering the environment, human and social resources, human rights, and the fight against corruption. By highlighting the diversity of information disclosed by the corporations (i.e., the economic, social, and environmental impact caused by the daily activities carried out), common benchmarks that determine the quality assurance are ascertained. Research methods include quantitative analysis of the sustainability reports, along with the authors' observation regarding the existing frame of reference. The results showed that some companies express their eco-sensitivity and are proactive, presenting many details in line with the pace of development of CSR, but on the other hand, we also notice some formalism of other companies that strive only to present a somewhat cosmetic facet to thus hiding duplicity. However, the reports on CSR referring to the practices and policies undertaken by companies seek to justify the aim of ensuring positive consequences globally, so companies must intensify their activities on pro-social objectives, as a sine qua non-factor, extremely important in addition to maximizing profits. As well, modeling a unitary reporting framework could be the keystone to which companies could relate to ensuring a good correlation with users' need for accurate, reliable, and relevant information.

An interesting business perspective on the main challenges of current e-accounting systems is revealed by Dan Ioan Topor, Umair Akram, Melinda Timea Fülöp, Sorinel Căpuşneanu and Constantin Aurelian Ionescu, the authors of the second chapter, "E-Accounting: Future Challenges and Perspectives." The objectives of this research are to present the conceptual approaches to e-accounting and ICT, their role and the determinants underlying the implementation of e-accounting systems in the business environment, the principles of security and processing of accounting information, the impact of implementation and the advantages and limitations of e-accounting. Based on the literature, the authors present the interpretations brought by specialists to the concept of e-accounting, analyze its role in terms of ICT and the factors that determine the acceptance of the concept in implementing various organizations. It can be seen that the scope of electronic accounting has expanded due to technological progress and therefore the use of new technologies has contributed to expanding the content area of the concept of e-accounting. By switching from offline to online and synchronizing with IoT, specialists talk about the e-accounting system through the two notions: accounting information system and computerized accounting system.

The premise of internalizing environmental costs in the investment decision making is illustrated by Mansi Shah, the author of the third chapter, "Reviving Green with Accounting in the Era of Sustainability." The author demonstrates the cost and benefits analysis for becoming environment friendly, the scope of environment costs, and capitalization of environmental expenditure, environmental liabilities, and environmental assets. Also the author presents the extensive role and importance of green accounting in the era of sustainability. Therefore, the costs and benefits which arise through the environment protection and depletion of the existing capital have been held forth. The management of companies must support the sustainability strategy, introduce it in their business and thus, they will see the value it can offer to them, but also to society in general.

The priorities of business people in the digital age, are presented by Ionica Oncioiu, Mihaela Mirela Dogaru and Manoela Popescu, the authors of the fourth chapter, "Using Digital Programs and Technologies to Simulate Business Development." As the changes are fast, in the digital age, the decision maker will not look for the optimal solution, but will stop at the first solution that he considers satisfactory and will put it into practice as soon as possible, given the fact that there is a high probability that the opportunity or the conditions for materializing the decision must change, even before the implementation of the decision. The use of digital programs and technologies to simulate the company's development decisions can circumvent these shortcomings, at least for a short period of time. This chapter shows that, in an increasingly digitized world, there is widespread recognition that a strong organizational goal is essential for any company. Also the proper management of the growing expectations of stakeholders contributes to building the confidence needed for an organization to survive and thrive.

In a descriptive manner, the interrelation of the environmental protection, environmentalism and the actions to slow down greenhouse effect is emphasized by Rauno Rusko, the author of the fifth chapter, "CSR and Greenwashing in Finland: Analysis About the Public Discussions of Greenwashing." The popularity of environmentalism tempts the firms to follow the direction of public opinion even though the actual environmental activities might be minor or even absent. This kind of quasi-environmentalism is called as greenwashing. This chapter focuses on greenwashing and CSR in the Finnish context via public discussions about greenwashing. This chapter is emphasizing the understandings and the sense-makings in the concepts of greenwashing and CSR and their numerous connotations based on the results of the textual analysis. The outcomes are completed and compared with the international contexts – and, therefore, they are also internationally robust.

In the sixth chapter, "CSR in the Tourism Industry," Andreea Marin-Pantelescu presents the scale of CSR activities in the tourism industry in three key areas, namely: CSR in hotels, CSR in travel agencies and CSR in airlines. Most environmental protection CSR programs are run by airlines. Companies with great economic and financial power also allocate money for social responsibility campaigns. On the other hand, environmental protection, fair working conditions for employees and contributing to the welfare of local communities are key issues in the strategies of international tourism corporations. The results show that investing more and more money from tourism companies' budgets for humanitarian projects would be a very important thing for CSR campaigns. As well, investing in employees and in providers' relationships will have a beneficial impact over CSR strategies. Informing tourists about all the CSR campaigns it will be a crucial and significant issue for all tourism companies.

The importance of flexible budgeting of expenditures is present by Mariana Zamfir, Constantin Aurelian Ionescu, Nicoleta Luminita Gudanescu Nicolau, Sorina Geanina Stanescu, Liliana Paschia, Mihaela Denisa Coman and Alexandra Delia Bugnariu, the authors of the seventh chapter, "Flexible Budget: Management Method for Cost Control and Monitoring the Performance of Economic Entities." The ever-changing business environment and the shorter product life cycle impose the need to develop new forecasting models and replace static budgets with flexible budgets. Thus, the analysis of deviations from budgeted costs becomes a desideratum of any entity. Flexible budgeting is based on the analysis of expenditure behavior and involves setting budgeted expenditure levels for different activity levels to monitor activity. In the face of changes both internally and externally, the forecasts and action plans of the budgetary process risk becoming more difficult to build, aging faster and becoming less useful for the enterprise. Due to future uncertainties, it is ideal to make budgeting flexible. Budget adjustments are required not only to change the use of production capacity. Budgets can also be changed in the event of price changes upstream (purchases from suppliers) or downstream (sales to customers). The research is addressed to the academic environment and the practitioners concerned with the enterprise's management through the budget system, having as motivation the desire to satisfy the need for information both in higher economic education and in economic practice.

The growth of the information society, the computer network, the increase in the number of users and the volume of information required by the public has resulted in a wide range of methods for transmitting and disseminating knowledge and information, all of which are appealing and simple to understand and use. In these circumstances, public and private legal institutions, businesses, professional groups, and non-profit organizations prefer to synthesize and exchange information via websites. Information, rather than tangible resources or money, is a considerably more essential element of production in the digital age. Ionica Oncioiu, Mihaela Mirela Dogaru and Manoela Popescu, the authors of the eighth chapter, "Business Model in a Time of Global Crises," present the increasing pressures for transformation - the shift from product-centric business models to new models focused on creating and capturing different sources of new value. Performing in this new global crisis context is the equivalent of disrupting, which economically requires, in addition to know-how and added value, their use in the most efficient way for innovation. The merging of various methods or systems of management accounting has created much more viable and efficient methods whose particularly important contribution is focused on providing real, substantiated, and effective information, necessary to ensure short-term or long-term decision-making efficiency. Thus, thanks to new methods, new alternatives for monitoring and measuring performance, including environmental performance, have been developed.

It often happens that the management of an economic entity fails to cope with the unique problems that have arisen as a result of money management situations of the institution, due to the practice of inaccurate accounting. Specifically, the information provided by the accounts is not accurately determined and this contributes to subsequent decision failure. In the chapter nine dedicated to "Top 7 Trends in Management Accounting," Gary Cokins describes how cost modeling has evolved over the last century. It describes the trends and obstacles that have helped or delayed developments. These evolving areas and trends include: (1) The expansion from product costing to include channel and customer profitability reporting and analysis; (2) the integration of managerial accounting with other enterprise and corporate performance management (EPM/CPM) methods; (3) The shift from historical reporting to predictive accounting; (4) Driver-based budgeting and rolling financial forecasts; (5) Imbedding analytics into managerial accounting (e.g., correlation and regression analysis); (6) Acceptance of two or more co-existing managerial accounting methods; (7) Chargebacks to internal users and service level agreements of information technology (IT) and shared services.

The global crisis affects the sectoral management strategies of businesses. Managerially, many stages in the process of the value chain such as supply, logistics, distribution, after-sales services have changed. Adaptation to these conditions requires new resources and sustainable management of existing resources. Professional organizations provide an important support service in this regard The authors of the tenth chapter, "A Qualitative Research on Sectoral Problems and Expectations," Fahri Özsungur and Himmet Karadal, investigate the sectoral market share of professional committees (occupational groups), the current situation, and expectations in terms of employment. From a sectoral perspective, the effects of the global crisis lead to a decline in entrepreneurship in the context of developing countries. According to the results, it was determined that there was a need for employment in agricultural products sales, textile, medical equipment, restaurants and cafes, insurance, private health services, advertising and media, paper, and packaging sectors. Assessing the observance of the environmental policy, achieving the environmental targets of an economic entity, and facilitating the managerial control of the practices with possible impact on the environment represent some of the main purposes of the environmental audit.

Increasing the impact of tourism on the economy as a whole justifies the assumption that value chains in tourism can play a significant role in paving the way for the transition to the bio economy. In the eleventh chapter, "A Vision Regarding the Role of Financial: Accounting Practices in Tourism," Traian Ovidiu Calotă brings forward a series of controversies on the opportunity and profitability of investments in this field, for which there is a constant need for accounting and tax information configured so as to meet all the necessary qualitative characteristics and, at the same time, express the specifics of tourism transactions. Also, from the same perspective, the author considers that there is a need to clarify the genesis of the main vulnerabilities faced by management and which affect performance in Romanian tourism. This requires the identification of new elements in the treatment of accounting information in tourism, including the effects of its impact on the relationship of accounting with taxation and management. All the aforementioned aspects highlight the need to find new directions in which to develop processes, techniques and other measures that will contribute in the future to the efficiency of the exploitation of accounting and fiscal information in the Romanian tourism management as a determining factor of achieving performance. The chapter includes some approaches on the specifics of information modeling in tourism, with emphasis on the actual modeling process and specific elements. Also, this chapter configures opinions on the impact of accounting policies on competitiveness and the specific elements of the elaboration of the manual of accounting policies in a tourist entity. Also included here are the logical schemes regarding the whole approach for the elaboration of the manual of accounting policies and the succession of the specific stages of the elaboration of this manual.

The problem of carrying out budgetary control over production costs is brought out by Alin Eliodor Tănase, the author of the twelfth chapter, "The Budget: The Basic Element of Management Accounting." The results show that knowing precisely the costs by sectors, products, activities, and functions helps locate in time and space the sub-units contributing to the improvement or, on the contrary, the depreciation of the results obtained by the company. Breaking down the costs by each function is another way to acquire knowledge about the internal accounting management conditions. A comparative analysis of expenditure by functions related to certain forecasts is the main way of identifying performant, efficient responsibility centers as well as those with deficient functioning. On the other hand, the budget may be seen as a correlation and streamlining instrument for the relationship between expenditures and income. Budgeting can also be seen as a systematic economic practice involving a formal process of allocating financial resources to achieve the objectives set for the following period of time. The revenue and cost budget is the object of managerial accounting and the instrument to control the costs and the income by comparing forecasts with achievements.

To be successful in their decision-making activity, managers must have at their disposal all the required instruments, to be able to distinguish between the relevant costs and the irrelevant ones and eliminate the latter from the decision-making process. In the final chapter, "Managerial Accounting: An Integral Part of the Decision-Making Process," Traian Ovidiu Calotă aims to discuss the role of managerial accounting. The results show that the costs play a determinant role in substantiating the decisions regarding the optimum production system and its adjustment in any competitive economic environment, as a special instrument determining the management of the company both as a whole and for each internal subdivision. But cost will only be able to play its true role if determined in a realistic and pertinent way. Consequently, the final objective of management from the point of view of forecasting, rational organization, information, analysis, prompt decision and constant control, is to obtain production at minimum costs.

This overview of this book highlights the fact that each chapter contains interesting elements whose potential and degree of interest open new directions for future research. Authorized analyses indicate that accounting practices act as a mechanism to facilitate environmental management through compliance with environmental legislation, stakeholders' communication, employees and management engagement, commitment to continuous improvement of environmental performance. Therefore, management accounting has a dual function in this respect: an environmental management facilitator and the benefit of an environmental management based on accountability.

Acknowledgment

Looking back, we wish to thank all the persons who made the publishing of the present volume possible: Jan Travers, Melissa Wagner, Erin Wesser, Christina Henning, Nicole Elliott, Kristina Byrne, Lindsay Johnston, Joshua Witman, Nick Newcomer, Jaimie Watts, Josephine Dadeboe, Jordan Tepper, Sean Eckman, Marianne Caesar, Gianna Walker and many other IGI Global team members, reviewers, collaborators, and all the contributing authors: without your efforts and dedication this editorial project would have never been possible.

Chapter 1
Ensuring the Quality of Information by Creating a Sustainable Framework in the Context of CSR Reporting

Nicoleta Farcane
West University of Timisoara, Romania

Ovidiu Constantin Bunget
West University of Timisoara, Romania

Rodica Blidisel
West University of Timisoara, Romania

Alin Constantin Dumitrescu
West University of Timisoara, Romania

Delia Deliu
https://orcid.org/0000-0001-5189-5607
West University of Timisoara, Romania

Oana Bogdan
West University of Timisoara, Romania

Valentin Burca
West University of Timisoara, Romania

ABSTRACT

This chapter aims to identify basic pillars around which issues related to non-financial reporting are going to be outlined by testing the quality of information presented by the top 50 largest listed companies according to non-financial reporting criteria, considering the environment, human and social resources, human rights, and the fight against corruption. By highlighting the diversity of information disclosed by the corporations (i.e., the economic, social, and environmental impact caused by the daily activities carried out), common benchmarks that determine the quality assurance are ascertained. Research

DOI: 10.4018/978-1-7998-8069-1.ch001

methods include quantitative analysis of the sustainability reports, along with the authors' observation regarding the existing frame of reference. Findings show that there is significant diversity in how non-financial information regarding CSR is disclosed. Modeling a unitary reporting framework could be the keystone to which companies could relate in ensuring a good correlation with users' need for accurate, reliable, and relevant information.

INTRODUCTION

Nowadays, the permanent development of the business environment is being witnessed, determining a continuous change regarding the needs of the interested parties, with the consequence of shifting the pole of interest from financial information to non-financial information. Companies' perceptions and ways of expressing themselves are the results of a wide variety of approaches, self-regulatory and co-regulatory processes being varied. Improving and monitoring the level of trust of companies and stimulating their degree of social involvement could be achieved by disclosing the key aspects and pillars, which present completeness, relevance, trust, and comprehensibility.

Numerous materials are being issued by various bodies that come to guide the issuer of non-financial information, but without a general framework and a set of standards issued, such as the IFRS referential, unevenness and differences of perception between users are being created. These are aspects that are not under the sign of fair-play if the right to correct, complete and relevant information is being considered. The vast variety of national and sub-national Corporate Social Responsibility (CSR) policies represent, in fact, a major obstacle to comparability. Thus, the need to standardize reporting methods by identifying a common reporting framework appears unavoidable.

On the one hand, the creation of added-value can be suddenly affected by certain catastrophes, epidemics, or crises. Can we distinguish the impact caused by them between the factors with long-term influence or can we talk about economic entities with long-term sustainable activities and resilient activities? Can economic utility be incorporated into social utility? On the other hand, companies are publishing annual reports that are becoming increasingly complex, the attention of organizations being directed towards sustainable and responsible development. But how is this non-financial information presented and measured, given that there is no uniform general reporting framework?

Currently we are witnessing more and more a permanent development of the business environment, determining a continuous change in the needs of the interested parties, with the consequence of shifting the pole of interest from financial information to non-financial information.

At the beginning of this debate, we consider it necessary to focus on the notion of *sustainability reporting* because behind every concept within the notion of *social responsibility* of a company, there are many interpretations and expressions, most of the time even contradictory. *Corporate social responsibility* (hereafter, CSR) is a conceptual dimension with a wide area of interpretation, and its substantiation is only possible over a long-time horizon. The dimensions of corporate governance are: a behavioral one – that regards the interactions, respectively a regulatory one – which includes the legal aspect of these interactions (i.e., namely on regulatory aspects with economic content), to which is added a predictive dimension – that involves the ability of rules and principles of corporate governance to anticipate future developments.

In the current era, we are in the presence of significant technological advances, in a process of globalization in full expansion, by manifesting a globalized market where companies develop individually in specific ways without resorting to global rules. To create more and more wealth than ever before, large companies use multiple practices with a strong social impact. They pollute, sometimes consume irrationally from natural resources, end up in discriminatory circumstances, cause social injustices, ignore local laws in some circumstances, practice corruption to facilitate and intensify certain activities that would otherwise prove socially irresponsible. Consequently, the issue of corporate responsibility became particularly important with the globalization of the markets, when multinational corporations gained new power internationally becoming even stronger than many states, manifesting themselves as the main player, taking over and increasing their responsibilities.

Worldwide, companies' sensitivity as regards social, moral, and ethical aspects of their activities is continually enhancing. Thus, CSR is inextricably linked to business identity and principles, even if it is expressed in various ways (i.e., ethics, morality, responsibility, and values) (Farcane *et al.*, 2019). In this context, corporate governance must now be built on sustainable development principles, involving not only the stakeholders' legitimate interests in corporate activities, but also the recognition of CSR (Deliu, 2020). Hence, CSR values should be integrated into corporate values, by also considering the moral, organizational, cultural, and strategic aspects of a business.

Some companies express their eco-sensitivity and are proactive, presenting many details in line with the pace of development of CSR, but on the other hand, we also notice some formalism of other companies that strive only to present a somewhat cosmetic facet to thus hiding duplicity. However, the reports on CSR referring to the practices and policies undertaken by companies seek to justify the aim of ensuring positive consequences globally, so companies must intensify their activities on pro-social objectives, as a sine qua non-factor, extremely important in addition to maximizing profits.

As Nikos Avlonas (Executive Director/Center for Sustainability & Excellence – CSE, 2010) pointed out, the idea behind CSR has obviously existed for thousands of years in various forms, different from the current ones, but in societies with a high level of culture and spirituality. This suggests not only its validity, but also its superiority mainly in the fact that the companies benefiting from the economic activities carried out must give something back to the society, so CSR must lead to a better society. So it can be concluded that the concept of social responsibility delineates new socio-economic and ecological guidelines, whose application enables a better coexistence between the stakeholders of a company.

Having, on the one hand, the diversification of guidelines, aspects regulated generically by international bodies and associations, and on the other hand, the reality estimated by reference to the reports disclosed by the main economic entities in the world (relevant from the stock market value), this chapter purposes to explore relevant common elements, related to the need for users of accurate information. Basic issues are outlined, along with pillars that support a future international non-financial reporting framework.

Ensuring qualitative non-financial information could be achieved by recommending a sustainable general framework on CSR that iterates the key elements, which cannot be ignored, as well as the degree of detail or explicitness of the content and presentation, to allow uniformity in regards to disclosure, at international level.

BACKGROUND

Individuals, at the international level, are increasingly concerned about sustainability and claim to be able to access information as transparent as possible from companies. As a result, companies are increasingly interested in developing their CSR strategies and are striving for better management, disclosing and transmission of information in the most accessible way, in terms of transparency and credibility, to reduce risk by ensuring reputation and be able to fulfill stakeholders' expectations.

Market regulators, through their involvement in sustainability reporting, are influenced by the public policy positions of their governments, manifesting themselves differently by region. We see more and more often that companies fail to clearly report the impact of climate change generated by their activities. There are also concerns about increasing regional and domestic regulatory requirements and their impact on global competitiveness.

The synopsis of sustainability reporting standards allowed us to illustrate a generous package of standards and frameworks, the most famous being GRI (Global Reporting Initiative), CDP (Disclosure Insight Action), SASB (Sustainability Accounting Standards Board), CDSB (Climate Disclosure Standards Board), IIRC (International Integrated Reporting Council), and TCFD (Task Force on Climate-Related Financial Disclosures). ESG reporting, respectively ESG reporting assurance are represented by ISO 26000 Social Responsibility, EU Directive 95/2014, ISO 14000 Environmental Management, UN Global Impact Principles, OECD Guidelines, AA1000 AccountAbility Principles, and ISAE 3000 International Standard on Assurance Engagements. In the international context, there can be found a wide range of tools (i.e., MSCI (Morgan Stanley Capital International), ISS (Institutional Shareholders Services Group of Companies), DJSI (Dow Jones Sustainability Indices), CSA (Corporate Sustainability Assessment), etc., set as ratings or indexes to serve as a reference for the disclosure of CSR information.

However, we note the existence of various ways of reporting sustainable development in the light of CSR. The way companies detail their CSR and sustainability policies can be achieved by using and complying with various standards – i.e., the GRI, ISO 26000, integrated reporting, or other standards. The certifications of these companies are guarantees regarding the credibility of these CSR and sustainability practices. The accessibility of information to report on the sustainability of companies is somewhat difficult because there are different situations of presentation and disclosure, some companies presenting a single consolidated report, others presenting distinct reports on differentiated topics: climate change, biodiversity, health, and welfare, etc. But all these forms of presentation are different depending on the standard referred to. Some standards have compliance requirements for which reports will have significant dimensions, even if some regular users only want to know some important aspects of companies' sustainability. There are also ways in which companies can present the CSR report based on a custom template, taking over the main points, and creating an attractive design, thus promoting their own custom CSR report. Companies' perceptions and ways of expressing themselves are the results of a wide variety of approaches, self-regulatory and co-regulatory processes are varied, there are a variety of national and sub-national CSR policies – all of which are a major barrier to comparability. We are faced with a great diversity of information disclosure on sustainability, which inevitably determines the need to standardize reporting methods by identifying a common reporting framework.

Several attempts to standardize standardization have already begun at the European level. There have been public consultations on the review of non-financial reporting, and it has emerged that mandatory sustainability reporting standards have a lot of support. Many parties emphasized that any sustainability reporting standards developed by the EU should be based on and compatible with the initiatives to create international standards. Stakeholders stressed the importance of clarifying the reporting requirement in line with the perspective of dual materiality – economic and social. Most SMEs and the organizations that represent them are opposed to mandatory regulations for SMEs, although they are receptive to the concept of fair and voluntary standards. One aspect is the detailed and prescriptive reporting requirements,

insurance related to a wide scope to meet the needs of users, but which is obviously more expensive for trainers. The goal is to get the best result as regards goals and costs.

The fundamental issue of our paper revolves around the need to ***uniformize*** existing reporting standards, so users can gain access to more comparative, applicable, and reliable sustainability data from a variety of companies. A package of universally valid standards would help other stakeholders (especially investors) to understand and compare the sustainability performance of one company with another, and will be able to appreciate the link between the performance of a company and value creation. Subsequently, the risks of investing in the financial system will be reduced, financial flows to businesses with positive social and environmental impacts will be increased, and corporations will be made more responsible. In our attempt to find optimal models for systematizing the diversity of sustainable reporting standards, respectively their convergence, we will continue to make an inventory of the current reporting standards and frameworks of GRI, SASB, CDSB, IIRC, CDP, and TCFD.

SYNOPSYS OF NON-FINANCIAL REPORTING REFERENTIALS

During the last century, a lot of research papers and independent global frameworks and standard-setters have been focused upon the concept of corporate social responsibility (CSR) pointing out on its central platforms, sustainability, and particularly sustainable development. In this context, Aras and Crowther (2009) in their research paper argued for a fuller debate about sustainability. Sustainability reporting refers to the disclosure and communication of environmental, social, and governance (ESG) goals and issues. The literature emphasizes that the sustainability report is not a legal requirement, but it may provide short- and long-term benefits to businesses. Moreover, non-financial reporting represents a tool for businesses to grow in a responsible and open manner (Perrini, 2005). In their study, Leuz and Wysocki (2016) the empirical research on the economic effects of transparency and financial reporting regulations, pointing out the frequency of standardization and mandatory information.

The combination of the financial and the non-financial perspective determines a more relevant assessment of a company's performance. A company that has an activity that harms the environment and implicitly the community will not be able to be sustainable. As De Nuccio (2020) emphasized, a sustainable society cannot be created if only a small percentage of top companies are practicing sustainable reporting, no matter how large and important they are in accordance with their market capitalization, revenues, and reputation. The growing globalization of financial markets has sparked debate over securities and transparency regulation reforms (Leuz and Wysocki, 2016).

The European Commission conducted an impact assessment and described one of the key issues as a lack of accountability and credibility of non-financial information (Kinderman, 2020), emphasizing the need to increase the transparency and comparability of information disclosed in sustainability reports. Moreover, researchers from a variety of countries were interested in examining the application of European Directive 95/2014 on non-financial reporting in national law, as well as the factors that influence non-financial reporting and the interrelationships between financial and non-financial indicators (Veltri, 2020).

In their paper, Idowu et al. (2016) stress the importance of including Sustainability elements and Corporate Social Responsibility (CSR) in the Integrated Reporting process, with a particular emphasis on voluntary CSR/ Sustainability/IR reporting initiatives. In the same light, in his research, Wagner (2018) scrutinized the European Directive 95/2014 from a number of viewpoints: the significance of

CSR and the rationale for non-financial reporting, challenges, and implementation of the non-financial reporting in Europe. The author points out the important step made by the European Directive in CSR implementation, with restraint in the assertion that it will not be able to improve reporting if uniform reporting requirements and strict penalties for those that do not reveal details properly and transparently are not in place. According to Aureli *et al.* (2020), CSR reporting includes not only the report writing process, but also the stages of the information flow that are significant to all stakeholders.

While there were divergent debates among developed EU member states, Kinderman (2020) pointed out the strong need to revise and harmonize the European Directive on non-financial reporting. Recently, in August 2020, the European Commission published a public consultation report on the revision of the European Non-Financial Reporting Directive, pointing out the support for requiring non-financial reporting to follow a consistent standard necessary for comparability and relevance. Reviewing non-financial reporting is essential to meet users' needs for relevant, comparable, and accessible information. Therefore, sustainability reporting needs to improve rapidly to progress as investors' interest in non-financial information is growing as our planet faces increasingly serious problems: environmental pollution, climate change, and population health problems. All these problems are caused by people and implicitly by the activities of the companies they run.

The European Directive 95/2014 was a starting point for companies in non-financial reporting, but the expectations of stakeholders are growing, as environmental, social, and economic issues arise. The non-financial information reported is not enough relevant, i.e. companies don't report all the information that stakeholders need to make certain decisions regarding that company. The content of social responsibility reports/statements is not sufficiently comparable and reliable. Due to the lack of a standardized social reporting report, material and values are presented in an unorganized manner.

Many existing indicators provide little information on how well a company minimizes its negative impact and often as a little perspective on the resulting impact on value creation for the enterprise. The information presented in the corporate social responsibility reports/statements is supposed to provide comparability between companies, but most, in fact, fail to do so in practice (Cho, 2020).

According to Dumitrașcu and Feleagă (2019), the sustainability practices depend mainly on the maturity of the business, the size of the company, and the business processes complexity. Reports on sustainability are becoming more well-known, the most common organizations internationally accepted as GRI (Global Reporting Initiative), SASB (Sustainability Accounting Standards Board), CDSB (Climate Disclosure Standards Board), CDP (Disclosure Insight Action), IIRC (International Integrated Reporting Council), and TCFD (Task Force on Climate-Related Financial Disclosures) sustaining the disclosure and assessment under certain standards and frameworks, assuring companies not only for greater visibility and marketing but also to increase their credibility to stakeholders.

GRI (Global Reporting Initiative)

GRI is a well-known independent international organization founded in 1997 that has pioneered non-financial reporting. GRI sets standards that address companies and governments all over the world to comprehend and report their impact on governance, human rights, climate change, and social welfare. This allows the creation of social, economic, and environmental returns for everyone. The guidelines published by GRI have reached the fourth generation, being nowadays the most widely utilized in the field of sustainability reporting.

The GRI aims to provide a global framework that allows for a standard approach to sustainable, transparent, and consistent reporting, facilitates the implementation of the EU Directive, thus creating an overview of how EU Directive's requirements can be linked to the G4 guide. "Linking the GRI Standards and the European Directive on non-financial and diversity disclosure document" (GRI, 2017) demonstrates how the GRI Standards should be used to conform with the European Directive on non-financial and diversity data disclosure, containing two parts: one with details on the European Directive in its broadest sense, and the GRI Standards.

SASB (Sustainability Accounting Standards Board)

SASB is an independent non-profit organization established in 2011 that establishes guidelines for corporations' disclosure of financial sustainability information to investors. Environmental, social, and governance (ESG) problems are defined by SASB standards. The SASB's key goal is to develop and enhance industry-specific standards on financially important governance, social, and environmental issues so that businesses and investors can exchange valuable information for decision-making (Busco et al., 2020). Hence, SASB standards allow the implementation of the integrated reporting framework providing comparability.

In the direction of clarity in the sustainability reporting the SASB and GRI started a collaborative work-plan in 2020, believing that helping others understand the sustainability performance issues is critical to meeting the needs of all stakeholders. At this moment the difference between SASB and GRI is that SASB has industry-specific standards, while the GRI focuses on economic, environmental, and social issues. SASB framework enables TCFD disclosure while they contain industry-specific metrics for evaluation of the company's exposure, including the management of climate-related threats and opportunities. From the standard analysis, we point out SASB as a specific industry standard and investor focus in terms of reporting requirements, oriented towards the future performance of companies. It has mainly US focus but it is embraced also by other global organizations widely spread in the US.

CDSB (Climate Disclosure Standards Board)

CDSB is an international consortium founded in 2007, formed by some environmental NGOs and nine companies, leading a global corporate reporting model. The CDSB's major goals are to assist businesses in translating their sustainability data into long-term value. The Framework is aligned with regulatory reporting requirements (e.g., the EU Non-Financial Reporting Directive) in accordance with TCFD. It is built on the most widely used reporting organizations, such as GRI, CDP, SASB, IFRS, and encourages environmental information reporting standardization (Climate Disclosure Standards Board, 2019). The presentation of environmental information must be clear, credible, and intelligible, being correlated with the financial information in the main report or with other aspects presented in various reports published by companies. The CDSB reporting framework induces companies to the idea of transparent reporting containing neutral information, devoid of subjectivism so as not to influence the users of the reports.

IIRC (International Integrated Reporting Council)

IIRC is a global association of regulators, companies, investors, standards-makers, the accounting profession, academia, as well as NGOs, having as a mission to elaborate reports and debates integrated into the business practice. The IIRC's integrated reporting framework provides a conceptual structure on financial position and performance. The integrated reporting framework was designed to provide information on how an organization can create value in different areas – social, environmental, and economic over the short, medium, and long term.

Applying the principles of integrated reporting makes a management report more meaningful and changes the way businesses think about creating and maintaining value (Idowu et al., 2016; Burlea-Schiopoiu and Mihai, 2019; Cosmulese et al., 2019). The last development of this regulator being related to various forms of the capital framework, the companies being advised to provide information on how social and environmental activities, employment issues, human rights, as well as corruption and bribery decrease are part of the value creation process. Integrated reporting is a set of principles that serve an organization's communication, integrated thinking about value creation to financial capital providers and other stakeholders. There were not identified among its conceptual framework any specific metrics for measuring climate-related threats and opportunities as well as the scope 1, 2, or 3 for greenhouse gas emissions.

CDP (Disclosure Insight Action)

CDP is a non-profit organization that helps companies, investors, cities to manage their impact on the environment. The CDP's key goal is to aid in the development of a sustainable economy by assessing and recognizing the effect of businesses on the environment. The CDP helps to improve corporate awareness for climate change management. According to CDP, the benefits of non-financial reporting would be: improving the company's reputation, gaining a competitive advantage, discovering environmental risks and opportunities, the possibility of comparing environmental performance with other companies in the same industry.

TCFD (Task Force on Climate-Related Financial Disclosures)

TCFD is a non-profit organization that was established in 2015 to advance a set of voluntary presentations of climate-related financial risks that can be adopted by companies based on the SASB standards and the general CDSB framework. The main objective of the TCFD is to help companies, through guidelines, identify and share both the risks and opportunities they face as a result of climate change. The information must be comparable to that of companies belonging to the same sector of activity or industry. Analyzing the framework, there is identified a complexity of the requirements.

As regards the strategy, all the standard-setters require climate impacts, risks, and opportunities disclosure. It can be observed that not all of them have generalized guidance related to associated financial impacts or their classification; instead, they provide industry-specific standards, referring to materiality topics and metrics. Moreover, as regards the metrics, some standards require the cover of the significant economic, environmental, and social topics, but each organization is able to establish what is considered important in their line of business, and, hence, the metrics could differ between organization (e.g. TCFD has specific Greenhouse Gas emissions metric - Scope 1, 2 and 3 based on the emission intensity, SASB and GRI focus materiality by industry). Compared to GRI, SASB, and IIRC, the CDP framework does not require data or provide guidance related to social and certain types of environmental factors. This comparison points out the similarity but also the difference in terminology, nature, and information across the frameworks. The TCFD and CDSB, in particular, are primarily concerned with climate change, while GRI and SASB have a broader ESG orientation, being focused on different industries and sectors. Despite the difference, the core objectives materially aligned with these standards are to help companies to provide consistent and reliable information about ESG variables and factors.

This unique moment in history, intensified by the COVID-19 pandemic, made governments, businesses, and NGOs think about a comprehensive and globally accepted corporate reporting system. More than ever, non-financial factors are seen as important for a company's long-term stability and growth, not only to report a set of universal ESG indicators useful for financial markets and the economy.

According to World Economic Forum (WEF, 2020) the CDSB, CDP, IIRC, GRI, and SASB standards-setters agreed to work toward a shared goal, and will present a paper at the IBC Summer Meeting 2020 on the components of a single, global ESG reporting framework, organized around four pillars: principles of governance, people, planet, and prosperity. The declaration of purpose for the Impact Management Project assumes that the five leading standard and process setters (CDSB, CDP, IIRC, GRI, and SASB) will work together to create a robust and standardized corporate reporting system.

As regards corporate sustainability reporting, the European Union has also started a process to comply with non-financial reporting, publishing in April 2021 the draft EU Directive amending Directive 2004/109/EC, Directive 2006/43/EC, Directive 2013/34/EU, and Regulation (EU) No 537/2014.

The public consultation on the revision of the Non-Financial Reporting EU Directive discusses the need for a clear stage between financial and non-financial reporting assignments (alignment of obligations). It was asserted that the same proportionate approach to non-financial reporting might be used for non-financial reporting, i.e. the boost in the reporting obligation as the company's size increases (European Commission, 2020).

The EU generally supports a view of businesses as key contributors to value creation in two dimensions: creating economic and financial value at the entity level that mainly affects financial capital providers and creating environmental and social value at the corporate level affects a broad range of stakeholders. The objective is to maximize the creation of value by businesses in both dimensions, recognizing the distinctions, relationships, and interdependencies between them.

Due to sustainability reporting consultations, IFRS Foundation administrators have committed to informally engage in sustainability reporting as the importance of stakeholders sharing the same interest has begun to grow: improving coherence and comparability in CSR reporting. A well-thought-out set of standards would help companies build public confidence in this information through greater transparency of sustainability initiatives, as society calls for initiatives to combat climate change (IFRS Foundation, 2020). Given the entire CSR reporting process in the EU since the adoption of European Directive 95/2014, the European Commission wishes to make a legislative proposal to revise the Non-Financial Reporting Directive in the spring of 2021 (European Reporting LAB - EFRAG, 2021).

The non-financial reporting frameworks, as mentioned above, deal with a wide range of topics, correlated with the target of each framework, but this diverse approach is a risk that in the future we will find a "dilution" of the consistency applicable to this non-financial reporting. It is necessary, more than ever, to align these frameworks to the real need for information of users, but also to create a sustainable and harmonious international business environment integrated with fundamental human values in which the environment plays a key role. The IFAC initiative to set up the SSB is a factor designed to pave the way for the creation of a general non-financial reporting framework, a framework to provide a true synergy of ideas and concepts presented in all these frameworks and to build an important position in relationship with the public and users of this information. A trend observed by analyzing the non-financial reporting of large international companies is the risk of pseudo-compliance that takes place at a more formal level and has a nuance in the service of marketing activities of companies rather than the background of sustainability issues and the importance of providing non-financial information to decision-makers.

In conclusion, the setting of standards should be based on sound EU conceptual guidelines, which are expected to address the alignment of qualitative information characteristics, relevant time horizons, clear boundaries, dual materiality, and connectivity between financial reporting and sustainability.

METHODOLOGY

Data Collection

Our study aimed to identify in what ways top companies disclose their non-financial information in the context in which a unitary reporting framework does not exist. Hence, sustainability reports may vary in structure and content since companies report the information regarding the economic, social, and environmental impact of their activities in different forms of presentation, according to their own custom. Our approach is similar to the one proposed by Dyer *et al.* (2017), aiming to study the textual characteristics of 10-K disclosures, published by US companies for almost 20 years. Following this approach, we check for the main topics derived from CSR reports selected. Those topics will be analyzed against the topics derived from the following list of conceptual frameworks defining a general framework of CSR reporting, listed in **Table 1**.

Data Analysis

European Directive 95/2014 regarding non-financial information disclosures and the frameworks elaborated by the most common organizations internationally accepted, namely GRI, SASB, CDSB, IIRC, CDP, and TCFD represent the starting point in our textual analysis. With the help of NVivo 12 software, respectively of word frequency criteria function, we extracted the 1000 most-used words from the frameworks and guidelines related to non-financial disclosures elaborated by the mentioned standard-setters, as reflected in the word-cloud presented in the following figure (**Figure 1**).

Table 1. CSR and Sustainability conceptual reporting frameworks

1. Sustainability reporting	GRI Sustainability Reporting Standards TCFD Implementation Guide SASB Conceptual Framework
2. Integrated reporting	International <IR> Framework
3. Climate reporting	CDSB Framework
4. ESG reporting	ISO 26000 Social Responsibility EU Directive 95/2014 ISO 14000 Environmental Management UN Global Impact Principles OECD Guidelines
5. ESG reporting assurance	AA1000 AccountAbility Principles ISAE 3000 International Standard on Assurance Engagements

Source: Own compilation

Figure 1. Word-cloud of the most frequent 1000 words
Source: authors processing using the NVivo 12 program

In order to establish the most relevant keywords for our study, we made a bibliometric analysis of scientific publications, focusing on the relevance of the CSR concept and the keywords used in the last 10 years. Hence, we extracted, with VOSviewer software, the information available in the Web of Science Core Collection database in the categories Economics, Business, and Business Finance, studying the distribution of the most intensively used keywords proposed by the authors, with a minimum threshold of 5 simultaneous occurrences. We identified 7,835 key-words, out of which 494 meet our imposed criterion of at least 5 occurrences. These words that exceed the established threshold are illustrated in **Figure 2**.

Taking into account these results and the aspects mentioned in the European Directive 95/2014 regarding some basic information that must be reflected in non-financial disclosures, namely (1) environmental, (2) social and employee matters, (3) human rights, (4) anti-corruption and bribery matters, we established, based on professional reasoning, the most relevant key words for our analysis, as reflected in the following table (**Table 2**):

Figure 2. CSR key word link network
Source: authors processing using the VosViewer program

Table 2. Selected keywords

1. Environmental matters	climate, emissions, water, waste, afforestation, biodiversity, pollution
2. Social and employee matters	poverty, optimization, safeguarding, unions
3. Human rights	health, well-being, expression, gender, discriminant, inequity, inclusion
4. Fighting against corruption	justice, bribery, favoritism, nepotism, corruption, conflicts

Source: authors projection

As underlined by Christensen *et al.* (2019), as well as Tsagas and Villiers (2020), shareholders and stakeholders decreased slightly their trust in CSR reports, as the practice does not seem to converge to a uniform and structured presentation of information, scattered information being presented in various ways by the companies. In the absence of a regional or global approach to CSR reporting standard-setting, it seems that the market-driven incentives model dramatically the form and the content of those corporate disclosures. Hence, CSR disclosures have become a core strategic communication tool for management, despite the externalities this type of reporting generates on all levels. Investors react positively to firms with stronger CSR disclosure, the reason why the way ESG information is presented can bring benefits or implicit costs on capital markets for listed companies.

As there is no unitary structure of presenting CSR information, not even requirements for minimal information to be disclosed, we considered it more suitable to analyze those reports from a CSR report topic analysis perspective. Main topics emphasized on CSR/sustainability reports and CSR reporting frameworks are extracted performing a Latent Dirichlet Allocation (LDA) analysis (Blei *et al.*, 2003). As underlined by Lewis and Young (2019) and Loughran and McDonald (2020), this automated textual analysis technique has become a core tool for analyzing the content of corporate disclosures. This textual analysis technique is based on Bayesian computational theory that makes abstraction of the disclosures structure and focus on a clustering approach of words that results in abstract notions, such as notations. Resulted topics represent latent constructs that reflect the essential message of different groups of words used in a different context, along with a set of multiple documents reviewed.

In order to describe shortly the LDA probabilistic model, we consider the following variables and notations:

- a vocabulary of *V* words used along the corpus analyzed: 1, …, V;
- a document that consists of Nw words denoted by w=w1,w2,…, wN ;
- a corpus that represents a collection of *M* documents denoted by D=w1,w2,…, wM;
- total number of words on the corpus defined as N=i=1MNi;
- a number of *K* topics extracted;
- the positive prior weight of topic k in a document is k, for k=1, …,K;
- the positive prior weight of word wn in a topic, for n=1, …,N;
- probability k,w is the probability of word wn occurring in topic k;
- the distribution of words in topic k is given by k;
- probability wn,k is the probability of topic k occurring in document wn;
- the distribution of topics in document wn is given by wn.

For each topic (latent attributes) a distribution over words is determined. The LDA model starts from several characteristics of the random process of using different words on different documents:

- N~Poisson, the distribution of words on each document follow a Poisson distribution, specific to counting variables;
- θ~Dir, the distribution of topics in document d has to follow a Dirichlet distribution, used to model random probability mass functions for the finite set of documents reviewed, with the properties i≥0, i=1ki=1;
- for each of the *N* words wn:
    - zn~Multinomial, each topic identified along the corpus follow a multinomial distribution consisting of a distribution of specific words found on document *n*;
    - pwn|zn, the multinomial probability of word wn conditioned on the topic zn.

The k-dimensional Dirichlet random variable is described by probability density below:

$$p(\theta \mid \alpha) = \frac{\Gamma\left(\sum_{i=1}^{k} \alpha_i\right)}{\prod_{i=1}^{k} \Gamma(\alpha_i)} \theta_l^{\alpha_1 - 1} \cdots \theta_k^{\alpha_k - 1}$$

where is a k-vector with components i>0.

Figure 3. Graphical representation of LDA
Source: Blei et al. (2003), Latent Dirichlet Allocation, p. 997

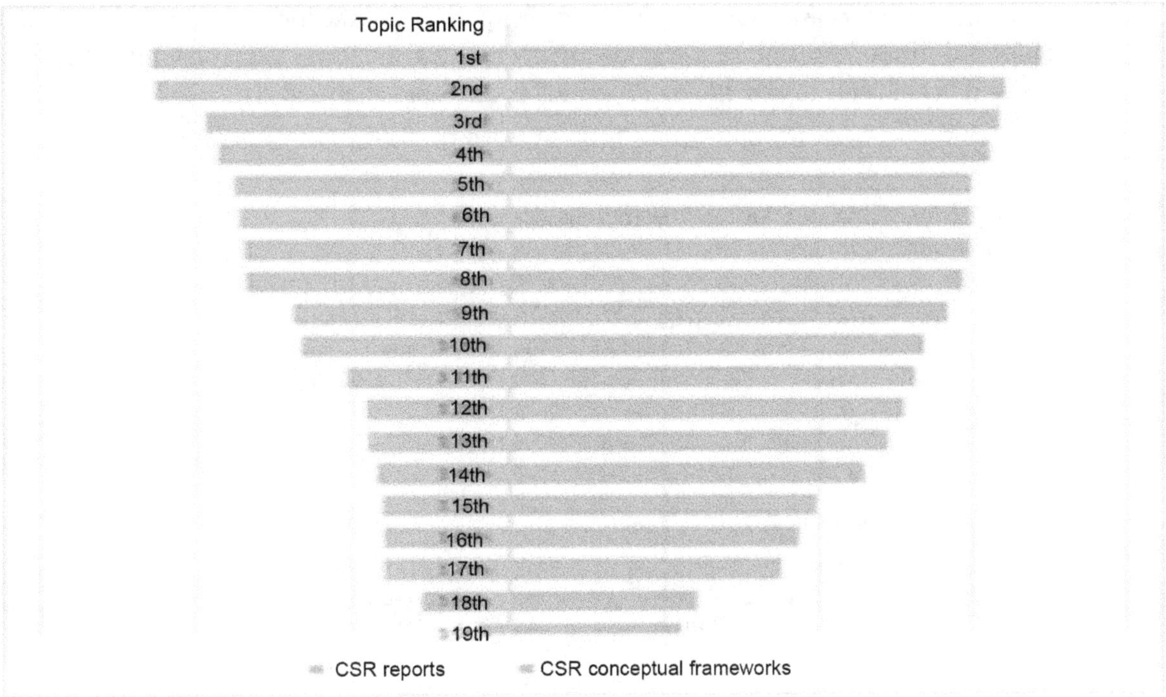

Figure 3 is a more representative description of the LDA model, on which Blei *et al.* (2003) defined the boxes as the replicates, the outer boxes as documents, while the inner boxes as the repeated choice of topics and words within a document.

Overall, the LDA probabilistic model looks for the identification of clusters of text that frequently appear in a corpus and that are used in a common context. We use this model as it is designed to determine proportions of content for documents that contain multiple topics. As a basis for the construction of our topic-based modeling, we will consider 20 topics to be extracted, starting from the number of the keywords selected after reviewing all relevant CSR and sustainability reporting frameworks and standards. However, we will perform separately LDA analysis of reviewed CSR reports, for other two different number of topics to check if significant improvement on avoiding topic overlapping can be made.

As a final step, we will proceed to a comparative analysis of the first 5 most robust topics extracted from CSR reports and respectively CSR/sustainability reporting frameworks considered in our analysis (**Figure 4**). The set of criteria considered when selecting the 5 most robust topics from the total of 20 topics extracted related to the part of Mallet LDA language processing metrics, respectively:

- *document entropy* that measures the frequency of a topic over all documents; a higher entropy of the topic related to a spread of the topic over many documents reviewed;
- *coherence* which reflects whether the words in a topic tend to co-occur together; as larger the value of this measure the lower the indication words co-occur in different topics simultaneously;
- *corpus distance* showing the marginal effect on words distribution of multiple topics selected, compared with a single topic selected model; the greater the distance means the more distinct is a topic from the other topics extracted;
- *uniform distance* is a measure based on Kullback-Leiber divergence, that shows topic's specificity, by determining the distance from a topic's distribution over words to a uniform distribution; the greater the distance means the more specific is a topic, compared with the other topics extracted;
- *exclusivity* metric that measures how many words from the list of the top words of a topic are common with words from the list of the top words of other topics; the lower the probability of common words shared by multiple topics, the more general is the topic analyzed.

Figure 4. Sample composition of CSR reports reviewed
Source: authors projection

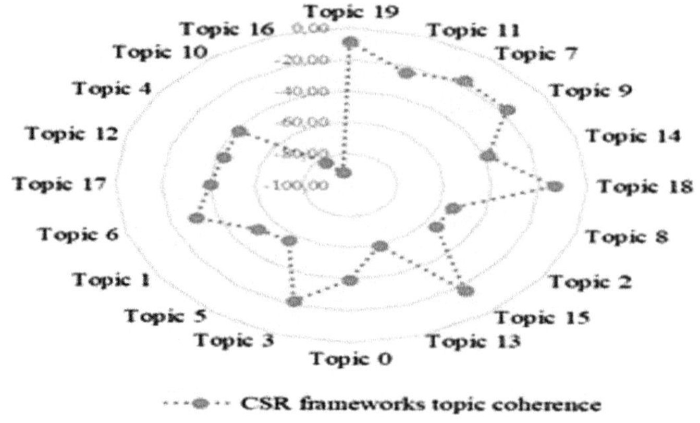

In our study, we analyzed the latest sustainability reports of the first 50 companies ranked by the stock market value in US dollars on 30 June 2020, from a global top elaborated by Bloomberg with PwC analysis (Bloomberg and PwC, 2020). We selected those companies because they represent the main economic entities in the world, and their published reports are in the spotlight. From those 50 CSR reports only 38 were considered for textual analysis (**Table 3**) as we could not extract information from the other 12 reports excluded, based on the procedure performed using RapidMiner Text analysis toolkit. The reports cover the period 2017 – 2020. In **Figure 4** is shown our sample composition which shows the prevalence of US companies. In our analysis, we will verify the differences in CSR reports characteristics, such as understandability and a complexity measure, as defined per Dyer *et al.* (2017). Such analysis is relevant if we want to see the effect of different approaches on CSR standard-setting. Additionally, the split of our sample per area of activities of the companies analyzed is essential for us to test if there are differences in CSR reporting practice, based on the specific of the operations. For instance, according to Carrots & Sticks (2020) report emphasized that half of the CSR provisions are issued by EU government bodies of capital market standard setters. Additionally, the same report has underlined that the focus of standard setters on CSR reporting is oriented especially towards heavy industries such as extraction, manufacturing or transport & storage.

Table 3. Sample of valid reports reviewed

1. Consumer goods	L'Oreal, LVMH, Nestle, PepsiCo, Proctle & Gamble, Toyota;
2. Consumer services	Alibaba, Comcast, Netflix, Walmart, WaltDisney
3. Financials	Berkshire, CCB, China Bank, JP Morgan, MasterCard, PayPal, PingAn, Visa
4. Healthcare	Johnson & Johnson, Merck, Novartis
5. Oil & Gas	Aramco, Exxon
6. Technology	Adobe Inc., Alphabet Inc., Apple, Cisco, Facebook, Intel, Microsoft, Nvidia, Oracle, Samsung, Tencent, TSMC
7. Telecommunication	AT & T, Verizon

Source: authors projection

For this purpose, we will check for the 50 CSR reports downloaded from companies' websites in pdf format, which allows textual analysis performed with RapidMiner package. Similar analysis will be performed for the CSR/sustainability frameworks and the results will be compared with the output related to LDA analysis for CSR reports.

RESULTS AND DISCUSSION

The current CSR reporting landscape raises a long list of conceptual and methodological challenges. As underlined by European Reporting LAB - EFRAG (2021), an increasing number of inconsistencies in reporting practice is reported, because of a proliferation of reporting requirements and frameworks that appear to be significantly heterogeneous, with implicit consequences on the relevance of CSR reports for shareholders and stakeholders as well.

It is well-known that the multiple CSR reporting frameworks, significantly heterogeneous in scope, objectives, and guidelines for implementation, provide an extremely scattered basis of reporting, with implications on the CSR reporting practice. Adding the challenges related to digitalizing increasing volumes of CSR information made public and correlating with the lack of mandatory requirements of assurance on data accuracy and materiality, lead preparers to the point that they face a high-cost burden on preparing those reports, while users seem to lose trust on CSR information made public (Christensen *et al.*, 2019).

This section is aimed to analyze the discrepancy between CSR practice and CSR frameworks, from the perspective of topics covered along the period analyzed. We consider this research approach more relevant compared with performing a holistic comparison of structure, volume, and content analysis on CSR reports. As long as there is no framework preparers can relate to when presenting CSR information in a more structured and well-referenced way, ensuring a proper connection between financial information and non-financial information made public, the topic modeling approach reveals conclusive information reviewing a high volume of textual information. The aim of this research is not to compare different CSR reporting frameworks, but to underline the effect of lack of coherence between them on the CSR reporting practice. Through the design of our analysis, we try to emphasize how important is to have a more robust CSR reporting framework that:

- aligns scope and objectives of CSR reports with a more unitary CSR reporting framework, that ensures a common global and regional approach on the concepts used (CSR reporting taxonomy; e.g.: business model, value continuum, ESG balanced scorecard, etc.), the scope, the objectives of CSR reporting and the way information is presented (e.g. of criteria to be considered: double materiality, information connectivity, forward-looking versus retrospective information, data validation rules, etc.);
- either structure one common framework or redesign existing CSR frameworks on separate layers of reporting, promoting differential reporting approach, that defines the level of degree of reporting requirements regulation gradually, based on these layers, as for example the models proposed by DiPiazza and Eccles (2002) highlighting the three layers of corporate reporting transparency model, which is promoted by European Reporting LAB - EFRAG (2021), which define a sector-agnostic layer of reporting, a sector-specific layer of reporting and an entity-specific layer of reporting;
- ask for a set of minimum information to be disclosed, similar to the IFRSs approach, and provide a guideline on some minimal checkpoints that ensure proper information connectivity (between quantitative and qualitative information, between content sections, between financial information and non-financial information, between past, present and future information, or between concepts used on the report);
- ensure higher coherence between standards with the purpose of reducing redundant and sometimes inconsistent requirements between standards, such the case of SASB standards;
- provide general principles on assessing ESG financial impact by connecting CSR reporting data to financial information presented on the annual report, in order to: (1) allow users to asses CSR value creation and firms' sustainable growth perspectives; (2) improve reputation; (3) show management long-term strategic orientation; (4) optimize risk management and controls, etc.;
- makes a clear separation between conceptual framework promoting concepts and general principles of CSR reporting, and the set of standards that address specific topics; here the SASB ex-

ample is a good example of CSR reporting framework architecture, which considers the industry-specific, compared with the EU NFRD Directive (Directive 95/2014) that seem to be too general;
- avoid inconsistencies between CSR reporting standards, issuing specialized standards, addressing strictly specific topics and that defines a clear scope, which should be coherent with the general CSR reporting conceptual reporting framework used for CSR corporate reporting purpose.

Review of CSR Reports Characteristics

In **Table 4** we provide the min descriptive statistics related to the 38 CSR reports reviewed in this study. The measure of complexity reflects the number of sentences per page, while the measure of understandability shows the number of words per sentence (Dyer *et al.*, 2017). The widespread of CSR reporting practice can already be easily observed looking at the measure of complexity, as the range between the minimum value (*3.79* sentences per page, specific for Oracle CSR report) and the maximum value (*27.78* sentences per page, valid for Cisco CSR report) is high. The same significantly high range is identified in the case of the measure of understandability as well, as the minimum value (*11.85* words per sentence, valid for L'Oreal CSR report) is far from the maximum value (*29.93* words per sentence, valid for TMSC CSR report).

Table 4. Descriptive statistics on CSR reports (textual analysis)

		No. Words	No. Sentences	No. Pages	Complexity	Understandability
Mean		18.737	1.129	88	13,02	16,73
Std. Error of Mean		2.324	134	9	0,81	0,63
Median		15.969	952	79	12,39	15,16
Std. Deviation		14.327	826	58	4,98	3,91
Minimum		1.869	91	17	3,79	11,85
Maximum		60.551	3.617	254	27,78	29,93
Percentiles	25	9.158	545	50	10,11	13,70
	50	15.969	952	79	12,39	15,16
	75	23.220	1.347	120	15,01	18,55

Source: calculation with SPSS 25

Firms prepare CSR reports of significantly different sizes, combining text content with graphical representation. Therefore, the small number of sentences per document does not necessarily mean a small size of the report, but data more represented in graphical format, the reason why the measure of complexity must be interpreted together with the measure of understandability. If the sentences per page have a higher number of words, this would lead to a lower understandability of the text as a higher volume of information is synthetized in a single sentence. However, as long as the information is presented with relevant graphical representation and with proper link to other related information, the information becomes more relevant for the users, instead of the case where long sentences are used with less graphical representation. From this perspective, as underlined by Lock and Seele (2016), the longer the length of the report, the higher the credibility will be, no matter the length of the sentences.

Table 5. ANOVA F-test on CSR reports characteristics

		Sum of Squares	df	Mean Square	F	Sig.
Region	Complexity	72,83	2	36,41	1,508	0,235
	Understandability	209,62	2	104,81	10,322	***0,000***
	ESG score	373,22	2	186,61	1,817	0,178
Sector	Complexity	46,57	6	7,76	0,276	0,944
	Understandability	32,28	6	5,38	0,313	0,925
	ESG score	1.544,5	6	257,42	3,293	***0,013***
Assurance	Complexity	33,25	1	33,25	1,353	0,252
	Understandability	0,34	1	0,34	0,022	0,884
	ESG score	47,28	1	47,28	0,434	0,514

Source: calculation with SPSS 25

The 1st and 3rd percentile for both measures show that approximately 75% of the sample reports reviewed have a closer value to the mean of the sample, showing that the CSR practice is heterogeneous in terms of the length of the reports, the length of the sentences, but the significant variation is limited to only a small part of the sample reviewed.

In **Table 5** we present a difference test of means for those measures, in order to identify within the three factors considered in the analysis, which is significantly impacting CSR reports textual quality. This way we seek for the outliers if they are more likely to be from a separate area of activity, or a region. The results show that the lack of an assurance auditor's opinion on the CSR reports does not significantly impact the quality of the report ($Sig. > 0.05$). The same results are valid for the area of activity, meaning that the specific operations conducted by companies publishing CSR reports are not necessarily impacting the quality of the reports ($Sig. > 0.05$). Those results show how important is the design of the CSR reporting framework on three layers of reporting, one of them being the industry-specific reporting requirements and guidelines. A good example of such a differential reporting layer can be the SASB standards, which are designed specifically for different areas of activity. However, SASB standards focus more on the financial materiality of the ESG topics (environment, social capital, human capital, business model and innovation, leadership, and governance), which is more aligned with the IIRC framework that stands for proper reporting of the value continuum (value creation – value preservation – value realization). On the other side, a framework of similar complexity, such as the GRI Guideline, try to have a balance between the core topics addressed (economic, environmental, social), with less focus on the value creation generated by human capital and innovative processes and technologies, unless they have an environmental and social impact. Instead, results from **Table 5** show that the regional approach on CSR reporting determines a significant influence on CSR reports understandability, from a textual analysis perspective ($Sig. = 0.00 < 0.05$).

To find the area of activity where companies with higher understandability of CSR reports operate, we provide in **Table 6** results of post-hoc statistical analysis on differences. The results of the Tukey

Table 6. Post-hoc test related to the impact of the specific activity on CSR reports

Area of Activity	Mean	Std. Dev.	Area of Activity	Mean	Std. Dev.	Mean Difference (I-J)	Std. Error	Sig.
Consumer goods	15,89	3,875	Consumer services	16,46	2,418	5.976*	1,915	0,010
			Financial services	17,36	2,942	5.437*	1,239	0,000

*the mean difference is significant at the 0.05 level.
Source: calculation with SPSS 25

HSD difference test show that the significant difference is between companies that operate on consumer goods area of activity and the companies that run operations on consumer services, respectively on financial areas of activities. Those results could be explained by the fact that consumers' trust is more sensitive to ESG related events, such as the negative effect to consumers' health, the technological process of production and packaging, or the way waste management is ensured, whereas products provided by companies working on trading area and financial area could have a more likely significant financial impact, but less probable social and environmental impact. Reviewing *The 2030 Agenda for Sustainable Development* official document issued by UN (2015), we observe that most of the new SDG targets related to social and environmental topics, which show that the main expectation of shareholders, investors, and stakeholders as well concentrate on those two components, the reason why companies operating in areas such as natural resources extraction, oil & gas extraction, transport, or even consumer goods are monitored more prominently.

Table 7. Post-hoc test related to the impact of the specific activity on CSR reports

Area of Activity	Mean	Std. Dev.	Area of activity	Mean	Std. Dev.	Mean Difference (I-J)	Std. Error	Sig.
Oil & gas	41,55	9,26	Consumer Goods	12,33	10,75	-29,22	7,22	0,005
			Financial services	14,00	10,52	-27,55	6,99	0,007
			Technology	17,61	8,56	-23,95	6,75	0,019

*. The mean difference is significant at the 0.05 level.
Source: calculation with SPSS 25

We have included on the ANOVA analysis the MSCI ESG score as well, to understand if the effect of the CSR reports message on investors' expectation and position. A higher score of ESG means that investors perceive positively the way CSR reports have covered the ESG topics, meaning that reports' complexity and understandability were enough to ensure the data presented are not misunderstood. In **Table 7** we provide the post-hoc Tukey HSD test to show the statistically significant differences in ESG score. As noted by Carrots & Stick (2020), areas of activity such as oil & extraction are subject to more CSR reporting requirements, which is confirmed by the results provided in **Table 7**, compared to the area of consumer goods ($Sig._{CG} = 0.005 < 0.05$), financial services ($Sig._{FS} = 0.007 < 0.05$), and technology ($Sig._{T} = 0.019 < 0.05$).

Figure 5. Heatmap on keywords occurrence on the CSR reports with highest occurrence
Source: projection with RapidMiner 9.8.00 package software

	Topic																			
	0	*1*	*2*	*3*	*4*	*5*	*6*	*7*	*8*	*9*	*10*	*11*	*12*	*13*	*14*	*15*	*16*	*17*	*18*	*19*
Topic 0	1																			
Topic 1	-0,187	1																		
Topic 2	-0,108	-0,150	1																	
Topic 3	-0,184	0,998	-0,106	1																
Topic 4	-0,258	0,738	-0,033	0,752	1															
Topic 5	0,050	-0,078	0,668	-0,013	0,176	1														
Topic 6	-0,161	-0,078	-0,170	-0,082	0,542	-0,077	1													
Topic 7	-0,088	-0,079	-0,176	-0,084	-0,174	-0,078	-0,078	1												
Topic 8	0,892	-0,078	-0,186	-0,083	-0,173	-0,077	-0,077	-0,079	1											
Topic 9	-0,031	-0,068	-0,185	-0,083	-0,103	-0,077	-0,077	-0,079	-0,078	1										
Topic 10	-0,089	-0,078	-0,105	-0,081	-0,121	-0,078	-0,078	-0,079	-0,078	-0,078	1									
Topic 11	0,059	-0,079	-0,159	-0,083	-0,126	-0,077	-0,078	-0,079	-0,078	-0,078	-0,079	1								
Topic 12	-0,038	-0,140	-0,437	-0,157	-0,220	-0,217	-0,096	-0,001	-0,187	0,365	0,255	0,769	1							
Topic 13	-0,305	-0,115	-0,044	-0,122	-0,185	-0,114	-0,112	-0,117	-0,110	-0,104	-0,116	-0,115	-0,260	1						
Topic 14	-0,278	-0,208	-0,035	-0,215	-0,345	-0,092	-0,199	0,093	-0,220	0,084	0,274	-0,169	0,184	-0,250	1					
Topic 15	-0,100	-0,078	-0,184	-0,082	-0,163	-0,077	-0,077	-0,078	-0,077	-0,077	-0,066	-0,078	0,114	-0,114	0,784	1				
Topic 16	-0,241	-0,139	0,494	-0,114	-0,156	0,339	-0,177	0,387	-0,230	-0,406	-0,002	-0,213	-0,429	0,451	-0,191	-0,189	1			
Topic 17	0,027	-0,080	0,512	-0,085	-0,154	-0,080	-0,080	-0,081	-0,080	-0,080	-0,081	-0,080	-0,219	-0,089	-0,104	-0,080	0,431	1		
Topic 18	0,235	-0,079	-0,145	-0,084	-0,068	-0,075	-0,064	-0,080	-0,079	-0,079	-0,079	-0,079	-0,085	-0,116	-0,209	-0,078	-0,186	-0,081	1	
Topic 19	-0,214	-0,079	0,339	-0,084	-0,131	-0,078	-0,078	-0,060	-0,079	-0,079	-0,079	-0,069	-0,214	-0,104	0,311	-0,078	-0,221	-0,080	-0,080	1

Looking at the CSR reports of those companies, we get a mean value of *16.38* for understandability measure and a mean value of *12.42* for complexity measure, which are close to the mean value of our sample. These results show that investors' perception does not resume only to the format of the information presented by to the content as well, as the highest ESG score for companies from our sample relates only to an average level of complexity and understandability of the CSR reports.

Instead, compared with companies from other areas included in our sample, there are no significant differences in the ESG score, such as companies operating in the consumer services area. Such companies concentrate the message of their CSR reports more likely on describing social topics, as for instance shown in **Figure 5**. Looking for the occurrence of family words related to our keywords, we observe that companies operating in the consumer services area, such as Walt Disney, Walmart (included on between Visa and Walt Disney in **Figure 5**), Comcast (included on between Cisco Inc. and Exxon Mobile on **Figure 5**), or Alibaba (included on between Adobe Inc. and Alphabet Inc. on **Figure 5**).

Analysis on Topics Emphasized on CSR Reporting Frameworks

Looking at the most frequent words on the corporate reporting frameworks considered in our analysis, we represent in **Figure 6** the heatmap that highlights the main concerns of standard-setters related to CSR reporting. We observe that the most frequent words seem to relate to reporting requirements and guidelines, while provisions related to the information to be included on the report (nature, users, relevance, materiality, quality) seem to be extremely scattered between different frameworks. If the SASB framework relates more to the *financial materiality* of ESG topics disclosed, GRI Guidelines seem to promote a more *balanced representation* of all ESG data on the CSR reports.

As expected, ISO standards show a clear focus on the *social responsibility* concerns (ISO 26000) and *environmental* data to be disclosed (ISO 14001). Inconsistencies seem to be not only between CSR reporting frameworks, but assurance standards as well.

Figure 6. Heatmap on keywords occurrence on the CSR reports with the highest occurrence
Source: projection with RapidMiner 9.8.00 package software

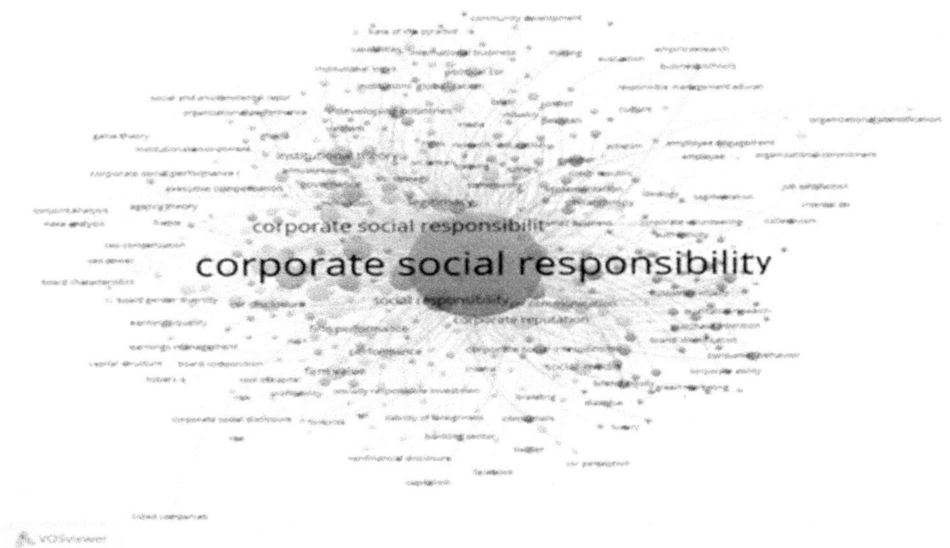

Figure 7. Heatmap on keywords occurrence on the CSR reporting frameworks
Source: projection with RapidMiner 9.8.00 package software

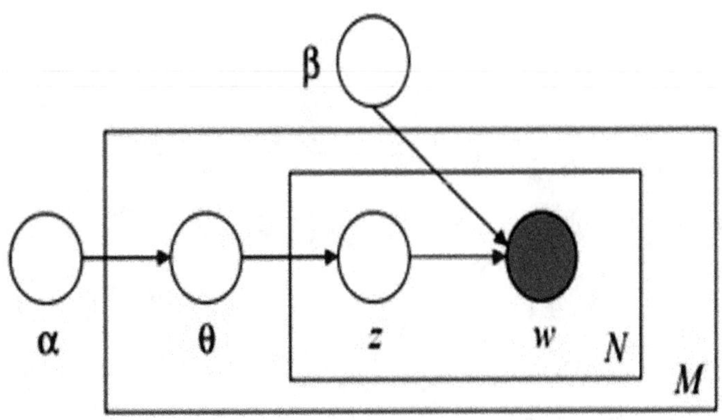

If the AA1000 standard shows higher preoccupation for the relevance of CSR reports for stakeholders, from the perspective of the impact of ESG special events, the ISAE standard relates more to the principles of CSR reports assurance and engagement definition basics.

The last observation related to **Figure 6** results is the lower occurrence of the "risk" word, compared with the" impact" word, which we infer to be a weakness of current CSR reporting frameworks, as seem that the focus of those frameworks is more on disclosure of the impact of ESG events than information providing data related to risk management. We consider this kind of approach to promote disclosure information that reflects more likely a reactive CSR reporting philosophy than a more proactive one. It is obvious that standard-setters have considered preparing the reporting frameworks companies' concerns related to proprietary costs or litigation costs (Christensen *et al.*, 2019). However, managers have to understand that the objective of CSR reporting is not to transform CSR reports into veritable strategic marketing tools, but rather to provide relevant and comparable data that allow investors and stakeholders as well to get an image of the externalities of CSR activities.

Starting from the keywords list retrieved from most relevant CSR reporting frameworks, we represent the heatmap of keywords occurrence in **Figure 7**. These results provide an overall indication of the orientation of those CSR frameworks. The results show a similar orientation of current CSR reporting frameworks with the 2030 agenda on SDGs targets set-up, emphasizing a prioritization on climate change concerns, and defending employees' rights. From this perspective, we underline that CSR reporting frameworks should continue to promote all aspects of social responsibility, including information related to business models that contribute to the sustainable development of the society and that describe better companies' impact on the circular economy structure.

Differences Analysis Between CSR Reports and CSR Reporting Frameworks

In **Figure 8** we provide a ranking of the families of words most frequently used on CSR conceptual reporting frameworks and respectively the CSR reports. Based on this ranking, we observe a slight difference in the topics addressed by each of those documents reviewed.

Figure 8. Heatmap on most frequent words used on CSR reports and reporting frameworks
Source: authors projection of words distribution

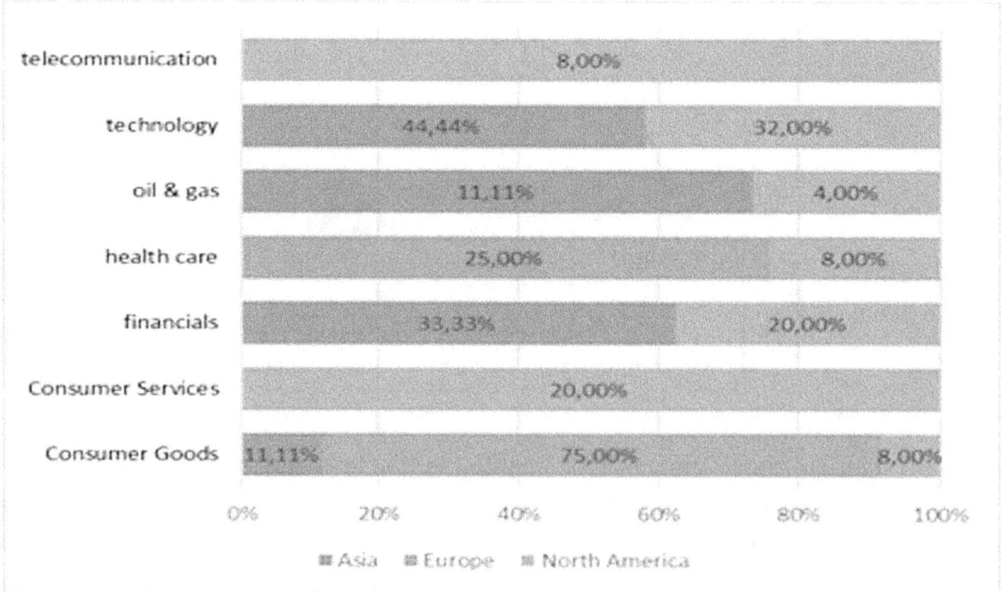

A first observation is related to the reference of each of the documents to the family of words assimilated to "development", such as "growth", "progress", "developed", which seem to be more frequently used on CSR reports. Through CSR reports, the management team wants to highlight the positive effects of

Figure 9. Word-cloud representation of CSR reporting frameworks
Source: projection with RapidMiner 9.8.00 package software

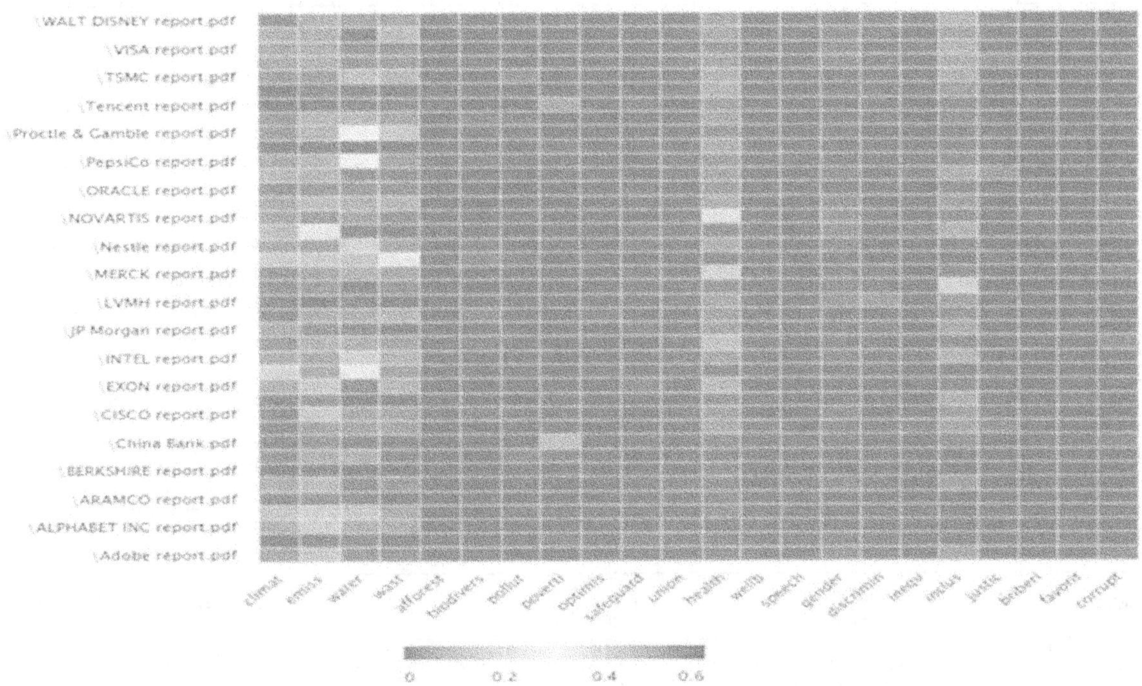

Figure 10. Word-cloud representation of CSR reports
Source: projection with RapidMiner 9.8.00 package software

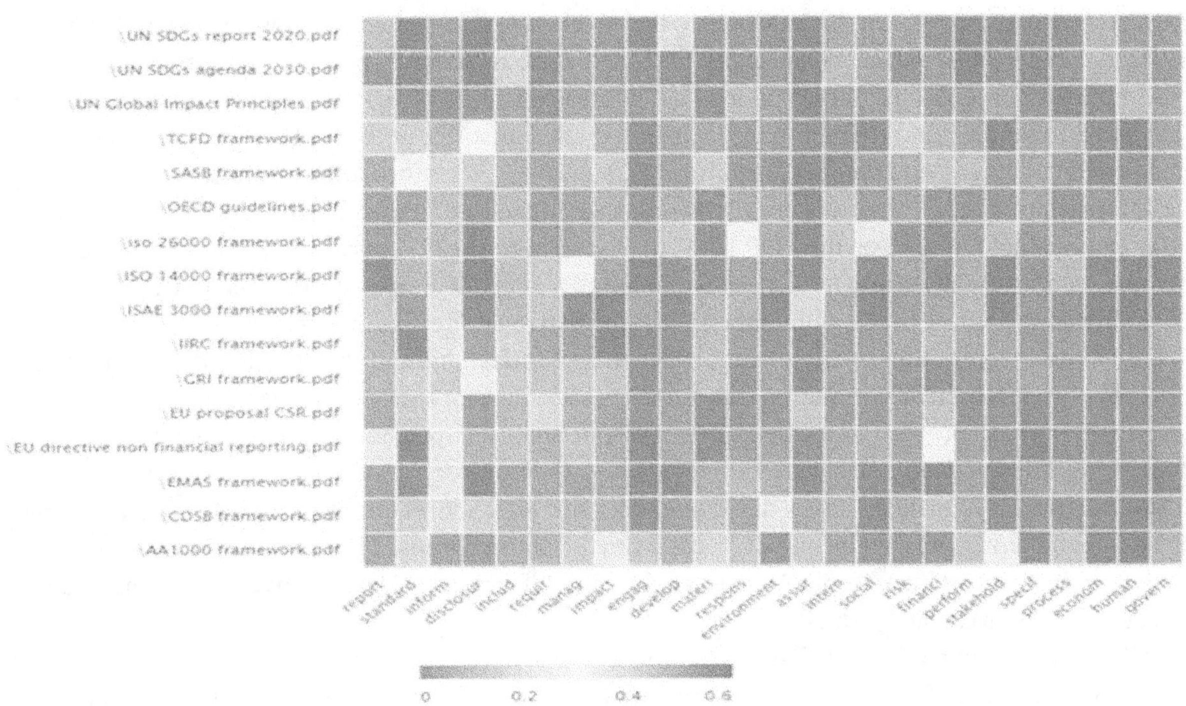

Table 8. Topics extracted from CSR reports, based on LDA model

Topic	Coherence	Exclusivity	Document Entropy	Uniform Distance	Words per Corpus
Topic_6	-11,90	0,338	3,45	3,56	5,06%
Topic_14	-12,45	0,252	3,21	3,97	6,11%
Topic_10	-11,70	0,202	3,18	3,74	7,49%
Topic_5	-49,01	0,339	3,11	3,68	6,66%
Topic_7	-12,70	0,286	2,99	3,69	5,83%
Topic_4	-8,13	0,321	2,99	3,87	6,86%
Topic	**Topic Generic Meaning Based on TOP Words List**		**TOP 10 Words Related to the Topic**		
Topic_6	*Strategic orientation*		global, make, people, systems, committed, plans, include, projects, time, increase		
Topic_14	*Objectives of CSR reporting*		global, business, ESG, financial, customers, employees, information, environmental, management, risk		
Topic_10	*Optimal use of human capital*		report, data, business, rights, human, social, performance, employees, security, governance, environment		
Topic_5	*Corporate governance and crisis management*		data, standards, diversity, impact, inclusion, governance, employees, company, workforce		
Topic_7	*Supply chain management and disruptive technologies*		suppliers, use, management, products, technology, process, product, global, facilities, program		
Topic_4	*Specific objectives of CSR reports*		energy, carbon, renewable, data, environmental, emissions, climate, use, scope, water		

Source: authors projection based on RapidMiner 9.8.00 output

CSR activities and companies' impact on the development of society (**Figure 9**). According to the social contract theory, companies must contribute to the development of society, otherwise, they will get lower motivation from social partners (especially the employees) to achieve their own objective (**Figure 10**).

Although CSR reporting frameworks do not address the topic of risk management enough, it seems that companies are willing to disclose information on this area, about the business model, supply chain management concerns, and product portfolio data. However, that information seems to be more descriptive than quantitative, as the frequency of words assimilated to "impact", such as "effect", "impact", "efficiency" is not included on the TOP 15 words list from the CSR reports analyzed. A simple descriptive approach, with only slight references to quantitative data, decreases users' trust in CSR reports, as this approach is not fact-based, but rather highly subjective and less audit-proof.

Keywords or top words list analysis indicates the essential nature of data disclosed by CSR reports. However, this approach has limitations, as it does not account for the context the words are used in, the reason why we will proceed to the second part of our analysis, focusing more on topic-based analysis of the two groups of documents analyzed.

Overall, the LDA analysis shows that documents analyzed address multiple topics, none of the most robust ones covering a higher weight of words from the entire corpus. These results lead to lower document entropy. For instance, Topic 16 extracted from CSR frameworks reviewed, reflecting financial impact, cover approximately 16.18%

In **Table 8** we summarize the TOP 5 most robust topics extracted from the CSR reports analyzed. In **Table 9** we present the TOP 5 most robust topics extracted from the CSR reporting frameworks analyzed.

Table 9. Topics extracted from CSR reporting frameworks, based on LDA model

Topic	Coherence	Exclusivity	Document Entropy	Uniform Distance	Words per Corpus
Topic_19	-8,67	0,466	2,28	3,34	4,64%
Topic_11	-24,35	0,411	2,26	3,66	3,20%
Topic_7	-17,20	0,385	1,94	3,95	4,24%
Topic_9	-17,71	0,450	1,85	3,28	4,56%
Topic_14	-38,55	0,445	1,75	3,24	3,01%
Topic_4	-8,13	0,321	2,99	3,87	6,86%

Topic	Topic Generic Meaning Based on TOP Words List	TOP 10 Words Related to the Topic
Topic_19	*Objectives of CSR reporting*	specific, context, process, standards, objectives, industry, identify, time, financial, services
Topic_11	*Value creation and risk management perspectives*	information, risks, report, include, activities, capitals, value, model, opportunities, reporting
Topic_7	*Materiality on CSR reporting*	principles, impact, standards, performance, stakeholders, disclosures, material, criteria, accounting, management
Topic_9	*Best practice on reporting metrics use of energy*	example, guidance, use, impact, policy, relevant, energy, including, consumption, development
Topic_14	*Supply Chain and Business conduct requirements*	business, global, support, supply, corruption, local, human, principles, reporting, rights
Topic_4	*Specific objectives of CSR reports*	information, water, include, economic, work, waste, nations, services, safety, health, emissions

Source: authors projection based on RapidMiner 9.8.00 output

Overall, results on entropy metrics show low values as documents analyzed on the same corpus share most of the topics identified. The issue is that those topics are presented in a combination that leads to poor structuring of information presented on CSR reports.

An essential observation, comparing the two lists of topics, is that the general description of reporting objectives seems to be distinctly presented on the CSR reports and CSR reporting frameworks as well, without any overlapping with other topics. Another common topic between the two corpuses of text analyzed, refer to supply chain management and related concerns, which seem to be extremely important nowadays in the context of COVID 19 pandemic restrictions, with its implications on supply chain disruptions and supporting technologies.

The rest of the topics, considered on the TOP 5 most robust topics extracted, differ between CSR reports and CSR reporting frameworks. CSR reporting framework aims to present distinct topics such as related to value creation and risk management and guidance on materiality, as topics that relate more to the principle-based conceptual framework. However, if we relate to our keywords list and the objectives achieved according to the 2020 SDGs progress status report, we observe that a better distinction on the CSR reporting frameworks is made only for energy-related CSR activities. Essential ESG information related to emissions, climate change, or water management is presented on an aggregate topic (Topic 4), as shown in **Table 8**. These results show that improvement on the separation within standards or reporting guidelines must be made to provide a clear set of criteria for data to be disclosed, for each SDG agreed

Figure 11. Topic ranking based on the score of entropy
Source: authors projection of words distribution

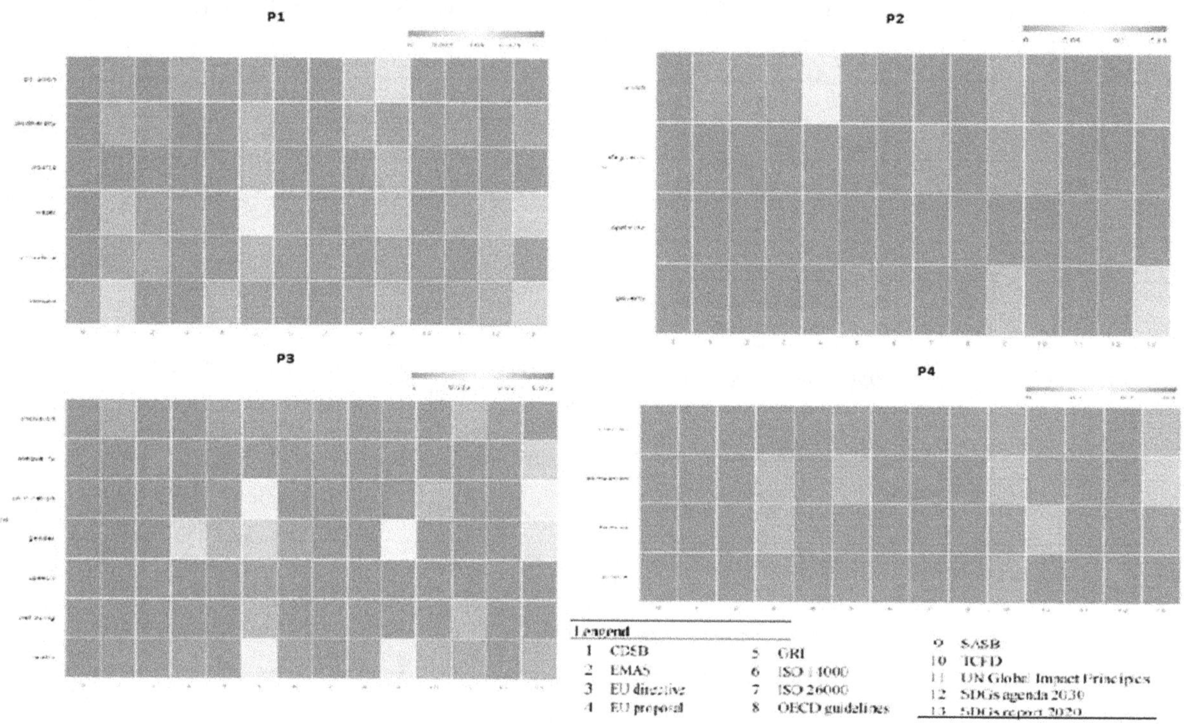

globally. For this purpose, the solution of three layers of standard-setting CSR reporting requirements could be a proper long-term solution.

On the other hand, CSR reports seem to present distinctly better than CSR reporting frameworks, the information related to human capital. The also a common approach to the presentation of companies' corporate governance information showing this way how managers understand the need for accountability and responsibility.

Instead, CSR reports do not have a common approach to presenting information related to the environment. This observation can be affected also by the sample composition we have considered in our analysis, as the number of companies operating in heavy industry, such as oil & gas is relatively small (approximately *5.26%*).

In **Figure 11** we represent on a pyramid chart the measure of information entropy of documents analyzed. The main observation on the results related to this measure of entropy is that CSR reporting frameworks have a lower degree of comparability on topics addressed, compared with the CSR reports analyzed. The higher the score of entropy the more present is the topics and all documents analyzed as a corpus. In our case, the topics addressed on the CSR reporting frameworks related corpus, seem to have a different presence on the frameworks. Similar results are shown in the case of the presence of topics on CSR reports related corpus, but with slightly better results, meaning that CSR reporting practice harmonization exceeds CSR reporting frameworks harmonization, with positive implications on the information comparability along with industries and in between.

Figure 12. Topic ranking based on topic coherence
Source: authors projection of words distribution

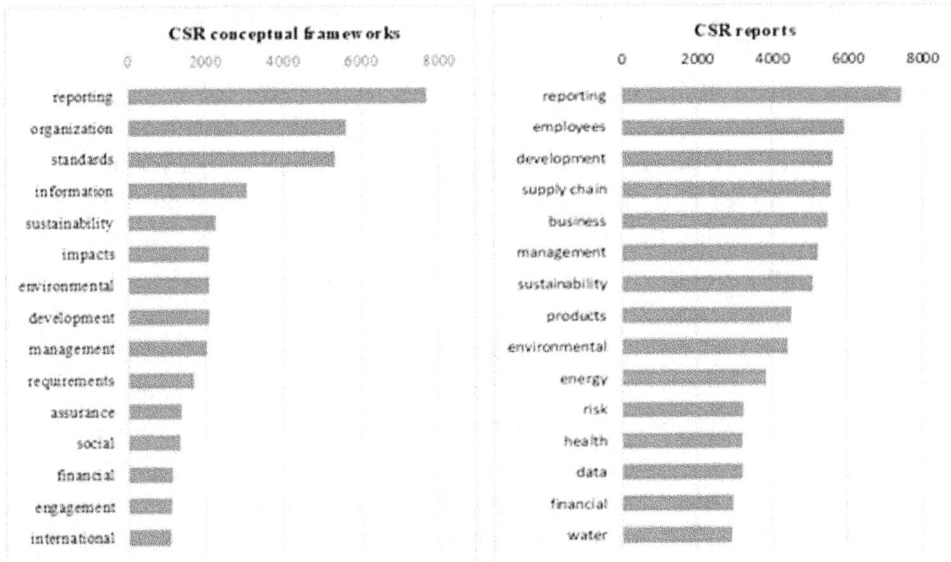

Figure 13. Correlation matrix on topics confidence metric (proportion of presence)
Source: authors projection based on RapidMiner 9.8.00 output

In **Figure 12** we provide an additional metric of topics extracted robustness, which shows the measure of whether words in a topic co-occur together, for the topics extracted from CSR reporting frameworks. This measure indicates the degree of harmonization between reporting frameworks analyzed, from a textual analysis perspective. Additionally, in **Figure 11** we present the correlation matrix related to the confidence metric of each topic that measures the presence of the respective topic on each document included on the corpus analyzed.

As expected, we observe several topics that share common words for CSR reporting as is the case of *Topic 19* which according to **Table 9** relate to the *objectives of CSR reporting*. However, the confidence of this principle-based topic is higher correlated only with *Topic 2* and *Topic 13*, which relate strictly to environmental information disclosed by CSR reporting. Instead, confidence for topics addressing the other classes of CSR information is weakly correlated with *Topic 19*. For instance, *Topic 3* relates to information about employees and the economic impact of their activity on the organization (i.e., the top 10 word-list corresponding to Topic 3 is: "information", "use", "organizations", "products", "employees", "human", "specific", "materials", "local", "negative"). Based on those results we appreciate a better separation between the section of generally accepted principles of CSR reporting and the sections that address a specific type of information (industry-based specific standards). SASB standards could be used as a reference for future projects of standard-setting, as they cannot be used as CSR reporting standards because their attention is more on financial materiality information concerning ESG data made public by companies.

Another case is of *Topic 18* that concern information about value creation (mainly specific for integrated reporting framework), which show that there is extremely low harmonization degree between integrated reporting model and CSR reporting model. CSR reporting frameworks do not address sufficiently the relevance of the value generated by high-quality CSR activities (the word "value" appears only *245* times from the total number of tokens of the corpus analyzed).

In the light of those results, we subscribe once more to Christensen *et al.* (2019) and Tsagas and Villiers (2020) opinion that a common approach to CSR reporting standard-setting is needed. Otherwise, as underlined on Carrots & Stick (2020) and European Reporting LAB - EFRAG (2021), users of CSR reports will lose confidence in the information disclosed, because of too heterogeneous reporting practice. It is not enough a material harmonization, reflected on a slight convergence of CSR reports from a topic-based analysis point of view. It is first essential that reporting requirements be coherent and provide sufficient guidance to preparers, to ensure a more uniform reporting practice. The first step is the project launched by EFRAG. Promising results are expected from the TCFD initiative as well, coordinated at a global level. Once a common conceptual framework is issued, the main pillars of the CSR reporting framework are created and a more homogenous topic-based orientation of CSR reports will be ensured, if countries' governance mechanism ensure reasonable compliance with the regulation, or capital markets incentives conditioned by the high quality of CSR reporting output will be sufficiently attractive for companies' management team.

Although there are initiatives that promote a scattered approach of CSR/sustainability reporting, such as the initiative, there have been recorded improvements in this area, at least looking at the increasing efforts of harmonizing different CSR reporting frameworks (Carrots & Sticks; 2020). In this direction we salute the efforts of EFRAG to outline the premises of a common regional project of standard-setting, that focuses on sustainability topics, detailed in their recent report *Proposal for a Relevant and Dynamic EU sustainability reporting standard-setting*. There are also efforts made by IASB who have launched a discussion if it is opportune to create a new board having the objective to *develop, in the public interest, a single set of high quality, understandable, enforceable, and globally accepted sustainability standards based upon clearly articulated principles* (IASB, 2021). Essential is that all involved organisms have shown willingness to work together. However, if the proposal Leuz (2010) has raised for a regional standard-setting body is less likely to happen, because of institutional and political factors related to national economies, there is still an open door for continuous cooperation between regulators and professional associations.

Instead, standard-setters and monitoring agencies in the area of CSR reporting will have to search for a long-term solution that addresses the problem of:

- the narrow scope of CSR reporting framework;
- lack of industry-specific sustainability standards;
- gaps on countries' enforcement framework;
- persistent lack of consensus related to the character of CSR reporting (voluntary versus mandatory) and the need for assurance, as the widespread of CSR practice made it more difficult for researchers' mission to performing a cost-benefit analysis.

CONCLUSION

Nowadays, while the whole world is facing limited resources, the conceptual dimension of sustainability gains more and more interest and attention. Our paper strives to highlight the need for information on how to report CSR information, determined by the significant diversity of national and sub-national corporate social responsibility (CSR) policies, which is a major obstacle to comparability.

In our paper, we aim to test the quality of information presented by top companies according to market value and in accordance with non-financial reporting criteria, taking into account the environment, human and social resources, human rights, and the fight against corruption. The validation of our working hypotheses highlighted the diversity of non-financial information presented by the top 50 listed companies, which confirmed that there is no unitary presentation of the economic, social, and environmental impact generated by the daily activities carried out. Based on the results obtained, we tried to identify common benchmarks that could ensure the quality of non-financial information presented by entities and that could support a future non-financial reporting framework that can be used internationally. Reviewing non-financial reporting is essential to meet the needs of users on relevant, comparable, and accessible information. CSR reporting needs to improve rapidly to progress as investors' interest in non-financial information grows, and in line with the evolution of the phenomena our planet is facing: environmental pollution, climate change, and public health problems.

Thus, we downloaded the sustainability reports from the companies' websites and performed the textual analysis with the RapidMiner package, as well as a similar analysis for CSR frameworks, and the results were compared with the results related to the LDA analysis for CSR reports. We did not aim to compare different CSR reporting frameworks, but to highlight the effect of the lack of coherence between them on reporting practice. By designing our analysis we were able to show the importance of a more robust CSR reporting framework that can bring together the scope and objectives of CSR reports with a more unitary CSR reporting framework that ensures a common global and regional approach to the concepts used: CSR reporting taxonomy, CSR reporting objectives and how the information is presented, criteria to be considered: double materiality, information connectivity, anticipatory versus retrospective information, data validation rules, etc.

We presented the minimum descriptive statistics regarding the CSR reports analyzed in this study, out of the 50 reports only 38 were considered for the textual analysis, the other 12 reports being excluded because we could not extract the necessary information. We have noticed that the most common words seem to be related to reporting requirements and guidelines, while the provisions on the information to be included in the report (nature, users, relevance, materiality, quality) are extremely scattered among different frameworks. By classifying the word families most frequently used in the CSR conceptual reporting framework and the CSR reports, respectively, we were able to make a ranking, which allowed us to observe a minimal difference on the topics addressed by each of the revised documents. The pyramid diagram regarding the measurement of the information entropy of the analyzed documents revealed that the CSR reporting frameworks have a lower degree of comparability on the approached topics, compared to the analyzed CSR reports.

The additional subject robustness metric allowed us to measure the words in a topic that appear together, for the topics extracted from the CSR reporting frameworks, this measure providing indications on the degree of harmonization between the analyzed reporting frameworks, from an analytical perspective. results that show that the separation of standards within reporting standards or guidelines needs to be improved to provide clarity on the set of criteria for the data to be disclosed. The solution of presenting three layers of standardized CSR reporting requirements has been highlighted as a possible appropriate long-term solution, CSR reports seem to present, for example, human capital information with better clarity than CSR reporting frameworks. The measure of informational entropy of the analyzed documents allowed the observation that the CSR reporting frameworks have a lower degree of comparability on the topics approached, compared to the analyzed CSR reports. The higher the entropy score, the more present the subjects and all the documents analyzed as a corpus are present. The topics we addressed in the corpus on CSR reporting frameworks seem to have a different presence than the reporting framework. Similar results are presented in the presence of topics in the corpus of CSR reporting, but with slightly better results, which means that the harmonization of CSR reporting practice goes beyond the harmonization of CSR reporting frameworks.

Accordingly, the common approach to the presentation of corporate governance information could facilitate how managers understand the need for accountability.

We also pointed out that the current reporting modalities do not sufficiently address the relevance of the value generated by high-quality CSR activities.

In the light of the results obtained, we can emphasize once again our rallying to the ideas presented by Christensen *et al.* (2019) and Tsagas and Villiers (2020), who consider that a common approach to setting CSR reporting standards is needed. Otherwise, as pointed out in Carrots & Stick (2020) and European Reporting LAB - EFRAG (2021), users of CSR reports will lose confidence in the information disclosed due to overly heterogeneous reporting practices. A material harmonization alone, reflected by a slight convergence of CSR reports in terms of thematic analysis, is not enough. First of all, it is essential that the reporting requirements are consistent and provide sufficient guidance to the preparers of these reports to ensure a uniform reporting practice. The first step turns out to be the project launched by EFRAG. Promising results are also expected from the globally coordinated TCFD initiative. Once a common conceptual framework has been issued, the main pillars for the CSR reporting framework will be created and a more homogeneous focus on CSR reports will be ensured if the country governance mechanism succeeds in ensuring reasonable compliance with regulations or incentives. in capital markets conditioned by the high quality of CSR reporting, the results will thus be able to be sufficiently attractive to company management.

Despite initiatives promoting a dispersed approach to CSR reporting, however, there have been some improvements in this area, at least based on an analysis of growing efforts to harmonize different CSR reporting frameworks (Carrots & Sticks; 2020). In this regard, we also highlight EFRAG's efforts to outline the premises of a joint regional standard-setting project, which focuses on sustainability issues, detailed in their recent report on the proposal for the development of relevant and dynamic EU sustainable reporting standards. There are also efforts by the IASB to launch a discussion on whether it is appropriate to create a new board with the aim of developing, in the public interest, a single set of high-quality, easy-to-understand sustainability standards. globally applicable and accepted, based on clearly articulated principles. The key is that all the bodies involved have shown their willingness to work together. However, if the proposal that Leuz (2010) raised for a regional standard-setting body is less likely to happen, due to institutional and political factors related to national economies, there is still an open door for ongoing cooperation between regulators and professional associations.

Consequently, standards preparers and monitoring agencies in the field of CSR reporting will have to look for a long-term solution that addresses issues related to: the narrow scope of the CSR reporting framework, the lack of industry-specific CSR standards, some gaps in countries, the persistent lack of consensus on the nature of CSR reporting (voluntary versus mandatory), and the need for assurance, the spread of CSR practice making it difficult for researchers to carry out a cost-benefit analysis.

Thus, we believe that in the sustainable reporting of companies, a clear correlation between the activities and responsibilities of the pillars involved is essential.

Further Research and Limits of Our Work

The inclusion of non-financial information requirements in international regulations requires transparency rules on the disclosure of non-financial information and the diversity of statements on environmental, social, and employee issues, respect for human rights, anti-corruption, and corruption. In an attempt to ensure the best possible transparency and accountability of a company to society and the environment, it will be necessary to impose more and more requirements that will affect unlisted entities in the future and it will be necessary to provide such a report externally, so as to increase the credibility and quality of the information provided.

However, the implementation of reference standards on the reporting of corporate social responsibility in a sustainable manner implies an analysis of the real costs and benefits in terms of financial and human resources, time, level of technology, costs related to process development, etc. We thus see as future avenues of research the conduct of research with a wide coverage area on significant economic sectors that will centralize the results of these impact analyzes where they will be carried out and thus be able to propose ways of standardized representation. We also believe that with the development of the digitization process, in order to ensure optimal access to useful information to stakeholders, those researches that will be able to identify possible ways to implement an integrated reporting platform will be very useful.

Limitations of Our Research

Our paper highlighted that CSR reports do not have a common approach to the presentation of environmental information, this observation may also be affected by the composition of the sample we considered in our analysis, the number of industry companies, such as oil and gas being insignificant.

REFERENCES

AccountAbility. (2018). *AA1000 AccountAbility principles*. Author.

Aras, G., & Crowther, D. (2009). Making sustainable development sustainable. *Management Decision, 47*(6), 975-988.

Association of Chartered Certified Accountants - ACCA. (2016). *Mapping the sustainability reporting landscape. Lost in the right direction*. ACCA.

Aureli, S., Salvatori, F., & Magnaghi, E. (2020). A country-comparative analysis of the transposition of the EU non-financial Directive: An institutional approach. *Accounting, Economics, and Law: A Convivium, 10*(2), 20180047.

Blei, D. M., Ng, A. Y., & Jordan, M. I. (2003). Latent Dirichlet Allocation. *Journal of Machine Learning Research, 3*, 993–1022.

Bloomberg & PwC. (2020). *Global Top 100 companies by market capitalization*. Author.

Burlea-Schiopoiu, A., & Mihai, L. S. (2019). An integrated framework on the sustainability of SMEs. *Sustainability, 11*(21), 6026. doi:10.3390u11216026

Busco, C., Consolandi, C., Eccles, R. G., & Sofra, E. (2020). A preliminary analysis of SASB reporting: Disclosure topics, financial relevance, and the financial intensity of ESG materiality. *Journal of Applied Corporate Finance, 32*(2), 117–125. doi:10.1111/jacf.12411

Carrots & Sticks. (2020). *Global trends in sustainability reporting regulation and policy*. Author.

Center for Sustainability & Excellence – CSE. (2010). News, CSE managing director, Nikos Avlonas, speaks on carbon footprint strategy & CSR at the 7th CSR Summit, Dubai. Author.

Cho, C. H. (2020). CSR accounting 'new wave' researchers: 'step up to the plate'… or 'stay out of the game'. *Accounting and Management Information Systems, 19*(4), 626–650.

Christensen, H., Hail, L., & Leuz, C. (2019). *Adoption of CSR and sustainability reporting standards: economic analysis and review*. NBER Working Papers, 26169, National Bureau of Economic Research.

Climate Disclosure Standards Board - CDSB. (2019). *Cadrul general CDSB- pentru raportarea informatiilor cu privire la mediu si schimbarile climatic*. CDSB.

Cosmulese, C. G., Socoliuc, M., Ciubotariu, M. S., Mihaila, S., & Grosu, V. (2019). An empirical analysis of stakeholders' expectations and integrated reporting quality. *Economic Research Journal, 32*(1), 3963–3986. doi:10.1080/1331677X.2019.1680303

De Nuccio, E. (2020). *Preparing future-ready professionals, from non-financial disclosure to integrated reporting*. Academic Press.

Deliu, D. (2020). The impact of a socio-economic crisis on corporate governance effectiveness and sustainable development. *Acumen: The current new Coronavirus (Covid-19) pandemic, 35th IBIMA (International Business Information Management Association) International Conference, 01-02.04.2020, Seville, Spain – Proceedings of the 35th International Business Information Management Association Conference*.

DiPiazza, S. A., & Eccles, R. G. (2002). *Building public trust. The future of corporate reporting*. Wiley.

Directive 2014/95 / EU of the European Parliament and of the Council amending Directive 2013/34/EU as regards the submission of non-financial information and diversity information by certain undertakings and large groups.

Dumitraşcu, M., & Feleaga, L. (2019). Mission, vision and organizational values, catalysts of social responsibility. *Financial Audit*, *17*(153).

Dyer, T., Lang, M., & Stice-Lawrence, L. (2017). The evolution of 10-K textual disclosure: Evidence from Latent Dirichlet Allocation. *Journal of Accounting and Economics*, *64*(2-3), 221–245. doi:10.1016/j.jacceco.2017.07.002

European Commission. (2020). *Summary report of the public consultation on the review of the Non-Financial Reporting Directive*. Author.

European Reporting LAB – EFRAG. (2021). *Proposals for a relevant and dynamic eu sustainability reporting standard setting*. Author.

Farcane, N., Deliu, D., & Bureană, E. (2019). A corporate case study: The application of Rokeach's value system to Corporate Social Responsibility (CSR). *Sustainability*, *11*(23), 6612. doi:10.3390u11236612

Global Reporting Initiative - GRI. (2017). *Linking the GRI Standards and the European Directive on non-financial and diversity disclosure document*. Author.

Idowu, S. O., Dragu, I. M., Tiron-Tudor, A., & Farcas, T. V. (2016). From CSR and sustainability to integrated reporting. *International Journal of Entrepreneurship and Innovation*, *4*(2).

International Accounting Standards Board - IASB. (2021). *ED/20215 Proposed targeted amendments to the IFRS Foundation constitution to accommodate an international sustainability standards board to set IFRS sustainability standard*. Author.

International Auditing and Assurance Standards Board – IAASB. (2013). *International standard on assurance engagements – ISAE 3000 Assurance engagements other than audits or reviews of historical financial information*. Author.

International Financial Reporting Standards (IFRS) Foundation. (2020). *Consultation paper on sustainability reporting*. Author.

International Integrated Reporting Council - IIRC. (2021). *International reporting framework*. Author.

International Organization for Standardization. (2010). *ISO 26000 – Guidance of social responsibility*. Author.

International Organization for Standardization. (2015). *ISO 14000 – Environmental management systems - Requirements with guidance for use*. Author.

Irish Fund - IF. (2020). *Sustainable finance comparing international sustainability reporting frameworks*. Author.

Kinderman, D. (2020). The challenges of upward regulatory harmonization: The case of sustainability reporting in the European Union. *Regulation & Governance*, *14*(4), 674–697. doi:10.1111/rego.12240

Leuz, C. (2010). Different approaches to corporate reporting regulation: How jurisdictions differ and why. *Accounting and Business Research*, *40*(3), 229–256. doi:10.1080/00014788.2010.9663398

Leuz, C., & Wysocki, P. D. (2016). The economics of disclosure and financial reporting regulation: Evidence and suggestions for future research. *Journal of Accounting Research*, *54*(2), 525–622. doi:10.1111/1475-679X.12115

Lewis, C., & Young, S. (2019). Fad or future? Automated analysis of financial text and its implications for corporate reporting. *Accounting and Business Research*, *49*(5), 587–615. doi:10.1080/00014788.2019.1611730

Lock, I., & Seele, P. (2016). The credibility of CSR reports in Europe. Evidence from a quantitative content analysis in 11 countries. *Journal of Cleaner Production*, *122*, 186–200. doi:10.1016/j.jclepro.2016.02.060

Loughran, T., & McDonald, B. (2020). Textual analysis in finance. *Annual Review of Financial Economics*, *12*(1), 357–375. doi:10.1146/annurev-financial-012820-032249

Organisation for Economic Co-operation and Development - OECD. (2011). *OECD Guidelines for multinational enterprises*. OECD Publishing.

Perrini, F. (2005). Building an European portrait of corporate social responsibility reporting. *European Management Journal*, *23*(6), 611–627. doi:10.1016/j.emj.2005.10.008

Sustainability Accounting Standards Board – SASB. (2017). *Convergența prevederilor privind riscul climatic: CDSB, SASB și TCFD*. Author.

Sustainability Accounting Standards Board – SASB. (2020). *Promoting clarity and compatibility in the sustainability landscape*. Author.

Sustainable Stock Exchanges Initiative – SSEI (2020). *ESG disclosure guidance database*. Author.

Task Force on Climate-Related Financial Disclosures – TCFD. (2019). *Implementation guide*. Author.

Tsagas, G., & Villiers, C. (2020). Why "Less is More" in non-financial reporting initiatives: Concrete steps towards supporting sustainability, *Accounting, Economics, and Law Convivium*, *10*(2).

United Nations. (2014). *The ten principles of the UN Global Compact*. Author.

United Nations. (2015). *The 2030 Agenda for sustainable development*. Author.

Veltri, S. (2020). *The mandatory non-financial disclosure in the European Union. In Mandatory non financial risk-related disclosure*. Springer. doi:10.1007/978-3-030-47921-3

Wagner, C. Z. (2018). Evolving norms of corporate social responsibility: Lessons learned from the European Union Directive on non-financial reporting. *Transactions: Tennessee Journal of Business Law*, *19*, 619.

World Economic Forum. (2020). *Measuring stakeholder capitalism: top global companies take action on universal ESG reporting*. Author.

Chapter 2
E-Accounting:
Future Challenges and Perspectives

Dan Ioan Topor
1 Decembrie 1918 University, Romania

Umair Akram
Jiangsu University, China

Melinda Timea Fülop
Babes-Bolyai University, Romania

Sorinel Căpuşneanu
https://orcid.org/0000-0003-3799-3993
1 Decembrie 1918 University, Romania

Constantin Aurelian Ionescu
https://orcid.org/0000-0001-6063-2921
Hyperion University of Bucharest, Romania

ABSTRACT

This chapter addresses the main challenges of current e-accounting systems and also some future perspectives. The main objectives of this chapter are to present the conceptual approaches to e-accounting and ICT, their role and the determinants underlying the implementation of e-accounting systems in the business environment, the principles of security and processing of accounting information, and the impact of implementation and the advantages and limitations of e-accounting. Based on the literature, the authors present the interpretations brought by specialists to the concept of e-accounting, analyze their roles in terms of ICT and the factors that determine the acceptance of the concept in the implementation of various organizations. The chapter ends with the general conclusions of the authors related to the challenges brought by e-accounting systems in managerial accounting and CSR in the conditions of current crises.

DOI: 10.4018/978-1-7998-8069-1.ch002

INTRODUCTION

Electronic accounting (e-accounting) is a new concept in the field of accounting, internationally accepted, in which source documents and accounting records exist in digital format and not on paper. Compared to traditional accounting which requires costs with paper consumables and a large volume of recording and processing time, electronic accounting contributes to saving consumables (paper), time and reduces the costs of an organization. Being a very important function of an organization, accounting and implicitly e-accounting, involves an education through various computer and internet-based accounting tools such as: web links, documentation and national and international resources on the Internet, databases data of institutions or companies on the Internet, software programs based on the Internet, digital tools etc. For increased performance and its many benefits, organizations need to adopt and use e-accounting as a replacement for traditional accounting.

The objectives of this chapter are: *(1) presentation of the concept of e-accounting and its role; (2) presentation of the concept of ICT and its role in accounting and e-accounting; (3) presentation of the determinants of the implementation of e-accounting systems; (4) presentation of the principles of security and proper processing of accounting information; (5) the impact of the implementation of e-accounting systems on business, SMEs and financial performance with effects on internal control systems; (6) the advantages, disadvantages, challenges and future prospects of e-accounting.*

BACKGROUND

Concept of e-Accounting and ICT

As a result of the developments in the field of technology, the evolution of the e-accounting concept was also noticed. Initially dedicated to computerized accounting, the concept of e-accounting has expanded to fulfill accounting functions by applying online, mobile and internet technologies. Different terms such as computerized accounting system or accounting information system are used in the description of the concept of e-accounting (Amidu et al., 2011). Thus, according to specialists, the concept of e-accounting is interpreted as: (1) books and documents used in accounting, bookkeeping, their preparation, supervision and transmission in electronic environment to relevant institutions but also supervision (Ak & Sönmez, 2007); (2) an accounting system that relies on computer technology for capturing and processing financial data in organizations (Amidu et al., 2011); (3) like any accounting system that relies on information and communication technology (ITC) to perform its information system functions (Relhan, 2013); (4) an accounting system that facilitates the management of the organization's activities in a more efficient, accessible and flexible way via the Internet (Guney, 2014).

It can be seen that the scope of electronic accounting has expanded due to technological progress and therefore the use of new technologies has contributed to expanding the content area of the concept of e-accounting. By switching from offline to online and synchronizing with IoT, specialists talk about the e-accounting system through the two notions: accounting information system and computerized accounting system.

Viewed through the prism of the accounting information system, the e-accounting system is defined as: (1) a tool incorporated in the field of information technology systems designed to help control the management of companies related to the economic and financial field (Grande et al., 2011); (2) a system that collects, stores and processes financial and accounting data useful for internal management decisions. This also includes the processing of non-financial data relating to financial transactions (Belfo & Trigo, 2013); (3) a set of tools, measures and processes that depend on information in decision making (Kloviene & Gimzauskien, 2015).

Compared to the computerized accounting system, the e-accounting system is considered by specialists as: (1) a system that manages financial and non-financial transactions, and which directly affects the processing of financial transactions (Muhrtala & Ogundeji, 2013); (2) system that is significantly activated by computer technology designed in accordance with techniques relevant to achieving the objectives of qualitative business decision making (Tijani & Mohammed, 2013); (3) the use of the computer as an accounting tool and the fulfillment of accounting tasks (Appiah et al., 2014).

In our opinion, e-accounting is that accounting system based on ITC tools and application devices that consists of collecting, recording, analyzing, processing, interpreting, communicating accounting transactions and information on events in accounting that allow stakeholders to take appropriate and effective decisions in the shortest possible time.

The Role of e-Accounting

Adopted internationally, e-accounting known as online accounting or digital accounting consists of the application of online and internet technology to perform the accounting function. Based on the creation of an account (with authentication ID and password) and a minimum monthly/annual fee, users can access an online database or server where they can record and store all transactions in the bookkeeping. This brings some benefits to users by giving up the use of separate licensed software that also involves some hidden costs (installation, upgrade, data exchange, backup, etc.) or failures in saving data on companies' computers.

In terms of business opportunities, e-accounting can provide some effective solutions related to: (1) increasing the satisfaction of the accountant and the employer by saving considerable sums of money on computer programs and their user manuals; (2) the accounting principles developed by IFAC, including the security of accounting information and the principles of accounting information can be respected by ensuring the provision of reliable information (IFAC, 2002); (3) e-business also has a significant impact on accounting systems, by changing the business processes and evidence available to support business transactions and leading to changes in maintained accounting records and accounting procedures (IFAC, 2002).

According to specialists, this electronic accounting system can be useful in streamlining the accounting process due to the following features: (1) universal access; (2) multiple access to the site; (3) large-scale business registration; (4) fast registration due to advanced technology; (5) zero system administration for end users; (6) possibilities for multiple database sharing; (7) improvements and remedies developed and installed continuously by the service provider (Fitriati & Mulyani, 2015).

The Role of Information Technology (ICT) in Accounting and e-Accounting

Today, the Internet has obviously become the main form of communication and sharing of the future (Seyal et al., 2002). The Internet is a technology that has emerged as a result of people's desire to store/share and easily, quickly, and securely access information produced in several fields (Akgül & Gökçöl, 1997). The Internet plays an important role in the development of global trade through the promotion through its websites of products and services offered by companies or organizations based on intranet technology, i.e., that media that only employees of a company can access and obtain information (Güney, 1998). The extranet is also linked to internet technology, a network open to cooperation that connects and interacts with suppliers, customers or other enterprises with which they share common goals (Algan, 1997).

The use of technology in accounting and e-accounting has increased amid technical progress due to computer technology to produce information for administrative purposes based on the integrated information system of accounting information of organizations. The importance of electronic document management became evident when using technology through documents produced or transferred to the electronic environment, while also providing versatile access facilities based on the content requested by users (MacKenzie, 1999; Sprehe, 2005). Due to the transfer and storage of accounting information in the electronic environment, electronic surveillance of the information environment has also become necessary.

Increased confidence in the use of technology in accounting and e-accounting has contributed to its widespread use in organizations or enterprises by facilitating the work of accountants and accounting staff. Compared to the traditional business environment, all the changes in the field of communication, the economic and social effects of globalization have required the participation of organizations in a dynamic environment by studying archives and stored documents. These factors oblige organizations to internal restructuring studies and to use international standards and applications (Duff & McKemmish, 2000).

The creation of systems for the use of information technologies by generating information for managerial purposes based on the integrated accounting information system has become a necessity in all enterprises. There are many accounting software to be used for unifying accounting but the tendency of companies is to switch to and use e-accounting applications (Alp, 2007). The development of information processing and technology transfer contributes to improving the individual quality of people, businesses, institutions and society.

Determinants of the Implementation of e-Accounting Systems

According to the specialists, among the determining factors of the implementation of e-accounting systems are: (1) management characteristics; (2) technological characteristics; (3) business characteristics; (4) external characteristics. In the following we will explain the most important meanings of the determinants of the implementation of e-accounting.

(1) Management Characteristics on the Implementation of e-Accounting

The adoption and implementation of e-accounting is directly influenced by the top management of an organization (senior management, owner or director) especially in the case of SMEs (Seyal et al., 2000) and on whose motivation and attitude depends the decision-making on future investments (Bruque & Moyano, 2007; Nguyen, 2009). According to specialists, there are other factors that influence the attitude of management regarding the implementation of e-accounting such as: (a) educational level, experience, degree of innovation, commitment (Padachi, 2012), (b) IT knowledge (Hussin et al., 2002) or knowledge in accounting (Ismail & King, 2007), (c) perception of future benefits (Caldeira & Ward, 2003), (d) commitment (Ghobakhloo et al., 2010), (e) commitment and support top management, technical training of employees, interdepartmental collaboration and communication, continuous improvement and continuous integration of processes and their expansion (Hernandez, 2020; Bukamal & Abu Wadi, 2016;

Ha & Ahn, 2014; Casanovas, 2013). There have also been studies of some specialists who denied the existence of a significant link or even its non-existence between the management of an organization and the implementation of e-accounting (Thong et al., 1997) and the fear of management to encourage the development of employees' positive interest and attitude towards e-accounting (de Guinea et al., 2005).

(2) Technological Features and Implementation of e-Accounting

The adoption and implementation of e-accounting viewed through the prism of technological features targets some influences such as: (a) relative advantages and ease of use (Pongpattrachai et al., 2013); (b) the level of compatibility between user requirements and the degree of perception on innovative business processes (Al-Majadi & Mat, 2011), corporate culture, value system and distribution channels (Zhu et al., 2006); (c) knowledge of the accounting system and theoretical and practical knowledge of software use in accounting (Cadez & Guilding, 2008; Amidu et al., 2011; Jalaludin et al., 2011; Ashrafi & Murtaza, 2013; Nikolić et al., 2020; Ibrahim et al., 2020) and strategic alignment of IT and Internet know-how (Damerji, 2020; Chao & Chandra, 2012); (d) bearing the technological costs with the commissioning of the necessary technologies and the effort made in the restructuring of the organization in order to adapt to the new technologies (Zhu et al., 2006).

(3) Business Characteristics and Implementation of e-Accounting

The business characteristics that underlie the implementation of e-accounting address issues such as: (a) international affiliation or the size of the organization (Ismail & King, 2007; Hajiha & Azizi, 2011); (b) internal expertise and staff turnover (Pongpattrachai et al., 2013), (c) organizational structure and financial constraints (Salehi & Abdipour, 2013); (d) the influence of liquidity, leverage, rate of return and human appearance which includes the audits to which the company is subject (Berumen & Arriaza, 2013; Alali & Yeh, 2012).

(4) External Features and Implementation of e-Accounting

Among the external features that underlie the implementation of e-accounting we can list: (a) assistance for consulting, assistance for the information system community (Ismail & King, 2007; Ven & Verelst, 2009; Baker et al., 2010); (b) support for suppliers, customer pressure or competition (Wanjau et al., 2012; Pongpattrachai et al., 2013; Baker, 2014); (c) government assistance or the assistance of accounting firms (Ismail & King, 2007; Hajiha & Azizi, 2011; Padachi, 2012); (d) environmental factors (Salehi & Abdipour, 2013); (e) system quality, quality of information, use of systems, user satisfaction, effect of individual and organizational impact (DeLone & McLean, 2003).

Principles of Security of Accounting Information

The most reliable accounting information is obtained from the processing of accounting data using high-performance systems that guarantee the reliability and security of the data stored and used. IT infrastructure plays a key role in ensuring data security and processing it in order to obtain the information needed to prepare accounting documents or tax returns. The management of an organization is directly responsible for fulfilling the premises for the security of accounting information. Management is also responsible for implementing, developing and maintaining the information security of the organization they lead. The security requirements that an IT system must meet in order to provide reliable accounting information are the following:

1. *Integrity.* The requirement of integrity of an IT system is ensured when the accounting data and information and also the system are complete and correct, all these being protected against unauthorized actions of manipulation and modification. The means by which the integrity of data, information and systems is ensured are appropriate testing procedures (firewalls and virus scanners). When IT data, information, applications and infrastructure are used in a particular configuration, with authorized change permissions, the reliability of IT-assisted accounting processes is improved and streamlined.
2. *Availability.* This requirement consists in the flexibility of an organization to constantly ensure the availability of hardware, software, data and information on business operations, accounting, but also the IT organization necessary to put it back into operation in case of temporary interruption (emergency interruption). In other words, the organization must be able to back up any situation of temporary interruption or malfunction of the IT system. The organization must also have the ability to quickly and easily and readily convert materials to digital format.
3. *Confidentiality.* This requirement refers to the way the information is transmitted to third parties or to the degree of unauthorized disclosure. To this end, in order to ensure the confidentiality of data transmitted to third parties, the organization shall use data encryption technology which includes, inter alia: (a) instructions for restricting the transmission of personal data; (b) the encrypted transmission of information to authorized third parties; (c) identification and verification of the data beneficiary; (d) deletion of personal data after a certain period of time.
4. *Authenticity.* This requirement refers to the traceability of a commercial transaction to its originator. Using an authorization procedure, it can be verified whether the data or information is exchanged electronically and whether the person initiating the commercial transaction uses a digital signature. For this purpose, trusted centers can also be used as an independent facility.
5. *Authorization.* This requirement refers to the appointment of a person responsible for accessing information and the IT system and this will benefit from password protection. This guarantees that only the responsible person has the right to access and manage the respective IT system to read, create, modify or delete the data and information from the system. In order to supplement security measures and authorize access to data and information, biometric systems will be used in the future.
6. *Non-rejection.* This requirement is linked to the ability of IT-assisted procedures to achieve binding legal consequences. A person/user initiating a transaction cannot refuse its validity due to unauthorization or erroneous intent as the authorization was made by an encryption key for which ownership or possession is responsible.

Principles of Proper Processing of Accounting Information

Accounting information resulting from electronic business processes becomes more reliable if the accounting system meets the principles of security of accounting information but also the principles of proper processing. The principles of proper processing of accounting information include:

1. *Completeness*. This principle refers to the volume and area of economic-financial transactions processed, such as the recipient of transactions who record all transactions in the electronic accounting system (each transaction is recorded separately and the record is kept throughout the running and processing of accounting information).
2. *Accuracy*. This principle refers to the accuracy of the recording and processing of all economic and financial transactions through the electronic accounting system that reflects the real events and circumstances in accordance with the applicable financial reporting framework.
3. *News*. According to this principle, all economic and financial transactions must be recorded in a timely manner so as not to require appropriate additional actions to determine the completeness and accuracy of the accounting records in the electronic accounting system.
4. *Evaluability*. According to this principle, each component of the financial statements must be verifiable and tracked at the level of the supporting documents as a result of the entries in the accounting records.
5. *Ordering in time*. According to this principle, the existing accounting records within an electronic accounting system must be organized in chronological order (by accounting function) or by their nature, assets or liabilities (in the Journal Register). The identification and conversion of this accounting information must be easy and as fast as possible for different users.
6. *Inalterability*. According to this principle, the original content of an accounting record in the electronic accounting system can no longer be changed after the date of its posting. However, there is also the possibility of the change provided that they are mentioned in a separate change log. All changes and control of accounting records are highlighted separately in a special register that is specially set up and parameterized for such operations.

Impact of the Implementation of e-Accounting Systems on Business, SMEs and Financial Performance with Effects on Internal Control Systems

e-Accounting and Financial Performance

Financial reporting is the process of presenting financial data about a company's financial position, operational performance and its cash flow (Rose & Hudgins, 2008). The evaluation of the financial performance of a business is judged in the light of the results of business strategies and activities carried out in monetary terms. The financial situation provided by e-accounting (Evans, 2005) underlies the evaluation of a company's profitability, operational efficiency and liquidity (Wang & Huynh, 2012). The production of corporate financial reports as relevant as possible for management and external users in order to make appropriate decisions has resulted in information technology progress, especially through the introduction of e-accounting. Any company or organization manages its business processes much easier and more cost-effectively using e-accounting which is designed to automate and integrate all the business operations carried out by them. Among the advantages of e-accounting are the ability to quickly and efficiently manage huge volumes of information, increase daily visibility or speed of access to vital information (Wang & Huynh, 2012).

ICS and Financial Performance

Internal control is defined as "the organizational plan and all methods and procedures adopted by the management of an entity to help achieve the objectives of management to ensure, as far as possible, the orderly and efficient conduct of its business, including compliance with management policies, asset protection, the prevention and detection of fraud and error, the accuracy and completeness of accounting records and the timely preparation of reliable financial information" (Gupta, 2007; SAP 6). The effectiveness of internal control over financial performance is very important for every organization or company, whereas the prevention and detection of fraud is the responsibility of internal control, and the flexibility of internal control must also be found in addressing the risks to the entity's mission and its general objectives: performance refers to the ability to operate effectively, profitably, increase survival and response to environmental opportunities and threats (Sunday Artur et al., 2013). In determining the performance, both financial performance and internal control become statistically significant (Muraleetharan, 2011). In other words, internal control promotes efficiency, reduces the risk of asset loss and helps ensure the reliability of financial statements and compliance with legislation (Ratcliffe & Landes, 2009). Determining operational performance is done using financial statements as the main diagnosis (Zender, 2011).

Advantages and Disadvantages of Implementing e-Accounting

Advantages of implementing an e-accounting system: (1) accurately obtaining and processing accounting data and information and ease in generating smart reports (financial statements, cash flow statement, budget statement, dashboards, etc.) (Birt et al., 2020; Arcega et al., 2015; Wadesango, 2015); (2) measuring the performance of post-adoption companies of ERP taking into account IT as a competitive tool (Moghavvemi et al., 2012; Ruivo et al., 2012); (3) the use of the new technology that benefits the internal control of the entity favors the rapid and accurate performance of audits within the company (Zakaria et al., 2011; Alali & Yeh, 2012); (4) providing accurate and timely information needed to improve decision-making, efficiency, effectiveness, internal control structure (Romney & Steinbart, 2009).

A particularly important study reveals the five major dimensions of the positive impact of e-accounting implementation (Table 1): (a) IT accounting benefits; (b) operating accounting benefits (time); (c) orga-

Table 1. Dimensions of the impact of e-accounting implementation

<table>
<tr><th>Operational Accounting Benefits (cost)</th><th>Operational Accounting Benefits (time)</th><th>Benefits of IT Accounting</th><th>Managerial Accounting Benefits</th><th>Organizational Accounting Benefits</th></tr>
<tr><td rowspan="4">Reduction of staff in the accounting department</td><td>Reducing the closing time of monthly, quarterly and annual accounts</td><td>Collecting data quickly and easily</td><td>Improving working capital control</td><td>Increasing flexibility in generating information</td></tr>
<tr><td rowspan="3">Reducing the time in issuing financial statements</td><td rowspan="3">Production and processing of information in a fast and easy way</td><td>Increasing use of financial report analysis</td><td>Improving decision-making based on reliable and timely information</td></tr>
<tr><td rowspan="2">Reducing the time to issue the payroll</td><td>Improving the quality of reports - account statements</td></tr>
<tr><td>Improving the internal audit function</td></tr>
</table>

Source: Processing and adaptation after Kanellou & Spathis (2013)

nizational accounting benefits; (d) managerial accounting benefits; (e) operational accounting benefits (cost) (Kanellou & Spathis, 2013).

The disadvantages or barriers to implementing an e-accounting system are: (1) lack of practical knowledge and inability to experience the potential benefits of new technologies and support strategies in achieving a company's operational objectives (Oduro, 2020; Pillay, 2016); (2) lack of financial resources, predominance of inexperienced staff in the use of new technologies, insufficient knowledge or inexperienced employees in the labor market (Turner et al., 2020; Janvrin et al., 2008); (3) employees' reluctance to the consequences of changing IT, increasing workload (Garcia et al., 2010) and the new responsibilities that come with it (converting data according to the new system, redesigning documents and reports) (Amidu et al., 2011). There are also a number of threats posed by the use of e-accounting such as: (a) security (illegal access to information and cyber-attacks with disruptive effects on the availability of IT services) (Elmaghraby & Lasavio, 2014); (b) risks (loss of data, distortion of confidentiality, system unavailability, user dissatisfaction, poor performance, etc.) (Brandas et al., 2015); (c) external intrusions into the information system that damage hardware, software and network (Jang-Jaccard & Nepal, 2014) or lack of ability to ensure security without affecting the life, property and rights of users (Elmaghraby & Lasavio, 2014).

The Challenges of e-Accounting

One of the great challenges of the accounting profession is Industry 4.0, which has rapidly transformed the way accounting and auditing functions were known a few years ago. E-commerce has increased the complexity of transactions, especially for the lesser-known business partners of an organization. Due to these transactional intensifications in the online environment, it is very important for an organization to ensure the quality and reliability of business partners, but also their financial viability, data security, or the reliability of electronic accounting systems. The most important challenges that e-accounting brings are: (1) the costs of developing and operating websites; (2) security threats (hacking, viruses) (3) threats to accounting information systems. In the following we will discuss some of the most important aspects of e-accounting challenges.

(1) Development and Operating Costs of Websites

In order to achieve e-commerce, it is necessary to create and develop a website that involves the following aspects: hiring organizational resources necessary for planning processes, building infrastructure, purchasing hardware, software tools, buying and managing a web domain, creating the website, its content and graphics. After the creation of the website, the process of staff training, data backup, creation of links for advertising, permanent updating of information, etc. begins. All of the above require a number of investments and operating costs.

(2) Security Threats (Hacking, Viruses)

Organizations need to take precautions when it comes to e-accounting security. This is to protect computer networks and software programs that are connected to the Internet. Due to the huge volume of data that is sent, stored and received, information security is a priority for any organization. There are also malicious people, hackers who take advantage of some breaches in computer systems to steal valuable information and then capitalize on it in exchange for monetary rewards. The hacking activity is very wide and includes several methods, among which the most common ones are: hacking websites, falsifying emails (sending emails as authorized by an organization and asking in return for various information that helps them hack a website or other systems), bombarding the website with e-mails in order not to have real control, etc. There are also various forms of fraud that can affect data security and thus the impossibility of securing every computer in the world on the Internet, which is why there will always be weaker links in e-accounting systems. Also, a number of computer problems are due to computer viruses that cause a lot of damage to computer and software networks by rewriting information or destroying data. The most effective method of protection against these cyber-attacks and computer viruses is to install a firewall, i.e., a hardware security device that is installed between a computer network and the Internet. It directs traffic, blocks external users from accessing an internal computer system. Also, another means of protection is the encryption of data sent or received in a network, the only way to read would be a key known to the parties who use it.

(3) Threats to Accounting Information Systems

Sources that pose threats to accounting information systems may come from a variety of sources, such as: (a) unauthorized access to modify, delete, corrupt, destroy or steal data; (b) misdirection or misuse of the computer; (c) incorrect processing of data due to computer viruses. Regardless of the stage at which data is collected or processed, an organization must establish security rules to ensure the integrity of transactions or events that occur within it.

Future Perspectives of e-Accounting

At this point it is very clear that the future of e-accounting depends on the evolution of Industry 4.0 and the new regulations that will be produced by legislation on measures to adapt accounting to the online system. Thus, accountants will have to adapt to new technological requirements in order to record, analyze and forecast business activities online. All this will have some repercussions on how e-accounting is perceived. For example, accounting summary documents or other reports (financial, non-financial, integrated) will have to switch from traditional to electronic form (published on the web) thus undergoing some changes in structure, form and content in the sense of their evolution. With huge amounts of online and up-to-date information, investors are aware that the organizations that own it can disclose certain information to a greater extent. This leaves its mark on the frequency of disclosure of the information that will be the subject of the integrated reports.

Due to technological developments, the dependence of the tax authorities on this will increase and the cost of auditing will decrease as the possibilities for fast processing are advantageous. The interactivity of the online environment will allow governments to better and more often audit compliance with tax and accounting laws and regulations, which will create a more difficult and alert environment among accountants and the government. The rapidity with which online consulting services, online accounting, online financial statement preparation or online auditing are propagated lead to obtaining advantages in the form of profit for the companies that have in their object of activity the provision of these types of services.

In other words, we will have to say goodbye to registers or paper journals and move on to the use of computer packages that integrate analytical databases (Big Data Analytics) that address customers / users according to their business requirements. Under these conditions, accountants and other stakeholders (investors) will have to design, manage, control and audit a vast amount of information from both the Internet and the Intranet. Remote auditing will become interactive and the costs of the audit process will decrease significantly. Auditors will need to report, make recommendations and certify them in a much shorter period of time, and their legal liability will change substantially.

SOLUTIONS AND RECOMMENDATIONS

Given the issues addressed during this chapter, we propose to specialists and all those interested, the following solutions for improvement:

- development of digital systems based on e-Security/e-Privacy, e-Business/e-Accounting;
- adoption and implementation of information technology (IT) type: Big Data Analytics (BDA), CloudComputing, Internet of Things (IoT) etc. (Oncioiu et al., 2019; Căpuşneanu et al., 2020; Turkes et al., 2020);
- application of accounting by organizing training sessions for staff employed at the level of each organization.

Based on the concepts debated in the international literature, we recommend specialists and all those interested in deepening the following aspects:

- research at national and global level of the impact produced by new innovative technologies and especially e-accounting both at the level of large organizations and at the level of SMEs or smaller entities (Cokins et al., 2020; Căpuşneanu et al., 2021);
- research of the specialized literature regarding the successful adoption and implementation of e-accounting;
- adapting and expanding the culture of accountants in the use of e-accounting within an organization.

FUTURE RESEARCH DIRECTIONS

Through the study objectives set at the beginning of this chapter but also through the target segment (academic and business environment) to which we addressed we consider that we have achieved our main goal and the topic is of current and future interest for very wide categories of users of accounting information. All the information presented in this chapter is based on existing studies in the international literature and synthesized by the authors to illustrate the main advantages, disadvantages, challenges and future trends in e-accounting. Being a limiting chapter from the point of view of the approached topic, we suggest to the specialists and to all those interested the following research directions:

- analysis of the possibilities to adapt and implement new innovative technologies to traditional accounting or to extend e-accounting;
- analysis of the position of accountants and management within an organization in the case of the adoption of new innovative technologies and in particular e-accounting;

- analysis of the impact of managerial decisions resulting from the adaptation or implementation of e-accounting, as well as the impact on cost management.

CONCLUSION

Through its structure, this chapter covers some segments dedicated to the conceptual approaches of e-accounting and information communication technology, as well as their role, two concepts in the current stage of development of Industry 4.0. The principles of security and proper processing of accounting information are also presented, as well as the advantages and disadvantages of e-accounting. The following can be mentioned as strengths of this chapter:

- fills some existing gaps in the application of the principles of security and proper processing of accounting information applicable to e-accounting;
- analyzes the main determinants in the implementation of e-accounting in organizations;
- presents the impact of e-accounting on business and internal control systems;
- presents the advantages, disadvantages, but also the challenges and some future perspectives of e-accounting as starting points in future analyzes of specialists.

By reaching these topics of future interest, we consider that our mission has been fulfilled and our contribution can be future starting points in the research of all those interested in business or academia, and not only, inciting new challenges in the implementation and development of e-accounting systems.

REFERENCES

Ak, F., & Sönmez, Z. (2007). *Fatura ve e-fatura*. Ak Denetim. Avalaible at: http://www.vergihesabi.com/ makaleler/2007/2007_06.htm

Akgül, M., & Gökçöl, O. (1997). Internet ve ilgili konularda çokça sorulan sorular: INET-TR.CSS. *Sürüm*, *2*, 5.

Al-Majadi, M., & Mat, M. K. (2011). Modelling the antecedents on internet banking service adoption (IBSA) in Jordan: A strutural equation modelling (SEM) approach. *Journal of Internet Banking and Commerce*, *16*(1), 1–15.

Alali, F., & Yeh, C. L. (2012). Cloud Computing: Overview and Risk Analysis. *Journal of Information Systems*, *26*(2), 13–33. doi:10.2308/isys-50229

Algan, S. (1997). Bilgi yolunda bildik yeni bir durak: Ekstranet. *BT Haber*, *111*, 54–55.

Alp, A. (2007). *Muhasebede kullanılan defter ve belgelerin elektronik ortamda izlenmesi* (Master's thesis).

Amidu, M., Effah, J., & Abor, J. (2011). e-Accounting practice in small and medium enterprise in Ghana. *Journal of Management Policy and Practice*, *12*(4), 146–155.

Appiah, K., Agyemang, F., Agyei, Y., Nketiah, S., & Mensah, B. (2014). Computerised accounting information systems: Lesson in state owned enterprises in developing economies. *Journal of Finance and Management in Public Services, 12*(1).

Arcega, C. K., Datinguinoo, E., Guerra, J., Guno, C., Mayuga, H. J., Villamena, E., & Manongsong, J. L. (2015). Computerized vs non-computerized accounting system of small and medium enterprises in Lipa City, Philippines: A comparative analysis. *Asia Pacific Journal of Academic Research in Business Administration, 1*(1), 48–55.

Ashrafi, R., & Murtaza, M. (2013). ICT adoption in SME in an Arab GCC country: Oman. In Small and Medium Enterprises: Concepts, Methodologies, Tools, and Applications. IGI Global.

Baker, E. W., Al-Gahtani, S. S., & Hubona, G. S. (2010). Cultural impacts on acceptance and adoption of information technology in a developing country. *Journal of Global Information Management, 18*(3), 35–58. doi:10.4018/jgim.2010070102

Baker, G. (2014). Ledgers in the cloud. *The Owner Manager's Magazine*, 26-32.

Belfo, F., & Trigo, A. (2013). Accounting information systems: Traditions and future directions. *Procedia Technology, 9*, 536–546. doi:10.1016/j.protcy.2013.12.060

Berumen, S., & Arriaza, K. (2013). Medición de la intensidad en el uso de las tecnologías de la información y la comunicación en Escandinavia. *Contaduría y Administración, 58*(1), 289–306. doi:10.1016/S0186-1042(13)71206-3

Birt, J., Chalmers, K., Maloney, S., Brooks, A., Oliver, J., & Bond, D. (2020). *Accounting: Business Reporting for Decision Making*. John Wiley & Sons.

Brandas, C., Megan, O., & Didraga, O. (2015). Global perspectives on accounting information systems: Mobile and cloud approach. *Procedia Economics and Finance, 20*, 88–93. doi:10.1016/S2212-5671(15)00051-9

Bruque, S., & Moyano, J. (2007). Organisational determinants of information technology adoption and implementation in SMEs: The case of family and cooperative firms. *Technovation, 27*(5), 241–253. doi:10.1016/j.technovation.2006.12.003

Bukamal, O., & Abu Wadi, R. (2016). Factors Influencing the Success of ERP System Implementation in the Public Sector in the Kingdom of Bahrain. *International Journal of Economics and Finance, 8*(12), 21–36. doi:10.5539/ijef.v8n12p21

Cadez, S., & Guilding, C. (2008). An exploratory investigation of an integrated contingency model of strategic management accounting. *Accounting, Organizations and Society, 33*(7-8), 836–863. doi:10.1016/j.aos.2008.01.003

Caldeira, M. M., & Ward, J. M. (2003). Using resource-based theory to interpret the successful adoption and use of information systems and technology in manufacturing small and medium-sized enterprises. *European Journal of Information Systems, 12*(2), 127–141. doi:10.1057/palgrave.ejis.3000454

Casanovas, A. (2013). Resistencia al cambio y conductas obstructivas. *Serie de Cuadernos Sobre Cumplimiento Legal*, 3-30.

Chao, C. A., & Chandra, A. (2012). Impact of owner's knowledge of information technology (IT) on strategic alignment and IT adoption in US small firms. *Journal of Small Business and Enterprise Development, 19*(1), 114–131. doi:10.1108/14626001211196433

Damerji, H. (2020). *Technology Readiness Impact on Artificial Intelligence Technology Adoption by Accounting Students* (Doctoral Dissertation). University of La Verne.

de Guinea, A. O., Kelley, H., & Hunter, M. G. (2005). Information systems effectiveness in small business: Extending a Singaporean model in Canada. *Journal of Global Information Management, 13*(3), 55–70. doi:10.4018/jgim.2005070104

DeLone, W., & McLean, E. (2003). The DeLone and McLean model of information systems success: A ten-year Update. *Journal of Management Information Systems, 19*(4), 9–30. doi:10.1080/07421222.2003.11045748

Duff, W., & McKemmish, S. (2000). Metadata and ISO compliance. *Information Management Journal, 34*(1), 4–15.

Elmaghraby, A., & Lasavio, M. (2014). Cyber security challenge in smart cities: Safety, security and privacy. *Journal of Advanced Research, 5*(4), 491–497. doi:10.1016/j.jare.2014.02.006 PMID:25685517

Evans, M. H. (2005). *Financial planning and forecasting, excellence in financial management.* Retrieved from www.exinfm.com/training/pdfiles/course02.pdf

Fitriati, A., & Mulyani, S. (2015). Factors that affect accounting information system success and its implication on accounting information quality. *Asian Journal of Information Technology, 14*(5), 154–161.

García, A. M., Álamo, F. R., & García-Barba, F. (2011). Antecedentes de la resistencia al cambio: Factores individuales y contextuales. *Cuadernos de Economía y Dirección de la Empresa, 14*(4), 231–246. doi:10.1016/j.cede.2011.02.007

Ghobakhloo, M., Zulkifli, N. B., & Azizi, F. A. (2010). The interactive model of user information technology acceptance and satisfaction in small and medium-sized enterprises. *European Journal of Economics. Finance and Administrative Sciences, 19*(1), 7–27.

Grande, E., Estebanez, R., & Colomina, C. (2011). The impact of accounting information system (AIS) on performance measures: Empirical evidence in Spanish SMEs. *International Journal of Digital Accounting Research, 11*, 25–43.

Guney, A. (2014). Role of technology in accounting and e-Accounting. *Procedia: Social and Behavioral Sciences, 152*, 852–855. doi:10.1016/j.sbspro.2014.09.333

Güney, Ü. (1998). İnternet, Intranet, Extranet. *Byte Türkiye, 116.*

Gupta, K. (2007). *Auditing and Assurance Standard, basic principles governing an audit.* Academic Press.

Ha, Y. M., & Ahn, H. J. (2014). Factors affecting the performance of Enterprise Resource Planning (ERP) systems in the post-implementation stage. *Behaviour & Information Technology, 33*(10), 1065–1081. doi:10.1080/0144929X.2013.799229

Hajira, Z., & Azizi, Z. O. (2011). Effective factors on alignment of accounting information systems in manufacturing companies: Evidence from Iran. *Information Management and Business Review*, *3*(3), 158–170. doi:10.22610/imbr.v3i3.929

Hernandez, A. A. (2020). *Exploring the factors to green IT adoption of SMEs in the Philippines, Start-Ups and SMEs: Concepts, Methodologies, Tools, and Applications*. IGI Global.

Hussin, H., King, M., & Cragg, P. (2002). IT alignment in small firms. *European Journal of Information Systems*, *11*(2), 108–132. doi:10.1057/palgrave/ejis/3000422

Ibrahim, F., Ali, D. N. H., & Besar, N. S. A. (2020). Accounting information systems (AIS) in SMEs: Towards an integrated framework. *International Journal of Asian Business and Information Management*, *11*(2), 51–67. doi:10.4018/IJABIM.2020040104

IFAC. (2002). *E-Business and the Accountant: Risk Management for Accounting Systems in an E-Business Environment*. Available at:https://www.icjce.es/images/pdfs/TECNICA/C01%20-%20IFAC/C.01.082%20-%20ITC%20-%20Other/E-Business_Book.PDF

Ismail, N. A., & King, M. (2007). Factors influencing the alignment of accounting information systems in small medium sized Malaysian manufacturing firms. *Journal of Information systems and Small Business, 1*(1), 1-19.

Jalaludin, D., Sulaiman, M., & Ahmad, N. N. N. (2011). Understanding environmental management accounting (EMA) adoption: A new institutional sociology perspective. *Social Responsibility Journal*, *7*(4), 540–557. doi:10.1108/17471111111175128

Jang-Jaccard, J., & Nepal, S. (2014). A survey or emerging threats in cyber security. *Journal of Computer and System Sciences*, *80*(5), 973–993. doi:10.1016/j.jcss.2014.02.005

Janvrin, D., Bierstaker, J., & Lowe, D. J. (2008). An examination of audit information technology use and perceived importance. *Accounting Horizons*, *22*(1), 1–21. doi:10.2308/acch.2008.22.1.1

Kanellou, A., & Spathis, C. (2013). Accounting benefits and satisfaction in an ERP environment. *International Journal of Accounting Information Systems*, *14*(3), 209–234. doi:10.1016/j.accinf.2012.12.002

Kloviene, L., & Gimzauskien, E. (2015). The effect of information technology on accounting system's conformity with business environment: A case study in the banking sector company. *Procedia Economics and Finance*, *32*, 1701–1712. doi:10.1016/S2212-5671(15)01476-8

MacKenzie, G. (1999). A new world ahead: International challenges for information management. *Informational Managment Journal*, *33*(2), 24–34.

Moghavvemi, S., Hakimian, F., Feissal, T., & Faziharudean, T. M. (2012). Competitive advantages through IT innovation adoption by SMEs. *Social Technologies*, *2*(1), 24–39.

Muhrtala, T., & Ogundeji, M. (2013). Computerised accounting information systems and perceived security threats in developing economies: The Nigeria case. *Universal Journal of Accounting and Finance*, *1*(1), 9–18. doi:10.13189/ujaf.2013.010102

Muraleetharan, P. (2011). *Internal Control and Impact of Financial Performance of the organizations special reference public and private organizations in Jaffna district*. University of Jaffna.

Nguyen, T. (2009). Information technology adoption in SMEs: An integrated framework. *International Journal of Entrepreneurial Behaviour & Research, 15*(2), 162–186. doi:10.1108/13552550910944566

Nikolic, G., Vitenberg, V., & Karanovic, B. (2020). Adoption of sustainable accounting practices among croatian SME's. *KnE Social Sciences, 4*(1), 456–480. doi:10.18502/kss.v4i1.6006

Oduro, S. (2020). Exploring the barriers to SMEs' open innovation adoption in Ghana. *International Journal of Innovation Science, 12*(1), 21–51. doi:10.1108/IJIS-11-2018-0119

Padachi, K. (2012). Factors affecting the adoption of formal accounting systems by SMEs. *Business and Economics Journal, BEJ-67*, 1–20.

Pillay, P. (2016). *Barriers to Information and Communication Technology (ICT) Adoption and use Amongst SMEs: A Study of the South African Manufacturing Sector* (Doctoral Dissertation).

Pongpattrachai, D., Cragg, D., & Fisher, R. (2013). IT infusion within the audit process: Spreadsheet use in small audit firms. *International Journal of Accounting Information Systems, 3*(9), 1–21.

Ratcliffe, T. A., & Landes, C. E. (2009). Understanding of Internal Control and Internal Control Services. American Institute of certified public accountants (AICPA).

Relhan, A. (2013). E-Accounting practices of SMEs in India. *International Journal of Technical Research, 2*(1), 1–10.

Romney, M. B., & Steinbart, P. J. (2009). *Accounting information system*. Pearson Prentice Hall.

Rose, P., & Hudgins, S. (2008). *Bank Management and financial services* (7th ed.). McGraw-Hill.

Ruivo, P., Oliveira, T., & Neto, M. (2012). ERP use and value: Portuguese and Spanish SMEs. *Industrial Management & Data Systems, 112*(7), 1008–1025. doi:10.1108/02635571211254998

Salehi, M., & Abdipour, A. (2013). Accounting information system's barriers: Case of an emerging economy. *African Journal of Business Management, 7*(5), 298–305.

Seyal, A., Noah, M., & Rahim, M. (2002). Determinants of academic use of the internet: Structural equation model. *Behaviour & Information Technology, 21*(1), 71–86. doi:10.1080/01449290210123354

Seyal, A., Rahim, M. N., & Rahim, N. (2000). An empirical investigation of the use of information technology among small and medium business organisations: A Bruneian scenario. *The Electronic Journal on Information Systems in Developing Countries, 2*(7), 1–17. doi:10.1002/j.1681-4835.2000.tb00014.x

Sprehe, J. T. (2005). The positive benefits of electronic records management in the context of enterprise content management. *Government Information Quarterly, 22*(2), 297–303. doi:10.1016/j.giq.2005.02.003

Standard Auditing Practices No. 6 (SAP 6). (n.d.). Available at: https://pcaobus.org/oversight/standards/archived-standards/pre-reorganized-auditing-standards-interpretations/details/auditing-standard-no-6_1834

Sunday, A., Turyahebwa, A., Byamukama, E., & Novembrieta, S. (2013). Financial Performance in the Selected Microfinance Institutions in Uganda. *International Journal of Engineering Research & Technology (Ahmedabad)*, *2*(2), 1–11.

Thong, J. Y., Yap, C. S., & Raman, K. S. (1997). Environments for information systems implementation in small business. *Journal of Organizational Computing and Electronic Commerce*, *7*(4), 253–278. doi:10.120715327744joce0704_1

Tijani, O. M., & Mohammed, A. K. (2013). Computer-based accounting systems in small and medium enterprises: Empirical evidence from a randomized trial in Nigeria. *Universal Journal of Management*, *1*(1), 13–21. doi:10.13189/ujm.2013.010103

Turner, L., Weickgenannt, A. B., & Copeland, M. K. (2020). *Accounting Information Systems: Controls and Processes*. John Wiley & Sons.

Ven, K., & Verelst, J. (2009). The importance of external support in the adoption of open-source server software. International Federation for Information Processing (IFIP). doi:10.1007/978-3-642-02032-2_12

Wadesango, O. V. (2015). The importance of record keeping to the growth of Small and Medium Scale Enterprises (SMEs) in Zimbabwe. *Corporate Ownership and Control*, *12*(4), 44–755. doi:10.22495/cocv12i4c7p5

Wang, D. H., & Huynh, Q. L. (2012). *Effects of Environmental Uncertainty on Computerized Accounting System Adoption and Firm Performance*. Feng Chia University.

Wanjau, K., Macharia, N. R., & Ayodo, E. M. (2012). Factors affecting adoption of electronic commerce among small medium enterprises in Kenya: Survey of tour and travel firms in Nairobi. *International Journal of Business. Human Technology*, *2*(4), 76–91.

Zakaria, W., Rahman, S., & Elsayed, M. (2011). An analysis of task performance outcomes through e-Accounting in Malaysia. *Journal of Public Administration and Governance*, *1*(2), 124–139. doi:10.5296/jpag.v1i2.946

Zender, J. F. (2011). *Evaluating Financial Performance*. University of Colorado. Retrieved from http://leedsfaculty.colorado.edu/zender/CEDIR/Session3-notes.ppt

Zhu, K., Dong, S., Xu, S. X., & Kraemer, K. L. (2006). Innovation diffusion in global contexts: Determinants of post-adoption digital transformation of European Companies. *European Journal of Information Systems*, *15*(6), 601–616. doi:10.1057/palgrave.ejis.3000650

ADDITIONAL READING

Căpuşneanu, S., Mateş, D., Tűrkeş, M. C., Barbu, C.-M., Staraş, A.-I., Topor, D. I., Stoenică, L., & Fűlöp, M. T. (2021). The Impact of Force Factors on the Benefits of Digital Transformation in Romania. *Applied Sciences (Basel, Switzerland)*, *11*(5), 2365. doi:10.3390/app11052365

Cokins, G., Oncioiu, I., Türkeş, M. C., Topor, D. I., Căpuşneanu, S., Paştiu, C. A., Deliu, D., & Solovăstru, A. N. (2020). Intention to Use Accounting Platforms in Romania: A Quantitative Study on Sustainability and Social Influence. *Sustainability*, *12*(15), 6127. doi:10.3390u12156127

Oncioiu, I., Bunget, O. C., Türkeş, M. C., Căpuşneanu, S., Topor, D. I., Tamaş, A. S., Rakoş, I.-S., & Ştefan Hint, M. (2019). The Impact of Big Data Analytics on Company Performance in Supply Chain Management. *Sustainability*, *11*(18), 4864. doi:10.3390u11184864

Türkeş, M. C., Căpuşneanu, S., Topor, D. I., Staraş, A. I., Ştefan Hint, M., & Stoenica, L. F. (2020). Motivations for the Use of IoT Solutions by Company Managers in the Digital Age: A Romanian Case. *Applied Sciences (Basel, Switzerland)*, *10*(19), 6905. doi:10.3390/app10196905

KEY TERMS AND DEFINITIONS

E-Accounting: Accounting that involves identifying measurement transactions (attaching a value) and reporting them through the website or the internet.

Encryption: Encrypting a message or electronic transmission to prevent unauthorized access.

Firewall: Hardware and software used to prevent unauthorized access to a computer or network.

Chapter 3
Reviving Green With Accounting in the Era of Sustainability

Mansi Shah
Amity University, Jharkhand, India

ABSTRACT

In the era of 'Reviving Green', sustainability is no longer a luxury; it has become a global necessity. The late 1990s saw the evolving concept of triple bottom line. The growing importance of the environmental agenda that 'sustainability' had been mainly focused upon to that point led to the inclusion of the environment as one of the defining factors of 'sustainability'. The new paradigm in the third millennium puts business in the driving seat. Consequently, their role and responsibility towards the environment is manifold. The tradeoff between economic growth and the environmental costs has become one of the major challenges for businesses. This chapter examines the traditional accounting practiced by organizations. The premise of internalizing environmental costs in the investment decision making is highlighted. The costs and benefits that arise through the environment protection and depletion of the existing capital have been held forth.

INTRODUCTION

The oldest human civilizations date back to 3500 BC and so do their dependency on natural resources for the wide array of activities. Meandering across the rivers for their primal survival to a full-scale economy relying on the extraction of natural resources, the fixation has only increased. Along with the ever existing eureka realization of its finite, mankind gained the sense to preserve it. Since centuries, redeeming nature at the behest of sustainability has managed to be a predominant theme making headway towards tracking the natural resources employed by economic agents. The requisite to gauge the sustainability of current economic activity underpins the motivation to account for all expenses, incomes, assets, and liabilities derived from nature. "The great source of both the misery and disorders of human life seems to arise from over- rating the difference between one permanent situation and another" urges the distinct necessity to estimate the true cost incurred to attain our objectives and sustainability of the current income. The need to assess income arises from the understanding that it is the amount which limits their

DOI: 10.4018/978-1-7998-8069-1.ch003

maximum consumption without causing eventual impoverishment (Hicks, 1946). The in-depth classification of accounting encompasses financial accounting, cost accounting and management accounting in its curriculum, with no formal mention of green accounting. In the absence of the structured techniques of green accounting, there is no mutually accepted definition. However, the continued edification has propelled different countries to maintain environmental accounts. The overarching macrocosm of green accounting, also referred as environmental accounting followed by different country includes:

1. Recording emission of harmful gases by the economic sector.
2. Accounting for actual expenditures incurred by the economic sector on environmental protection.
3. Accounting for hypothetical expenditures to further reduce pollution.
4. Recognizing natural resources like forests, energy sources, minerals, fish, land etc as physical assets.
5. Monetary and physical flow accounts for natural resources along with the whereabouts of their use.
6. Consistency of structure in monetary asset and physical asset account.
7. Monetary valuation of the non-marketed environmental goods and services.
8. Monetary valuation of the cost due to environmental degradation.
9. Maintaining physical resource asset and flow account, physical input/output tables (PIOTS), physical pollutant emission accounts.
10. Calculation of green GDP, sustainable national income, or genuine savings.

The shared purpose of accounting for these items aims to link the extensive role of environment in economic performance (Hecht, Joy E., 2000). Most production and consumption activities have some effect on the physical environment. The growing population and economy have increasingly put pressure on the physical environment. Conventional accounting techniques and national accounts have considered man-made assets like machineries and buildings as productive assets, while recording natural resource assets only partly. Environmental accounting reexamines the ways in which we assess our social responsibility towards our environment and future generations.

It lays the framework for recording the existing value and usage of environmental and natural resources assets pertaining to economic activity (WGEA,2010).

It aims to provide organized information and tools to link environmental and economic data. It seeks to evaluate environmental impacts of economic activities, at a regional, sectoral and national level. It entails the inclusive study of resource management and expenditures on environmental protection, which can be used for macro-economic policy making and sector wise anatomization. The non-renewability, the partial renewability and the time needed to find the substitutes of exhausted resources makes it an intergenerational issue. Dereliction of natural resources needs to be hedged. Resource management requires the rational allocation of natural resources over generations, internalizing the externalities long before the effects of negative externalities can be felt like global warming. Externalities occur while producing or consuming a good affect the welfare of economic agents not directly related to the transaction. For example: Air travel increases air pollution. Expenditures incurred to hedge against the negative externalities of our extraction and consumption is also known as defensive expenditures (Alfsen, K. H., 1994) (Dieren W., 1995).

The time series data presented in the account allows comparative analysis and trend analysis. The data produced as a result of green accounting on a regular basis trails the course of path we have deflected from.

OBJECTIVE

The growing challenges and requirements of considering the environmental costs into the financial results of operations are studied. Premise of internalizing environmental costs in the investment decision making is highlighted in the chapter. The costs and benefits which arise through the environment protection and depletion of the existing capital have been held forth. Underlying the cost and benefits analysis for becoming environment friendly, the scope of environment costs, and capitalization of environmental expenditure, environmental liabilities, environmental assets, and environmental benefits has been demonstrated. Environmental accounting helps inaccurately estimating the costs and benefits of companies' environmental conservation measures. It provides a common framework for organizations to identify and account for future, present and past environmental costs in support of taking decision or we can say management decision-making, control, and disclosure.

Green accounting is considered to be an important tool for understanding the influential aspects of the natural environment related to the economy. The data and information provided by environmental accounts have been determined in relation to the involvement of natural resources in economic development and costs caused by pollution or deterioration of resources. The benefit of an environmental accounting initiative for companies is identified as the ability to determine and create environmental costs, which in turn helps identify the techniques to reduce and avoid such costs. This makes it advantageous function; the environment performance is also improved. The environmental costs that arise as a result of the financial results of the business operations can be determined by means of a green accounting tool. The operational performance of the organization can be determined using certain processes such as documentation and reporting of greenhouse gas emissions. However, it is stipulated that the conventional accounting system is not eligible for new or existing demand for natural resources. This demand for natural resources can destabilize the sustainability of economic performance and growth, depletion of natural capital, environmental degradation as social costs of economic activity and also destabilize the account of non-market goods in gross domestic product.

The severity of environmental problems as a global phenomenon has a negative impact on the quality of our lives. Measures are being taken both at national and international level to reduce, prevent and limit their impact on social, economic, and political issues. The emergence of environmental reporting for companies in India has been an important development, both for better environmental management and for overall corporate governance. Global stakeholder awareness of corporate environmental performance has already made traditional reporting redundant.

Commercial homes risk losing the confidence of their stakeholders if they save the environment in future performance information that is not included in their regular reporting. Environmental accounting is in the preparatory phase in India and what can be seen in the accounts in this regard is more or less compliance with the relevant rules and regulations in law. In fact, the development of accounting in this regard is a bit questionable unless the ordinary people of India are not made aware of the safety of the environment. It is the call of the times that companies prepare a solid environment policy, take steps to combat pollution, comply with the associated laws and regulations and report adequate details about environmental aspects in the annual accounts. For sustainable development of country, a well-defined environmental policy and good follow-up and correct accounting procedures are a must. Environmental accounting practices are still not widespread and there is no clarity and transparency regarding policy frameworks for national, state and even corporate reporting levels. Due to increased stakeholder awareness and other practices, it is becoming a segment of financial reporting. Most companies publish the environmental initiative in their annual reports, but such a practice is only nominal, does not disclose the financial implications and environmental cost policies, as it is unable to calculate both environmental liabilities and assets in terms of monetary value, as it is not.

In the past two decades, both academics and practitioners have begun to question prevailing traditional management accounting thinking. Changes in the competitive and production environment, changes in the cost structures of companies and the rapid development of advanced technologies have been advocated for putting pressure on changes in management accounting practices.

The objectives of this chapter are:

- The extensive role and importance of green accounting in the era of sustainability.
- To provide measures and practices that should be taken into consideration worldwide by finance managers, policy makers, and stakeholders in order to prefer growth sustainably.
- To improve and enhance the understanding of practitioners and the academicians towards the challenges and limitations being faced by various industries in terms of green accounting.

BACKGROUND

The limitedness of natural resources and the myopic measures of growth have prompted nations to save themselves from unforeseen disruptions of an economy dependent on natural resources. The history of green accounting dates to 1970 when Norway diagnosed the allocation of resources to be Pareto optimal. They led the vanguard of the natural resource accounting system in 1978, considering the resources which were economically and politically important. The resources were classified into two major groups:

1. Material resources
2. Environmental resources.

The distinction between the two considered their renewability, marketability, substitute options and the degree of their importance. Environmental resources are conditionally renewable and cannot be substituted like air, water, and soil. The quality or state of the resources determines their usefulness. Therefore, the mismanagement of environmental resources has consequential ramifications. Environmental resources comprise mostly nonmarketable resources, unlike material resources.

Material resources have several attributes which are taken into account. It entails location of the stock, price, extraction cost, size of the stock, usefulness of the resource and its level of impact on human welfare. They are broadly classified into:

- Minerals account- It includes accounts for crude oil, coal, natural gas, zinc, titanium, together with other minerals, metals, and non-renewable materials. The production sectors using these minerals as raw materials records extraction and conversion of material in physical units. For e.g.: Iron account, Crude oil account.
- Biotic account- It comprises living species and partially renewable resources like forest account and fish account. Norwegian production sectors dependent on these resources emphasizes on extraction rate and the rate at which it gets replenished. Fish have a reproduction time between 3-7 years whereas forest takes 20- 80 years to reproduce itself. Thus, the age structure of stocks acts

as a determining factor. The existing reserves and extraction rate are considered to deduce the 'optimal' extraction rate. Fish being an important export commodity for the Norwegian economy entails detailed accounting and has been developed over years.

- Inflowing account- Amidst multifarious classifications of natural resources, the one that has been considered, segregates at the stage where it has been utilized first. Thus, the same resource can be segmented differently based on where and how the resources first enter the production or consumption process. For e.g.: water is considered as an inflowing resource for hydro power generation, but for inland recreation fishing it is segmented under environmental resources. Ocean currents, gravitational field of the earth, hydrological cycle, solar radiation is counted as inflowing resources.

Environmental resources- The major attributes of environmental account comprise conditional renewability, non-marketability, difficulty to substitute. Unlike material resources, there are no property rights and direct costs associated with consumption of the services. It included accounts of pollutants emission in air and land use at various sectoral and regional levels. The primal optimality of land utilization for infrastructure, manufacturing units, agriculture or for housing and recreational activities has always been at conflicts. In the 70s policymakers of Norway could not make decisions in the absence of data on availability and quality of land. Land use account was designed to aim at documenting the quality of land and the land use in rural and urban areas. It provided the data by using sampling techniques on existing economic maps and air photos, which proved to be very time consuming and expensive. The pre-existing point sampling method made headway towards using remote sensing data (satellite) for classification purposes.

Another environmental resource air and the increasing emission of pollutants necessitated the accounting for emissions of nitrogen oxide, sulphur dioxide, carbon monoxide and lead at the sectoral level from 1976. Emissions to air accounts obtain their data from closely linked accounts like energy accounts, technical information on emissions coefficients, cleaning process of emissions and data on factor use by different economic agents. The continuous monitoring of emission components aided in determining the pollutant components to be added in account or to be removed from account. Expected impact of a pollutant on the ecosystem, industrial statistics of pollutants emitted and the enlarging data on pollutants has helped the policy makers, industries, and investors in administering corrective measures.

The overarching emphasis on integration of traditional economic and environmental issues has further convoluted the macrocosm of social planning. The exposition of social planning was no more just limited to rapid economic growth and regional equity of income. It extensively includes management of natural resources and internalization of externalities (Alfsen, Bye & Lorentsen, 1987) (Kuszewski & Crowther, 2012)

Norway made headway for further developments in environmental accounting. In 1983, the UN set up the World Commission on Environment and Development, also known as Brundtland Commission and examined the exploitation of natural and environmental resources by countries. Consequently, the report accentuated the concept of sustainable development. Sustainable development obtained its definition as "development that meets the needs of the present without compromising the ability of future generations to meet their own needs."

Continual significance of economic data by policy makers, economists and politicians has made the national income a measure of gross national product, gross domestic product (GDP) and net national product (NNP) as the measure of growth and development. The extensive calculation of national accounts aggregates the final monetary value of all economic activities regardless of their role in production and consumption, failing to serve its purpose of measuring true income. However, the era of sustainability addresses that welfare is not limited to monetary measure of income and accounting should not be limited for solely for financial reporting. The predicament between accounting for stakeholders and sustainability accounting have given rise to the concept of 'Accounting for sustainability and stakeholders' (Vardon, Castaneda, Nagy, & Schenau, 2018). The scope of accounting comprises matching of supply and uses. It accounts all changes between opening and closing stock. Sustainability accounting aims to maximize the quality of data provided by the system. There are six dimensions of data quality: relevance, accuracy, timeliness, accessibility, interpretability, and coherence.

1. Relevance- The data should be able to help the users with the information on the population represented.
2. Accuracy- It measures the extent to which data correctly measures the phenomenon they were designed for.
3. Timeliness- It is the duration gap between data of reference period and the actual date at which data become available.
4. Accessibility- The data should be made available to be used by different stakeholders through different mediums like journals, newspapers, library, etc.
5. Interpretability- The quality of data which represents how insightful the data is.
6. Coherence- It represents the internal consistency of data collected and presented so that it can help in longitudinal analysis and time series analysis.

The availability of data is the first step towards preparation of production accounts. Sustainability accounting emphasizes the need to extend the scope of conventional accounting and broaden it to incorporate range of social and environmental topics (Burritt and Schaltegger, 2010; Schaltegger and Wagner, 2006). The broadened scope of sustainability accounting integrates the environment into national accounts.

In the recent years, the countries have started compiling and using environment accounts to substantially upgrade economic statistics. The linking of economic and environment data renders a coherent and relevant information system which is taken into consideration by the government and business in policy making. The use of it not merely helps the stakeholders in identifying issues, policy response and monitoring but also equips them with increased data quality by providing a comprehensive framework to record relevant information on economy and environment.

Accounting for shareholders acknowledges that organization consist of network of relationships between different stakeholders and the views of additional stakeholders which goes beyond profit making should be integrated to create superior value for stakeholders (Freeman, Harrison, Wicks & Parmar, 2010) (Silva, 2019).

Accounting for sustainability and stakeholders selectively includes more stakeholders in accounting for sustainability. It emphasizes on including non-financial value creation in accounting, related to environmental and social issues. It calls for not separating financial, environmental, and social reports, thus creating a separate account for each different kind of value, but for issuing value creation reports, which include all types of value creation relevant for the company and each respective stakeholder (Horisch, Schaltegger, & Freeman, 2016)

For the purpose of measuring true income, the concept of sustainable income should be clear. It comprises net of all costs of natural capital as well as man-made capital intact. The encompassing framework of national accounts and adequate progress to link environmental accounting to System of National Accounts requires a system of environment statistics to complement the already existing systems of economic statistics (United Nations, 1975)

Sustainable national income circumvents the shortcomings of the existing System of National Accounts (SNA). It considers environmental protection costs and degradation and depletion of natural resources. Along with the defensive expenditures, it considers the consumption of natural capital like air, water, soil and so forth in the measurements of national income. The separate classification of environmental transactions like the cost of land improvement, housing and sanitation, forestry, water supply etc. is taken. Norway's version of accounting resources emphasized on politically and economically important natural resources and extended the SNA balance sheets to cover the total stock, including non-marketed stocks of the respective natural resources in physical units. Concurrently, French 'patrimony' approach included ecological processes that are not directly affected by human intervention that is interactions among the physical components of the environment and its biota. The data collected in all the approaches were limited to physical units. While physical indicators elevated the policy makers towards the corrective measures, it could not be integrated with national accounts. Consequently, physical measures remained limited to environmental and resource management (Peskin, 1989); (Alfsen, & Lorentsen, 1987).

GREEN ACCOUNTING PRACTICES AND ITS RELEVANCE

The pioneering work of National Accounts Matrix including Environmental Accounts (NAMEA) and System of Environmental and Economic Accounts 2003 (SEEA) has orchestrated the way framework of environmental accounting evolved from the collection of physical data to estimation of sustainable national income (WGEA,2010)

The efforts to link environment and national income accounts has created quite a few ecological indicators and descriptive statistics to monitor the environment's contribution to the economy and economy's impact on the environment. The National Accounts Matrix including Environmental Accounts (NAMEA) was developed to avoid the complete disruption of national income accounts. The framework of NAMEA is built on input/output substructure of national income accounts by introducing additional columns of physical data. It expands national accounts by adding environmental and social dimensions for different economic sectors, which can be called as satellite accounts. It incorporates environment and economic data of industry and household categories. The substructure helps in identifying the source of emissions. It is a hybrid flow account which records a combination of statistics on the economy and environmental pressure expressed in physical and monetary units (Eurostat 2006). Although it has extensively created data to record air emissions enabling comparison across countries, the input/output tables of other compartments and extraction of natural resources has been ignored. NAMEA- Air comprehensively integrates the monetary data of supply and use tables of the ordinary national accounts (NAM) as well as the physical data of production activities that result in emissions (EA).

The left side of the figure 1 represents NAM while the right side represents EA. There is no compulsion on recording of the recognized pollutants only. For instance, the French NAMEA- Air includes 10 pollutants 10 pollutants: carbon dioxide, Sulphur oxides, nitrogen oxides, nitrous oxide, ammonia, methane, carbon monoxide, non-methane volatile organic compounds, lead and particulate matter [Tudini and Vetrella 2004]. Databases available at Eurostat network cover emissions of nitrogen oxides, methane, nitrous oxide, carbon dioxide and Sulphur oxides. Netherlands NAMEA considered themes

Figure 1. NAMEA components
(Adapted from [Source: Eurostat 2001b])

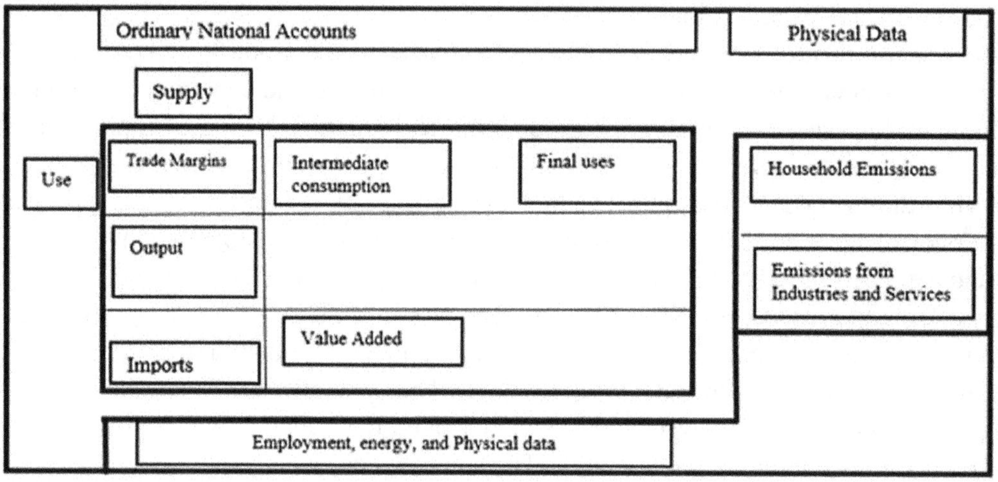

like greenhouse effect, ozone layer depletion, eutrophication, wastewater, acidification, solid waste, and the exploration of crude oil and natural gas from 1990-2005.

European Union and SEEA (2003) officially adopted input/output analysis of NAMEA tables to provide data for researchers and decision makers which was not available earlier. The System of Environmental and Economic Accounts (SEEA) provides a framework to account for environmental information and systematically link it to economic data. The information presented in an account form helps to derive indicators for policymakers and researchers. It integrates economic information and environment statistics to circumvent the shortcomings of System of National Accounts. Environmental accounts usage can span from supervising sector-based policies like forests, water, and energy to more complex areas of cross sectoral policies for climate change and green growth (Bass, Ahlroth, Rujis, & Vardon 2017). SEEA has been implemented by various nations like Netherlands, Guatemala, and United Kingdom with few changes to adjust to their specific environmental requirements. A key issue in the production of accounts is availability of data.

The central framework of SEEA (2012) extensively includes:

1. Measurement of physical units to record flow of energy and material within the economy and between the environment and economy- Flow of energy and materials have been classified in three phases- natural inputs, product flows, residuals. Natural inputs flow from environment to the economy (e.g., flow of water, minerals, and fish). Product flows are flows within the economy (e.g., additions to the stock of fixed assets). Residuals flow from economy to the environment (e.g., air emissions and solid waste)

The supply and use tables are prepared in physical and monetary terms in figure 3 and figure 4 to exhibit the flows of natural input, product flows and residuals.

Figure 2. Overview of the different environmental accounts in the Netherlands, implemented and under development
P = Physical measures, M = Monetary measures, P + M = Physical and monetary measures.

	Implemented	Work in progress
Flow accounts		
Energy flow accounts	P	
Water flow accounts	P	
Material flow accounts	P	
Air emission accounts	P	
Water emission flow accounts	P	
Waste accounts	P	
Asset accounts		
Subsoil accounts for oil and gas	P+M	
Water asset accounts		P+M
Environmental activity accounts		
Environmental goods and services sector	M	
Environmental expenditure accounts	M	
Resource management expenditure accounts		M
Environmental tax accounts	M	
Environmental transfers accounts		M
Ecosystem accounts		
Extent account		P
Condition account		P
Ecosystem services (supply and use)		P+M
Asset account		M
Carbon account		P
Biodiversity account		P

2. Measurement of environmental assets- The living and non-living components (e.g., mineral resources, water resources, land.) of the biophysical environment provided to the economy are measured in both monetary and physical terms. The balances of stocks of individual environmental assets are recorded at the beginning and the end of each accounting period along with the changes in stock as shown in figure 5.

Figure 3. Basic form of monetary supply and use table
(Adapted from [Source: Nations, U] (2014) System of Environmental-Economic Accounting 2012])

	Industries	Households	Government	Accumulation	Rest of the world	Total
Supply table						
Products	Output				Imports	Imports
Use table						
Products	Intermediate consumption	Household final consumption expenditure	Household final consumption expenditure	Gross capital formation (including changes in inventories)	Exports	Total use

Figure 4. Basic form of physical supply and use table.
(Adapted from [Source: Nations, U. (2014) System of Environmental-Economic Accounting 2012]).

	Industries	Households	Accumulation	Rest of the world	Environment	Total
Supply table						
Natural inputs					Flows from the environment	Total supply of natural inputs
Products	Output			Impor ts		Total supply of products
Residuals	Residuals generated by industry	Residuals generated by final household consumptio n	Residuals from scrapping and demolition of produced assets			Total supply of residuals
Use table						
Natural inputs	Extraction of natural inputs					Total use of natural inputs
Products	Intermedia te consumpti on	Household final consumptio n	Gross capital formation	Expor ts		Total use of products
Residuals	Collection and treatment of waste and other residuals		Accumulation of waste in controlled landfill sites		Residual flows direct to environment	Total use of residuals

3. Economic transactions and activity related to the environment- The activities undertaken to protect the environment; resource management and production of environmental goods and services are recorded under the central framework of SEEA (e.g., - device to reduce water pollution). Functional accounts are prepared to separately identify economic activities undertaken for environmental purposes.
4. Economic accounts are compiled in a sequence- The account starts with the Production account comprising intermediate consumption and output from the monetary supply and use table. The balancing aggregate of production accounts is total disposable income, distributed as compensation

Figure 5. Basic form of an asset account
(Adapted from [Source: Nations, U. (2014) System of Environmental-Economic Accounting 2012])

Opening stock of environmental assets
Additions to stock
Growth in stock Discoveries of new stock Upward reappraisals Reclassifications *Total additions of stock*
Reductions of stock
Extractions Normal loss of stock Catastrophic losses Downward reappraisals Reclassifications *Total reductions in stock* (only applicable for asset accounts in monetary terms)
Revaluation of the stock
Closing stock of environmental assets

of employees and on flows of further income and payments such as rent for the use of environmental assets, interest, tax and subsidies as shown in figure 6. The balance of income accounts gives operating surplus and savings which is utilized under capital account in the acquisition of produced and environmental assets. If expenditure on acquisition is less than savings then an economy will have resources to lend to the rest of the world, else it will have to borrow from the rest of the world. The sequence gets completed in the financial account which records the lending and borrowing of an economy.

Accounting rules and principles followed:

1. Principle of consistency is followed in recording of transactions in different economic units.

Figure 6. Basic SEEA sequence of economic accounts
(Adapted from [Source: Nations, U. (2014) System of Environmental-Economic Accounting 2012])

Production account (elaborated in supply and use tables)	
Main entries	Output, intermediate consumption, consumption of fixed capital, depletion
Balancing items/aggregates	Gross value added, gross domestic product, depletion-adjusted net value added, depletion-adjusted net domestic product
Distribution and use of income accounts	
Main entries	Compensation of employees, taxes, subsidies, interest, rent, final consumption expenditure, consumption of fixed capital, depletion
Balancing items/aggregates	Depletion-adjusted net operating surplus, depletion-adjusted net national income, depletion-adjusted net saving
Capital account	
Main entries	Acquisitions and disposals of produced and non-produced assets
Balancing items/aggregates	Net lending/borrowing
Financial account	
Main entries	Transactions in financial assets and liabilities
Balancing items/aggregates	Net lending/borrowing

2. Principle of double and quadruple entry accounting is applied. Since the framework is not for individual units but for the entire economy, each transaction is recorded by both the parties which is known as quadruple entry accounting.
3. All the transactions which can be expressed in monetary terms are recorded. The account compiled in physical terms will be recorded separately depending on their units of measurement.
4. Transactions are recorded on accrual basis.
5. Transactions are recorded at market price. Market prices of non-produced assets (e.g., timber, water resources and minerals) are estimated using SNA techniques.
6. Prices are classified into three subtypes- Basic price, producers' price and purchasers' price. While compiling monetary supply and use tables, basic price is used. Retail margin, wholesale margin and transport charges are allocated to the relevant services (retail services, wholesale, and transport) rather than deducting from the table.

While SEEA Central Framework (SEEA CF) has broadened the scope of assets as compared to the definition of asset in SNA, SEEA CF accounts the environmental assets as individual component. It fails to address these assets as media ecological health and growth. For example: cutting of trees at exorbitant rate can affect the ecosystem's potential to regenerate. SEEA CF will account for the changes in stock, but it does not address the damage that propagates as trees are cut. In the same way, SEEA CF records air emissions but it does not provide any data on how ecosystem has been affected because of it. It does not provide enough information for retroactive analysis of sustainable management of natural resources or to infer correlations to continue with forward planning (A. La Notte and C. Rhodes, 2020) System of Environmental-Economic Accounting – Experimental Ecosystem Accounting (SEEA EEA) was endorsed in 2013 to bridge this gap, which is being actively worked upon.

AGGREGATES AND INDICATORS OF SEEA CENTRAL FRAMEWORK

The Central Framework conjointly lends itself to the derivation of vital aggregates and indicators within the same method because the national accounts are renowned for the vital aggregates that are derived from the accounting structure, as an example, GDP and NNI.

The breadth of the Central Framework allows several aggregates and indicators to be sourced from the element tables and accounts. this section introduces the vary of aggregates and indicators that are either embedded within the framework or simply derived because the magnitude relation between variables among the frameworks. knowledge might also be wont to compile additional complicated indicators that need a variety of assumptions and coefficient patterns for his or her derivation.

Descriptive Statistics

Totals and Aggregates

The Central Framework contains a variety of totals (for the economy) and aggregates (balancing items) that will be of interest in observance changes in environmental and economic activity:

1. From the physical flow accounts, total physical flows like total flows of water, energy, air emissions and solid waste, for the economy as an entire or for individual industries and households, will be obtained.
2. From quality accounts, total physical flows of natural resources, together with extractions and natural losses, will be obtained, yet as total values of natural resources and any associated depletion.
3. From the sequence of economic accounts, the key financial aggregates within the Central Framework are the depletion-adjusted equalisation things like depletion adjusted web worth side and depletion-adjusted web saving.
4. From the useful accounts, EPEA and EGSS statistics, totals like national expenditure on environmental protection and total production, worth side, and employment of environmental product and services is also obtained.

Structural Statistics

Another variety of descriptive statistics which will be obtained from the accounting structures are statistics on the structure of various physical and financial flows and stocks. the very fact that the accounting structures are complete in their coverage of economic units and geographical areas allows shares of various variables to be derived. for instance, the share of total emissions by households and therefore the share of water use by agriculture may be calculated in an exceedingly easy manner from the relevant physical flow accounts. Indicators associated with land management, as well as land cowl and land use indicators, also are thought-about structural statistics. These indicators might offer data on the share of total space being employed for the upkeep and restoration of environmental operate or the share of land owned by completely different industries.

Other samples of structural statistics embody the share of environmental taxes in total taxes, the share of employment within the production of environmental product and services in total employment, and therefore the share of energy provide from renewable sources. Specific mention is formed of the power to derive shares at intervals purposeful accounts, since the totals concerning expenditure and production may be directly associated with typical national accounts aggregates, like GDP and business worth more.

Environmental Aggregates and Indicators

Asset accounts in physical terms regarding individual environmental assets will offer indicators on availability of those assets and changes in availability through the comparison of the amounts extracted with the remaining stock. Such data is also relevant within the management of demand and provide of environmental assets. Moreover, accounts in financial terms may be accustomed derive indicators for each individual environmental assets and for mixtures of those assets since summation across assets is feasible in financial terms. A summation will offer estimates of environmental plus wealth that successively may be compared with estimates of the worth of different assets, as well as created and monetary assets. Estimates of total national and institutional sector wealth may also be calculated.

The sequence of accounts will offer data on the depletion of environmental assets and on the share of resource rent accruing to varied sectors concerned within the extraction of resources, significantly mineral and energy resources.

By combining these indicators with population statistics and descriptive statistics on households like annual financial gain, it is conjointly potential to think about the employment of resources on a per capita basis and therefore the distribution and use of resources by completely different social unit sorts.

Aggregates Related to Financing and Cost Recovery of Economic Activity Related to the Environment

Data contained within the sequence of economic accounts will give necessary insights on however economic activity associated with the atmosphere is supported and on the complete value of providing access to resources, notably water and energy. The finance aspects will be thought of through analysis of subsidies and alternative transfers for environmental functions, notably flows from government and the remainder of the planet. it is going to even be relevant to think about the gathering of atmosphere taxes as a way of supporting economic activity associated with the environment.

Estimates of the complete value of supply resources should incorporate the overall in operation prices like intermediate consumption of materials and compensation of staff, and alternative current and capital prices. These embody payments of rent and interest, as applicable, and the prices of any relevant infrastructure and instrumentation. The estimation of capital prices ought to embody each the consumption of fastened capital and the cost of finance within the assets that is corresponding to estimating a rate of come back on the assets. the popularity of all prices is very important in guaranteeing that investment choices square measure soft on each short- and semipermanent prices in mind. All the relevant variables for these estimates square measure contained within the sequence of economic accounts.

Environmental Magnitude Relation Indicators

The aggregates and indicators represented directly higher than emerge from accounts and tables in either physical or financial terms. There are necessary indicators of carry mental pressures and responses which will be derived from combined physical and financial shows. they are generically named here as environmental magnitude relation indicators. the current section describes 3 main styles of these combined indicators.

Productivity and Intensity Indicators

Productivity and intensity indicators square measure necessary indicators which will be derived from environmental and economic data. Productivity indicators represent the magnitude relation of AN economic combination, like output or GDP, to a physical flow, like the energy content of energy merchandise used. Intensity indicators represent the magnitude relation of a physical flow to AN economic combination, i.e., they are the inverse of productivity indicators. of these indicators specialize in the assembly method and changes within the extent to that natural resources and natural inputs square measure getting used by industries to supply product and services.

In the derivation of those styles of indicators, it is necessary that the economic combination used be measured in volume terms, if the intention is to live changes over time. Otherwise, the image given of the degree of productivity or intensity is also dishonourable.

Decoupling Indicators

Decoupling indicators show the extent to that growth in financial gain and consumption is going on with a decreasing use of environmental resources, e.g., ablated energy use, or reduced emissions. they are derived by dividing a relevant economic combination (e.g., social unit consumption or GDP) by a relevant physical flow, for instance, air emissions. This square measure basically productivity indicators, however the main target is on the divergence of the environmental and economic aggregates.

As for productivity-type indicators, the economic aggregates ought to be measured in volume terms for time-series functions. Also, to assess the relative significance of the decoupling, it is necessary to gift decoupling indicators alongside the values of the dividend and divisor.

Polluter Pays Indicators

Polluter pays indicators relate physical data on emissions to payments, primarily environmental protection expenditures and environmental taxes, that square measure created in reference to those emissions. These indicators facilitate show the extent to that environmental protection prices square measure internalized, and whether or not taxation and alternative payment schemes square measure influencing the number of emissions. AN example of this sort of indicator is that the implicit charge per unit for energy that comes by dividing energy taxes by joules of energy used.

CONCLUSION

Economic growth and its immediate impact on the environment have led to discern the growth of a nation through the lens of sustainability. The one-dimensional definition of economic growth without the consideration of natural capital and assets has been found to be constrained. International organizations and industrialized nations have recognized the importance of recording environmental aspects. The recording of environmental accounts has challenged the spectrum of conventional national accounting. The conceptual framework of green accounting has provided the policy makers with statistics to monitor the interaction between economy and environment by integrating the monetary as well as physical aspects of the transactions. The adjustments to conventional national accounting have extensively covered the shortcomings of traditional measurements of growth with a lot of flexibility. The flexibility has helped nations to embark upon the paths of the SEEA framework in the way it suits their nation's requirement. The physical accounts prepared in SEEA is difficult to interpret in an economic way and thus do not provide an easy comparison with various forms of capital. Therefore, until expressed in monetary terms, it is difficult to assess the true worth of environmental assets. On the other hand, monetary environmental assets express the assets in monetary terms. The difficulty that monetary accounts pose is the estimation of complex and non-marketable assets like ecosystem and air. The subjective approach adopted by nations in valuing these assets question the legitimacy of various valuation approach. The empirical and conceptual challenges in valuing natural assets which are generally not traded in markets such as clean air and water requires further work to be done. The implementation of framework does not mention of its application in green capital budgeting which is very essential to evaluate the sustainability of investment projects. The green capital budgeting has the potential to increase the efficiency and effectiveness in project selection. The study in future should be in the direction of linking green accounting with green capital budgeting. Environmental accounting has been adapted by nations in a very fragmented manner due to the constant seesaw between short term economic growth and sustainable economic growth. The complex measurements unit and diverse agendas of humankind have made it difficult to come to one conclusion. Environmental accounting as a discipline is still evolving. The United Nations along with the Organization for Economic Cooperation and Development has made formative accounting structure to be adopted by nations. Further research needs to be done in identifying the challenges being faced by countries that are not maintaining environmental accounts. Nations face challenges specific to their location, therefore, framework should be made accordingly.

REFERENCES

Accounting, E. (2010). *Current Status and Options for SAIs.* INTOSAI. Working Group on Environmental Auditing.

Alfsen, K. H., Bye, T., & Lorentsen, L. (1987). *Natural Resource Accounting and Analysis. The Norwegian Experience 1978-86.* Central Bureau of Statistics of Norway.

Bass, S., Ahlroth, S., Ruijs, A., & Vardon, M. (2017, October). Natural capital accounting for policy–a global view of achievements, challenges and prospects. In Forum on Natural Capital Accounting for Better Policy Decisions: Taking Stock and Moving Forward (p. 17). World Bank WAVES.

Craig, P., & Glasser, H. (1994). Transfer models for 'green accounting': an approach to environmental policy analysis for sustainable development. *Assigning Economic Values to Natural Resources*, 67-110.

Eurostat. (2001b). *NAMEAs for air emissions. Results of pilot studies.* Detailed Tables. Eurostat.

Freeman, R. E., Harrison, J. S., Wicks, A. C., Parmar, B. L., & De Colle, S. (2010). *Stakeholder theory: The state of the art.* Cambridge University Press. doi:10.1017/CBO9780511815768

Gajos, E., & Prandecki, K. (2016). National Accounting Matrix with Environmental Accounts (NAMEA)-an Overview of Environmentally Extended Input-Output Analysis. *Acta Scientiarum Polonorum. Oeconomia, 15*(4).

Hecht, J. E. (2000). *Lessons learned from environmental accounting: findings from nine case studies.* IUCN.

Hicks, J. R. (2017). From 'Value and Capital'. In Bond Duration and Immunization (pp. 57-61). Routledge.

Hörisch, J., Schaltegger, S., & Freeman, R. E. (2020). Integrating stakeholder theory and sustainability accounting: A conceptual synthesis. *Journal of Cleaner Production, 275*, 124097. doi:10.1016/j.jclepro.2020.124097

Kuszewski, J., & Crowther, Y. (2012). *Canada and the green economy.* Academic Press.

La Notte, A., & Rhodes, C. (2020). The theoretical frameworks behind integrated environmental, ecosystem, and economic accounting systems and their classifications. *Environmental Impact Assessment Review, 80*, 106317. doi:10.1016/j.eiar.2019.106317 PMID:31902970

Nations, U. (2014). *System of Environmental-Economic Accounting 2012*. The World Bank.

Peskin, H. M. (1989). A proposed environmental accounts framework. *Environmental Accounting for Sustainable Development*, 65-78.

Schaefer, F., Luksch, U., Steinbach, N., Cabeça, J., & Hanauer, J. (2006). *Ecological footprint and biocapacity. In The world's ability to regenerate resources and absorb waste in a limited time period. Eurostat*. Luxemburg.

Schaltegger, S., & Burritt, R. L. (2010). Sustainability accounting for companies: Catchphrase or decision support for business leaders? *Journal of World Business*, *45*(4), 375–384. doi:10.1016/j.jwb.2009.08.002

Schaltegger, S., & Wagner, M. (2006). Integrative management of sustainability performance, measurement and reporting. *International Journal of Accounting, Auditing and Performance Evaluation*, *3*(1), 1–19. doi:10.1504/IJAAPE.2006.010098

Silva, S., Nuzum, A. K., & Schaltegger, S. (2019). Stakeholder expectations on sustainability performance measurement and assessment. A systematic literature review. *Journal of Cleaner Production*, *217*, 204–215. doi:10.1016/j.jclepro.2019.01.203

Tudini, A., & Vetrella, G. (2004). Italian NAMEA: 1990–2000 air emission accounts. ISTAT final report.

Ullmann, A. A. (1976). The corporate environmental accounting system: A management tool for fighting environmental degradation. *Accounting, Organizations and Society*, *1*(1), 71–79. doi:10.1016/0361-3682(76)90008-8

United Nations Statistical Office. (1975). Towards a system of social and demographic statistics. New York: United Nations.

Van Dieren, W. (1995). Defensive Expenditures. In *Taking Nature into Account* (pp. 175–186). Springer. doi:10.1007/978-1-4612-4246-8_12

Vardon, M., Castaneda, J. P., Nagy, M., & Schenau, S. (2018). How the System of Environmental-Economic Accounting can improve environmental information systems and data quality for decision making. *Environmental Science & Policy*, *89*, 83–92. doi:10.1016/j.envsci.2018.07.007

KEY TERMS AND DEFINITIONS

Gross Domestic Product: It is the monetary value of goods and services produced by an economy in one accounting year.

National Accounts Matrix Including Environmental Accounts: Was developed to avoid the complete disruption of national income accounts. The framework of NAMEA is built on input/output substructure of national income accounts by introducing additional columns of physical data.

Sustainability: It aims to achieve the needs of present generation without compromising the ability of future generations to meet their needs. It is inclusive of economic, environmental, and social factors.

Sustainable National Income: It considers environmental protection costs and degradation and depletion of natural resources, the consumption of natural capital like air, water, soil and so forth in the measurements of national income, which is not considered under system of national accounts.

System of Environmental and Economic Accounts: It provides a framework to account for environmental information and systematically link it to economic data. The information presented in an account form helps to derive indicators for policymakers and researchers. It integrates economic information and environment statistics.

System of National Accounts: It is an overarching framework to account for all the economic activities of a country with an objective to prepare national accounting systems to promote comparability across nations.

Chapter 4
Using Digital Programs and Technologies to Simulate Business Development

Ionica Oncioiu
Titu Maiorescu University, Romania

Mihaela Mirela Dogaru
Titu Maiorescu University, Romania

Manoela Popescu
Independent Researcher, Belgium

ABSTRACT

The priorities of business people in the digital age are human capital and innovation. As the changes are fast, in the digital age, the decision maker will not look for the optimal solution, but will stop at the first solution that he considers satisfactory and will put it into practice as soon as possible, given the fact that there is a high probability that the opportunity or the conditions for materializing the decision must change, even before the implementation of the decision. The use of digital programs and technologies to simulate the company's development decisions can circumvent these shortcomings, at least for a short period of time. This chapter shows that, in an increasingly digitized world, there is widespread recognition that a strong organizational goal is essential for any company, as well as an awareness that trust is becoming increasingly difficult to gain. Also, the proper management of the growing expectations of stakeholders contributes to building the confidence needed for an organization to survive and thrive.

INTRODUCTION

Globalization affects the sphere of influence of economic and social change, so that no company can consider itself independent of the global evolution of the economy and society.

The competition between companies extends from the regional level to the global level and, implicitly, moves, under the impact of the digital age, in the virtual environment. The companies that hold the power

DOI: 10.4018/978-1-7998-8069-1.ch004

given by digital technology are the competitive ones, which can cope with the exponential changes that characterize the current business environment.

The priorities of business people in the digital age are human capital and innovation. As the changes are fast, in the digital age, the decision maker will not look for the optimal solution, but will stop at the first solution that he considers satisfactory and will put it into practice as soon as possible, given the fact that there is a high probability that the opportunity or the conditions for materializing the decision must change, even before the implementation of the decision.

The use of digital programs and technologies to simulate the company's development decisions can circumvent these shortcomings, at least for a short period of time. It is known that business people have at their disposal a multitude of methods of developing the company / business, among which innovation and investment are among the most efficient, taking into account the fact that innovation is the foundation of the digital age. Innovation, which is of several types, can be manifested even in the proactive presence of a company in the online environment, not only passive through a website presenting the company and products. The presence that directly generates sales is the online store, as a way of doing business in the virtual environment.

BACKGROUND

In the digital age, businesses with fast Internet and modern technology can access the global market. So, it is much easier for a businessman to develop a business in the digital age. The digital age has also transformed traditional businesses by having to explore opportunities to move to the next level for development. Knowing that technologies and new business models have fundamentally threatened the value and relevance of traditionally offered products and services.

New businesses are present in all areas, especially in trade, intermediation and the provision of online solutions. Most are established in the field of technology, thus attracting funds dedicated to the field. However, it is known that the big challenge for businesses is to keep them on the market and develop them in the long run. (Bari, 2003)

DIGITAL ERA - SUPPORT FOR BUSINESS DEVELOPMENT

The digital age should benefit society as a whole, putting people first and opening up new opportunities for businesses. In the age of globalization, digital solutions are absolutely necessary for the development of all entities, but also for combating climate change and ensuring the transition to a green economy (Dunning, 1997). In other words, the digital solutions offered by the digital age open new opportunities for businesses, encourage the development of reliable technologies, promote an open and democratic society, create a dynamic and viable economy and contribute to combating climate change and transitioning to a green economy.

The European Union wants to become a global role model in the digital economy, support the digitization of developing economies and develop digital standards to promote internationally. Regarding opportunities for businesses in a digital society, access to high quality data is expected to lead to lower costs and manufacturers can optimize their production. For example, in agriculture, the analysis of data on crops, seeds and the use of fertilizers can increase the efficiency of agricultural activity, so that farmers could earn EUR 225 more per hectare. In terms of agricultural production, data-driven optimization can lead to savings of EUR 90 billion worldwide.

Digitization provides businesses with a better framework for conducting business online. At the same time, it gives economic entities equal access to markets in order to start an economic activity, to expand or develop economic activity, to innovate, as well as to compete on a level playing field. This is because innovation will be a key factor and a precondition for productivity and economic progress. Usually, the innovation starts within the company in which it was developed, but the greater benefits appear when the innovation is taken over by other companies and communities along the value chain.

It is true that digital technologies are changing the image of the industry and the way business is done. They enable economic actors to be more proactive and give workers new skills. This is because the traditional sectors are obliged to modernize at least their production, thus creating new opportunities for the whole economy and allowing all companies, especially SMEs, to access new technologies.

The digital age also offers real opportunities for the development of individuals, who can acquire the digital skills needed to fill better-paying jobs or the 1 million vacancies that are currently limiting economic growth. Experts consider that the development of employees' digital skills is fundamental in the perspective of the transformations that the European economy and, implicitly, the economy of our country will go through.

The digital age is said to have been facilitated by the phenomenon of globalization. But, according to other experts, globalization, seen as a progressive concentration of national economies in the hope of creating a coherent global economy, is a process facilitated by the unprecedented development of digital technology. It seems that the two phenomena, processes are interdependent. Specifically, the unprecedented development of digital technologies obviously contributes to facilitating the connections between the states of the world.

In fact, globalization influences almost all aspects of life, only the way this phenomenon is felt differs from one country to another, from one region to another, from one individual to another. Globalization facilitates universal access to basic infrastructure and services, contributes to enhanced global connectivity, improves the free movement of people, capital, goods and information, and supports the creation of an educated and skilled workforce, which means facilitating research and the emergence of new digital technologies.

For example, according to 76% and 71% of directors globally and in Central and Eastern Europe, respectively, I believe that this globalization contributes to increasing the employment rate and changing the structure of jobs. Although there are voices that believe that the phenomenon of globalization causes job losses in certain sectors and economies due to internationalization. The main factors of globalization being the internationalization of business through mass production, product standardization, development and modernization of communications, improving the banking system.

In other words, for them, globalization is a factor that determines the erosion of traditions and identities. Instead, for others, especially young people, globalization gives them access to opportunities around the world. (https://marplo.net/, 2021) It is true that the manifestation of the correlated effect of globalization and technological evolution in the digital age has led to an increase in the demand for skilled labor, leading to a reduction in the number of jobs available to people with a lower level of skills.

Also, a significant percentage of CEOs are convinced that globalization has beneficial effects on the harmonization of regulations, the protection of personal data and the management of geopolitical risks. On the other hand, business leaders are a little more skeptical about the success of the globalization process in mitigating climate change and promoting fairness and coherence in tax systems.

However, few (30%) agree that globalization also has the capacity to reduce the income gap between rich and poor. Also, more than half of CEOs (58% globally) argue that it is becoming increasingly difficult to compete in a globalized market but with increasingly narrow, increasingly restrictive national policies.

Today, under the effect of rapid technological developments, this phenomenon is increasingly based on knowledge and digital technologies. In fact, technological advances and the development of emerging economies have further accelerated global trade and transformed their nature. In this context, of the use of new technologies, of the Internet, globalization materializes in the form of liberalization and deregulation of the market of products and services, capital and labor.

At the same time, globalization has an important feature, namely integration (simultaneous integration of the three markets: the market for goods and services, the capital and technology market and the labor market). Integration is possible due to the use of digital technologies in all aspects of socio-economic life. What is certain is that globalization is a result of quantitative and qualitative processes over time, starting with the economy (structurally addressed: production, agriculture, trade, finance, investment, etc.) and continuing with technology, culture and the environment, with impact on all socio-economic entities, regardless of location, size, objectives, potential, synergy, etc.

The process of globalization cannot be stopped, as such it is necessary to take into account the particularities of this process revealed by the digital economy. Thus, the digital economy requires innovation and creativity on the part of Member States in strategic technologies, as well as supporting citizens in acquiring the appropriate skills needed for easy access to the labor market.

Today, more and more companies operate worldwide via the Internet (http://e-training.iatp., 2021) or use computer programs to grow their business. Moreover, thanks to technology, people have become more aware of the opportunities offered worldwide. What is certain is that business development opportunities depend on the speed and quality of the internet connection, as well as on investments in state-of-the-art technology. So we will be more and more connected. Of course, a more interconnected world will bring with it new opportunities, but also new threats or the growth of existing ones.

Globalization has been shaken in the last ten years by two major events that have affected its essence and future. For example, the global economic crisis of 2008 has brought very harsh reactions to globalization and there is already a tendency to isolate some countries and regions. Even countries that have campaigned for a world economy have shown interest in limiting immigration, slowing imports and boosting domestic production.

Thus, the growth of world trade has slowed down. It is the turn of 2020 to institute other harsh reactions to globalization. For example, sceptics have highlighted the harmful effect of globalization on the spread of the virus that has led to more than 200,000 deaths globally. However, the whole phenomenon of the unification of the countries of the world allowed the rapid transfer of aid, the rapid access to the results of medical research, to the transfer of funds necessary for the fight against Covid-19. Therefore, globalization can be considered both an inevitable historical process and an advantage for the human species. Regardless of the criticism, global economic integration also means huge opportunities for humanity.

Definitely, all this was possible due to digitization. Currently there are applications that notify the user if he is around a person who is a carrier of the virus. Digital technology has also made it possible to maintain jobs and telework. But what is the digital age? Information technologies have generated digital communication and information explosion and have led to changes in the paradigms of work, management, organization and economy. New business development models, new forms of work organization and digital citizens (those who use the Internet regularly and efficiently) have emerged.

In fact, major changes have occurred in all areas, regardless of what they are called: telemedicine, telework, reinsurance, remote election. In the field of education have appeared and developed learning platforms, virtual libraries, e-Learning, e-Teaching, which facilitated the access of individuals to unlimited learning resources and the possibility of continuing the learning process in conditions of physical distance and movement restrictions, the result of the Covid-19 pandemic.

As already mentioned, traditional businesses have started to develop in the virtual environment through company websites or e-stores, and most businesses have started to use applications, programs, platforms and IT solutions for development. The history of the emergence of the digital or information economy or the knowledge economy is well known among theorists.

It is known that in the period after 1994, productivity growth in the United States was even faster than in the past periods of high economic growth, which led many experts to say that a "new economy" emerged in equal importance. with the industrial revolution or, even more, similar to the second industrial revolution of the period 1860-1900, a remarkable period in terms of implications for human development.

Since then, attempts to define what economists originally called new economy have materialized in the use of terms such as: digital or computer economy, information economy, electronic economy, globalized economy, network or communications economy, etc. It has been called digital economy, information or information economy due to the role of this factor of production in creating wealth: information. It is known, it is not a secret, the one who has the information has the power. Information being a much more important factor of production than material resources or capital. Thus, the digital economy manages a new factor of production along with labor and capital, information, either as a distinct factor or as a factor attached to one of the two factors mentioned (Popescu, 2013).

As such, over the past two decades, the world has witnessed profound transformations as a result of globalization and technological change. Although all countries of the world know the defining characteristics of the digital economy, not all economies are structured and operate in accordance with its trends or not to the same degree. The Digital Single Market Strategy was based on ensuring better access for consumers and businesses to digital goods and services across Europe, creating the right conditions for the development of digital networks and services and maximizing the growth potential of the digital economy.

The Digital Single Market (PUD) creates prosperity and opportunities for European citizens and businesses, especially SMEs. A functioning single market stimulates competition and trade, improves efficiency, increases quality and contributes to lower prices.

PUD has reduced trade margins and increased productivity: for EU Member States, the gains from the single market amount to around EUR 427 billion per year. The single market has also boosted competition, making a fundamental contribution to increasing the EU's competitiveness and its green and digital transformation. The single market can only work for the benefit of citizens and businesses if its rules are applied effectively and strictly complied with. At the same time, the single market helps European companies to compete in world markets.

By deepening and consolidating the single market, Europe will become more attractive to international trading partners, and the EU will have additional levers on the international stage.

The European Union encourages the economy, businesses and the workforce to make the most of digitalization. In this regard, Europe intends to strengthen its global competitive advantage in 2020-2030 on the basis of state-of-the-art technologies, associated with global partnerships and investments in human resources and environmental protection.

Definitely, the digital economy is the cornerstone of the development of national economies. This is essential for the modernization of traditional industry. The EU is working to create the right environment for the digital economy to flourish, offer more choice to consumers and promote social inclusion. For our country, digitalization is at least a short-term solution to reducing the labor shortage. Before the pandemic, experts predicted that for a 3.5% increase in 2022, Romania needed an additional 1 million employees.

All European Commission reports say the same thing, the success of states in the digital economy will be increasingly determined by how they succeed in driving technological innovation, entrepreneurship, education, specialized skills and the transition of all public and private organizations from bureaucratic hierarchy in learning networks.

The digital economy, resulting from the interaction between the personal computer, telecommunications, Internet and electronics, is characterized by a series of features completely different from the traditional economy. Clearly, digitalization brings major benefits to large companies and digital entrepreneurs, new technologies, robotics, iCloud services and smart systems are the main factors that can contribute to increasing business efficiency and, therefore, business development. In the age of globalization, one cannot "run away" from digitalization.

BUSINESS - PROFITABLE ORGANIZATION IN THE ERA OF DIGITALIZATION

The major institution of the economic sphere with the key role in producing the goods and services needed to maintain a certain standard in society is the profitable organization, ie the business. In market-oriented societies, business organizations compete with each other to meet the needs and requirements of consumers. (Boian, 2004)

In any economy there are different organizations, they differ depending on their nature, the purpose of establishment, the form of organization. Organizations that aim for social goals are organized as foundations and associations. Usually, what differentiates organizations from each other are mainly the objectives. Such objectives change, from one period to another, for the same organization depending on certain conditions of the environment in which they operate.

Usually, with a plan, human, material and financial resources, as well as a team of efficient managers, any organization can achieve its goals. Definitely, the reason for the existence of business organizations is to obtain the highest possible profits in the shortest possible time. However, not all people's needs can be met through goods and services. Currently, the needs at the top of the needs pyramid are met through social networks, offered by the digital age. Organizations come to meet these needs, either directly or indirectly. Thus, recently, the effectiveness of organizations is no longer measured in terms of economic performance, but in terms of economic and social performance.

Big business (Dunning J. H., 1997), viewed by the general public as conservative, is the main means of transforming science and technology into the goods and services needed by society. In order to fulfill this role towards society, they have also undergone a series of significant social changes, especially with the use of digital technologies.

In general, over time, business organizations, although job-creating, thus generating economic growth, value and prosperity, are criticized by some individuals. Currently, business organizations are struggling with the economic environment to properly adapt to the highly competitive environment, but also to respond to the demands imposed by society. In the digital age, business organizations use analogy information that has been digitized. This digitized information can then be integrated into various software applications with good premises for automation. All people want business organizations to contribute more to the well-being of the society in which they live.

People's aspirations, whether they are members of those organizations or not, in terms of the social and economic performance of organizations depend on the dynamics of the environment in which they live. These aspirations increase as organizations reach them, an increase that is not always perceived as such, which leads to the perception and recording of the performance of organizations as having a downward evolution.

Although business organizations are purely economic, profitable systems, they are also economically and socially responsible. It is said that only organizations that have high economic performance, have the opportunity and willingness to engage in social responsibility activities. Of course, commitments that ensure, over time, much more stable relationships with the main stakeholders of those business organizations.

Some companies cannot respond to the social and economic needs of their own employees, much less of society in general. However, according to some authors, the economic performances of commercial companies are, in fact, their first social responsibilities, which precede the legal, ethical and discretionary ones (optional). The economic performance of commercial companies is considered the most important social responsibility because it involves safe and well-paid jobs, providing consumers with environmentally friendly goods and services, of high quality, at adequate prices, according to their purchasing power.

The digital economy is increasingly asserting the idea that business exists in a national framework to meet social needs and not just material ones. According to this approach of business, from a macrosocial perspective, it is necessary to take into account the concept of CSR (Corporate Social Responsibility), because the purpose of business, more precisely their socio-economic function is to meet the best social needs not only of consumers, but all stakeholders (employees, suppliers, partners, social organizations, residents of local, zonal, regional, national communities).

The social responsibility of commercial companies began to be discussed with the transition from the purely economic to the socio-economic model. Social responsibility is intended to be a new form of self-control and control over the activities carried out by commercial companies, other than the market, government regulations, trade unions and the pressures of different interest groups. The social responsibility of commercial companies can be approached both by reporting the results of the company's activities in terms of social responsibility, and by reporting the processes and phenomena within the companies. This means that companies must assume a certain social responsibility in terms of products / services, the information they provide to the market, but also an ethical behavior towards its internal and external customers.

It can be stated that business organizations, which are considered to have economic and social performance, are those that try to satisfy all stakeholders (shareholders, employees, neighbouring communities, suppliers, customers, state, unions); have a higher purpose (job creators and suppliers of goods and services); are dynamically connected to the economic and social environment; have high standards.

The business organization (firm or company) must be profitable, so efficient in producing goods and services. In this sense, society has laid the necessary foundations for business: regulations, rules and laws that allow them and help them in achieving their economic and social mission. Such a system of laws and regulations is considered to be the one that will direct the managerial policies regarding the economic and social responsibility of the business organizations. Also, the undesirable effects of the activity of certain commercial companies can be overcome by means of certain laws and governmental decrees.

Business organizations today are the main source of power and influence of any human society. In developed countries, the business organization has become the most important economic institution and the strongest force of social change. The set of values in a company must include the acceptance of business in order to have them. Without a well-defined set of business values, they risk losing the positions accepted by individuals and the legitimacy of their existence in society.

Currently, along with all the traditional values of business culture, joins the managerial concept of the set of values of business culture. According to all traditional business values, individuals are responsible for their own material well-being. Initiative, saving, diligence, honesty, honesty, discipline, imagination and risk-taking are rewarded. It is considered that failure and lack of success are deserved by some individuals. The values found as part of the set of values of a successful business culture are: individualism, moral responsibility and freedom; materialism and productivity; practical realism; sustained progress; optimism and adventurous spirit; taking risks; competition; equal chances; sustained activity; social responsibility; serving society. Spiritual and moral values are limited to those related to freedom.

Within the digital economy, businesses know new horizons and infinite forms and possibilities for development. Digital transformation redefining business. In order to achieve the assumed goal (making a profit), the organization must use digital technologies. First, business organizations need to digitize their business processes. In other words, all information is collected and then passed on in digital format, i.e. it is accessible to those who use it in a digital format.

Thus, centralized data about customers, suppliers, product information (presentation materials, catalogues, features, video tutorials, etc.), financial information can be used much more easily in electronic format by those interested, in order to streamline business. Once the processes of a business are digitized, they can be easily accessed on different platforms, devices, interfaces, which means that business people can use different programs, platforms or technological solutions to develop their business.

This is how new business models can appear, because digital companies generate very large profit margins. The next step for businesses in the digital age is digital enterprises, with a digital architecture, that use digital technologies to manage and control the complexity of the business. Thus, many areas of the digital enterprise will be subject to digital transformation, namely: leadership, sales channels, communication, information, operating model and workforce.

At the level of a business that wants to be profitable in the digital age, it is imperative to develop a digital culture that involves change and digital governance. Thus, at the management level, changes will be needed such as the acceptance and adoption of innovation as a business model, the adoption of digital models for planning and governance, the adoption of criteria to assess the rationale for strategic digital initiatives.

In terms of sales activity, important for any business, regardless of the object of activity or the field in which it operates, knowing the needs, desires and expectations of customers is the major goal. At the same time, it is well known that, through digital technologies, consumption and buying habits are evolving towards simplification, convenience and rapid satisfaction.

As such, through digitalization, the company must ensure that it can offer its customers all these facilities, but also fast contact points (interaction) (www.marplo.net, 2021). Online communications (emails, mobile messaging, social media, video chats) are ways to eliminate physical operators and streamline communication with customers, but also to streamline sales (customers needing only a mobile phone and connectivity).

Digitizing the information of a business is an element of supporting an easy and efficient experience of selling, buying or communicating. The information in digital format allows, with the help of some programs, the realization of statistics with the value and utility, analyzes and forecasts necessary for the development of the business. The decision-making process becomes more efficient using digital solutions.

Moreover, businesses in the digital age can use digital business models to make business operations more efficient by using digitally connected products / services, resources, people and partners.

In the age of digitalization, optimizing employee productivity and flexibility is a challenge, as in any economy. Although digital technologies may take over some activities, they should be seen as facilities for employees to work and not as obstacles to streamlining the work. But the human resource, the most valuable resource of business organizations, must follow skills development programs in order to effectively fulfill their digital work roles. What is certain is that the digital transformation of business generates valuable savings for companies related to time and money.

SIMULATION - ROLE AND IMPORTANCE IN BUSINESS DEVELOPMENT

Individuals have a great ability to create patterns, including patterns of development.

Models are used when it is desired to represent, understand and anticipate the behavior of an existing legal entity, i.e. a business. Usually, in business, decision makers are tempted to use the computer often only to assess customer preferences that are based on previous experience and knowledge gained over time, in different ways.

In all these situations the decision maker can use with good results the simulation models and the associated computer tools. (www.gpec.ro, 2020) Templates can be used in the information gathering phase or in the selection phase. Thus, in the information gathering phase, a simulation model can be useful in assessing the situation and assessing possible developments in the absence of the decision to act. In the election phase (its procedural model H. Simon), the simulation model offers possible courses of action (sometimes called alternatives) or sensitivity analyses of preferred alternatives based on human judgment or the solutions provided by computerized optimization algorithms.

Classical theories are based on several assumptions, namely the ability to know all the options, the ability to understand the consequences of elections, the certainty of being able to assess the impact of these choices, the ability to draw comparisons through a single indicator.

According to this concept, the individual tries to maximize his earnings, based on complete and relevant information (homo economics), to which he has unrestricted access. In this way the individual can make optimal decisions. Therefore, the neoclassical view makes the decision the result of a calculation. The decision maker is fully rational in his decision (omniscience). H Simon theorized the concept of "delimited rationality", which is now used in sociology, psychology, microeconomics and political philosophy.

Confronting the hypotheses of classical theory with reality and taking into account the limited capabilities of the decision maker, Herbert Simon decomposed the decision-making process into key stages (problem identification, choice and evaluation of solutions). However, such a process is influenced by several personal, organizational and environmental factors that can influence the decision-making process. Decision-making ability can actually be altered by a set of constraints such as lack of information, cognitive bias or even lack of time. Such uncertainty explains the impossibility of making a perfectly rational and objective decision.

The famous procedural model of decision-making activities proposed by H Simon is based on the idea that the decision-maker is endowed with limited rationality, due to his inability to understand all the elements related to the decision. satisfactory rather than optimal solutions After H Simon, in a decision-making process, the decision-maker will not look for the optimal solution, but will stop at the first solution he considers satisfactory. the one of maximum (optimal) utility Contrary to the classical theory, H Simon will therefore insist on personal and intuitive factors (deliberation and invention) in decision making. Thus, it places the individual in front of the requirements of the situation, in which the calculation and analysis capacities prove to be insufficient, which leads him to an acceptable and not optimal choice.

Introducing the concept of limited rationality, Herbert Simon placed the decision-making process in a procedural and realistic perspective, questioning the idea of clearly defined objectives and the ability of actors to understand all constraints (wordpress.org, 2020). As such, the search for an optimum cannot be accomplished when the individual is confronted with the realm of facts.

On the other hand, the process followed by the actors in the decision-making process must allow satisfactory decision-making, through appropriate deliberation. Rationality is therefore procedural (the search for an acceptable method) and not substantial (optimal logic). The individual cannot be compared to a method of calculation (absolute rationality).

His reduced abilities lead him to reasonable actions (strategies, coordination, heuristics), able to solve a problem adequately (limited rationality). Simon's analysis thus fits into the theses on the analysis of behaviors and organizations, emphasizing the necessary organizational adaptation of economic agents (resources, availability, information) in a situation of uncertainty.

It also contributed to the change in economic thinking, by presenting new approaches (implicit contracts, agency theory, transaction costs) as elements of response to the imperfections of market regulation.

There are several definitions of simulation in the literature. Thus, it can be approached from a procedural and technological perspective. Simulation as a process is a set of activities designed to represent reality through a model and to systematically experience the models of various decision-making activities.

As such, predictions can be made about the future evolution of the business under the influence of the environment, sensitivity analyses can be performed or the impact of different possible alternatives (decision solutions) can be evaluated (through analyses such as What would have happened if).

Regarding the definition of simulation as a technology offered by the digital age, simulation is a set of methods, techniques and tools ICT (Information and Communication Technology) designed to make simulation possible as a process. The simulation can be used to study an existing entity, to better understand a decision situation and to predict the future evolution of a process. However, the simulation can also be used to assess possible human interventions to change the environment to extend the controllable part of the entity and estimate the impact of design / management / leadership decisions. (www.linkedin.com, 2020)

So, it can be stated that simulation models are used when it is not possible to use optimization ones and / or when the decision maker wants to check the solutions he wants to adopt based on his own judgment. This is because simulation models allow time compression and / or expansion and are associated with intuitive visualization techniques.

Also, the simulation models do not require simplifications to be solvable, they can be built independently (they are not conditioned), but without guaranteeing the optimal solution. Decision making is based on a "passive" way of evaluating a limited number of alternatives proposed by the user. This means that simulation models are largely application-dependent and oriented towards an input / output approach, and the results are only valid for a given set of input data.

The man being the one who establishes criteria that he introduces in the respective program in order to obtain possible variants. Of course, digital technology has evolved, today we are talking about AI (Artificial Intelligence), which makes qualified employees to be replaced by high-performance computers. In fact, the nature of work has also changed, with the emergence of a wide range of professions specific to their digital nature (www.profit.ro, 2020). Today some companies use the digital algorithm to appoint the board of directors.

It is known that the decision is the result of the conscious activities of man to choose one of the alternatives available to him to achieve a goal or goals. Any decision involves the allocation of necessary resources and is the result of the processing of information and knowledge carried out by a person or group of persons, who have been designated for this purpose.

Usually, a business simulation is a constitution, a decision-making model that has as a starting point a model represented by a real business or a probable business. For example, a production business has the following essential components: employees, related technology, specific methods and techniques, product stocks, capital reserves, customer groups, partners, suppliers. Obviously, the business cannot function if one of these components is missing.

In order to simulate, all the components of the company will be analyzed in detail, then a faithful mathematical model will be built, a numerical and / or visual representation with a high degree of similarity. Thus, business simulation will capture the essence of the business or industry you are studying. Thus, in business and management, a simulation is a mathematical imitation of a real-world system.

Once completed, with the help of this new resource, participants will be able to interact with each component of the business and will be able to propose approaches in the company's decision policy in a risk-free environment. The simulation can be used as a training model, the business simulation aiming in this case to improve decision-making skills and understand the key indicators of business success (www.themegrill.com, 2020). The feasibility and profitability of business initiatives, both functional and strategic, can be studied quickly and without consequences. The team that will participate in the simulation can consist of general or functional managers or even new employees in the company.

In a simulation you can act on increasing the costs associated with staff in order to increase the company's capacity. During the simulation, personnel costs can be analyzed relative to the evolution of staff productivity. Also, during the simulation, the prices of the products / services can be reduced, which will lead to the increase of orders in a significant way.

The simulation parameters can be adapted to current market conditions. A high degree of realism can be achieved through simulation so that managers can identify the characteristic elements of the market in which their business is present. Various promotion decisions can be proposed in the simulation in order to study the impact on the company's sales and to discuss alternatives to the organization's strategy. (www.creativebloq.com, 2020)

Also, if a company completed a large-scale project but did not bring an estimated value, either by the fact that there were budget and time overruns, or by the fact that the beneficiaries were not satisfied with the results, then by a management simulation, participants can go back in time and identify key situations or critical points that could be changed to get a better result. Participants in a management simulation can detect signs and symptoms of potential problems and mitigate them using limited resources.

The groups of people who act for decision-making are differentiated by: the location of the members: in the same place or in different places; moment of interaction: synchronous or asynchronous; type of interaction: direct, indirect, or mediated; size: small teams or large and very large groups.

Usually, the first reaction of the participants in the management simulation is that you can't please everyone. The idea is that a balance must be struck between the needs of key actors and end users of the organization, in order to create the maximum value of the business.

Today, many business organizations use simulation to assess current performance or predict the future of the business process. Thus, business people can discover new ways to improve their business processes by using mathematical, statistical and other analytical methods.

SOLUTIONS AND RECOMMENDATIONS

In an increasingly digitalized world, there is widespread recognition that a strong organizational goal is essential for any company, as well as an awareness that trust is becoming increasingly difficult to gain (ec.europa.eu, 2018). And the proper management of the growing expectations of stakeholders contributes to building the confidence needed for an organization to survive and thrive.

More and more managers are increasingly aware of the need for an organizational goal that reflects the needs of all stakeholders. The technology has created a new dynamic between companies and customers, offering enormous benefits for both parties. However, the lack of trust in the business environment is a constant threat of recent years, almost four out of five (79%) of executives in our country (and 69% globally) considering that, in the digital age, it is increasingly difficult for companies to gain and maintain public trust.

Although business organization managers recognize that digitization is also an opportunity, not just a risk: 78% of Romanian respondents (and 64% of their global counterparts) believe that the way their organization manages customer and employee data will be a differentiating factor in the market. Public opinion influences the business environment by giving them their trust, thus legitimizing the existence of business. Lack of trust leads to eroding the long-term performance of organizations.

That is why a new paradigm is needed - that of a business environment that really contributes to the creation of a better society, through an inclusive global growth. Understanding the main causes of mistrust is a first step, essential for promoting the benefits that organizations can provide to society. And the challenge for company managers will be to develop a deeper and lasting relationship, based on dialogue and trust, with stakeholders (customers, suppliers, employees, state institutions, media, local communities, etc.) and to find a balance between the often divergent or competing interests of shareholders and society, between immediate results and long-term vision.

The impact of technology and digitalization on industries is increasingly diverse and profound. Thus, the implications of digitization are manifested on recruitment techniques, development strategies, redefining competition, specific digitization skills, etc. Also, digitization could affect the relationships developed by the business organization with its partners (customers, suppliers, employees, communities, state institutions, population, etc.). Businesses that pay attention to customers, their satisfaction and develop an honest behavior are the ones that win in thc digital agc.

The pace of technological change will continue to accelerate, and disruptions caused by the widespread use of automation and artificial intelligence will increase uncertainty and gaps between those who understand and use by adapting and thriving from new technologies and those who do not. understand and use technology. However, most managers are familiar with digital technologies, aware of the competitive advantage of businesses that have the ability to turn technology into a competitive advantage in the market.

In this context, traditional industries will be significantly (http://e-training.iatp., 2021) transformed and established business models will be rethought. Also, traditional jobs will look completely different in the coming years. People will work more and more from their favorite places, outside the office, and virtual meetings and representation through "avatars" and "holograms" will be widely used. The benefits of digitization will be huge in the coming years in various industries, especially in medicine and the improvement of living conditions.

Today, for many economists, entrepreneurship has become synonymous with starting and developing an individual's personal business (www.softline.ro, fără an). Which means that business development requires a business plan. On the other hand, business development involves the development of business organizations, which leads to the idea of organizational development.

Any development of an organization involves a planned process of change, which will generate changes in all or certain aspects of organizational life. Usually, any development involves and requires a change in organizational culture. Digital technologies being elements of the material culture of the business organization.

However, the purpose of any development of the business organization is to ensure the increase of its performance and competitiveness. Business development is a planned effort, coordinated by senior management, which targets the entire organization and aims to increase efficiency through intervention on processes.

Theory and practice clearly show that organizational development is a planned process, which is based on a wide range of methods, techniques, managerial and behavioral tools, in order to increase the performance of the organization. In the most general way, the goal of organizational development is the successful achievement of organizational change, in order to achieve high organizational performance. In other words, organizational development aims at designing, designing and implementing changes that favor the efficient use of resources and increase economic efficiency.

In the digital age there are several ways to do business. For more and more business people, organic growth is an effective business development strategy. They intend to develop new strategic alliances or joint ventures, while others plan new mergers and acquisitions. In Romania, significantly more managers focus on organic growth than on cost reduction.

Also, to stimulate revenue growth and profitability, some managers are considering new alliances and partnerships, as well as new mergers and acquisitions (www.marplo.net, 2021). According to a PWC (Global CEO Survey) study, collaboration with entrepreneurs and start-ups is on the agenda of only 15% of respondents in Romania, a lower percentage than that recorded globally (28%) and in Central Europe and East (24%). In our country with all the factors that can threaten the growth prospects - the degree of regulation, social instability, inadequate infrastructure, fiscal burden and climate change and environmental issues it is quite difficult for companies to be concerned about development. Romanian businessmen being especially concerned about the fiscal burden and the inadequate basic infrastructure. Also, other issues faced by business people who want to develop their businesses are those related to the availability of staff with key skills and the speed of technological change reaching record levels.

About two thirds (69%) of managers in our country are concerned about the reaction capacity of the organization in case of a crisis. 15-20 years ago, public trust in organizations was not one of the key concerns of executive managers, but 2019 brings this fear to the forefront. Thus, 58% of responding managers globally (and 47% in Romania) fear that lack of trust in the business environment will negatively affect the development of companies.

In the business environment there are solutions offered by specialists for transforming companies into successful business models. It is important that business development starts from the inside. Starting from the inside, value can be created, which can materialize in the business environment in an increase of competitiveness and performance. And this growth from within can be achieved by focusing on digital and circular strategies for business growth, customer satisfaction and business excellence.

FUTURE RESEARCH DIRECTIONS

The priorities of business people in the digital age are human capital and innovation. This is because the degree of capitalization of new opportunities on the market is represented by human capital. Talent management for identifying and capitalizing on new opportunities in the context of global changes in the technology age is an important part of company management.

Business organizations can reap the benefits of technology and globalization if they pay attention to the human factor and issues related to inclusion both in the workplace and in society as a whole. Preserving and enhancing the human element in an increasingly virtual and technology-driven world will be an essential condition for ensuring the next stage of long-term development worldwide. Human resource strategies are changing, and automation and artificial intelligence have entered the agenda of CEOs, with business leaders wanting an agile and versatile workforce. This is because innovation is specific to the individual. At the organizational level, the individual is the one who creates and innovates. Therefore, all types of innovations must be built on the creative and inventive spirit of employees.

Five are the qualities an individual need to innovate according to the Harvard Business Review: association (the ability to connect information, seemingly unrelated, from different fields of activity), questioning (the ability to ask questions), observation (the ability to perceive attitudes, behaviors, changes), experimentation (active and repeated) and relationship (social and professional). In other words, an innovator needs to know how to ask the right questions, questions like "Why?", "Why not?" and "What if?", to know how to notice behavioral nuances, to anticipate change, to experiment, to test theories, concepts and products, to validate ideas, to associate with specialists in different fields of activity.

According to the managers surveyed by PWC, adaptability and problem-solving orientation are the most important skills for organizations. Therefore, beyond the technical expertise specific to each field of activity, business leaders in Romania and around the world also appreciate the adaptability of employees, problem-solving orientation, leadership skills and their ability to collaborate in teams. Also, given the speed and magnitude of technological change, other qualities of future employees such as creativity, innovation and emotional intelligence are equally appreciated.

The literature presents several types of innovation: product innovation (improving existing products or creating new products), process innovation (improving processes either by simplifying them or by introducing new technologies, a process that does not necessarily influence and products or services), innovation at the level of the business model (obtained by changing industry or sources of income).

Harvard Business Review proposes four types of innovation that take into account the degree to which the business model and technological skills change (innovation model at organizational level): routine innovation (the company can innovate using the current business model and technological skills it already has), radical innovation (the company innovates by investing in new technologies and developing new technological skills), disruptive innovation (involves changing the business model, using existing technological skills), architectural innovation (business model and technological skills are changed /

improved) (www.tutoriale-html5, 2018). Taking into account the market, we can talk about the following three types of innovation: basic innovation (involves the use of existing products with minor changes, for example, change of packaging or packaging design for existing markets), adjacent innovation (change of products already existing in order to enter adjacent markets, knowing the consumer behaviors in those markets) and transformative innovation (creating new markets and identifying new consumer needs for which products or services will be created to meet them).

At the level of companies, innovation is present in the form of redesigning their organizational structures, depending on the breadth of functional requirements specific to each stage of their maturation and evolution.

In the digital age, innovation is a success factor in all sectors of a business organization and at all stages of the product / process life cycle (research, development, manufacturing, distribution and marketing, maintenance, product recall and disposal or recycling), as well as in the organizational field. (www.it-ebooks., 2018) The development of an optimal and systematic innovation process requires that at the level of the organization to define and implement an innovation management. Innovation management is a component of the general management of the organization which through its policy and strategy determines the management of an innovation process.

Any business organization must constantly evaluate its current and potential innovation capacities taking into account the following aspects: existing practices in the field of innovation management, skills and knowledge in innovation culture and organizational culture, equipment performance and investment opportunities from sources internal and / or external related to innovation, external collaborations, business models, product improvements for ecological, economic and ethical reasons. The innovation process must be substantiated, planned and implemented.

Also, the monitoring of the process as well as the control represent important steps if it is desired to achieve the planned objectives by implementing the respective innovation. The specific activities of the innovation process must be determined by the size and particularities of the business organization. The innovation process must also be in line with the organization's policy, strategy, vision and objectives, including in the field of innovation.

CONCLUSION

In conclusion, the future is neither predictable nor predictable, and innovation has become the key element that can provide added value in any context, be it individual, organizational or societal.

Digitization should benefit society as a whole, putting people first and opening up new opportunities for businesses. Digital solutions in the age of globalization contribute to the development of all physical and legal entities, by opening new opportunities for businesses, encouraging the development of reliable technologies, promoting an open and democratic society and creating a dynamic and viable economy. Digitization provides businesses with a better framework for conducting business online. Today, more and more companies operate worldwide via the Internet or use computer programs to grow their business. business development opportunities depend on the speed and quality of your internet connection, as well as investments in state-of-the-art technology.

Although all countries of the world know the defining characteristics of the digital economy, not all economies are structured and operate in accordance with its trends or not to the same degree. The Digital Single Market (PUD) creates prosperity and opportunities for European citizens and businesses.

All European Commission reports say the same thing, the success of states in the digital economy will be increasingly determined by how they succeed in driving technological innovation, entrepreneurship, education, specialized skills and the transition of all public and private organizations from bureaucratic hierarchy in learning networks.

It is known that the major institution of the economic sphere with the key role in producing goods and services necessary to maintain a certain standard in society is the profitable organization, i.e. the business. Definitely, the reason for the existence of business organizations is to obtain the highest possible profits in the shortest possible time. Big business, viewed by the general public as conservative, is the main means of transforming science and technology into the goods and services needed by society. In order to fulfill this role towards society, they have also undergone a series of significant social changes, especially with the use of digital technologies.

Currently, business organizations are struggling with the economic environment to properly adapt to the highly competitive environment, but also to respond to the demands imposed by society. In the digital age, business organizations use analogy information that has been digitized. This digitized information can then be integrated into various software applications with good premises for automation. The digital economy is increasingly asserting the idea that business exists in a national framework to meet social needs and not just material ones.

The business organization (firm or company) must be profitable, so efficient in producing goods and services. In order to achieve the assumed goal (making a profit), the organization must use digital technologies. First, business organizations need to digitize their business processes. Once the processes of a business are digitized, they can be easily accessed on different platforms, devices, interfaces, which means that business people can use different programs, platforms or technological solutions to develop their business.

This is how new business models can appear, because digital companies generate very large profit margins. At the level of a business that wants to be profitable in the digital age, it is imperative to develop a digital culture that involves change and digital governance. Thus, at the management level, changes will be needed such as the acceptance and adoption of innovation as a business model, the adoption of digital models for planning and governance, the adoption of criteria to assess the rationale for strategic digital initiatives.

In terms of sales activity, important for any business, regardless of the object of activity or the field in which it operates, knowing the needs, desires and expectations of customers is the major goal. Digitizing the information of a business is an element of supporting an easy and efficient experience of selling, buying or communicating. The information in digital format allows, with the help of some programs, the realization of statistics with the value and utility, analyses and forecasts necessary for the development of the business. The decision-making process becomes more efficient using digital solutions. The technology has created a new dynamic between companies and customers, offering enormous benefits for both parties.

Businesses that pay attention to customers, their satisfaction and develop an honest behavior are the ones that win in the digital age. In the digital age there are several ways to do business. For more and more business people, organic growth is an effective business development strategy. They intend to develop new strategic alliances or joint ventures, while others plan new mergers and acquisitions.

In the business environment there are solutions offered by specialists for transforming companies into successful business models. It is important that business development starts from the inside. The priorities of business people in the digital age are human capital and innovation.

Business organizations can reap the benefits of technology and globalization if they pay attention to the human factor and issues related to inclusion both in the workplace and in society as a whole. Preserving and enhancing the human element in an increasingly virtual and technology-driven world will be an essential condition for ensuring the next stage of long-term development.

In general, we can talk about the following three types of innovation: basic innovation (involves the use of existing products with minor changes, for example, change of packaging or packaging design for existing markets), adjacent innovation (change of existing products for entry on adjacent markets, knowing the consumer behaviors in those markets) and transformative innovation (creating new markets and identifying new consumer needs for which products or services will be created to meet them).

REFERENCES

Bari, I. (2003). *Probleme globale contemporane.* Bucureşti: Editura economică.

Boian, F. (2004). *Tehnologii fundamentale Java pentru aplicaţii Web.* Cluj: Editura Albastră.

Dunning, J. (1997a). *The Advent of Alliance Capitalism, "The New Globalism and Developing Countries.* United Nations University Press.

Dunning, J. H. (1997). The New Globalism and Developing Countries. In *The Advent of Alliance Capitalism.* New York: United Nations University Press.

Popescu, M. (2013). *Comunicarea şi negocierea în afaceri – esenţa succesului antreprenorial.* Bucureşti: Editura Pro Universitaria.

Chapter 5
CSR and Greenwashing in Finland:
Analysis About the Public Discussions of Greenwashing

Rauno Rusko
University of Lapland, Finland

ABSTRACT

Due to the general tendency to express environmental protection, environmentalism, and the actions to slow down the greenhouse effect in the world, the enterprises have noticed the importance of environmental values in their public announcements, documents, and homepages. In other words, corporate social responsibility (CSR) is a very important and topical theme of the firms. The popularity of environmentalism tempts the firms to follow the direction of public opinion even though the actual environmental activities might be minor or even absent. This kind of quasi-environmentalism is called as greenwashing. This chapter focuses on greenwashing and CSR in the Finnish context via public discussions about greenwashing. This chapter is emphasizing the understandings and the sense-makings in the concepts of greenwashing and CSR and their numerous connotations basing on the results of the textual analysis. The outcomes are completed and compared with the international contexts, and, therefore, they are also internationally robust.

INTRODUCTION

Scandinavian study (Rusko, 2020) noticed that in Scandinavian the firms are expressing values instead of strategy in their homepages. This outcome was evident regardless the industry of the firm. The homepages and "About us" -pages emphasized corporate social responsibility (CSR) or the connotations of CSR, such as responsibility, sustainable development or sustainability, among others.

This study focuses on the role of greenwashing in the society and in the part of the corporate social responsibility (CSR) discussions. The phenomenon of greenwashing is analyzed using Finland as a case

DOI: 10.4018/978-1-7998-8069-1.ch005

study example. However, the chapter will finally compare the found results of Finland with the international findings about greenwashing phenomenon.

This chapter will analyze this phenomenon described above using Finland, which is part of Scandinavian, as an example (or case study). Analysis is based on public discussions about CSR and especially greenwashing. Greenwashing is "a deliberate act by an organization to obscure potentially harmful information or deliver information in a way that portrays a false image that the organization is green or eco-friendly (cares about the environment)." (Mitchell & Ramey, 2011). This study takes into account the definition above but also the possibility that part of the public discussions about greenwashing are overemphasized or even "false news". Therefore, especially important is to study the contexts of these discussions, why term greenwashing have been mentioned and what are the aims of the particular news, blog or announcement, where term greenwashing is included in.

Due to fact, that greenwashing is seemingly linked with the concept of corporate social responsibility, this chapter will consider also CSR, especially understandings of CSR in these contexts, where greenwashing has also been mentioned. Thus, in addition to greenwashing, this chapter finds meanings of CSR and its connotations among greenwashing discussions.

In Finland, greenwashing discussions are very popular (in Finnish greenwashing is "viherpesu"). This research process of this chapter covered 200-300 blogs, news or announcement of greenwashing. The referenced number of sources in text is 20. The main focus is on the discussions, which consider especially the role of firms in greenwashing, not of political parties, for example.

As an outcome, this chapter clarifies the concept of greenwashing especially related to CSR. This study finds the different nuances of greenwashing concept. Furthermore, it classifies the various contexts, where term greenwashing has been used. Though the outcomes are based on Finnish context the results have been compared with the outcomes of international studies of greenwashing.

LITERATURE REVIEW - ENVIRONMENTALISM AND GREENWASHING

Environmentalism and Corporate Social Responsibility

The contemporary global discussions emphasis global warming and greenhouse effect. Environmentalism is not a new phenomenon, however. There are two important early milestones in the development of environmentalism:

1. The Limits to Growth report for the Club of Rome 1972 (Meadows et al., 1972)
2. Our Common Future report of Brundtland Commission 1987 (WCED, 1987)

The Club of Rome have published several reports, but The Limits to Growth is the most famous one. It based on computer simulations and it forecasted the various global problems, for example in the growth of economy, due to lack of natural resources (Meadows et al., 1972). Partly the popularity of the report based on the oil crisis in 1973, which also turned eye toward natural resources.

Sustainable development is an important theme in the branch of environmentalism. Brundtland Commission published the report named Our Common Future in 1987, which launched sustainable development concept into the public discussion. (WCED, 1987).

These two reports have wide effects on the public and scientific discussions, which have enlarged and developed in different disciplines (Lumley & Armstrong, 2004). Gradually the role of environmentalism has increased as a part of everyday life, business and economy. One reason for the rise of the contemporary environmentalism is based on the market changes in the price of natural resources, such as the rise of oil price in the beginning of the 21st century (Furlow, 2010). Environmentalism has several nuances and branches, and this sub-chapter will introduce the most known branches and concepts, and differences between them. Cunha, Rego and Vieira da Cunha (2008) noticed that in the mid1990s a number of scholars, such as Paul Shrivastava, incorporate the natural environment in management theorizing and especially in ecocentric management.

Thus, ecocentrism is one of the concepts, which has connotations with environmentalism. Ecocentrism is, according to Zelezny, Chua and Aldrich (2000, 446), "a fundamental belief in the inherent value of natural, the biosphere, and all living things". They are emphasizing in this context the gender socialization theory, and especially feminine socialization. They noticed that during the decade (1988-1998) females have stronger ecocentrism than males (Zelezny et al., 2000). Emetumah (2017) see that ecocentrism points out the relevance and intrinsic value of ecological entities. Furthermore, he expresses the need to take into account, in addition to ecocentrism, also technocentrism in the developing countries, such as Nigeria (Emetumah, 2017).

The perspectives of Emetumah (2017), where we consider technology and economy with environmental issues, are typical, for instance, to Corporate Social Responsibility (CSR) or corporate environmental orientation. According to Banerjee (2002), corporate environmental orientation is a corporate value, akin to corporate social responsibility. Both of them involve respecting and caring for the environment and being responsive to external stakeholders as well as being good corporate citizens. Banerjee see that, similar to corporate environmental orientation, also stakeholder theory, business ethics, and corporate social responsibility are avenues for internalizing environmental costs from the perspective of a business firm (Banerjee, 2002; see also Gladwin et al., 1995).

There are differences between the understandings of CSR. Cunha et al. (2008), for example, see that in CSR the term "capture" explains the limited ability of the corporate social responsibility philosophy to improve corporate accountability: the environmental issues are a source of competitive advantage or a condition to be competitive. That is, the neoclassical model of corporate control remains untouched: companies should create value mostly for shareholders (Cunha et al., 2008, see also Valor, 2005, 199).

CSR discussions emphasize, in addition to gains in business, the marketing potential and gains of CSR to consumers. According to Lee and Shin (2010), CSR research trend has flourished and has developed as the marketing potential of corporate responsibility initiatives, including corporate environmentalism, corporate citizenship, and corporate sustainability.

Greenwashing

Greenwashing has several alternative definitions. According to Delmas and Burbano (2011, 64), greenwashing is "misleading consumers about their environmental performance or the environmental benefits of a product or service". Another definition is that "Greenwashing is disinformation disseminated by an organization so as to present an environmentally responsible public image" (Ramus & Montiel, 2005; see also 10th edition of Oxford dictionary). Furlow (2010) defines greenwashing as "the dissemination of false or incomplete information by an organization to present an environmentally responsible public image". According to European Commission (2021), greenwashing is "the practice by which companies claim they are doing more for the environment than they actually are". In other words, greenwashing has elements of misleading and disinformation. These kinds of activities are harmful to environmentalism. Especially "skyrocketing incidence of greenwashing", which can have profound negative effects on consumer and investor confidence in green products (Delmas & Burbano, 2011,64). Delmas and Burbano (2011) have noticed two levels in greenwashing: firm-level greenwashing and product-level greenwashing, that is the act of misleading consumers in the environmental practices of a company or the environmental benefits of a product or service.

Delmas and Burdano (2011) emphasise in greenwashing two elements: environmental performance and communication. In the case of bad environmental performance, the firms have two alternatives with communication: their either have no communication about environmental performance or positive communication. Greenwashing firms are following positive communication with bad environmental performance (silent brown firms). Actually, it is in the principle a possibility to have bad environmental performance with negative communication, but this is not realistic alternative – or it might be possible after revealed greenwashing. Delmas and Burdano (2011), do not take into consideration this alternative, however. They introduce two alternatives in the case of good environmental performance: vocal green firms and silent green firms without communication (Delmas & Burdano, 2011).

Ramus and Montiel (2005, 409) emphasize in the conclusion of their study the easiness to make environmental policy statements and stakeholders want companies to make them, and "it is hard to control whether they are implemented, companies may be committing to them without a serious intent to implement the policies". Ramus and Montiel (2005) also notice the absence of regulation and without a business rationale for implementation, they see that it is unlikely that even those companies that claim to be committed to sustainable development will move closer to this illusive goal. That is, active environmental communication of the firms may be mostly misleading, and therefore, communication in the form of environmental policy commitment may often be a form of greenwashing.

Delmas and Burdana (2011) consider in their remarkable study also drivers of greenwashing. They focus on the drivers that lead brown firms with bad environmental performance to communicate positively about their environmental performance. They find four levels: individual level, organizational level, nonmarket external drivers and market external level drivers. They name the following individual psychological drivers: optimistic bias, narrow decision framing and hyperbolic intertemporal discounting. Optimistic bias, the tendency for individuals to over-estimate the likelihood of positive events and under-estimate the likelihood of negative events, narrow decision framing, the tendency to make decisions in isolation and hyperbolic intertemporal discounting, characterized by an impatient relatively high discount rate over short horizons (Delmas and Burdana, 2011).

According to Delmas and Burdana (2011), organizational drivers of greenwashing are firm characteristics, incentive structure and culture, effectiveness of intra-firm communication and organizational inertia; market external drivers are consumer demand, investor demand and competitive pressure; and nonmarket external drivers in regulatory/monitory context are lax and uncertain regulatory environment, and activist, NGO (non-governmental organization) and media monitoring. On the contrary to Ramus and Montiel (2005), Delmas and Burdana (2011) do not evaluate whether environmental communication of the companies may be mostly greenwashing or not.

Furlow (2010) emphasizes the problems of greenwashing. Due to skepticism of consumers, that is they may become confused about which products actually do help the environment, legitimate attempts by companies to become less environmentally harmful will lose any competitive edge they might have gained. According to Furlow (2010), if "the consumer finds the claim to be unreliable, they are likely to disregard all environmental claims, thereby avoiding any product that may in fact be better for the environment". (See also Mayer, 1993).

METHODS

This study leans on case study approach: case study strategy enables several forms of research methods (Yin, 1981; Eriksson & Kovalainen, 2015). In this study the cases are textual materials, which consider greenwashing in the form or other. Textual material of analysis is mainly coming from Finnish popular articles, but there are also some international cases about greenwashing. Furthermore, some Finnish materials are focused on the international greenwashing cases.

Empirical material has following criteria:

1. It contains word "greenwashing" or "viherpesu" in Finnish
2. It contains text in the form of (popular) article
3. It contains companies, general examples or attitudes about greenwashing.

Thus, the empirical material includes names of the firms, which have environmental activities, which are or are not greenwashing. Furthermore, it contains some NGOs, campaigns and competitions, which are directed against greenwashing.

OUTCOMES

International Seminal Examples of Greenwashing

Though the focus of this chapter is on the Finnish cases of the greenwashing it is good to introduce also some known international cases of greenwashing in order to compare Finnish findings of this chapter. Furlow (2010), for example, have introduced some international actions of greenwashing, such as Ford Motor Company's "It Isn't Easy Being Green" campaign for the hybrid Escape SUV, General Electric with "EcoImagination" campaign and BP (British Petroleum) with "Beyond Petroleum" slogan as part of its green campaign. Furthermore, Bowen and Aragon-Correa (2014) named some examples in 2014, such as Nestle with the recycling program for Nespresso disposable coffee pods and Unilever with its Twitter campaign about its partnership with the Guardian newspaper (Table 1). resent your perspective on the issues, controversies, problems, etc., as they relate to theme and arguments supporting your position. Compare and contrast with what has been, or is currently being done as it relates to the chapter's specific topic and the main theme of the book.

These examples in Table 1 show the difficulties of the traditional firms, which mainly have non-environmental brand, to change the image towards an environmental firm. These kinds of minor steps without remarkable positive environmental effects turned easily out to be greenwashing in the public discussions. The examples above are relatively old, but the situation is the same even in the year 2021. According to European Commission (2021), National consumer protection authorities believe that in 42% of cases the environmental claims were exaggerated, false or deceptive and could potentially qualify as

Table 1. International examples of greenwashing

Company/Companies	Campaign	Reason for Greenwashing
Ford Motor Company	It Isn't Easy Being Green (for the hybrid Escape SUV)	Ford's cars were considered the worst carbon emitters and had the worst fuel efficiency trend of any major automaker (Friedman & Mackenzie, 2004)
General Electric (GE)	"EcoImagination"	GE's environmental practices have been largely criticized. In 2000, GE went as far as the Supreme Court to fight the new clean air EPA requirements; EPAordered clean up of the Hudson River where it dumped PCBs between 1940 to 1977, not to mention the other fights (Source Watch, 2008).
British Petroleum	Beyond Petroleum	The company was named as one of the 10 worst companies in 2005 by Multinational Monitor.
Nestle	recycling program for Nespresso	disposable coffee pods, has only a negligible overall waste reduction impact
Unilever (and Guardian newspaper)	Unilever with its Twitter campaign about its partnership with the Guardian newspaper	a sustainable living online engagement platform did not accurately reflect the firm's true environmental impacts.

(according to Furlow, 2010; Bowen and Aragon-Correa, 2014)

unfair commercial practices under EU rules. European Commission (2021) see that greenwashing has increased due to fact that consumers increasingly seek to buy environmentally sound products.

Next this chapter consider Finnish greenwashing discussions, their connotations, expressions and meanings.

Examples of Greenwashing Discussions in Finland

Finnish discussions about greenwashing are not focused only on Finnish companies and their greenwashing, but the companies, which are known and popular among Finnish customers. This is the case, for example, in the article of Finnish popular tabloid, Iltalehti, in April 21, 2021 (Harju, 2021). This popular article noticed, basing on the comments of some national environmental organizations, six alarming marks of greenwashing:

1. Marketing with vague expressions, such as responsibility and ethicalness. Check whether salaries of the firm are high enough, where the product is produced and what kinds of international certificates and agreements it follows.
2. Only "good" part of the product is expressed. E.g. what is the actual share of recycling and carbon footprint in the product.
3. The firm use only own certificates and credits of ethicalness. The firms are creating own standards for ethical actions and products, which actually need critical consideration.
4. Over-emphasized carbon neutrality in marketing. It is need to check the targets and actions of the firm, such as whether emissions are already decreased or is there only compensation payments without diminished emissions.
5. Request to buy new product instead of recycled product.

6. Production information is difficult to find. Typically, good details are expressed and bad details are hidden. (Harju, 2021)

Actually, several Finnish blogs have nearly the same content. They are listing the typical features of greenwashing and actually the content of these lists is similar with each other regardless the author or publisher. Thus, this list above is possible to consider as presentative list of Finnish blogs about greenwashing.

The same popular tabloid article named several international and national greenwashing examples. Zalando is the most popular online store in Europe. According to Harju (2021), Finnish environmental association Eetti ry have noticed in the category of "sustainable development" greenwashing among several cloth brands of Zalando. Only part of the materials in the products are classified as responsible. For some of these cloths the share of organic fiber is not mentioned, which might mean low share. Furthermore, the production country has not been mentioned in online store. (Harju, 2021.)

In the same article, two international shoes producers have been named in the context of greenwashing: New Balance and Reebok. New Balance has emphasized in their marketing video in the responsible way produced product and also the makers of the products are proud of them. However, company do not tell about the actual working conditions or salaries of the sewers. Reebok has introduced in their responsibility pages figures about seaweed, plastic garbage of sea and text Reebok constructs new future, giving second life to plastic. However, the responsibility report of Reebok does not tell the share of responsible material (Harju, 2021.)

Article of Iltalehti tabloid finds also some Finnish cases about greenwashing. The largest Finnish retail chains Kesko, S-group, (Finnish) Lidl and Tokmanni have climate targets, which contains carbon neutrality of own activities in 2025, but this do not contain the products for sale in the shops, but own emissions of the buildings e.g. in the form of electricity and heating. The largest emissions of the retail chains are linked, however, with the life cycles of the products from the shops. Some of the Finnish firms have (only) long-term aims, such as milk producer Valio, which aims zero carbon footprint of milk production by 2035. (Harju, 2021.)

Finnish public broadcasting company/organization Yleisradio has 16 articles with the label "viherpesu (PR)" (greenwashing (PR) in English). These articles are between April 21, 2021 and 2010. The content of the articles is introduced in Table 2. The activities of Yleisradio are financed by public taxes, which might have effects on the content of the published articles of Yleisradio.

The content of Table 2 shows the position of Yleisradio as a public organization, which is financed by taxes. The role of other public organizations, such as European Union and/or European Commission is important in several articles of greenwashing. These articles describe international trends of CSR, which have effects on Finland, too. Yleisradio has wide local networks, and therefore several articles are focused on local Finnish cases of CSR. The general tone of the articles is neutral and some cases in the context of greenwashing are favourable to the named companies of the articles. They are not following, but avoiding greenwashing.

DISCUSSIONS

In the Finnish context, greenwashing discussions are focused on local, national and international levels. International cases consider the attitudes and experiences of customers and audience about the

Table 2. Greenwashing articles in the Finnish public broadcasting company/organization Yleisradio (Translated from Finnish)

Headline of Article, Year	Company/Companies	Campaign/Context	Reason for Greenwashing/Details
Nuclear power and gas dropped from the list of green investments- Commission introduced the first ever eco-classification for investments in the world. 21.4. 2021	Considers industry level greenwashing. Nuclear power and gas are doubted as greenwashing, wind and solar power are emphasized positively.	Classification introduced by European Union.	Classification is based on scientific results.
Responsibility of firms is also the benefit of investors – responsible firms are successful and more profitable during the Corona crisis. 2020	Danish Maersk (the greatest chipping company in the branch of container ships) British Petroleum (BP) and Shell, Stora Enso.	Allied investors pressure BP and Shell to improve reporting in oil business and in mining. Norwegian insurance company insisted to Maersk improve the process of dismantle for the old decommission ships. The investors of Stora Enso emphasized several problems, which Stora Enso have to react and fix, such as land use in Brazil, land hiring in China, wastepaper process with children in Pakistan. Actually, Stora Enso is now more responsible company.	BP, Shell, Maersk and Stora Enso had good brand, but investors noticed these faults and companies have to change their activities more responsible.
Company from Halsua rents forest as carbon sink and plants saplings for other companies – specialist: "promises have to keep, it may not be greenwashing". 2019	Co2 Compensate Finland Oy	Co2 Compensate Finland Oy is a rental agent, which rents forest and leases further for the purpose of carbon sink. Forests remains untouched.	It is difficult to investigate how much the movement from clearcutting to continuous -cover silviculture will increase carbon sink. Logging might also adjourn.
Plastic is now arch enemy, next megatrends perhaps food and movement- how can consumer separate greenwashing from actual responsibility? 2019	S-Group, Kesko, Lidl, Varusteleka, Neste	S-Group and Kesko have informed to erase the plastic handle of swap in ears cleaning and Lidl have informed to erase plastic straws and disposable containers during the year due to aims of EU to forbid disposable plastic products.	(Too) small environmental activities is easy to interpret as greenwashing
Ikea abjures disposable plastic products – the annual waste for the giant of furniture is nearly similar to 60 Eiffel towers 2018	Ikea, Ica, Coop ja Axfood, Lidl, Lego and Hennes & Mauritz (H&M).	Several firms have decreased use of plastic products and materials (or especially oil-based plastic materials, such as in Lego). The share of recycled plastic will increase. However, H&M is focused on short-term, nearly disposable cloths.	Small steps of large firms might resemble greenwashing, but they have large total positive effects. H&M criticized because of greenwashing.
"Environmentalists are not anymore so much criticized" -50 years old environmental association of East Savonia is the resource for the society. 2016	Potentially forthcoming biofuel factory in Savonlinna.	East Savo environmetal association will organize discussion event about potential biofuel factory.	Doubts about the factory to be greenwashing. Solar energy might be more progressive and reasonable.

continued on following page

Table 2. Continued

Headline of Article, Year	Company/Companies	Campaign/Context	Reason for Greenwashing/Details
Selective consumer will get money moving? 2015	No companies mentioned	Focused on LOHAS-consumers (lifestyle of health and sustainability)	LOHAS consumers appreciate sustainable development, healthy and ethical production. They will notice easily potential greenwashing.
Researcher about the cheap cloths chains: "Quality do not mean anything, but quantity"2014	No companies mentioned	Halpavaateketjujen lanseeraamat ekologiset tuotelinjat eivät vakuuta tutkijaa.	Cheap cloths chains are launching ecologic production lines, which are not impressive, but resembling greenwashing: environmentalism have to cover all the activities of the firms.
Perspective: Office without paper- big joke or unnecessary hype? 2013	No companies mentioned (only GreeenOffice)	Offices are aiming to decrease the use of paper, e.g. GreenOffice.	Offices aim to get rid of paper and they are saving electricity in the name of environmentalism. Some claim these action to be greenwashing.
Discuss: is the blog of nickel mine greenwashing? 2012	Talvivaara mining company	Talvivaara nickel mine company is starting blogs "Paikan päällä" about environmental issues.	Problematic mining company starts internet discussions about environmentalism, which action is possible to interpret to be greenwashing.
Eco-bakery of Järvenpää is tanking with paste	Primula (and city of Järvenpää)	Primula bakery is located in the neighborhood of mill and raw materials are coming from mill via pipe. Surplus products are going to biofuel.	Instead of information manipulation it is important to follow transparency and the principle of real environmental actions and information.
The main group of young consumers is becoming greener	15/30 Research oy (subname:Nanohabits)	Article introduces the outcomes of new survey of 15/30 Research oy about the environmental attitudes of 15-30 years consumers. Most of them claim to think about environment.	Young consumers do not believe environmentalism of companies. This kind of environmentalism is doubt to be marketing trick (i.e. greenwashing)
Popped marketing bubbles remind of natural values 2010	McDonalds	Vastamainos (in English subvert) campaign, Marketing bubble competition	Winning works in competition focused on greenwashing, such as the vagueness of environmental programs in big companies (e.g. McDonalds) and problems of environmentalism among carrier companies.
Do not buy anything -day challenges to consider consumption habbits 2010	Luonto-Liitto (Finnish Nature League)	Vastamainos (in English subvert) campaign, Marketing bubble competition	The theme of Marketing bubble competition was "bright green values" in order to express greenwashing in advertisements and quasi ecoactions. Whether consumption can be ecological at all?
Carbon neutral company is still rarity in Finland 2010	Primula bakery, Green Office	Consider the situation of carbon neutrality among Finnish companies	Only company, which have been mentioned to aim carbon neutrality is Primula bakery.
Energy of Jyväskylä (Jyväskylän energia) asserts to green- with the customers 2010	Jyväskylän energia, Jyväskylän Voima oy, Tampereen sähkölaitos, Tampereen Energiantuotanto Oy Tampereen Sähkömyynti Oy	Jyväskylän Energia produce more green energy as the customers want to buy.	Article finds greenwashing among the network of Tampereen sähkölaitos, Tampereen Energiantuotanto Oy Tampereen Sähkömyynti Oy, but not between Jyväskylän energia and Jyväskylän Voima oy.

Source: Yleisradio, 2021 (https://yle.fi/uutiset/18-77418)

environmentalism of big international companies. Mostly these international examples are some kinds of warnings about greenwashing: do not do like this. Local and national examples consider both successful and unsuccessful environmentalism. The most typical themes for greenwashing are from energy industries. There seems to be a lack of good examples about environmentalism due to fact that the same firms, especially Primula bakery, has been introduced in several articles. Noticeable is that the same firms might have activities resembling greenwashing and actual environmentalism. Delightful is the noticed possibilities to change the direction: the most obvious greenwashing firms have partly changed their practices and activities towards actual environmentalism.

Examples show the importance to prevent from overstating even the actual (small) action of environmentalism. Audience easily interpret them (incorrectly?) to be greenwashing. However, little strokes fell great oaks: small environmental activities of big international company might have large total effects due to large magnitude of the company. Especially young Finnish consumers are critical about small steps of environmentalism in the companies. This finding is similar to Furlow (2010): the skepticism of consumers will increase due to noticed greenwashing, they may become confused about which products actually do help the environment and doubt generally all environmental activities of the company to be as greenwashing. This will actually be harmful for environmentalism and environment, as also Furlow (2010) noticed.

International level of environmentalism is also linked with international regulations and aims of the European Commission or European Union. Also, some environmental phenomenon is international and it is adopted also in the Finnish context. Examples show strongly the powerfulness of international environmental trends also in Finland.

Environmentalism is strongly based on the actions of NGOs internationally and in Finland. Environmental campaigns and competitions are arranged mainly by associations, sometimes also by governments and companies. Several international environmental associations and NGOs have also activities and organization in Finland.

Delmas and Burdana (2011) noticed external drivers of greenwashing to be consumer demand, investor demand and competitive pressure. Empirical material also shows their importance in greenwashing. However, these same drivers proved to be actors, which fight against greenwashing. Finnish customers are skeptic against the environmental actions of the companies. Small activities of CSR are interpreted to be greenwashing. Investors are more enlightened in the branch of CSR. Several large investors, such as insurance companies, do not allow greenwashing, but actual environmentalism of the firms. Due to need for transparence in the environmental actions of the firms, also competitive pressure is directed against greenwashing and towards actual actions of CSR. If the competitors do not practice greenwashing, it is not wise to the particular company either to have greenwashing activities.

Generally, it seems due to increasing transparency, activities of NGOs and media, that greenwashing is only a temporary step of (quasi) environmentalism. The next (and partly already contemporary) step is the actual environmentalism of the firms. This trend is threatened by greenwashing, however. If the greenwashing is too usual tool of marketing, ALL the environmental and quasi environmental activities of the companies will be interpreted to be as greenwashing by the consumers. There are several alternative results for this tendency. Two main paths might be following: either all of the firms have some environmental activities (real or pretended) or none of the firms have even these minor actions, because the audience is believing them to be only greenwashing.

However, the public pressure due to climate change is so strong that it possible that gradually companies have to make remarkable steps towards environmentalism. These kinds of large steps are impossible to see as greenwashing. It might be even harmful to the companies, in this sense, to have only incremental environmental improvements instead of strong transformative environmental improvements.

In principle, consumers have following alternatives to consider marketing campaigns and advertisement of the firms about environmentalism:

1. Believe all of them
2. Believe none of them
3. Believe some of them

Especially interesting is the case, where the consumers believe some of the marketing campaigns of environmentalism and do not believe the rest of them. It is easy to suppose that the strong actual environmental activities are easier to accept than weaker activities because of the increasing transparency of the society for example in social media.

Similarly, companies have following alternatives in the announcing and implementing environmental activities:

1. Strong marketing campaign with minor environmental activities
2. Strong marketing campaign with major environmental activities
3. Minor marketing campaign with major environmental activities
4. Minor marketing campaign with minor environmental activities
5. No campaign and no environmental activities

It depends on the type consumers whether a), b), c) or d) will be interpreted as greenwashing or not. In the consumer type of 1) all rational companies will choose strategy d) or a) depending on the power of marketing for demand. The consumer type of 2) causes rational firms to choose strategy e), which means the end of environmentalism (in ceteris paribus). The consumer type of 3) is fruitful for environmentalism: the firms will choose easily strategy b) or c) depending on the effectiveness of marketing efforts.

One interesting perspective for greenwashing is the discussions about traditional viewpoints theory in use and espoused theory with greenwashing. Theory in use means actual activities of the entity and espoused theory consider informed (announced) activities of the entity. Bowen and Aragon-Correa (…) compressed this shortly in greenwashing: what we say and do. However, they do not actually consider theory in use and espoused theory perspectives in the text. However, marketing of environmental activities is front yard strategy of the firms, that is a part of the espoused theory of the firm, it will not necessarily be part of the theory in use or backyard strategy of the firm (cf. Argyris and Schön, 1978).

If the difference between the environmental front yard strategy and backyard strategy of the firm is remarkable, there is some kind of greenwashing. However, reasonable question might be whether firm have to redirect its actual environmental actions towards the front yard strategy in order to reduce the gap between theory-in-use and espoused theory – or to have parallel front yard and backyard strategies. According to Argyris (1976, 367) a model of the theory-in-use "was hypothesized that human behavior, in any situation, represents the most satisfactory solution people can find consistent with their governing values or variables, such as achieving a purpose as others define it, winning, suppressing negative feelings, and emphasizing rationality".

Though theory-in-use and espoused theory perspectives are rarely used in the discussions of greenwashing, it might be fruitful to enlarge and develop greenwashing research using them. Generally, greenwashing is multifaceted research branch, which have to take into account seriously. Environmentalism, CSR, sustainable development, responsibility and other connotations have close relationship with greenwashing. Greenwashing is some kind of spook, which is all the time present in environmentalism. Environmentalism activities and studies without the greenwashing is only half-truth.

CONCLUSION

Greenwashing is a common concept, which is closely related to corporate social responsibility and its connotations, such as environmentalism, sustainability, sustainable development, responsibility, among others. Different nuances of environmentalism in the companies are difficult to understand without greenwashing. Textual material of this chapter shows that environmentalism of the companies is practically evaluated using greenwashing as an instrument: environmental activities of the companies are either greenwashing or not, or at least they are resembling greenwashing or not. Also, the marketing actions and campaigns linked with environmental activities are part of greenwashing phenomenon: strong environmental marketing might be even harmful: especially young Finnish consumers do not believe in marketed environmentalism of the companies.

One of the environmental tendencies of the companies is to achieve carbon free production. This aim is proved to be problematic. Only a couple of Finnish companies are believable with this aim and the same companies have been mentioned several times in the Finnish media texts. European Union and European Commission have a hegemony in Finnish environmentalism. These international institutions have effects on the aims of the companies and the themes of the media texts in Finland. Also, international NGOs have effects on Finnish environmentalism of the firms. Though several environmental activities of the Finnish companies are remarkable, the ideas of the environmentalism are coming abroad. In this sense, there are greenwashing among environmental activities of the Finnish companies. The firms are following environmentalism because several international companies do the same. Finnish companies want to be "model pupil" in the national and international markets.

REFERENCES

Argyris, C. (1976). Single-loop and double-loop models in research on decision making. *Administrative Science Quarterly*, *21*(3), 363–375. doi:10.2307/2391848

Argyris, C., & Schon, D. (1978). *Organizational Learning: A theory of action approach*. Addision Wesley.

Banerjee, S. B. (2002). Corporate environmentalism: The construct and its measurement. *Journal of Business Research*, *55*(3), 177–191. doi:10.1016/S0148-2963(00)00135-1

Bowen, F., & Aragon-Correa, J. A. (2014). *Greenwashing in corporate environmentalism research and practice: The importance of what we say and do*. Academic Press.

Cunha, M. P. E., Rego, A., & Vieira da Cunha, J. (2008). Ecocentric management: An update. *Corporate Social Responsibility and Environmental Management*, *15*(6), 311–321. doi:10.1002/csr.169

Delmas, M. A., & Burbano, V. C. (2011). The drivers of greenwashing. *California Management Review*, *54*(1), 64–87. doi:10.1525/cmr.2011.54.1.64

Emetumah, F. C. (2017). Modern perspectives on environmentalism: Ecocentrism and technocentrism in the Nigerian context. *Asian Research Journal of Arts & Social Sciences,* 1-9.

Eriksson, P., & Kovalainen, A. (2015). Qualitative Methods in Business Research: A Practical Guide to Social Research. *Sage (Atlanta, Ga.)*.

European Commission. (2021). *Screening of websites for 'greenwashing': Half of green claims lack evidence*. https://ec.europa.eu/commission/presscorner/detail/en/IP_21_269

Furlow, N. E. (2010). Greenwashing in the new millennium. *The Journal of Applied Business and Economics*, *10*(6), 22.

Gladwin, T. N., Kennelly, J. J., & Krause, T. S. (1995). Shifting paradigms for sustainable development: Implications for management theory and research. *Academy of Management Review*, *20*(4), 874–907. doi:10.5465/amr.1995.9512280024

Harju, E. (2021). Näin meitä huijataan Valmistajan vastuullisuuspuheet voivat olla vain tyhjää sanahelinää. Tässä jutussa asiantuntijat neuvovat, mistä tunnistat viherpesun. *Iltalehti*.

Lee, K. H., & Shin, D. (2010). Consumers' responses to CSR activities: The linkage between increased awareness and purchase intention. *Public Relations Review*, *36*(2), 193–195. doi:10.1016/j.pubrev.2009.10.014

Lumley, S., & Armstrong, P. (2004). Some of the nineteenth century origins of the sustainability concept. *Environment, Development and Sustainability*, *6*(3), 367–378. doi:10.1023/B:ENVI.0000029901.02470.a7

Mayer, R., Scammon, D., & Zick, C. (1993). Poisoning the well: Do environmental claims strain consumer credulity? *Advances in Consumer Research. Association for Consumer Research (U. S.)*, *20*, 698–703.

Meadows, Meadows, Randers, & Behrens. (1974). *The Limits to Growth: A Report for the Club of Rome's Project on the Predicament of Mankind* (2nd ed.). New York: Potomac Associates.

Mitchell, L., & Ramey, W. (2011). Look how green I am! An individual-level explanation for greenwashing. *Journal of Applied Business and Economics*, *12*(6), 40–45.

Ramus, C. A., & Montiel, I. (2005). When are corporate environmental policies a form of greenwashing? *Business & Society*, *44*(4), 377–414. doi:10.1177/0007650305278120

Rusko, R. (2020). Values or Strategy? Comparative Study About the Roles of Values and Strategy in the Web Pages of the Largest Scandinavian Firms. In Sustainability Reporting, Ethics, and Strategic Management Strategies for Modern Organizations (pp. 63-77). IGI Global.

Valor, C. (2005). Corporate social responsibility and corporate citizenship: Towards corporate accountability. *Business and Society Review*, *110*(2), 191–212. doi:10.1111/j.0045-3609.2005.00011.x

WCED (The World Commission on Environment and Development). (1987). *Our Common Future*. Oxford University Press.

Yin, R. K. (1981). The case study as a serious research strategy. *Science Communication*, *3*(1), 97–114.

Yleisradio. (2021). https://yle.fi/uutiset/18-77418

Zelezny, L. C., Chua, P. P., & Aldrich, C. (2000). New ways of thinking about environmentalism: Elaborating on gender differences in environmentalism. *The Journal of Social Issues*, *56*(3), 443–457. doi:10.1111/0022-4537.00177

ADDITIONAL READING

Alves, I. M. (2009). Green spin everywhere: How greenwashing reveals the limits of the CSR paradigm. *Journal of Global Change and Governance*, *2*(1), 1–26.

Gatti, L., Seele, P., & Rademacher, L. (2019). Grey zone in–greenwash out. A review of greenwashing research and implications for the voluntary-mandatory transition of CSR. *International Journal of Corporate Social Responsibility*, *4*(1), 1–15. doi:10.118640991-019-0044-9

Lee, H. C. B., Cruz, J. M., & Shankar, R. (2018). Corporate social responsibility (CSR) issues in supply chain competition: Should greenwashing be regulated? *Decision Sciences*, *49*(6), 1088–1115. doi:10.1111/deci.12307

Mahoney, L. S., Thorne, L., Cecil, L., & LaGore, W. (2013). A research note on standalone corporate social responsibility reports: Signaling or greenwashing? *Critical Perspectives on Accounting*, *24*(4-5), 350–359. doi:10.1016/j.cpa.2012.09.008

Parguel, B., Benoît-Moreau, F., & Larceneux, F. (2011). How sustainability ratings might deter 'greenwashing': A closer look at ethical corporate communication. *Journal of Business Ethics*, *102*(1), 15–28. doi:10.100710551-011-0901-2

Vollero, A., Palazzo, M., Siano, A., & Elving, W. J. (2016). Avoiding the greenwashing trap: Between CSR communication and stakeholder engagement. *International Journal of Innovation and Sustainable Development*, *10*(2), 120–140. doi:10.1504/IJISD.2016.075542

Willers, C., & Kulik, A. (2011). CSR as Corporate Strategy vs."Greenwashing": CSR as a New Paradigm of Brand Management? In *Trends and Issues in Global Tourism* (pp. 301–313). Springer. (Original work published 2011)

Wu, Y., Zhang, K., & Xie, J. (2020). Bad greenwashing, good greenwashing: Corporate social responsibility and information transparency. *Management Science*, *66*(7), 3095–3112. doi:10.1287/mnsc.2019.3340

KEY TERMS AND DEFINITIONS

Club of Rome: A scientific association or Non-Governmental Organization (NGO), which focuses on the future challenges, such as environment and economy, of the world.

Ecocentrism: A perspective, which emphasizes the inherent value of natural, the biosphere, and all living things.

Environmentalism: A perspective, which takes care of nature conditions and the challenges of global warming, for example.

Espoused Theory: The actual actions and activities are not (exactly) similar to public message about them.

Greenfashing: A quasi-environmentalism, where the actual environmental activities might be minor or even absent.

Sustainability: The (business) actions or activities, which follows the principles of environmentalism and sustainable development.

Theory-in-Use: The actual actions and activities are similar to public message about them.

Chapter 6
CSR in the Tourism Industry

Andreea Marin-Pantelescu
Bucharest University of Economic Studies, Romania

ABSTRACT

CSR in the tourism industry aims to bring to the fore social responsibility initiatives. The decline in the first 10 months of the year 2020 represents 900 million fewer international tourist arrivals compared to the same period of the year 2019, and translates into a loss of US$ 935 billion in export revenues from international tourism. According to the World Tourism Organization, international arrivals will drop by 75% in 2020. This would mean that international tourism has returned to the levels of 30 years ago. In order to restore tourism, extensive social responsibility campaigns involving stakeholders should be launched. The main stakeholders in the tourism industry carry out social responsibility campaigns that take into account employees, guests, the environment, and the local communities. Environmental protection, fair working conditions for employees, and contributing to the welfare of local communities are key issues in the strategies of international tourism corporations and will be explored in the chapter on CSR in the tourism industry.

INTRODUCTION

Corporate social responsibility (CSR) in tourism can be defined as a business policy that guides tourism companies to integrate social and environmental concerns in their own mission, in their business strategies and operations, as well as in their interaction with stakeholders (Ahn, 2020).

CSR is now seen as a multi-stakeholder approach, in which stakeholders are not only beneficiaries of CSR initiatives, but also collaborators in their implementation. In the strategies of tourism companies, the CSR concept has become a core element. Environmental sustainability, fair working conditions for employees, and contributing to the well-being of local communities are key aspects emphasized in the strategies of international tourism corporations (Ahn & Kwon, 2020).

Tourism is an economic and social activity with a strong impact on society through income and prosperity brought to local communities. The tourism industry represented in 2019 a total international tourist arrival of 1,460 million and a total international tourism receipts of 1,481 billion USD (UNWTO, 2021).

DOI: 10.4018/978-1-7998-8069-1.ch006

Tourism is an industry that encompasses different fields from lodging and transport, to attractions and travel companies. In its broadest sense, tourism is defined as when people travel and stay in places outside of their usual environment for less than one consecutive year for leisure, business, health, or other reasons.

Tourism has seen continued expansion over time, despite occasional shocks, underlining the sector's strength and resilience.

Nowadays, more than ever, tourism is struggling to survive due to the Covid-19 pandemic that froze international travel. International tourist arrivals (overnight visitors) declined 65% in the first half of 2020 over the same period last year, with arrivals in June down 93%, according to data reported by destinations. The massive fall in international travel demand during the first half of 2020 translates into a loss of 440 million international arrivals and about USD 460 billion in export revenues from international tourism. This represents over five times the loss in receipts recorded in 2009 amid the global economic and financial crisis. Based on the three UNWTO scenarios published in May 2020 pointing to declines of 58% to 78% in international tourist arrivals in 2020, current trends point to a decline in international arrivals closer to 70% for 2020.

Extended scenarios for 2021-2024 point to a strong rebound in the year 2021 based on the assumption of a reversal in the evolution of the pandemic, significant improvement in traveller confidence and major lifting of travel restrictions by the middle of the year. Nonetheless, the return to 2019 levels in terms of international arrivals would take 2½ to 4 years.

BACKGROUND

The European Commission presents the multidisciplinary nature of CSR, pointing out the areas covered: human rights, labor, and employment practices (training, diversity, equal opportunities for women and men, health and well-being of the employees) environmental issues (biodiversity, climate change, effective use of resources, life cycle assessment, and pollution prevention), combating bribery and corruption, consumer interests, community involvement and development, integration of people with disabilities. Cross-cutting issues are also addressed: social promotion and environmental responsibility through supply chains and the reporting of non-financial data (EU, 2021; The role of CSR in business strategy, 2018).

According to the EUROPEAN COMMISSION (2017) tourism companies report CSR actions, so appreciated by tourists.

Companies in the tourism industry are becoming increasingly concerned about their role in terms of social responsibility, which implies ethical behavior in conducting business (Köseoglu, et al., 2021).

In figure no.1 entitled: *The essence of corporate social responsibility on different levels: economic, legal and ethical* there can be observed the different levels in social responsibility that companies in the tourism sector should fulfill.

Responsible tourism targets objectives related to economic viability, local prosperity, quality of workplaces, social equity, visitor experience, local control, life quality of the local community, cultural richness, the physical integrity of the environment, biological diversity, efficient use of resources, purity of the natural environment (Nazir & Islam, 2019).

Figure 1. The essence of corporate social responsibility on different levels: economic, legal and ethical
Source: created by the author

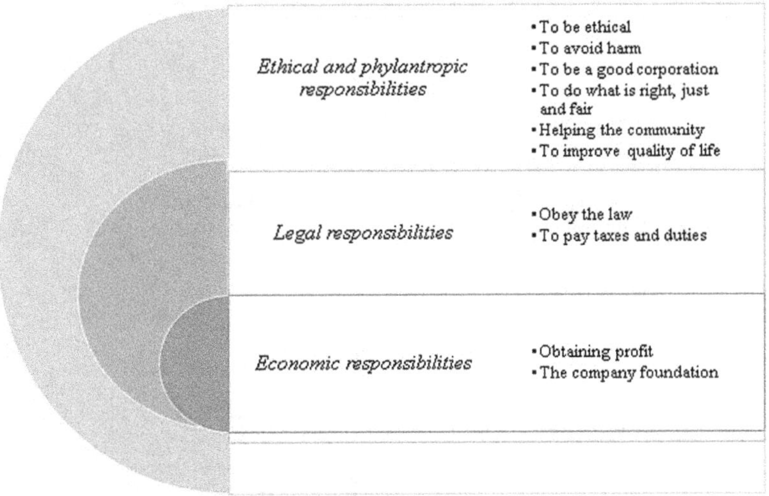

Awareness of the economic, social, and ecological issues generated by the business operation has led, on one hand, to the need of taking responsibility for sustainable development, and on the other hand, to the understanding that CSR can be seen as a source of competitive advantage (Manente, Minghetti, & Mingotto, 2014; Higgins-Desbiolles, 2018; Farmaki & Farmakis, 2018; Buckley & de Vasconcellos Pegas, n.d).

Tourism is a dynamic, diverse, multiple, and powerful sector of activity. According to the World Tourism Organization in the year 2019, tourism continued expansion and diversification to become one of the largest and fastest-growing economic sectors in the world.

Growth in tourism was driven by a relatively strong global economy, growing middle classes and rapid urbanization in emerging economies, affordable travel and visa facilitation, as well as technological advances and new business models.

Tourism, consisting of both inbound and domestic tourism represents a major part of gross domestic product for many economies around the world. This proportion is largest in Macao (China) where tourism accounts for 48% of GDP.

In Jordan, Spain, Croatia and Mauritius, tourism accounts for 10% or more of those countries' GDP. In France, the world's top tourism destination, tourism represents 7% of GDP.

Tourism also generates millions of direct and indirect jobs, with a high share of women and young people.

Most tourism enterprises (around 80%) are micro, small and medium sized enterprises (MSMEs) which employ a high share of women and young people.

Women make up 54% of the tourism workforce (as compared to 39% in the overall economy).

Tourism has several components that are shown in *figure no.2 The main components of the travel and tourism industry.*

This chapter mentions social responsibility campaigns for hotels, tourism agencies, and airlines to highlight their intense concerns.

Figure 2. The main components of the travel and tourism industry
Source: created by the author

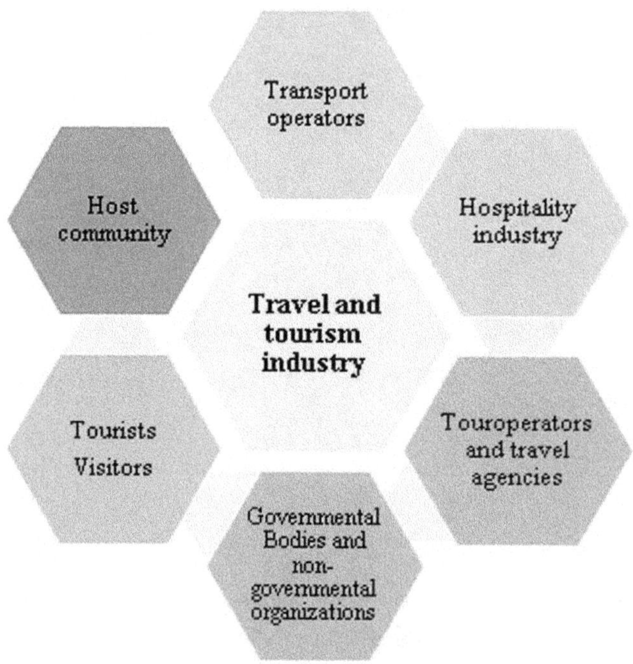

SOCIAL RESPONSIBILITY CAMPAIGNS CARRIED OUT BY HOTELS

Large international hotels have intense concerns in reducing the seasonal nature of the demand for tourism services, increasing the quality of services provided, maintaining and consolidating market share, increasing the life quality of employees, increasing shareholder dividends, intense promotion, creating loyalty programs, saving energy, reducing to a minimum the use of resources and waste production, protecting the environment, saving energy and providing value to the natural and cultural heritage, improving the quality of jobs in the hotel sector.

CSR Campaigns of Orbis' Hotels

The first example is one of the oldest and most famous Polish brands – Orbis S.A. it the largest hotel chain in Poland and Central Europe. It offers 10,5 thousand rooms in almost 60 hotels in 24 Polish cities and in Vilnius, Lithuania (Orbis Hotel Group, 2017).

ORBIS S.A. together with Accor Group tries to link its development with respect for local communities and the environment. To do this, they have launched an international program, PLANET 21, that encourages all hotels and customers to participate in it. This program is based on Agenda 21, a document adopted in 1992 at the UN Conference on environment and development in Rio de Janeiro. PLANET 21's strategy consists of 21 commitments in seven areas, such as:

- Health - in a time when life is threated by epidemics and obesity, represents a goal in the Orbis Hotels CSR strategies, offering hygienic interiors, which are equipped with eco-labeled products, promotes balanced nutrition by preparing food using local and natural products and participates in the international program of HIV / AIDS – HIV, combating HIV in 6 steps;

- Local development – the area that refers to the protection of children against sexual abuse, the protection of ecosystems, and support of responsible trade;
- Activity – actions in this field focus on promoting the development of employees and their skills, improving the professional quality of life, and promoting diversity. Orbis Hotel Group has introduced the Accor "International Diversity Charter" which defines priorities such as diversity of origin, gender, age diversity, disabilities, and dialogue in all hotels from Poland;
- The actions are focused on transparent and open activity. It is manifested, among other things, by the publication of periodic reports, as well as by the involvement of suppliers of private companies and hotel companies in the idea of CSR activity;
- Natural environment - this domain includes commitments on reducing water use, biodiversity conservation, and waste recycling;
- Carbon dioxide - activities in this field are based on reducing energy consumption and carbon dioxide emissions, as well as increasing the use of renewable energy;
- Energy innovation - activities are based on promoting a sustainable building; stimulating eco-design and the application of sustainable technologies.

ORBIS Hotel Group also takes environmental aspects into account in its activities. During Earth Guest Day, a program run by the Accor Group, more than 3,000 Orbis employees were involved in environmental activities. In addition to planting trees and flowers and clearing forests, there were lectures for children and adults on healthy eating, waste segregation, and ecosystems. Also, environmental activities are supported by the OPEN operational program which controls energy and water consumption, and waste management.

CSR Campaigns of Polski Pod Białym Orłem Hotel

Polski Pod BiałymOrłem considers social responsibility. Its activities mainly support environmental initiatives. Actions for the community include the promotion of Polish culture and tradition and the protection of national heritage. In 2004, being one of the first hotels in Poland, it received a clean tourism certificate (CSR Hotel Polski Pod Białym Orłem, 2021).

People in Poland are increasingly aware that companies need to play an active and positive role in society. Their focus must not only be on prices, but also on the social and environmental consequences of their work.

Good CSR practices, recognized as a long-term investment, do not have a cost, are ultimately beneficial both to the hotel and society, along with each party involved.

CSR activities in the hotel industry focus on the health and safety of employees and guests, reducing the negative impact on the environment and respecting the social and ethical norms of the company and the local community.

CSR Campaigns of Hilton Hotels Group

Hilton Worldwide has decided to offer paid parental leave to all hotel employees, including those from top management, as well as housekeepers and restaurant staff. Given the wide range of possible responsible activities in hotels, from adopting a green practice to participate in community engagements, social responsibility campaigns have an impact on the employees' lives and influence their quality of life, leading to job satisfaction in hotels where human capital is a key to gaining a competitive advantage (Hilton Corporate Responsibility Report, 2017).

CSR Campaigns of Marriott International Hotels Group

The hotel industry player has set ambitious sustainability goals, which by 2025 will have a significant difference in terms of their environmental and social footprint (MARRIOTT SERVE 360 REPORT, 2020).

Over the next five years, Marriott International, which operates a global portfolio of 7,200 properties under 30 brands, aims to:

Decrease by 45% of waste to the landfill;

- Decrease by 50% of food waste
- Decrease by 15% of water consumption
- Decrease by 30% in carbon intensity
- Use of at least 30% of renewable energy
- 100% of hotels certified according to a recognized sustainability standard.

The vehicle used to drive change and operational evolution throughout the hotel network is a global program called Serve 360: Doing Good in Every Direction, which the group launched in 2017.

Two years after the program, Marriott International also sees a series of innovative workplace sustainability initiatives and has a positive impact at local, regional and global levels.

The president of the Marriott International Asia Pacific group, Craig Smith, declared that properties across the region are actively participating in the program and work to reduce their carbon footprint by investing and implementing operational changes, including initiatives involving guests and local community groups.

As the world's largest hotel group, Marriott International will continue to use its size and scale to drive positive social and environmental change to meet the changing mindset of staff, guests, corporate customers, and the wider industry of travellers.

Marriottt International CSR in Relation to the Environment

Marriottt International Reducing Food Waste

The evolution initiatives of management and recycling waste, with a focus on reducing waste consumption and waste, is a key focus for the hotel group. Leveraging the size and scale of the group, Marriott's priority has been a series of sustainability initiatives to eradicate disposable plastic materials. As part of its Serve 360 program, the group is working to remove disposable plastics from all of its global properties and replacing the small disposable bathroom bottles from rooms with larger, pumped bottles.

When implemented globally, Marriott International's extended toilet program will prevent overcoming 770 tons of plastic from being dumped in landfills, which translates into a 30% annual reduction from current levels.

Local and Responsible Supply for Marriott International

By 2025, Marriott International aims to supply 50% of all its products locally, with 95% of the top 10 priority categories coming from ethical and sustainable suppliers. This includes companies that supply their hotels - meat, eggs, cleaning products, bottled water, cocoa, coffee, toiletries for rooms, paper products, seafood, sugar, and textiles.

By the end of 2020, the hotel group will require all contracted suppliers in these top 10 categories to provide information on product sustainability, including social and human rights impact, and by 2025 all suppliers (centrally contracted) will have to provide this information.

Reducing Water Consumption for Marriott International

With the increasing pressure on Asia Pacific water resources, Marriott International has also implemented water-saving strategies to reduce water and energy consumption. By 2025, the company will reduce its water intensity by 15% through reduction, water treatment, and collecting initiatives.

JW Marriott Phuket Resort & Spa has installed a Generation Water system that extracts drinking water from moisture in the air to reduce the need for bottled water in the hotel. The system replaced over 2 million plastic bottles in 2019.

Recycling at Marriott International

The Manila Marriott Hotel makes disposable plastic chairs for the School of the Deaf in the Philippines and the Red Cross in the Philippines, providing better learning opportunities for students in the community.

Ritz-Carlton, Millenia Singapore turns the threads from the aluminum drink cans of the guests into artificial limbs for those in need.

Minimize Food Waste for Marriott International

The Bangkok Marriott Marquis Queen's Park Hotel contributes an average of about 38 kg of food to the Thailand Scholar of Sustainability Foundation (SOS) network, which redistributes meals to disadvantaged people in Bangkok.

Conference and Ecological Events Organized by Marriott International

Athenee Hotel, a luxury collectible hotel in Bangkok, was the first hotel in the world to reach a standard of event sustainability management system (ISO20121). The hotel offers a "Green Meeting Package", which includes eco-friendly materials and soft drinks. All of the hotel's conference and meeting rooms operate with minimal energy.

Pier One Sydney Harbor has made its half-size banquet notebooks and offers conference guests organic wheat straw pens.

Local and Responsible Supply Within Marriott International

Hong Kong Ocean Park Marriott has designed all menus to meet World Wildlife Fund standards, using only sustainable seafood in all its restaurants.

Sustainable Water Solutions

Le Méridien Mahabaleshwar Resort & Spa in India has installed high-efficiency showers in the guest rooms and treats wasted water for use in hotel washing systems.

CSR Campaigns of Accor Hotels Group

Solidarity Week brings together the Group's employees every year around the same goal: sharing the values of humanity and solidarity through committed initiatives. Christmas markets, clothing collections, charity lunches, snacks, donations, orphanage visits, table distributions. For this new edition on December 7-13, while the health crisis has led to the temporary closure of headquarters and hotels in some countries, the group's employees continue their solidarity actions and give them a new impulse. These initiatives are part of the ongoing exceptional mobilization of the units and their owners in recent months to support those most affected by the crisis. Since its creation in 2008, the Accor Solidarity endowment fund has been involved in the fight against the economic and social exclusion of people in great precariousness through professional integration. Although its areas of intervention have not changed in 2020, the teams have worked to better respond to the needs of the crisis and current events (Accor CSR & Performance, 2021).

Accor Solidarity has been specifically involved in maintaining contact with Heartists employees and the group's partner NGOs. To ensure the support given to NGOs – from some of which are in great difficulty with the crisis to carry out new projects. With ALL - Accor Live Limitless, the endowment fund has joined forces with the Pasteur Institute to support research in the fight against Covid-19. Loyalty program members were able to donate their reward points thanks to the operation "Burn for Covid", making it possible to collect over EUR 360,000 in 2 months. And thanks to the matching of this amount by Accor, over 660,000 euros were donated to the Pasteur Institute.

CSR in Relation to Customers Within the Accor Group

Most guests already operate daily in their own homes. And a majority would like to continue these responsible gestures when they stay in Accor hotels.

- 85% of Accor's guests try to avoid wasting food at home
- 82% buy energy efficient appliances
- 81% sort waste
- 76% buy locally made products

ACCOR guests are willing to help:

- 70% of Accor guests are as concerned about the sustainable development of the hotel as they are in their homes
- 2 out of 3 guests are willing to pay a little more for a hotel that takes responsible action
- 64% are willing to receive the invoice by e-mail
- 61% are willing to sort their waste at the hotel
- 57% are willing to use their towels and sheets for two or three days

CSR in Relation to Accor Partners

Accor's goal is to co-innovate with partners to open new horizons and give concrete shape to their vision of positive hospitality. The hotel's business and performance are both closely related to those of its partners, meaning suppliers and properties of Accor units operated under management and franchise agreements.

The Accor commitments for 2020 were:

- Every year, a major innovation to develop alternative and responsible models
- Accor "CSR & Ethical Risk Management" process is implemented among 100% of their partners

What Is the Accor Group Already Doing?

In 2010, they were looking for eco-labeled cleaning products that could be implemented in all their hotels around the world. Diversey, one of the suppliers of cleaning products, wanted to grow its business with Accor. Together, they created a global partnership, which gave them global access to a range of eco-labeled cleaning products. This collaboration is one of the main reasons why 97% of their hotels now use environmentally friendly cleaning products.

Benefits:

- a significant reduction in the environmental impact of their water discharges and the quantities of packaging used.
- a reduction of health and safety risks for employees that are handling cleaning products.

PUR PROJET, an organization that works to protect the climate by supporting reforestation and forest conservation schemes implemented by local communities, is helping the Accor Group to develop and coordinate the 2012 Plant for the Planet program.

This partnership allows them to innovate in customer communication, in supporting business for farmers and in a new approach to food supply.

Accor Solidarity Support

Accor Solidarity, the Accor Group's endowment fund, has been working side by side with its employees since 2008.

Each year, it provides financial and technical support for approximately 30 local projects sponsored by the hotels that work with local NGOs and charities. Its general purpose is to counteract the economic and social exclusion of the most vulnerable, allowing for professional integration.

Redistribution of Buffet Residues (Accor Bangkok)

Eight of Accor's hotels in Bangkok have set up a Food for Thought operation. Twice a week, the teams collect leftover buffets and donate them to Good Shepherd Sisters, a charity organization that works with children and women living in leisure towns. Volunteers at our hotels in Thailand take care of the logistics.

What Is the Accor Group Already Doing?

Accor has been a pioneer in the fight against the sexual exploitation of children in the hospitality sector.

In 2001, it was the first hospitality group to partner with ECPAT, an international NGO at the forefront of the fight to end the commercial sexual exploitation of children. In 2002, they began setting up training programs for our employees to deal with this problem. ACCOR initiatives are based on the Code of Conduct for the Protection of Children against Sexual Exploitation in Travel and Tourism. 1,200 professionals in tourism from 46 countries have signed it. Companies sign in each of the host countries. By the end of 2015, 38 Accor host countries had signed it. This Code of Conduct requires Accor to take a variety of measures to combat the sexual exploitation of children. Example:

- employee training,
- traveler information,
- includes clauses in this regard in contracts with suppliers.

WATCH: keeping your eyes open

WATCH means "We act together for children".

It is the program they introduced in 2014 to step up efforts to eradicate child sexual exploitation.

NGOs, children's rights organizations, police services and embassy networks are on deck to respond quickly and synchronously if hotels alert them. Watch is adapted to the local situation and to the extent of the scourge in each country.

WATCH provides hotels with awareness films, training modules and various other tools for:

- Keep employees constantly alert
- Helps to respond to suspect situations,
- Aware guests.

Specifically, if an employee realizes or suspects that a child is being sexually exploited, he or she informs the general manager of the hotel or the service manager, who assesses the situation.

If the suspicions are confirmed or the situation is not clarified, the manager warns the police and they take over immediately. The child is entrusted to local child protection organizations.

CSR Campaigns of NH Hotels Group

NH Hotel Group has always given solid support to the internal development of employees, where talent management has taken on special importance, along with the need to proactively identify and develop professionals to ensure management and succession in the company in the medium and long term (NH Sustainable Business Annual Report, 2021).

NH Hotel Group has established the "Hotel with heart" more than 15 years ago, in order to help foundations and NGOs to cover their needs in hotels group. The company has strengthened this commitment through agreements with hospitals and foundations in a variety of countries to support children with serious illnesses and their families with limited resources when they need to be housed away from their own cities.

Several NH Hotel Group employees also participate in this initiative, acting as the true hosts of these families and "ambassadors" of the program in each of the hotels. Since the program began, more than 2,000 employees each year have become true hosts of these families, helping to turn the hotel into a second home for them. The company also has its own special rate for NGOs, which offers discounts of up to 30% of the best rates, which are available to organizations that have been evaluated and approved in advance by the corporate responsibility department. Since its inception, the program has donated over 25,800 hotel nights.

NH Group Projects

- Youth career initiative

They are the only multinational company in Spain engaged in this innovative international initiative which, together with Intercontinental, Marriott and Starwood, provides training each year to over 400 young people at risk of social exclusion in catering / hotel industry out of 53 hotels in the world. The support, knowledge and experience of the volunteer staff were essential during the 24-week training.

- Sprint program

In 2012, the first edition of this program was launched to cover jobs with qualified staff for their business unit in Central Europe. Together with the Tomillo Foundation and the support of the Barclays Foundation, their volunteer employees participated as mentors at the destination hotels.

- Jinc

Jincai collaborates with providing training for young people from disadvantaged neighborhoods in 2009 focused on improving the employability of their integration into the labor market through visits and workshops at hotels in cities like Amsterdam, Amersfoort and Utrecht.

- Spanish Red Cross

Introduces women at risk of social exclusion, identified by the Spanish Red Cross in a training program as housekeeping staff. Also, volunteers participate in the course offered to participating women.

- Pantar In Amsterdam

In 2020, under the slogan "Together with Love" NH Hotel Group has organized for the second time a week of corporate volunteering worldwide. This is a global initiative focused on sustainability and strengthening relations with the local communities in which the Group is present, and all Company teams have been invited to participate. In this way, NH Hotel Group has joined the annual volunteer initiative of Minor International, with which it shares a strong commitment to the development of its corporate social responsibility strategy.

Since the beginning of the pandemic, NH Hotel Group has been aware of the need for food and commodities and has therefore endeavored to help vulnerable families and others who, due to the current situation, have seen their incomes cut sharply and have not never thought he would end up living such a complicated situation.

With all the necessary safety measures and without endangering the health of its team members, NH Hotel Group has launched the NH Runners initiative, aimed at all employees, to raise funds for meals during the kilometers traveled by volunteer employees. The commitment to food donations continues today, thanks to the 5,600 meals funded by this initiative. In the second week of June 2020, NH Hotel Group proposed the idea to run for help during a pandemic. All employees of the Company (including those affected by temporary suspensions of the contract) had the option to donate the kilometers they covered for a week, with a conversion rate of 1 km = 1 meal.

CSR Campaigns of Hyatt Hotels Group

CSR in relation to the employees from Hyatt Group of Hotels. In their intensive work, it is vital to take care of the employees - in mind, body and spirit. Caring for their minds means providing the tools to stay present and support lifelong learning, including school reimbursement and travel benefits. Taking care of employees' bodies means supporting their energy and health, including exercise options, relaxation and snack spaces and healthy meals at discounted prices or meals in canteens. And caring for their spirit means allowing them to build relationships and connect with their communities through flexible working arrangements, networking opportunities, volunteering and other channels. The Employee Welfare Council helps to assess and shape how they can continue to energize them through the feedback gathered from their work to discover staff well-being (Hyatt Corporate Responsibility, 2021).

With colleagues from over 50 countries, Hyatt embraces all cultures, races, ethnicities, genders, sexual orientations, ages, abilities, perspectives and ways of thinking. All colleagues bring something unique and special to the Hyatt family. Their culture is the one that empowers each individual to be their best, and such a genuine connection inspires the way they care for each other and their guests.

Hyatt Hotels Offers a Wide Range of Benefits

It offers staff competitive salaries, health care, retirement savings and performance-based incentives, while providing industry-leading benefits to eligible colleagues, including free hotel stays. In the US, benefits include short-term disability paid by the employer, coaches to help colleagues quit smoking, free medical advice from health experts, advocacy services to help staff with questions about their benefits, and easy access. at a low cost, to doctors for employees and their families.

Supporting Families

Hyatt understands that each person is unique and thus allows the flexibility to work for different needs through programming options. In addition, they were among the first companies of our size in the hotel industry to offer a comprehensive family care policy, offering primary caregivers or domestic partners free time after birth or adoption, as well as financial assistance for adoption.

Helping People Reach Their Potential

Their competitive advantage comes from people and focuses on attracting and retaining the best. Hyatt offers significant learning and development initiatives to help employees explore their passions and reach their full potential.

In an industry with a historically high turnover, Hyatt has over 14,000 employees with over 15 years of service - proof of the positive impact of their efforts.

CSR in Relation to Local Communities for Hyatt Hotels Group

With hotels in hundreds of cities around the world, the needs of each community are different. Since 2008, the Hyatt Community Grants Program has empowered Hyatt hotels to identify the most pressing issues in their communities and to support nonprofits that provide meaningful local solutions. Through this unique program, our employees have the opportunity to nominate local non-profit organizations to receive grants that support local social and environmental priorities.

Helping People Start their Careers at Hyatt Hotels

Hyatt's global RiseHY program provides career opportunities for young people to help them reach their full potential.

To achieve this, it is working on a number of programs that address the lack of unemployment and qualifications:

- Youth Career Initiative (YCI) - Hyatt Hotels receive and provide training to develop the skills of young adults from disadvantaged backgrounds. 85% of YCI participants won a job or returned to education. Hyatt Hotels have supported this program since 2008 in countries such as India, Mexico, Brazil, Nepal and Jordan.
- The 100,000 Opportunities Initiative - Hired hundreds of people under the age of 25 in the US living in areas with a high youth unemployment.
- Hands On Education - They have been collaborating since 1998 to provide training and jobs for people with intellectual and physical disabilities.
- In addition, through the International Partnership for Tourism (ITP), the tourism industry comes together to strengthen youth employment.

Hyatt has adopted two schools in the Back of the Yards community, a low-income, high-risk neighborhood, and supports them through book discussions, career workshops, work days, college trips and other projects.

Setting Hyatt Goals to Address Environmental Challenges

In 2014, Hyatt launched its 2020 vision to address the most pressing global environmental issues it can influence.

Using Data to Increase Performance

Hyatt use a global environmental management database, Hyatt EcoTrack, to collect and analyze sustainability data from hotels around the world. The database provides hotels with easy-to-read dashboards for data analysis and includes projects and best practices for further improvement.

Identification and Planning Solutions

All Hyatt hotels face various operational and environmental opportunities and challenges, depending on the type of building, age, climate, layout and local infrastructure, among other factors. Therefore, they use energy audits to identify and prioritize property-specific projects to improve performance. We review hotel locations against water risks using the World Resources Institute Aqueduct tool and prioritize water efficiency, especially for hotels in areas with water stress.

Typical property-specific projects include, but are not limited to, lighting and water upgrades, upgrades to older heating and cooling systems, installation of new and efficient air treatment systems, upgrades to kitchen and laundry equipment, use of sources water alternatives or water recycling, renewable or low-carbon energy generation and the implementation of building automation and energy optimization systems.

Waste approach - They have a number of recycling and waste management strategies that we apply, including steps such as working with Clean the World to donate lightly used soaps and shampoos.

Collaborating to reduce food waste - Food waste is often a large part of a hotel's waste stream. In collaboration with other hotel companies, the American Hotel and Lodging Association, the World Wildlife Fund, and with the support of the Rockefeller Foundation, Hyatt helped create and launch a toolkit developed to promote industry-wide food waste prevention. It also works with a variety of organizations that assist hotels in establishing donation programs for excess edible food.

To accelerate progress in this area, the goals for food waste are:

- All hotels will complete Hyatt's training in food waste prevention and implement prevention plans.
- They will double the percentage of hotels in North Amcrica with food donation programs.
- If possible, alternative methods of inedible food waste management will be used.
- The International Tourism Partnership (ITP) working groups on climate change and water management contribute to the development of sustainability in the tourism industry.
- The Sustainability Committee of the American Hotel and Lodging Association helps them advance best practices and raise awareness of environmental issues throughout the industry.

- Hyatt is a signatory of the Hotel Owners Coalition for Tomorrow, which sets out commitments and five actions to promote sustainability among Asian hotel owners, focusing on raising awareness to address climate change risks and opportunities for developments and investment.
- The CEO of the Paulson Institute for Sustainable Urbanization in China brings together companies from the US and China to establish a more sustainable way forward for China's extensive urbanization programs. Hyatt has also been a leading sponsor of the Paulson Institute's China Mayor Training Program, an initiative that brings Chinese mayors to the United States for a two-week immersion training to teach sustainable urban approaches and last generation.

Providing transparent data:

- They have participated in the CDP Climate Change since our 2013 report, so that investors and analysts can access detailed information on GHG emissions and our climate change strategy.
- Hyatt and other hospitality companies came together through ITP to develop the Hotel Carbon Initiative (HCMI) and the Hotel Water Measurement Initiative (HWMI). They standardize the industry's methodology for reporting carbon emissions and water use, especially for corporate customers.
- yatt has worked with peer-to-peer hotel chains to launch a comparable evaluation index available free of charge through Cornell University's Hospitality Research Center. Established in 2013, it is the only global coverage comparison tool based on real and revised data for 10,000 hotels.

CSR Campaigns of Radisson Hotels Group

Radisson Hotel Group are ethical businesses practiced based on their culture, which is evident in the way he treated its customers, team members, suppliers and business partners. It believes in providing meaningful jobs, developing talents and increasing the employment capacity of young people. Radisson promotes human rights, business ethics and diversity in hotels, their business network and supply chain (Radisson Hotel Corporate Social Responsibility, 2021).

Youth Career Initiative is an employment program that works with local hotels to give disadvantaged young people (aged 17 to 24) the chance to learn a range of skills in a variety of departments. Since the launch of the partnership, they have trained over 200 students and over 85% of them either get a job or continued their education, proving the incredible success of this program. By offering career opportunities to vulnerable young people, the company is gaining new, young and dynamic colleagues.

Radisson Hotel Group CSR in Relation to the Local Community

Radisson Hotel Group empowers team members to contribute to their local communities. In partnership with SOS Children Villages, they ensure the development of children in a safe and caring environment, so that they can reach their full potential. We are also investing in our future, assisting with programs for vulnerable young people, helping them to develop their personal and professional life skills.

Radisson Hotel Group believes in positive and meaningful actions. Team members support this initiative at every level, from individual hotels to corporate offices. It focuses primarily on helping children, young people and families and provides them with educational opportunities and sustainable shelter. In

2019, team members supported nonprofits around the world, donating over 43,000 hours of volunteering and over $ 1.3 million.

Every June, they celebrate Community Action Month by finding ways to make a positive impact on local communities. Their goal is to draw attention to local initiatives that can make a real difference in each community. In 2019, for the 16th year in a row, Radisson Hotel Group members were proud to demonstrate their continued commitment to their communities by organizing 1,000 activities and raising nearly $ 500,000 in cash and in-kind donations to children's villages, SOS and other local charities.

When a community crisis arises, Radisson hotels are on the front line and intervene to help when needed. Local teams donate furniture, provide and serve meals and water, and collect and donate clothing and items for those affected by natural disasters. They were there for those affected by typhoons in the Philippines, wildfires in Alberta and floods in Louisiana, among other devastating events that affected communities around the world.

SOS Children Villages is the largest non-profit organization in the world dedicated to building loving and stable families for orphaned, abandoned and vulnerable children. Radisson Hotel Group has set a goal for more than 1,100 hotels: asking each hotel to sponsor a child, which will ensure that the child has what he or she needs and an education to secure a promising future. This sponsorship has the added benefit of establishing more meaningful local relationships with SOS Villages around the world. Less than two years after the launch of our global partnership, hotels have already sponsored 686 SOS and counting copies.

RadissonBlu Hotel Krakow, as part of the Rezidor Group that considers sustainable development, acts in the field of corporate social responsibility in the field of three programs:

- The Think Planet - draws attention to minimizing the ecological footprint;
- The ThinkPeople - is geared towards health and safety of guests and the employees;
- The ThinkTogether - is related to the acceptance and observance of ethical and social norms in the company and in the local community.

In 2011, Forbes magazine awarded RadissonBlu Hotel Kraków the title of "Leader in Sustainable Development" for obtaining the BS 8901 certificate.

CSR Campaigns of InterContinetal Hotels Group

One of the most famous hotels in Romania is Hotel InterContinental and is located in Bucharest. It is known as an architectural symbol of the Capital, highlighting both the quality of services and the uniqueness for that view offered to guests in hotel rooms. With its imposing construction, the hotel has 257 rooms and suites, 13 function rooms, two restaurants, two bars and a summer terrace, as well as a Health Club 22 and Club InterContinental, from where guests can admire the panorama of the city, right from its center.

InterContinental Bucharest has been supporting the WWF EarthHour event since 2009, but this year it has joined other people, companies and institutions from over 7000 cities, from 180 countries, participating in EarthHour (Earth Hour). On March 30, 2019, between 20:30 and 21:30, the exterior lighting of the hotel was turned off, as well as in the public areas of the hotel, and guests were invited to follow this example, being invited to a cocktail light candles on the 21st floor of the hotel or at specially organized dinners in restaurants (InterContinental Hotels Group Corporate Responsibility IHG, 2021).

Dana Chiriac, who is the Marketing & PR Manager of the hotel, stated that they decided to create the hotel logo, this being the letter "I", made of lighted candles on the terrace on the 2nd floor, representing a symbol that could be admired from the upper floors. He continues to support the Earth Hour event for 10 years, during which time he fulfilled more and more thoroughly the promises to recycle, to control the consumption of utilities and to separate the waste, but also to urge both guests., as well as colleagues to change their consumption habits with sustainable ones.

It is Green Globe certified for environmental protection, recycling and community support. The hotel participates in the IHG Green Engage program, which monitors the energy and water consumed on a monthly basis, as well as the amount of waste produced, while offering recommendations and solutions to conserve energy and minimize carbon footprint.

The most recent actions in support of environmental protection are the replacement of plastic straw in restaurants and bars with biodegradable cardboard straw, informing colleagues about the moderate use of electricity and introducing Britta filtered water at breakfast and colleagues' restaurants, to replace water consumption in glass or plastic drums.

SOCIAL RESPONSIBILITY CAMPAIGNS CARRIED OUT BY TRAVEL AGENCIES

Paralela 45 is a travel agency in Romania, which was founded in 1990 by Alin Burcea and Adrian Grigorescu. For 30 years, this agency has built a prestigious name, which offers its tourists: trips in the country and abroad, group or individual, reservations for transport tickets (plane, bus, train), hotel reservations, obtaining tourist visas, specialized guides, car rental (Paralela 45Actiuni CSR, 2021).

Over the years, Paralela 45 has been part of, but also supported, numerous Corporate Social Responsibility (CSR) projects. The most recent took place near Christmas, giving innocent souls the emotion and joy of this holiday. They became Santa Claus to the over 70 children from Vaslui. Through the association Alexandra Timar - Angels for souls, Paralela 45 offered clothes, toys, school supplies, shoes, hygiene products, sweets.

Travel agencies have become increasingly involved in the implementation of CSR measures, due to increasing consumer awareness and sensitivity to ecological and social behavior.

Tour operators, who usually combine different travel components, such as transport, insurance, onsite visits, etc. in order to create a travel package, they face extraordinary challenges when implementing CSR in their business, as they not only have to evaluate CSR measures within their own enterprise, but also along the value chain.

The big tour operators have initiated simple donations, campaigns to help in case of natural disasters, association with non-profit organizations that protect the environment, volunteer campaigns to collect garbage from many holiday destinations, energy saving at offices, paper recycling, technology.

Recognizing deserving employees and rewarding them with vacation incentives for them and their families are the best CSR actions undertaken by travel agencies.

Travel agencies value the environment because a tourist destination does not withstand a large flow of tourists over time unless it is protected.

Travel agencies have focused on energy use green / renewable water use, waste management, recycling, reduction of toxic emissions, ecological policy office and business travelers .

Travel agencies are concerned with CSR in the field of local community and interaction with it.

The main projects of the travel agencies in the field of relations with local communities were charitable actions in the tourist destination, sponsorship of local events, organization of holiday destination cleaning campaigns, volunteering in schools and community projects help for old people's homes and endowment of hospitals.

The Sustainable Development Tour Operator Initiative (TOI) is a network of over 20 international tour operators of all sizes and specialties who are committed to incorporating the principles of sustainability into their business operations. The initiative was developed with the support of the United Nations Environment Program (UNEP). Together with TOI, these groups created the report, Integrating Sustainability into Business - A Management Guide for Responsible Tourism Operations. The report recognizes that tour operators have the ability to influence a wide range of stakeholders and provides an overview of the economic, environmental and social impact of tourism. It outlines key indicators for each perspective, but is not prescriptive about how they should be integrated into a sustainability strategy. The key areas addressed are internal operations, product development of sustainable destinations and holiday packages, sustainability standards for supply chain supply, customer relationship communication and education. Another study of the Romanian market found that mass tour operators do not yet adhere to the principles of CSR in any structured and systematic form, however, a social approach may be the determining factor for additional CSR initiatives. So far, CSR awareness is evident among Romanian tour operators, but there is low participation and there are no measures or disclosures of initiatives aimed at protecting the areas in which these tour companies operate. Furthermore, most major tour operators in Europe, especially the United Kingdom, seem to have embraced CSR and sustainable development policies more broadly.

Key Issues Affecting Tour Operators

Package holiday marketing puts constant pressure on the bottom line of tour operators and the main concern of the business is to be profitable. Along with this challenge, tour operators face a number of challenges, including climate change, in particular with regard to managing new legislative requirements, high costs, environmental instability and changes in consumer behavior. Additional challenges are the effects of the economic downturn and the resulting financial crisis, rising fuel costs, fears about security at home and in destinations, political instability in the areas where it operates and global pandemics. As consumers now have the ability to assemble their own holiday packages through web-based technology, operators who have had low direct distribution have also cited disaggregation as a threat to the traditional model of tour operators.

In 2011, with the drafting of the National Strategy for the Promotion of CSR, the public authorities recognized the importance of raising awareness and supporting the development of the CSR field in Romania, identifying gaps and setting objectives in line with the EU strategy. However, since joining the EU and with funding, public institutions and authorities have initiated and developed a number of awareness-raising initiatives, as well as research studies, seminars, conferences and websites on one or more several topics specific to the field of CSR. Examples include initiatives to prevent or reduce pollution, promote equal opportunities for women and men and non-discrimination in the workplace, promote road safety, social inclusion of people with disabilities, reduce bribery and corruption. in public institutions and authorities.

Initiatives of interest in the field of CSR are still few in number, with public institutions and authorities often being a secondary partner in projects and campaigns, not the main initiator.

There are several initiatives in Romania, CSR and sustainable development networks, forums, blogs and websites, many of which have developed in recent years, including:

CSR Romania (www.csr-romania.ro) has developed a specific CSR / SR specific website that delivers daily news and information to the public, promoting the concept of "ethical management" and in particular that of CSR / SR, in order to increase the competitiveness of companies and enterprises. The latter is achieved by communicating the concept of CSR / SR, as well as what responsible business practices mean (CSR ROMANIA, 2021).

Ştiri ONG is the most important database and information platform on civil society. It was developed by the Foundation for Civil Society Development within the project "Catalog of Civil Society 2008" in order to facilitate social partnerships between civil society, the private sector, public institutions and citizens, providing information, news about various projects and events, opportunities public or private funding, and organizing capacity building courses and training (Stiri.ong, 2021). The portal hosts the largest and most up-to-date database of Romanian NGOs (associations, foundations, unions and other similar structures) and issues one of the most well-known newsletters in the field.

The general concerns of regular tour operators are to maintain profitability in a fragile global economy and in a highly competitive and disaggregated travel market. This includes reducing costs, increasing market share, creating differentiation in tourism products and services, and reducing exposure to business risk. In the future, where CSR and the general problems of climate change are becoming more widespread, these tour operators may want to consider a number of issues that will also affect their medium and long-term operations. First, it should examine ways in which climate change mitigation can reduce energy costs and increase the efficiency of their home and destination assets, as well as their air, land and sea operations. Second, regular tour operators can seek to leverage sustainability initiatives in resorts to develop niche travel products that help local communities preserve their cultural and environmental heritage, thus potentially increasing market share and profit margins through a differentiation strategy. Third, mass tour operators can seek to hire all their employees in CSR to increase loyalty. Finally, they should be an active participant in greening their supply chain to reduce energy and water consumption and waste issues, thus ensuring the future viability of the product they benefit from.

SOCIAL RESPONSIBILITY CAMPAIGNS CARRIED OUT BY AIRLINE COMPANIES

Aviation-related charities are people dedicated to providing care, kindness and frequent transportation. Some services are related to health, caused by emergencies, and others are related to encouraging emotional well-being.

Examples of organizations that provide assistance in various global issues are the following.

Air Charity Network

Air Charity Network is a charity that provides access to people in need seeking free air transportation to specialized health care facilities or remote destinations due to family, community or national crisis. Air Charity Network serves all 50 states, and its volunteer pilots use their own aircraft, fuel and time to provide free air travel to medical facilities for citizens in financial difficulty or unable to travel on public transport. Air Charity Network members also coordinate flights to fly organ transplant candidates, people involved in clinical trials, chemotherapy or other repetitive treatments, victims of relocation abuse, families receiving help from Ronald McDonald Houses, Shriners Hospitals, and many other charities, children with disabilities or the sick at special summer camp programs and for many other humanitarian reasons. Combined, the airline charity is the largest unified volunteer organization in the nation, consisting of thousands of pilots flying tens of thousands of passengers to the United States each year.

Angel Flight

Angel Flight Soars arranges free air travel for people who have to travel to receive rescue medical treatment but do not have the means. "We believe that the disease is not stopped by borders and there should be no remedies - whether the boundaries are geographical or monetary. We help families focus on improvement, instead of worrying about how to get there. That's why we coordinate 9 missions a day, 7 days a week, 365 days a year (Air Charity Network, 2021).

Parkwater Foundation

The Parkwater Foundation is a high-impact, non-profit organization that changes lives by combining educational and aviation opportunities (Parkwater Foundation, 2021).

The Covid-19 pandemic brought us closer and opened us up to offering help to those left without a job, home or even food. To help those who do not have the opportunity to cover their minimum expenses, charitable funds have been created. All over the world, various organizations have been looking for ways to raise as much money as possible to make the pandemic's burdens a little easier for others. One of their ideas was to create a website called SmarterTravel where companies such as tourism (hotels, agencies) and transportation (airlines) can donate some of the profits.

Two airlines offer ways to do good by doing good. American offers its Advantage program members 250 bonus miles for donations of at least $ 50 to the American Red Cross and 500 bonus miles for donations of $ 100 or more.

Spirit Airlines offers a 5,000-mile bonus to the first 200,000 Free Spirit members who donate at least $ 5 to the American Red Cross, UNICEF or Yele Haiti.

In addition to such special bonuses, most major airline and hotel programs allow their members to donate money, miles or points to selected charities, some of which will be on the front lines in Haiti in the coming days and weeks.

Starwood, for example, allows Preferred Guest members to redeem 4,000 points for a $ 50 donation to the American Red Cross, 8,000 points for a $ 100 donation (Starwood Hotels and Resorts CSR & sustainability, 2021).

Miles Dividend members of US Airways also donate miles to the airline's Miles of Hope program, which distributes miles to various charities to offset travel expenses.

Airlines are involved in CSR activities that aim is employees, communities, environment.

Airlines are committed to complying with certain corporate social responsibilities, the first being environmental conservation. This involves the conservation of the natural environment, as well as measures to minimize air pollution, water pollution, land pollution and noise pollution. Environmental conservation is essential for airlines. Environmental conservation has become a concern for airlines operating airlines because they emit a large volume of greenhouse gases.

The huge amount of non-renewable energy consumed by airlines is a source of air pollution and carbon emissions. Globally, there is a growing need for conservation of the environment and natural resources. This leads to the creation of policies governing issues related to environmental conservation and climate control. Airlines such as British Airways, Virgin Airlines and KLM have come up with corporate social responsibility programs aimed at conserving the environment.

For example, *British Airways* has a carbon offsetting program through which the company provides resources to organizations that advocate for environmental conservation through activities such as planting trees, rehabilitating forests and developing greenhouse projects. Environmentally oriented corporate social responsibilities aim to achieve three major objectives that influence the company's profit. The first being the desire to make the company look positive in the eyes of customers (British Airways Corporate Responsibility Report, 2010/2011).

This means that customers and the public look at the company in a positive light, because it is concerned about the sustainability of well-being. Such a positive attitude gives the company a good reputation.

Second, environmentally oriented corporate social activities offer the company the opportunity to save resources through greenhouse projects.

Third, corporate social responsibilities related to the environment lead to the creation and development of resources and activities that minimize waste through projects such as green projects, recycling of waste materials and minimal use of energy in offices during working hours.

Many airlines are committed to supporting the tourism sector, as a way to attract more customers, and to be in a better position to influence the movement of tourists.

Wizz Air is an airline and was conceived in June 2003, when six people with extensive experience and extraordinary results in aviation teamed up with József Váradi, the company's CEO. In just three months, it was already registered and ready to fly. A decade of solid development followed, in which it became the largest low-cost airline in Central and Eastern Europe (Wizz Air Holdings CSR & sustainability, 2020).

The company says it is striving to make it the greenest choice of airlines and striving to continuously reduce its environmental impact by saving fuel, but also having the lowest carbon emissions rate in the airline industry in Europe. According to the annual report, since 2012, they have implemented several projects, including: improving flight speed, understanding and optimizing the network which means almost 100,000 tons of CO 2 emissions per year (3% per aircraft). A major initiative is the use of sharklets, being a type of device that improves the efficiency of a

aircraft and reduces interference resistance. On average, sharklets can reduce fuel consumption by up to 4% compared to other older options for aircraft wings, which can correspond to an annual saving of 900 tonnes of CO 2 / aircraft.

At the end of fiscal 2020, 71% of the Wizz Air fleet was equipped with sharklet devices. As we replace the older aircraft and as all new Airbus A321ceo and A320neo Family aircraft will be delivered 100% of their fleet, which will be equipped with sharklet by 2024.

SOLUTIONS AND RECOMMENDATIONS

Corporate social responsibility in the hospitality and tourism industry discusses the problems and challenges faced by organizations implementing responsible business practices in the travel, hotel, leisure and hospitality industries.

The essence of CSR includes environmental concerns, respect for local communities, the use of technology and energy consumption.

Investing more and more money from tourism companies' budgets for humanitarian projects would be a very important thing for CSR campaigns. As well, investing in employees and in providers relationships with have a beneficial impact over CSR strategies. Informing tourists about all the CSR campaigns it will be a crucial and significant issue for all the tourism companies.

FUTURE RESEARCH DIRECTIONS

Now more than ever, all operators in the tourism industry: hoteliers, travel agencies and airlines have demonstrated involvement in CSR campaigns which has demonstrated a genuine commitment to the greater good.

The budgetary impact should be studied in terms of companies' CSR campaigns, because there is a lack of these studies in specialty literature.

CONCLUSION

At the heart of the chapter's concerns was to see clearly the scale of CSR activities in the tourism industry in three key areas, namely: CSR in hotels, CSR in travel agencies and CSR in airlines. Most CSR campaigns at all levels (employees, environment, local community) are carried out by the hotel industry. Most environmental protection CSR programs are run by airlines. Most CSR programs in relation to local communities are run by hotels. Companies with great economic and financial power also allocate money for social responsibility campaigns. That is why we have multiple CSR projects carried out by Marriott International, Hyatt Hotels Group, Hilton, British Airways, etc.

REFERENCES

Accor CSR & Performance. (2021). https://group.accor.com/en/commitment/sharing-our-knowledge/csr-and-performance

Ahn, J. (2020). Role of hope and compulsion for CSR activities in hotel customers' engagement. *Current Issues in Tourism*, 1–7. doi:10.1080/13683500.2020.1839026

Ahn, J., & Kwon, J. (2020). CSR perception and revisit intention: The roles of trust and commitment. *Journal of Hospitality and Tourism Insights*, *3*(5), 607–623. doi:10.1108/JHTI-02-2020-0022

Air Charity Network. (2021). https://aircharitynetwork.org/about-us/

Angels of Flight Community Involvement. (2021). https://www.angelsofflightcanada.com/community-involvement/

British Airways Corporate Responsibility Report 2010/2011. (n.d.). https://www.britishairways.com/cms/global/pdfs/environment/ba_corporate_responsibility_report_2010-2011.pdf

Buckley, R., & de Vasconcellos Pegas, F. (n.d.). *Tourism and CSR*. The Routledge Handbook of Tourism and the Environment., doi:10.4324/9780203121108.ch46

CSR Romania. (2021). *Forum for International Communications*. http://www.csr-romania.ro/

EU. (2021). *Corporate social responsibility & Responsible business conduct*. https://ec.europa.eu/growth/industry/sustainability/corporate-social-responsibility_en

European Commission. (2017). *Information from European Union Institutions, bodies, offices and agencies. EU directive 2017/C215/01 for reporting its performance in relation to non-financial information.* https://ec.europa.eu/anti-trafficking/sites/antitrafficking/files/guidelines_on_non-financial_reporting.pdf

Farmaki, A., & Farmakis, P. (2018). A stakeholder approach to CSR in hotels. *Annals of Tourism Research*, *68*, 58–60. doi:10.1016/j.annals.2017.11.009

Higgins-Desbiolles, F. (2018). Sustainable tourism: Sustaining tourism or something more? *Tourism Management Perspectives*, *25*, 157–160. doi:10.1016/j.tmp.2017.11.017

Hilton, C. R. R. (2017). *Hilton Hotels CSR Programs and Initiatives – Research*. https://cr.hilton.com/wp-content/uploads/2018/05/Hilton-Corporate-Responsibility-2017-1.pdf

Hotel Polski Pod Białym Orłem, C. S. R. (2021). *Corporate social responsibility in hotel industry – CORE*. https://core.ac.uk/download/pdf/230306873.pdf

Hyatt Corporate Responsibility. (2021). https://about.hyatt.com/en/hyatt-thrive.html, https://about.hyatt.com/content/dam/HyattStories/thrive/HyattEnvironmentalSustainabilityHighlights20192020.pdf

InterContinental Hotels Group Corporate Responsibility IHG. (2021). https://www.ihg.com/content/us/en/about/corporate-responsibility

Köseoglu, M. A., Hon, A., Kalargyrou, V., & Okumus, F. (2021). Hiring People with Disabilities As a Csr Strategy in the Tourism Industry. *Tourism Analysis*, *26*(1), 41–55. doi:10.3727/108354220X15758302602547

Manente, M., Minghetti, V., & Mingotto, E. (2014). Responsible Tourism. *Responsible Tourism and CSR*, 3–13. doi:10.1007/978-3-319-06308-9_2

Marriott Serve 360 Report. (2020). *Serve 360 Corporate Social Responsibility– Marriott*. https://serve360.marriott.com/wp-content/uploads/2020/12/2020-Serve360-Report.pdf

Nazir, O., & Islam, J. U. (2019). Influence of CSR-specific activities on work engagement and employees' innovative work behaviour: An empirical investigation. *Current Issues in Tourism*, *23*(24), 3054–3072. doi:10.1080/13683500.2019.1678573

Orbis Hotel Group. (2017). *Corporate Social Responsibility ReportCSR Report 2017 4/10/18 / 7910kB - Orbis SA*. https://www.orbis.pl/en/download/filedisplay/csr-report-2017

Paralela 45Actiuni CSR. (2021). https://www.paralela45.ro/actiuni-csr/

Parkwater Foundation. (2021). *Corporate Social Responsibility Annual Report 2016-2017*. https://dq7j3ns0e24fe.cloudfront.net/uploads/45ea9ad985a49a523fc556322291befe6-026739600-1500371378.pdf

Radisson Hotel Corporate Social Responsibility. (2021). https://www.radissonhotels.com/en-us/social-responsibility/community

Starwood Hotels and Resorts CSR & Sustainability. (2021). https://www.csrhub.com/CSR_and_sustainability_information/Starwood-Hotels-and-Resorts-Worldwide-Inc

Stiri.ong. (2021). *The Foundation for Civil Society Development*. https://www.stiri.ong/

Sustainable Business Annual ReportN. H. (2021). https://www.nh-hotels.com/corporate/sites/default/files/files-rsc/einf_nhhg_2020_en.pdf

The role of CSR in business strategy. (2018). *Strategic Direction, 34*(10), 13–15. doi:10.1108/SD-07-2018-0156

UNWTO World Tourism Organization. (2020). *World Tourism Barometer and Statistical Annex, August/September 2020, UNWTO World Tourism Barometer*. https://www.e-unwto.org/doi/abs/10.18111/wtobarometereng.2020.18.1.5

Wizz Air Holdings CSR & Sustainability. (2020). https://wizzair.com/en-gb/information-and-services/about-us/sustainability

KEY TERMS AND DEFINITIONS

Airline Companies: Commercial enterprises that provides scheduled flights or charters for passengers.

CSR: Represents a management concept whereby companies integrate social and environmental concerns in their business operations and interactions with their stakeholders.

Global Code of Ethics for Tourism: A fundamental frame of reference for responsible and sustainable tourism and encompass a comprehensive set of principles designed to guide key-players in tourism development.

Hotel Strategies: An overview of the hotel services offered to their customers.

Hotels: A place to sleep and eat and other services for tourists offered for a sum of money.

Tourism Industry: A complex concept, which includes several fields of activity: travel agencies, airlines, hotels and restaurants, entertainment activities, professional associations and tourism state bodies.

Travel Agencies: Creator and seller of holiday packages.

Chapter 7
Flexible Budget:
Management Method for Cost Control and Monitoring the Performance of Economic Entities

Mariana Zamfir
Valahia University of Targoviste, Romania

Constantin Aurelian Ionescu
https://orcid.org/0000-0001-6063-2921
Hyperion University of Bucharest, Romania

Nicoleta Luminita Gudanescu Nicolau
Romanian Academy, Romania

Sorina Geanina Stanescu
Valahia University of Targoviste, Romania

Liliana Paschia
Hyperion University of Bucharest, Romania

Mihaela Denisa Coman
Valahia University of Targoviste, Romania

Alexandra Delia Bugnariu
1 Decembrie 1918 University, Romania

ABSTRACT

The ever-changing business environment and the shorter product life cycle impose the need to develop new forecasting models and replace static budgets with flexible budgets. Thus, the analysis of deviations from budgeted costs becomes a desideratum of any entity. Flexible budgeting is based on the analysis of expenditure behavior and involves setting budgeted expenditure levels for different activity levels to monitor activity. The chapter highlights the importance of flexible budgeting of expenditures. It presents a comparison between static budgets and flexible budgets, the methodology for preparing flexible budgets, exemplifying how to prepare them for more predictable levels of activity, and budgetary control based on flexible budgets. The research is addressed to the academic environment and the practitioners concerned with the enterprise's management through the budget system, having as motivation the desire to satisfy the need for information both in higher economic education and in economic practice.

DOI: 10.4018/978-1-7998-8069-1.ch007

INTRODUCTION

Any activity of an economic entity requires the knowledge of the objectives to be achieved, fulfilled, but also the knowledge of the resources needed for those objectives to be achieved. In order to cope with the intensification of competition, the changes of the business environment, the economic entities must increase their degree of monitoring and control of the business. Forecasting tools are inevitably the starting point of the control process. Forecast information is grouped in forecasts on increasingly narrow horizons. A complete planning process comprises three levels (Alazard & Sépari, 1998): a strategic plan (long-term forecast), an operational plan (forecast for a horizon of 2-3 years, represents the articulation between long-term and short-term) and an ensemble of budgets. Thus, one of the tools used to monitor and control performance is the budget, as a management method and as a management tool. Bouquin (1994) mentioned that the budget is necessary "to lead, to manage the complex information system of an enterprise, to meet the imperative need to anticipate ".

The budget is the short-term result of the planning process initiated at the strategic level (Costello, 2011). The current decisions of the managers must take into account their effect on the achievement of the objectives from the strategic plan. It is obviously tempting for managers to prioritize short-term performance over long-term performance, but short-term forecasting without reference to long-term plans is a big mistake. The construction of budgets without highlighting the expectations regarding the activity in the next financial year, but the objectives established by the strategic plan, as well as the performance judgment taking into account the real activity conditions and future perspectives, make the analysis of verifying the fulfillment of budgeted values give added value to the forecasting process (Shane et al., 2009).

Flexible budgeting is one of the budgeting techniques that can be used in forecasting. Flexible budgeting is a major tool of managerial accounting. The benefits that are obtained through the use of flexible budgets almost always exceed the costs that are incurred for the organization of the budgetary system, the budgetary management being integrated into a wider set of performance appraisals. In addition to forecasting which is an undeniable advantage of the budget, the use of budgeting in business management has many other advantages: communication, coordination, authority, responsibility, mobilization, motivation, support in substantiating decisions.

BACKGROUND

The word budget is a generic term that refers to short-term plans of any kind. Over time, many authors have defined it. Burlaud and Simon (2003) consider that the budget is both a quantitative management tool, for budgetary control, and a way of organizing responsibilities and transmitting orders - or objectives - the latter term being considered much more motivating. Budgets are, by definition, forecast situations (Dupuy & Rolland, 1991). The budgetary process must be seen as a stage in the fulfillment of the long-term plan. The budget shows the ways forward to achieve the goals proposed for next year's financial year (Ionescu, 2015). The budgets establish the activity programs for one year and allocate the necessary resources for the realization of the programs. In order for the next year's budget to be reliable, it is necessary to know the characteristics of the current period and the conditions in which the current activity takes place. Bouquin (1994) considers that the main function of the budget is to capitalize and, particularly, to balance the relationship between means and results. At the level of an enterprise, the financial balance involves ensuring the necessary financial resources to achieve the objectives. This balance must be foreseen and achieved through the budget both on the whole enterprise and on each subdivision of the organizational structure or economic activity of the enterprise.

The budget shows how the profit will be obtained. It allows the identification of its generating factors so that managers can act on the controllable elements that influence the achievement of this priority objective (Aslău, 2001). Selmer (2014) says that in order to be efficient and effective, the budgetary mechanism must be in line with the company's economic management. Gervais (1994) mentions that a budget system fully fulfills its mission if it manages to cover all the company's activities and integrate well into the global information system (thus facilitating the comparison of achievements with forecasts) and if it is well adapted to the nature of the company's activities and structure.

It is necessary to distinguish between budget and budgetary control. The budget is a forecast, budgetary control involves comparing forecasts with achievements. Together, the budget and budgetary control form the budgetary system, which occupies an important place in the information system of an economic entity. Badea & Dobrin (2006) believe that budgetary control must be present before, during and after the launch of an action or a decision. Budgetary control is, first and foremost, a practice that has evolved with economic, technological and cultural changes (Dunk, 2011). If its foundations remain relatively stable over time, the techniques used must adapt to new information technologies (J. Forget, 2005). Deviation analysis should focus on understanding the causes of deviations and how this understanding can be used to learn from experience and improve performance (Horngren, Datar & Foster, 2006). Deviations are not analyzed separately from each other, they are often interdependent. Deviations that are identified in one segment of the value chain may be the result of decisions made in another segment of the value chain. Hofstede (2012) argues that the process of budgetary control is one of the forms of managerial control, and this is a necessity for business. Mintzberg quoted by Albu & Albu (2003), specifies that in order to function, the budgetary system must meet the following conditions: to translate the company's strategy; to respect the organizational structure; to forecast objectives, means and resources; to carry out an a priori control; to ensure the pursuit of achievements; to ensure a posteriori control.

The budget must uickly adaptable to the environment. For Xiaobei & Shengli (2011), flexibility is the ability to adapt to environmental changes. A certain flexibility is necessary, one of the methods of applying this idea being the flexible budget method. Flexible budgeting is used to analyze cost behavior for different levels of activity. Richard Pearson, Romfh, Habib, & Frieling (1985) have shown that this tool provides much more information than classical budgeting procedures. Boyabatli, Leng & Toktay (2016) studied budgetary flexibility versus technology choices and investment decisions in the presence of budgetary constraints. The authors mention that there can be many situations in which companies cannot achieve everything they want, due to the existence of limited resources and restrictive factors. Chod and Zhou (2014) examined the relationship between a company's resource flexibility and its financial leverage.

Building flexible budgets takes longer than building static budgets. Branke & Elomari (2012) identify optimization techniques for adjusting the parameters of the flexible budgeting algorithm, thus saving time that can be dedicated to other activities in the enterprise. Selmer (2014) shows that in building budgets one can opt for either the bottom-up approach or the top-down approach. In the bottom-up approach, the needs of each analysis center are translated into partial budgets and then integrated at the enterprise level into the general budget. In the top-down approach, which is also the fastest approach, the company's objectives are transferred to the analysis centers and transformed into specific objectives for them, on the basis of which the budgets will be built.

FROM STATIC BUDGETS TO FLEXIBLE BUDGETS

Budgetary control is often criticized for deviations from budgeted values sometimes due to changes in real operating conditions compared to those taken into account when preparing budgets, due to poor forecasts or poor managerial performance. The most effective budget for evaluation should be designed and made to take into account the impact of uncontrollable or unpredictable events (Barrett & Fraser, 1977, quoted by Sponem, 2004). Barrett and Fraser hypothesize that an effective budget is a fair budget, that is, it takes into account the factors on which the person responsible cannot act. They start from the premise that organizational justice favors performance. Using such a budget could, however, reduce managers' motivation if they know a priori that they will be held accountable for uncontrollable things (Sponem, 2004). The more the budgeted value is loaded with uncertainty, the less economically significant the deviation found. When standards are set in a certain economic environment, the analysis of deviations is not a problem. But when the environment is uncertain, the standards are elaborated without knowing perfectly their possibilities of realization. A deviation is important to be assessed by distinguishing between what comes from the malfunctioning of the responsibility center and what comes from the uncertainty of forecasts (poor knowledge or estimation of the future or insufficient formulation of the forecast model). The level of analysis performed when building the budget has an important role in the significance of the deviations. A budgeted value can be the influence of a single variable, or, as it is most often the case, it can be the influence of several factors (Zamfir, 2017). Some of these factors are related to the operation of the responsibility center, other factors may vary independently of the decisions of the responsibility center. Poor conception of the forecasting model can lead to deviations caused by factors over which managers have no power and which should not be attributed to them.

Manufacturing technology and the type of activity leave their mark on the correctness of the forecast and therefore on the way in which the budgetary control is performed (Berland, 2009). In enterprises with homogeneous and mass production, or in enterprises where customer demand and behavior are relatively stable, the projected level of activity is easier to determine and the budget will be easier to establish, unlike enterprises with production to order where customer requests may vary from time to time and where meeting consumer needs forces the company to frequently change certain activities to customize their customers' products. Budgetary control is also more difficult to carry out in the enterprises of the second category. Besides the changes in the internal environment, there are added the changes in the external environment that lead to the multiplication of the hypotheses that must be taken into account in the construction of budgets. Thus, there is a need to create several possible scenarios in the preparation of budgets, which aim to prepare the company to cope with changes in the internal and external environment. With the increasing dynamism of modern society, the techniques of drawing up budgets and carrying out budgetary control have diversified. According to the criterion of adaptability to changes in the company's activity, we distinguish two categories of budgets: static budgets and flexible budgets. Static budgets, also called fixed budgets, are characterized by the fact that they are drawn up for a single degree of use of production capacity. They have a single level of expenditure. Flexible budgets, also called variable budgets, are characterized by the fact that they are drawn up for several degrees of use of production capacity, taking into account possible fluctuations in production during the period for which they are drawn up. They present several levels of expenditure, corresponding to the possible levels of activity for which they were developed.

Static budgets are drawn up for the degree of utilization of the production capacity that is most expected in the budget year, and which is usually less than 100%. Being a relatively simple method, static budgeting saves time and the resulting budgets are often less accurate. Static budgeting is recommended for economic entities characterized by stability, in which there are no fundamental changes from one year to another. Regular, static budgeting starts from the premise that the environment can be easily forecasted and from the fact that the people who carry out the budgeting have at their disposal information that allows an accurate forecasting (Horvath & Partners, 2009). As the business environment is constantly changing and the life cycle of products tends to become shorter and shorter based on increasing competition, the accurate forecasting of the activities of economic entities tends to become increasingly difficult to perform. Rapid changes in the environment have led to the need to develop new forecasting models. Replacing static budgets with flexible budgets and analyzing deviations from budgeted costs must become a desideratum of any economic entity.

FLEXIBLE BUDGET PREPARATION METHODOLOGY

Budgeting techniques differ across enterprises. In small enterprises, where the structure of the company is centralized, there are no built budgeting models. Here, starting from the directives formulated by the management of the enterprise, the accounting managers prepare the necessary figures and elaborate different budget variants. Based on the advice of employees and various discussions related to these options, the management committee or manager of the company will choose one of them. In large enterprises, in which the structure of the company is decentralized, and which have a significant experience in building budgets and a developed organizational culture, they use complex budgeting methods that are adapted to the specifics of the company's activity.

In the face of changes both internally and externally, the forecasts and action plans of the budgetary process risk becoming more difficult to build, aging faster and becoming less useful for the enterprise. Due to future uncertainties, it is ideal to make budgeting flexible. Budget adjustments are required not only to change the use of production capacity. Budgets can also be changed in the event of price changes upstream (purchases from suppliers) or downstream (sales to customers). When prices fluctuate from period to period, flexible budgeting becomes a pressing economic necessity. The flexible budget thus becomes an important tool of the management, both in terms of control and analysis of the way of carrying out the activity, and in terms of knowing the causes of deviations (Epuran, Băbăiţă, 1999).

Building budgets requires dialogue within the hierarchy. The budgeting process can start 3-4 months before the start of the year for which the budget is drawn up. A first stage is the setting of *objectives for the next year*, in accordance with the content of the strategic plan, but taking into account the evolution of the business environment. The annual budget is to be divided into quarterly and monthly budgets. As flexible expenditure budgets present expenditures in relation to the different levels of activity in a range considered relevant for the following year, a first step for their preparation is to identify the range within which the volume of activity is considered to vary in the period under review, and which aims to prepare the company to deal with different situations. The sales process is what determines the production. The role of managers and management controllers is, starting from the level of budgeted sales, to substantiate the way in which the company's production will cover this level, so that the long-term profit is maximum. Flexible budgeting is based on the analysis of expenditure behavior, and involves establishing budgeted expenditure levels for different levels of activity in order to monitor activity. This tool provides much more information than the traditional budgeting procedure. The people in charge of building the budget identify the information necessary for the elaboration of the budgets, identify the missing information and the possibilities of their collection with the help of the existing structures, and if these are not enough, through newly created mechanisms (Cucui, Horga & Radu, 2003). The main data sources used for budgeting are forecasts of possible levels of various activities and accounting records containing indicators specific to past and present operations.

Based on this information, the management control service will create a series of scenarios and draft budgets, for the different foreseeable levels of activity, which estimate the possible results for the budget year, resources and costs for achieving the objectives. The decision-maker is faced with a large number of choices to be made in building his budget. From the draft budget submitted to it, the Directorate-General shall select the project which it considers best, ie the one which allows the annual objectives to be achieved under certain conditions and which best ensures the congruence with the strategy.

The pre-budget draft for the whole enterprise is to be divided into detailed budgets on the responsibility centers. The managers from the higher hierarchical levels set the objectives for the managers of the departments from the lower hierarchical levels, within the interval within which it is considered that the volume of activity will vary. Each responsible person determines the consequences of the budget on the department he leads and establishes an action plan that will allow him to achieve the objectives set for each level of activity provided. Discussions and negotiations take place to clarify the divergences that may occur between the different types of budgets or between the heads of the analysis centers and the general management. The detailed budgets (operational and financial) that were elaborated in the previous stage, are consolidated in a general budget. Then follows the approval by the budget committee of this generalization document. From the moment the budget is approved, its follow-up becomes a component part of the manager's activity.

The flexible budget takes into account the change of expenses when changing the volume of activity. Thus, it becomes necessary to determine the behavior of the expenses according to which they are divided into fixed expenses and variable expenses. It is recommended that this classification of fixed and variable expenditures be combined with the classification of direct and indirect expenditures. Direct expenditures can be unambiguously attributed to calculation objects (product, work, service), indirect expenditures are common to several calculation objects, and additional calculations for their distribution in the cost of goods are necessary to be performed.

Variable expenditures tend to follow the behavior of the volume of activity expressed in work units. The following can be used to assess the volume of activity in an analysis center as work units for budgeting indirect costs: the volume of production obtained (when production is homogeneous and can be summed), the number of hours of operation of machinery (machine hours), the number of direct labor hours (human hours). The category of variable expenses may include: expenses with raw materials and direct materials, expenses with direct labor, fuel consumption, water, electricity for motor purposes, various expenses with maintenance and operation of machinery and tools, devices, verifiers, overhauls and current repairs, transport costs, etc. Variable expenses will change when the volume of activity changes (when the number of work units changes). In general, the category of fixed expenses includes: depreciation of fixed assets, taxes borne by the company, various expenses incurred under contracts, etc. Fixed expenses will remain unchanged at all levels of activity. The assumptions regarding the behavior of expenditures (total value of fixed expenditures and unit cost for variable expenditures) are kept within the budgets prepared for several degrees of activity (Radu & Gîju, 2015). The fixed budget is drawn up for a single volume of activity, and it is valid only for this volume. Its utility is thus reduced compared to that of the flexible budget (Brault & Giguère, 2003). Flexible budgeting involves the ability to change forecasts as a result of unexpected events. The greater the flexibility incorporated in the budget, the less the danger involved in unexpected events (Simionescu, Buşe, Bud & Purcaru Stamin, 2006). It adapts to several different volumes of work units following predictable changes (Epuran, Băbăiţă & Grosu, 1999).

Efficient use of budgets leads to cost control and increased revenue. The higher the share of variable expenditures in total expenditures, the more flexible budgeting is required. The total budget expenditure for activity grade "x" is expressed as an equation of the form:

$$BC_x = cv_u \bullet A_x + CF$$

In which:

BC_x - total budgeted expenditures for the degree of activity „x";
cv_u – unit variable cost of work unit;
A_x – the volume of activity expressed in work units, for the degree of activity x;
CF – the total amount of fixed expenses.

The most important purpose of the flexible calculation of budgeted expenditures is, however, cost control. Budgetary control is facilitated by the use of flexible budgets, thus becoming a key tool in performance management. Deviations are useful to managers in making planning and control decisions, as well as in evaluating performance. The execution of budgets is followed by the elaboration of reports, called "Budgetary Control Reports". They contain information about the budgeted level and about the results obtained. Through them, the deviations from the budgeted values are calculated and analyzed (Radu, 2009). Within the static budget, at the end of the management period, the revenues and expenditures from the static budget do not adjust to changes in the actual volume of activity. Deviations from budgeted values involve the comparison of indicators that refer to different volumes of activity, and their analysis is irrelevant. The flexible budget adjusts to changes in activity level. Regardless of the budgeted volume of the activity, for performing the budgetary control activity, the actual revenues and expenditures will be compared with the budgeted revenues and expenditures recalculated on the basis of the real activity, keeping the norms on which the initial budget was founded. Thus, indicators related to the same level of activity are compared. By neutralizing the effect of changing the volume of activity, the causes of deviations can be accurately identified and the efficiency of resource use can be assessed. The recalculated flexible budget for the volume of real activity can be expressed in the form of the following equation (Zamfir, 2017):

$$BC_r = cv_u \bullet A_r + CF$$

in which:

BC_r - expenditure budget recalculated to the volume of real activity;
cv_u – unit variable cost of work unit;
A_r – the volume of real activity expressed in units of work.
CF – the total amount of fixed expenses.

Deviation analysis must be done for each level of decision making, ie for each production section, workshop, production line, etc. In order to carry out budgetary control of expenditure on raw materials, the list of products to be manufactured contains, for each product, the list of raw materials required, the quantities budgeted and actually consumed, as well as the list of raw materials used in the production process comprising for each raw material, budgeted and real supply price. Budgetary control of direct labor expenditure calls for the list of products to be manufactured which contains, for each product, the list of operations required, the budgeted and actual time per operation, skill level or job, as well as the list of skill levels and the hourly salary budgeted and realized per operations. In order to carry out the budgetary control of the indirect production expenses, the following indicators are used: the budgeted and effective values of the variable and fixed indirect expenses; to the volume of activity measured in work units which, depending on the specifics of the activity, can be: labor hours, machine hours, quantity of finished products, etc .; to yield, ie the ratio between activity and production.

Badea & Dobrin (2006) consider that budgetary control must be present before, during and after the launch of an action or a decision. Three types of control can be performed (Simionescu, Buşe, Bud & Purcaru Stamin, 2006): i) preliminary control (it is the control exercised before the action or decision to finalize the budget, focuses on preventing possible qualitative and quantitative deviations of resources used in the organization); ii) concomitant control (takes place during the actions, helping to substantiate new forecasts or new decisions that will correct any dysfunctions that may occur during the actions); iii) feedback control (post-control, takes place after the launch of an action, allows the evaluation of the performances achieved, the way of achieving the objectives, the way in which the company was within the volume of resources it had at its disposal, as well as the identification of the causes leading to possible deviations from what was initially established). Performance and results data are returned to managers who have the ability to make corrections.

CASE STUDY ON FLEXIBLE BUDGETING AND BUDGETARY CONTROL

A patrimonial unit wants to draw up the budget of production expenses for year N. The company produces and sells two products: A and B. The quantities of finished products to be obtained in the budget year are 40,000 pieces product A and 60,000 pieces product B. However, due to an unstable market, the company may not be able to realize and sell the entire desired quantity. For year N, following the estimates made by the management control department, it was concluded that the projected volume of activity will be in the range of 70% - 100% of the maximum level of activity which is 262,000 hours of direct labor. The company decides to develop a flexible budget for 70%, 80%, 90% and 100%.

In order to achieve a unit of finished product, the standard consumption norms and the budgeted supply prices of the raw materials to be used in the production process were identified, as well as the budgeted working time and the budgeted remuneration tariffs for each operation (Table 1).

For the elaboration of the flexible budget of the indirect production expenses, we start from the volume of activity and from the indirect expenses from the previous year, presented in table 2. The unit of work used is the number of direct labor hours.

Production Expenditure Budgeting

Expenditure is budgeted separately, for each category of production costs: raw material costs, direct labor costs and indirect production costs.

Table 1. Information necessary for budgeting direct expenditure

Name of Raw Material	Product A		Product B	
	Consumption norm (kg / pc)	Consumption Norm (kg / pc)	Consumption Norm (kg / pc)	Budgeted supply Price (EUR / kg)
Raw material 1 Raw material 2 Raw material 3	0,5 0,4 -	7 9 -	0,6 0,3 0,2	7 9 5
Labour	**Budgeted time (h / pc)**	**Budgeted tariff (EUR / h)**	**Budgeted time (h / pc)**	**Budgeted tariff (EUR / h)**
Operation 1 Operation 2	1 1,5	16 17	1 1,7	16 17

For the budgeting of the expenses with the raw materials, the quantitative standards (consumption norms) are weighted with the budgeted supply prices. For the entire physical volume of production expected to be achieved, the calculation relationship is as follows:

$$CMD_j = \sum_{i=1}^{n} \left(Qp_j \times Nc_{ij} \times p_i\right)$$

In which:

CMD_j – expenditure on raw materials for the entire quantity of products j expected to be obtained;
Qp_j – the physical volume of production j expected to be achieved,
Nc_{ij} – the norm of consumption of the raw material i for the product j,

Table 2. Level of indirect production costs in year N-1

No.	Name of Expenses	Values N-1
1	Activity volume (direct labor hours)	**260.570**
2	Fixed expenses (EUR)	**184.085**
2.1	Depreciation of fixed assets	160.085
2.2	Rent	24.000
3	Variable expenses (EUR)	**487.846**
3.1	Salaries of management and administration staff	230.571
3.2	Material expenses	42.470
3.3	Repair expenses	38.967
3.4	Electricity costs	95.752
3.5	Transportation costs	36.758
3.6	Other variable expenses	43.328
4	Total indirect production costs (EUR)	**671.931**
5	Indirect costs per hour of activity (EUR / h)	**2,58**

p_i – budgeted supply price of raw material i;
i – the kind of raw material;
j – the type of product.

For year N, it starts from the calculation of the budgeted expenditures for the maximum degree of activity, and then the expenditures will be budgeted for the other foreseeable degrees of activity.

Table 3. Calculation of budgeted expenditures with raw materials for the maximum degree of activity (40,000 pcs. A and 60,000 pcs. B)

No	Raw Materials	Product A		Product B		Total	
		Quantity Consumed (kg)	Expenditure on Raw Materials (EUR)	Quantity Consumed (kg)	Expenditure on Raw Materials (EUR)	Quantity Consumed (kg)	Expenditure on Raw Materials (EUR)
1	Raw material 1	20.000	140.000	36.000	252.000	56.000	392.000
2	Raw material 2	16.000	144.000	18.000	162.000	34.000	306.000
3	Raw material 3	-	-	12.000	60.000	12.000	60.000
4	Total	36.000	284.000	54.000	414.000	90.000	698.000

The calculation of budgeted expenditures for direct labor involves the weighting of execution times with budgeted remuneration rates. For the entire physical volume of production expected to be achieved, the calculation relationship of budgeted expenditures with direct labor is as follows:

$$CMD_j = \sum_{i=1}^{n} \left(Qp_j \times t_{ij} \times s_i \right)$$

In which:

CMD_j – direct labor costs for the entire quantity of products j expected to be obtained;
Qp_j – the physical volume of production j expected to be achieved;
t_{ij} – budgeted execution time of operation i for product j;
s_i – budgeted salary per unit of time for operation i;
i – type of operation;
j – the type of product.

In order to determine the expenses with raw materials and the expenses with direct labor for the other degrees of activity (CMD_x), the expenses related to the maximum degree of activity (CMD_{max}) were weighted with the different degrees of activity (X%) for which the budgeting was decided.

$$CMD_x = CMD_{max} \bullet X\%$$

Table 4. Calculation of budgeted expenditures with direct labor for the maximum degree of activity (40,000 pcs. A and 60,000 pcs. B)

No	Operations	Product A		Product B		Total	
		Time (h)	Salary Expenses (EUR)	Time (h)	Salary Expenses (EUR)	Time (h)	Salary Expenses (EUR)
1	Operation 1	40.000	640.000	60.000	960.000	100.000	1.600.000
2	Operation 2	60.000	1.020.000	102.000	1.734.000	162.000	2.754.000
3	Total	100.000	1.660.000	162.000	2.694.000	262.000	4.354.000

The result of the calculations performed can be found in table 7.

For the **budgeting of indirect production expenses**, the methodology is different on the two types of expenses: fixed expenses and variable expenses.

The fixed expenses budgeted for year N will remain at the same value from the previous year, on all foreseeable activity levels.

Table 5. Budgeted fixed expenses

No	Name of Expenses	(EUR)
1	**Fixed expenses**	**184.085**
2	Depreciation of fixed assets	160.085
3	Rent	24.000

Variable expenditures for year N are determined by correlating the actual variable unit expenditures from the previous year with the volume of budgeted activity. The calculation steps are:

The unit variable expenses from the previous year are determined:

$$cv_u = \frac{CV_{N-1}}{H_{N-1}}$$

in which:

cv_u - variable expenses per hour of activity;
CV_{N-1}- total variable expenditure in the reference period (previous year);
H_{N-1} - the volume of activity in the reference period (in the example presented the volume of activity is expressed in hours direct labor).

The budgeted variable expenditures are determined by applying the relationship:

$$CV_b = cv_u \cdot H_b$$

in which:

CV_b – budgeted variable expenditures;
H_b – volume of activity in the budget (expressed in hours direct labor).

For the example presented, the volume of activity (H_b) on the four degrees of activity proposed for the budget, is:

$$H_b = H_{max} \bullet X\%$$

in which:

H_{max} – maximum volume of activity
X% - degrees of activity.
pentru gradul de activitate 100%, H_b = 262.000 h.
for the degree of activity 90%, H_b = 262.000 h x 90% = 235.800 h.
for the degree of activity 80%, H_b = 262.000 h x 80% = 209.600 h.
for the degree of activity 70%, H_b= 262.000 h x 70% = 183.400 h.

One can also choose the option in which the variable expenses are first budgeted for the maximum degree of activity (CV_{max}), and for the other degrees of activity (X%) the variable expenses will be calculated based on the relation:

$$CV_x = CV_{max} \bullet X\%$$

in which:

CV_x – budgeted variable expenditures for activity level x;

Budget calculations for indirect variable expenditure are performed in Table 6.

After performing the budgeting calculations of the indirect expenses for different degrees of activity, the flexible budget for the company subject to analysis can be prepared (table 7).

In order to draw up the unit cost budget for the two products (Table 9 and Table 10), it is necessary to allocate indirect production costs to their cost. The distribution is done using as a basis for distribution (unit of work) direct labor. The distribution calculations are performed in Table 8.

It is observed, from the performed calculations, that on the total economic entity the budgeted expenditures decrease with the decrease of the activity level. For the proposed case study there is a difference of 1,662,757 EUR between the expenses related to the maximum degree of activity and the expenses related to the minimum predictable degree of activity of 70% (5,726,608 EUR - 4,063,851 EUR). At the product level, however, the unit cost increases as the production volume decreases.

Table 6. Indirect variable expenditures budgeted by predictable degrees of activity

No	Indicators	Salaries of Management and Administration Staff	Material Expenses	Repair Expenses	Electricity Costs	Transpor-tation Costs	Other Variable Expenses	Total Variable Expenses
1	Variable expenses from the previous year (EUR)	230.571	42.470	38.967	95.752	36.758	43.328	487.846
2	Previous year's activity volume (h)	260.570	260.570	260.570	260.570	260.570	260.570	260.570
3	Variable unit expenditure from previous year (EUR / h) (1/2)	0,88487	0,16299	0,14955	0,36747	0,14107	0,16628	1,87223
4	Maximum budgeted activity volume (h)	262.000	262.000	262.000	262.000	262.000	262.000	262.000
5	Budgeted indirect variable expenditure related to maximum degree of activity (EUR) (3 x 4)	231.836	42.703	39.181	96.277	36.960	43.566	490.523
6	Budgeted indirect variable expenditure related to activity level of 90% (EUR)	208.653	38.433	35.263	86.650	33.264	39.209	441.472
7	Budgeted indirect variable expenditure related to the degree of activity of 80% (EUR)	185.469	34.162	31.345	77.022	29.568	34.853	392.419
8	Budgeted indirect variable expenditure related to activity level of 70% (EUR)	162.285	29.892	27.427	67.394	25.872	30.496	343.366

Performing Budget Control

To exemplify how to carry out budgetary control, January was chosen, year N. At the beginning of the month, the company predicted that it would sell, that month, 3,100 pieces of product A and 4,200 pieces of product B. Even if the time horizon was relatively reduced (only one month), the forecasts were not exactly correct, at the end of the month, the production obtained and sold being 3,000 pieces product A and 4,000 pieces product B.

In carrying out the budgetary control, we started from the calculation of the total deviation on each item of expenditure (raw material expenditure, direct labor expenditure and indirect production expenditure), and then the total deviation to be broken down into sub-deviations corresponding to different cost elements, the purpose being the identification and triggering of the corrective actions that are necessary. The cost deviation was calculated based on the relation:

Cost deviation = Real cost - Budgeted cost

Table 7. Flexible expenditure budget for year N

No	Indicators	Budgeted Values by Degrees of Activity			
		100%	90%	80%	70%
1	**Production volume (pcs)** - A - B	**100.000** 40.000 60.000	**90.000** 36.000 54.000	**80.000** 32.000 48.000	**70.000** 28.000 42.000
2	**Activity volume (hours)**	262.000	235.800	209.600	183.400
3	**Direct costs (EUR)**	**5.052.000**	**4.546.800**	**4.041.600**	**3.536.400**
3.1	Expenditure on raw materials	698.000	628.200	558.400	488.600
3.2	Direct labor	4.354.000	3.918.600	3.483.200	3.047.800
4	**Total indirect production costs (EUR)**	**674.608**	**625.557**	**576.504**	**527.451**
4.1	**Fixed expenses (EUR)**	**184.085**	**184.085**	**184.085**	**184.085**
4.1.1	Depreciation of fixed assets	160.085	160.085	160.085	160.085
4.1.2	Rent	24.000	24.000	24.000	24.000
4.2	**Variable expenses (EUR)**	**490.523**	**441.472**	**392.419**	**343.366**
4.2.1	Salaries of management and administration staff	231.836	208.653	185.469	162.285
4.2.2	Material expenses	42.703	38.433	34.162	29.892
4.2.3	Repair expenses	39.181	35.263	31.345	27.427
4.2.4	Electricity costs	96.277	86.650	77.022	67.394
4.2.5	Transportation costs	36.960	33.264	29.568	25.872
4.2.6	Other variable expenses	43.566	39.209	34.853	30.496
5	**Total expenses (EUR)**	**5.726.608**	**5.172.357**	**4.618.104**	**4.063.851**

The concept of budgeted cost often creates confusion. It can be:

χ budgeted cost for the quantity of budgeted production;
χ budgeted cost for the actual production quantity (recalculated cost).

Difference: Real cost of real production - Budgeted cost of budgeted production, is not very significant in the economic analysis because it compares the associated cost of two different production volumes. On the other hand, the difference: Real cost of real production - Budgeted cost of real production, is significant for management control and must be analyzed.

Actual consumption as well as budgeted consumption of raw materials for budgeted production (static budget) and for production actually obtained per month (recalculated budget), as well as their supply prices, can be found in table 11. Expenditure on actual direct labor as well as expenditure on direct labor budgeted for the budgeted production (static budget) and for the production obtained in January (recalculated budget) are found in table 12.

The actual and budgeted values of indirect production costs are summarized in Table 13.

Table 8. Distribution of budgeted indirect production costs IPC

No	Indicators	Degrees of Activity			
		100%	90%	80%	70%
1	Indirect production costs to be allocated (EUR)	674.608	625.557	576.504	527.451
2	Distribution base (direct labor), of which:	4.354.000	3.918.600	3.483.200	3.047.800
	- product A (EUR)	1.660.000	1.494.000	1.328.000	1.162.000
	- product B (EUR)	2.694.000	2.424.600	2.155.200	1.885.800
3	Distribution coefficient (Ks = CIP / Total direct labor)	0,15494	0,15964	0,16551	0,17306
4	IPC allocated to product A (Ks x Direct labor A)				
	- total (EUR)	257.200	238.499	219.797	201.095
	- unitary (EUR / pc.)	6,43	6,62	6,87	7,18
5	IPC allocated to product B (Ks x Direct labor B)				
	- total (EUR)	417.408	387.058	356.707	326.356
	- unitary (EUR / piece)	6,96	7,17	7,43	7,77

Table 9. Unit cost budget for product A

Indicators	UM	Quantitative Standard	Budgeted Price (Tariff) (EUR / UM)	Value (EUR/buc)			
				100%	90%	80%	70%
I. Raw materials							
Raw material 1	kg/buc kg/buc	0,5 0,4	7 9	3,5 3,6	3,5 3,6	3,5 3,6	3,5 3,6
Raw material 2		-	-	7,1	7,1	7,1	7,1
Total raw materials							
II. Direct labor	h/buc h/buc	1 1,5	16 17	16,0 25,5	16,0 25,5	16,0 25,5	16,0 25,5
Operation 1	h/buc	2,5	-	41,5	41,5	41,5	41,5
Operation 2							
Total direct salaries				**48,6**	**48,6**	**48,6**	**48,6**
				6,43	**6,62**	**6,87**	**7,18**
III. Total direct expenditure (I + II)				**55,03**	**55,22**	**55,47**	**55,78**

Table 10. Unit cost budget for product B

Indicators	UM	Quantitative Standard	Budgeted Price (Tariff) (EUR / UM)	Value (EUR/buc)			
				100%	90%	80%	70%
I. Raw materials							
Raw material 1	kg/buc kg/buc kg/buc	0,6 0,3 0,2	7 9 5	4,2 2,7 1,0	4,2 2,7 1,0	4,2 2,7 1,0	4,2 2,7 1,0
Raw material 2		-	-	7,9	7,9	7,9	7,9
Total raw materials							
II. Direct labor	h/buc h/buc	1 1,7	16 17	16,0 28,9	16,0 28,9	16,0 28,9	16,0 28,9
Operation 1	h/buc	2,7	-	44,9	44,9	44,9	44,9
Operation 2							
Total direct salaries				**52,8**	**52,8**	**52,8**	**52,8**
				6,96	**7,17**	**7,43**	**7,77**
III. Total direct expenditure (I + II)				**59,76**	**59,97**	**60,23**	**60,57**

Table 11. Expenditures on raw materials - January N

Indicators	Quantitative Consumption (kg)			Supply Price (EUR/kg)		Raw Material Costs (EUR)		
	Static Budget	Recalculated Budgeted	Realised	Budgeted	Realised	Static Budget	Recalculated Budgeted	Realised
Product A								
Raw material 1 Raw material 2	1.550 1.240	1.500 1.200	1.530 1.210	7 9	7 8	10.850 11.160	10.500 10.800	10.710 9.680
Total product A	2.790	2.700	2.740	-	-	22.010	21.300	20.390
Product B								
Raw material 1 Raw material 2 Raw material 3	2.520 1.260 840	2.400 1.200 800	2.360 1.210 805	7 9 5	7 8 4	17.640 11.340 4.200	16.800 10.800 4.000	16.520 9.680 3.220
Total product B	4.620	4.400	4.375	-	-	33.180	31.600	29.420
Total	7.410	7.100	7.115	-	-	55.190	52.900	49.810

Table 12. Expenses with direct labor - January N

Indicators	Time (h)			Salary (EUR/h)		Direct Labor Costs (EUR)		
	Static Budget	Recalculated Budgeted	Realised	Budgeted	Realised	Static Budget	Recalculated Budgeted	Realised
Product A								
Operation 1 Operation 2	3.100 4.650	3.000 4.500	3.100 4.520	16 17	16 16	49.600 79.050	48.000 76.500	49.600 72.320
Total product A	7.750	7.500	7.620	-	-	128.650	124.500	121.920
Product B								
Operation 1 Operation 2	4.200 7.140	4.000 6.800	4.050 5.750	16 17	16 16	67.200 121.380	64.000 115.600	64.800 92.000
Total product B	11.340	10.800	9.800	-	-	188.580	179.600	156.800
Total	19.090	18.300	17.420	-	-	317.230	304.100	278.720

Table 13. - Indirect production costs - January N

No	Expenses	Static Budget (EUR)	Realised (EUR)
1	**Total indirect production costs**	**51.080**	**50.492**
2	**Fixed expenses**	**15.340**	**15.340**
2.1	Depreciation of fixed assets	13.340	13.340
2.2	Rent	2.000	2.000
3	**Variable expenses**	**35.740**	**35.152**
3.1	Salaries of management and administration staff	16.892	16.215
3.2	Material expenses	3.111	3.500
3.3	Repair expenses	2.855	2.545
3.4	Electricity costs	7.015	6.956
3.5	Transportation costs	2.693	3.150
3.6	Other variable expenses	3.174	2.786

1. Deviations From Budgeted Raw Material Costs

For raw materials, the *total cost deviation* is calculated.

ΔCT = Real cost of raw material related to real production - Budgeted cost of raw material related to real production.

$$\Delta CT = C_r - C_b = Q_r \text{ x } cs_r \text{ x } p_r - Q_r \text{ x } cs_b \text{ x } p_b$$

in which:

C_b – budgeted expenditures on raw materials;
C_r – actual raw material costs;
cs_b– budgeted specific consumption of raw material;
cs_r– actual specific consumption of raw material;
p_b – budgeted unit price of raw material supply;
p_r – real unit price of raw material supply.
Q_r – the amount of product made.

The total deviation breaks down into two sub-deviations:

1. 1. *Deviation from budgeted consumption (quantity deviation)* (A_C)

$$\Delta_C = (cs_r - cs_b) \text{ x } Q_r \text{ x } p_b$$

2. 2. *Price deviation* (A_P)

$$\Delta_P = (p_r - p_b) \text{ x } Q_r \text{ x } cs_r$$

The total cost deviation can also be calculated as the sum of the two sub-deviations (quantity and price).

$$\Delta CT = \Delta_C + \Delta_P$$

On a daily basis or at certain intervals, the people in charge of tracking costs draw up the "Report on deviations from budgeted costs for raw materials" (Table 14).

Table 14. Report on deviations from budgeted raw material costs / 1-31 January N

No	Material Name	Quantities Consumed (Kg)		Supply Price (EUR/kg)		Expenditure on Raw Materials (EUR)		Deviations (EUR)		
		Real	Budgeted	Real	Budgeted	Real	Budgeted	Total	of Quantity	of Price
0	1	2	3	4	5	6 = 2 x4	7 = 3 x 5	8 = 6 - 7	9=(2-3)x5	10=(4-5) x2
1	Raw material 1	3.890	3.900	7	7	27.230	27.300	-70	-70	0
2	Raw material 2	2.420	2.400	8	9	19.360	21.600	-2.240	180	-2.420
3	Raw material 3	805	800	4	5	3.220	4.000	-780	25	-805
4	**Total**	-	-	-	-	49.810	52.900	-3.090	135	-3.225

As the actual consumption of raw materials was higher than the consumption in the budget for two of the raw materials used, an unfavorable quantity deviation of EUR 135 resulted. By contrast, the actual supply price of raw materials, lower than budgeted, led to a favorable price deviation of EUR 3,225. In total, the deviation from budgeted raw material costs is favorable, with actual costs being lower than budgeted by EUR 3,090.

2. Deviations From Budgeted Costs With Direct Labor

For direct labor the total cost deviation ΔC is determined based on the relation:

$$\Delta CT = C_r - C_b = Q_r \text{ x } t_r \text{ x } s_r - Q_r \text{ x } t_b \text{ x } s_b$$

in which:

C_b – budgeted expenditures on raw materials;
C_r – actual raw material costs;
t_b– budgeted time per unit of product;
t_r – actual time worked on the product unit;
s_b – budgeted salary per unit of time;
s_r – the real salary per unit of time.
Q_r – the amount of product made.

The total deviation can be broken down into two sub-deviations:

1. 1. Time deviation (efficiency):

$$\Delta t = (t_r - t_b) \text{ x} Q_r \text{x } s_b$$

2. 2. Remuneration rate deviation (salary):

$$\Delta s = (s_r - s_b) \text{ x } Q_r \text{x } t_r$$

The total deviation can also be calculated as the sum of the two sub-deviations (time and salary):

$$\Delta CT = \Delta t + \Delta s$$

Every day or at certain intervals, the people in charge of tracking the costs draw up the "Report on the deviations from the budgeted costs with direct labor" (table 15).

The total deviation from budgeted direct labor costs is favorable, with actual expenditure being lower than budgeted by EUR 25,380. This is due both to the shorter processing time of the products than in the budget, which led to a favorable time deviation of EUR 15,110, but also to the consequence of a lower remuneration rate in operation 2, compared to the budgeted tariff, which determined a favorable salary deviation of EUR 10,270.

Table 15. Report on deviations from budgeted costs with direct labor / 1-31 January N

No	Operation Name	Total Processing Time (h)		Salary Rate (EUR/h)		Labor Costs (EUR)		Deviations (EUR)		
		Real	Budgeted	Real	Budgeted	Real	Budgeted	Total	of Time	of Salary
0	1	2	3	4	5	6 = 2 x 4	7 = 3 x 5	8 = 6 - 7	9 = (2-3)x5	10=(4-5)x2
1	Operation 1	7.150	7.000	16	16	114.400	112.000	2.400	2.400	0
2	Operation 2	10.270	11.300	16	17	164.320	192.100	-27.780	-17.510	-10.270
3	**Total**	17.420	18.300	-	-	278.720	304.100	-25.380	-15.110	-10.270

3. Deviations From Budgeted Indirect Production Costs

For indirect production costs, the total deviation (ΔCIP) is calculated based on the formula:

$\Delta CIP = CIP_r - CIP_{br}$

in which:

CIP_r - real indirect production costs related to real production
CIP_{br} - budgeted indirect production costs related to real production, respecting the budget yield

In economic theory and practice, there are several models for calculating deviations from indirect expenditures. For the present case study, the decomposition of the total deviation into yield deviation and cost deviation was chosen. The cost deviation is, in turn, broken down into activity deviation and volume deviation.

1. Yield deviation (Δr)

$\Delta r = (H_r - H_{br}) \text{ x } cuh_b$

In which:

H_r – total effective labor hours;
H_{br} – total labor hours budgeted for actual production in compliance with budgeted efficiency;

cuh_b – unit labor cost according to budget data.

2. Cost deviation (from the change in the unit cost of labor time) (Δcuh)

$\Delta cuh = (cuh_r - cuh_b) \text{ x } H_r$

in which:

cuh_r – the actual (actual) unit cost of the labor hour;

2.1. *Activity deviation* (Δa) is calculated using the method of rational imputation which measures the overabsorption or subabsorption of fixed expenses in the unit costs determined by the variation of the activity level.

$\Delta a = CF_n - CF_{fnc}$

in which:

CF_n - normal fixed expenses;
CF_{fnc} - fixed expenses incorporated in the cost.
$CF_{fnc} = CF_r \times k$, where:
CF_r – real fixed expenses;
K - coefficient of rational imputation of fixed expenses.

$$k = \frac{The\,volume\,of\,real\,activity}{Volume\,of\,normal\,activity} = \frac{H_r}{H_n}$$

When the volume of budgeted activity corresponds to the volume of normal activity, as in the case study presented, in the formulas for calculating the deviation of activity it can be replaced H_n with H_b, and CF_n with CF_b.

The activity deviation can be calculated according to the relation:

$$\Delta a = \left(H_b - H_r\right) \times \frac{CF_b}{H_b}.$$

2.2. *Expenditure deviation, also called volume or budget deviation (ΔCh).* The effect of the level of activity being isolated, it is then possible to analyze which are the savings or the excesses of expenses in relation to the budget, that is to say the effective deviation of the cost can be determined.

$\Delta Ch = CIP_r - CIP_{rec}$

CIP_r - actual indirect production costs (actual)
CIP_{rec} - recalculated indirect production costs

For this, the budgeted expenses for the volume of real activity must be recalculated. A distinction is made between fixed expenses that remain unchanged (as in the initial budget) and variable expenses that change when the volume of activity changes. Recalculated variable expenses are determined by the relationship:

$$CV_{rec} = \frac{CV_b}{H_b} \times H_r$$

in which:

CV_b - variable expenditures according to the initial budget (static budget)
H_b - the volume of budgeted activity
H_r - the volume of real activity.

For the proposed case study, the calculation of the deviations of the indirect production costs starts from the figures in table 16.

The number of labor hours budgeted for the actual production volume respecting the budget yield H_{br} (2.5 hours for product A and 2.7 hours for product B) is calculated as follows:

Table 16. January indicators N

No	Indicators	Budgeted Values	Real Values
1	Production obtained (pcs)	7.300	7.000
	- product A	3.100	3.000
	- product B	4.200	4.000
2	Direct labor hours (h)	19.090	17.420
3	Variable expenses (EUR)	35.740	35.152
4	Fixed expenses (EUR)	15.340	15.340
5	Total indirect production costs (EUR) (3 + 4)	51.081	50.492
6	Cost per hour of labor (EUR / h.) (5: 2)	2,67575	2,89851

$$H_{br} = \sum_{i=1}^{n} \left(Q_{ri} \times h_{bi}\right)$$

in which:

Q_{ri} - the quantity manufactured from product i;
h_{bi} – budgeted labor hours for making a piece of product i.

H_{br} = 3.000 buc x 2,5 h/buc + 4.000 buc x 2,7 h/buc = 18.300 h

Table 17. Calculation of the total deviation for indirect production costs

Indicators	Budgeted Values Related to Real Production	Realized Values	Deviations
Volume of activity in man-hours (h)	18.300	17.420	-880
Unit labor cost (EUR / h)	2,67575	2,89851	0,22276
Total indirect production costs (EUR)	48.966	50.492	1.526

$CIP_r = H_r$ x cuh_r

$CIP_{br} = H_{br}$ x cuh_b

in which:

H_r – total effective labor hours;
cuh_r – the actual (real) unit cost of the labor hour;
H_{br} – total labor hours budgeted for actual production in compliance with budgeted efficiency;
cuh_b – unit lsabor cost according to budget data.

$CIP_r = H_r$ x cuh_r = 17.420 h x 2,89851 EUR/h =50.492 EUR

$CIP_{br} = H_{br}$ x cuh_b = 18.300 h x 2,67575 EUR/h = 48.966 EUR

ΔCIP = 50.492 – 48.966 = +1.526 EUR – unfavorable deviation

There is, in January N, an overrun of actual indirect production costs compared to what was budgeted at EUR 1,526.

1. 1. Yield deviation

$\Delta r = (H_r - H_{br})$ x cuh_b = (17.420 – 18.300) x 2,67575 = -2.355 EUR – favorable deviation

The decrease of the number of hours worked by 880 compared to those established by the budget (17,420 h– 18,300 h) determined a decrease of indirect expenses by the amount of 2,355 EUR.

2. 2. Cost deviation

$\Delta cuh = (cuh_r - cuh_b)$ x H_r = (2,89851 - 2,67575) x 17.420 = +3.881 EUR – unfavorable deviation

Table 18. January N expenses

Costs	Budgeted (EUR)	Realized (EUR)
Fixed expenses	15.340	15.340
Variable expenses	35.740	35.152
Total expenses	51.080	50.492

An actual unit cost per hour of labor higher than budgeted led to an increase in indirect production costs of EUR 3,881.

Deviation of Activity

The actual and budgeted indirect production costs in January N are:

According to the budget data, the actual production requires 17,420 man-hours, while the budget provided 19,090 hours. It is a sub-activity, with a rational imputation coefficient of:

$$k = \frac{H_r}{H_n} = \frac{17.420}{19.090} = 0,91252$$

The fixed expenses incorporable in cost for this level of activity, according to the rational imputation, are:

Incorporable CF = total CF x k = 15,340 x 0.91252 = EUR 13,998

The deviation of activity is:

$\Delta a = CF_b - CF_{înc} = 15.340 - 13.998 = +1.342$ EUR – unfavorable deviation

or:

$$\Delta a = \left(H_b - H_r\right) \times \frac{CF_b}{H_b} = \left(19.090 - 17.420\right) \times \frac{15.340}{19.090} = 1.670 \times 0,80356 = +1.342 EUR$$

Due to a sub-activity of 1,670 direct labor hours (19,090 h - 17,420 h), the indirect cost of labor hours was increased by EUR 1,342.

Volume or Budget Deviation

In order to determine the volume deviation, the budgeted expenses for the volume of the real activity are recalculated.

Fixed expenditure remains at EUR 15,340 as in the static budget.

The recalculated variable expenses are:

Table 19. Volume deviations for indirect production costs - January N

Indirect Expences	Recalculated Budget (EUR)	Realized (EUR)	Volume Deviations (EUR)
Fixed expenses	15.340	15.340	0
Variable expenses	32.613	35.152	2.539
Total	47.953	50.492	2.539

$$CV_{rec} = \frac{CV_b}{H_b} \times H_r = \frac{35.740}{19.090} \times 17.420 = 32.613EUR$$

$\Delta Ch = CIP_r - CIP_{rec} = 50.492 - 47.953 = +2.539$ EUR

In the case of fixed costs, the deviation is zero, while variable costs increased by EUR 2,539. Of the total indirect costs, the volume deviation is unfavorable.

The volume deviation can be determined on each item of expenditure separately. For this purpose it is necessary to recalculate all variable expenses and all fixed expenses for the volume of real activity. If we add to the indirect production costs the direct costs, the result is Table 20, which includes the volume deviations calculated for all production costs, deviations related to the actual production of 3,000 pieces A and 4,000 pieces B.

Centralized, the deviations found in January N in production costs, by cause, are presented in table 21.

It is found that on the total economic entity, in January N, the production expenses decreased compared to what was budgeted, with the amount of EUR 26,944. This is a consequence of the reduction in direct expenditure (favorable deviation of EUR 28,470), which includes direct labor expenditure (a favorable deviation of EUR 25,380). On the other hand, indirect production costs had a negative effect on the total deviation, rising from the budget by EUR 1,526.

CONCLUSION

The flexible budget takes into account the possible fluctuations of the production in the period for which it is drawn up, it adapts to the foreseeable changes that may arise during the development of the company's activity. It is important to manage budgets in a flexible way, allowing budgets to be revised when necessary.

The flexible budget is a tool to support decision-making. Before setting the final budget, managers measure the impact that a decision or change in the business environment may have on the forecast result. It can be said that the flexible budget is a "simulation tool", through which several hypotheses can be tested, obtaining as many variants of the corresponding forecasts.

The flexible budget ensures the control of the company's performance. Through control, the budget contributes to increasing profits, increasing profitability and saving resources. The budget recalculated to the volume of real activity allows the correct comparison of the forecasted expenditures with those actually realized, referring to the same volume of activity. It is possible to analyze and control the efficiency of

Table 20. Total volume deviations - January N

No	Indicators	Static Budget	Realized	Recalculated Budgeted	Volume Deviations
1	**Production volume (pcs)**	7.300 3.100 4.200	**7.000** 3.000 4.000	**7.000** 3.000 4.000	X X X
2	**- A**	19.090	17.420	18.300	-880
3	**- B**	**372.420**	**328.530**	**357.000**	**-28.470**
3.1	Activity volume (direct labor hours)	55.190	49.810	52.900	-3.090
3.2	Direct costs (EUR)	317.230	278.720	304.100	-25.380
4	**Expenditure on raw materials**	**51.080**	**50.492**	**47.953**	**2.539**
4.1	**Direct labor**	**15.340**	**15.340**	**15.340**	0
4.1.1	Total indirect production costs (EUR)	13.340	13.340	13.340	0
4.1.2	Fixed expenses (EUR)	2.000	2.000	2.000	0
4.2	**Depreciation of fixed assets**	**35.740**	**35.152**	**32.613**	**2.539**
4.2.1	Rent	16.892	16.215	15.414	801
4.2.2	Variable expenses (EUR)	3.111	3.500	2.839	661
4.2.3	Salaries of management and administration staff	2.855	2.545	2.605	-60
4.2.4	Material expenses	7.015	6.956	6.401	555
4.2.5	Repair expenses	2.693	3.150	2.457	693
4.2.6	Electricity costs	3.174	2.786	2.897	-111
5	**Transportation costs**	**423.500**	**379.022**	**404.953**	**-25.931**

Table 21. Total deviations - January N

Name of Deviations	Amount (EUR)
Total deviation, of which:	-26.944
1. Deviation from direct expenses	-28.470
1.1. Deviations from budgeted raw material costs, of which: 1.1.1. Quantity deviation 1.1.2. Price deviation	-3.090 +135 -3.225
1.2. Deviations from budgeted costs with direct labor, of which: 1.2.1. Time deviation 1.2.2. Salary deviation	-25.380 -15.110 -10.270
2. Deviations from budgeted indirect expenditure, of which: 2.1. Yield deviation 2.2. Cost deviation, of which: 2.2.1. Deviation of activity 2.2.2. Volume deviation	+1.526 -2.355 +3.881 +1.342 +2.539

resource use, to accurately identify the causes of deviations, neutralizing the effect of changing activity. However, drawing up flexible budgets is more expensive than drawing up static budgets. Therefore, it is achieved only if the level of costs involved is lower than the expected benefits.

REFERENCES

Alazard, C., & Sépari, S. (1998). *Management control. Manual & Applications* [Contrôle de gestion. Manuel&Applications] (4th ed.). Dunod.

Albu, N., & Albu, C. (2003). *Performance management tools. Management Control* [Instrumente de management al performantei. Control de gestiune]. Economica.

Aslău, T. (2001). *Management control beyond appearances* [Controlul de gestiune dincolo de aparenţe]. Economica.

Badea, F., & Dobrin, C. (2006). *Budgetary management of production systems* [Gestiunea bugetară a sistemelor de productie] (2nd ed.). Economica.

Berland, N. (2009). *Measure and drive performance* [Mesurer et piloter la performance]. Retrieved from: http://www.crefige.dauphine.fr/publish/berland/performance.pdf

Bouquin, H. (1994). *Fundamentals of management control* [Fondements du contrôle de gestion]. PressesUniversitaires de France.

Boyabatli, O., Leng, T., & Toktay, L. B. (2016). The Impact of Budget Constraints on Flexible vs. Dedicated Technology Choice. *Management Science*, *62*(1), 225–244.

Branke, J., & Elomari, J. A. (2012, July). Meta-optimization for parametertuningwith a flexible computing budget. *Proceedings of the 14th annual conference on Genetic and evolutionary computation*, 1245-1252. 10.1145/2330163.2330336

Brault, R., & Giguère, P. (2003). *Management accounting* [Comptabilité de management] (5th ed.). Presses Université Laval.

Burlaud, A., & Simon, C. (2003). *Management accounting. costs / control* [Comptabilité de gestion. coûts/contrôle] (3rd ed.). Vuibert.

Chod, J., & Zhou, J. (2014). Resourceflexibilityand capital structure. *Management Science*, *60*(3), 708–729. doi:10.1287/mnsc.2013.1777

Costello, T. (2011). Better budget planning. *IT Professional*, *13*(5), 64–63. doi:10.1109/MITP.2011.78

Cucui, I., Horga, V., & Radu, M. (2003). *Management Control* [Control de gestiune]. Niculescu.

Dunk, A. S. (2011). Product innovation, budgetary control, and the financial performance of firms. *The British Accounting Review*, *43*(2), 102–111. doi:10.1016/j.bar.2011.02.004

Dupuy, Y., & Rolland, G. (1991). *Management control* [Contrôle de gestion]. Dunod.

Epuran, M., Babaita, V., & Grosu, C. (1999). *Accounting and management control* [Contabilitate şi control de gestiune]. Economica.

Forget, J. (2005). *Gestion budgétaire: Prévoir et contrôler les activités de l'entreprise*. Éditions d'Organisation.

Gervais, M. (1994). *Budget Management: Plan and control the company's activities* [Contrôle de gestion par le système budgétaire] (3rd ed.). Librairie Vuibert.

Hofstede, G. H. (Ed.). (2012). *The game of budget control*. Routledge. doi:10.4324/9780203714874

Horngren, C. T., Datar, S. M., & Foster, G. (2006). *Cost Accounting: A Managerial Emphasis* [Contabilitatea costurilor, o abordare managerială]. 11th ed.). Chisinău, Moldova: ARC.

Horvath & Parteners. (2009). *Controlling* (2nd ed.). Bucuresti, Romania: C.H. Beck.

Ionescu, C. A. (2015). Using Flexible Budgets to manage organizational performance and cost. *Annals of the Academy of Romanian Scientists*, *1*(1), 87–96.

Radu, M. (2009). *Standard cost method. Theoretical and practical aspects* [Metoda standard cost. Aspecte teoretice şi practice]. Valahia University Press.

Radu, M., & Giju, G. C. (2015). The flexible budget–basic tool of the management control in the economic entities. *ScientificBulletin: Economic Sciences*, *14*(1), 3–10.

Richard Pearson, J., Romfh, P. C., Habib, J. M., & Frieling, M. J. (1985). The Flexible Budget Process - A Tool for Cost Containment. *American Journal of Clinical Pathology*, *84*(2), 202–208. doi:10.1093/ajcp/84.2.202 PMID:4025225

Selmer, C. (2014). *Build and defend your budget. Tools, methods and behaviors* [Construire et défendre son budget. Outils, méthodes et comportements] (3rd ed.). Dunod.

Shane, J. S., Molenaar, K. R., Anderson, S., & Schexnayder, C. (2009). Construction project cost escalation factors. *Journal of Management Engineering*, *25*(4), 221–229. doi:10.1061/(ASCE)0742-597X(2009)25:4(221)

Simionescu, A., Buse, F., Bud, N., & Purcaru Stamin, I. (2006). *Managerial control* [Control managerial]. Editura Economica.

Sponem, S. (2004). *Diversity of the budgetary practices of the French companies: proposal of a typology and analysis of the determinants* [Diversité des pratiques budgétaires des entreprises françaises: proposition d'une typologie et analyse des déterminants]. Retrieved from: https://tel.archives-ouvertes.fr/tel-00465697/document

Xiaobei, L., & Shengli, D. (2011). Research on flexible budget of marketing expenditure. In *Proceedings of the 8th International Conference on Innovationand Management* (pp. 1309–1313). Retrieved from http://www4.pucsp.br/icim/ingles/downloads/papers_2011/part_7/part_7_proc_50.pdf

Zamfir, M. (2017). *Management control through the budget system* [Controlul de gestiune prin sistemul de bugete]. ProUniversitaria.

Chapter 8
Business Model in a Time of Global Crises

Ionica Oncioiu
Titu Maiorescu University, Romania

Mihaela Mirela Dogaru
Titu Maiorescu University, Romania

Manoela Popescu
Independent Researcher, Belgium

ABSTRACT

Globalization has created complex production chains, in which many countries contribute to the creation of added value. Globalization influences almost all aspects of life, but the way this evolution is felt differs from one country to another, from one region to another, from one individual to another. Globalization is an objective process that is taking place with astonishing speed, covering all the states of the world. It was determined and favored by the ultra-fast advances of technology, especially information technology, but also by the manifestations of the digital economy or information economy. Digitization has fundamentally changed the way companies operate while providing new entities with opportunities for survival and development. Websites have become powerful advertising and commercial tools, being used in all areas of activity. The technologies used to create and develop websites have diversified and become increasingly complex.

INTRODUCTION

Globalization has eroded traditions and identities, but it has also offered and continues to provide enormous opportunities, particularly for young people (Ahearne, Lam, Mathieu & Bolander, 2010). Any new technology is now accessible to everyone as a result of the dynamic process of developing interdependencies (Ben-Asher & Gonzalez, 2015). As a result, we are seeing the digital age's unparalleled

DOI: 10.4018/978-1-7998-8069-1.ch008

progress, which gives the instruments needed to ease access to a simple and informative existence. The knowledge society has provided mankind with new business models as a result of digitization.

The growth of the information society, the computer network, the increase in the number of users and the volume of information required by the public has resulted in a wide range of methods for transmitting and disseminating knowledge and information, all of which are appealing and simple to understand and use (Li, Xu & Zhao, 2018). In these circumstances, public and private legal institutions, businesses, professional groups, and non-profit organizations prefer to synthesize and exchange information via websites. Information, rather than tangible resources or money, is a considerably more essential element of production in the digital age.

The ease with which information is provided requires attention to the manner and quality of information disseminated online (Orzan, 2001). Economic agents have at their disposal a wide range of forms of manifestation of their presence in the virtual environment, depending on the assumed objectives. Sites being the easiest way to present and / or develop a business.

There are numerous promotional sites, despite the fact that the majority of sites are either business or product presentations or e-stores (Davila, 2012). Personal and creative websites, on the other hand, serve less apparent goals, such as establishing an online presence. It is generally known that in the age of electronic media, company and product promotion, as well as direct marketing, have taken on new meanings. Currently, the Internet is providing limitless opportunities for action in order to attract clients, gain their loyalty, and, most importantly, create beneficial connections with worldwide organizations.

In the digital era, it is no longer optional to have a presence on the Internet, regardless of the kind of physical or legal body, the sector of activity, or the goals pursued (Alstete & Beutell, 2018). According to the literature, some sites are designed to provide information, such as an online magazine or a blog, while others aim to present a company or service in a clear and concise manner, while others have a retail network, accessibility, and schedule for each unit, and still others have as their primary goal the generation of leads for potential sales. Last but not least, there are electronic stores, which are websites dedicated solely to the selling of goods.

BACKGROUND

Globalization has resulted in complicated manufacturing chains in which many nations participate to added value development. Globalization has an impact on nearly every area of life, yet how this change is perceived varies from country to country, region to region, and person to individual.

Globalization is associated with employment loss, social inequity, and low environmental, health, and privacy standards for some individuals. Globalization, they argue, is a factor that contributes to the destruction of traditions and identities. Globalization, on the other hand, provides young Europeans with access to possibilities all around the world.

Globalization of the economy is defined as a particularly dynamic process of increasing interdependencies between nation states as a result of the expansion and deepening of transnational ties in ever broader and more diverse spheres of economic, political, social, and cultural life, resulting in global rather than national solutions (Akgün, Keskin & Byrne, 2009). This indicates that human civilization faces global issues for which global solutions are required.

Globalization is the process of increasing the number of linkages and interconnections between nations and societies that are now part of the global system (Ashkanasy, 2011). It refers to the process through which events, choices, and actions in one area of the globe have far-reaching implications for persons and communities in other parts of the world. The field of activity (extent) and the intensity of globalization are two separate characteristics (or depth).

On the one hand, it describes a group of processes that span virtually the whole globe or function globally, giving the phrase a spatial meaning. On the other hand, it indicates that the degrees of contact, connectivity, and interdependence between the nations and communities that make up the global community are intensifying. As a result, global processes are strengthening in tandem with the growth of links (Agha, Alrubaiee & Jamhour, 2012)

Globalization is an objective process that is unfolding at breakneck pace and affecting every country on the planet. It was shaped and promoted by ultra-rapid technological developments, particularly in information technology, as well as manifestations of the digital economy or information economy, or knowledge-based economy. Globalization manifests itself in the form of liberalization and deregulation of the product and service markets, as well as capital and labor markets, in this context of the use of new technologies, such as the Internet. Interference between domestic and global markets has risen as a result of the free movement of people, goods, and capital. In the current time, the promotion of new means of continual development of the system of trade-consumer relations is accompanied by contemporary systems of supply realization, penetration, and demand migration.

If the EU is to continue to be able to leverage these global value chains to produce prosperity and benefit all European people, whether they importers, exporters, employees, consumers, and so on, removing trade barriers is critical (Alhyari, Alazab, Venkatraman, Alazab & Alazab, 2013).

Closing the EU market or erecting protectionist barriers would have an impact not just on the EU's well-integrated economy, but also on the economies of its partners, particularly the world's poorest countries. The EU has the capacity to influence globalization in the spirit of multilateral governance as the world's biggest trade union and a dedicated international participant.

Trade has a beneficial impact on employment, with exports accounting for one in every seven jobs (or 31 million) in the EU. Export-related employment is also better compensated on average in the EU, with salary premiums reaching up to 16%. Globalization, on the other hand, can have negative consequences in particular industries and areas.

The EU's "Trade for All" policy is evolving in response to changing economic realities and strives to seize new trade possibilities (de Waal & Kourtit, 2013). Free access to products, services, personnel, and money is required to ensure EU firms' capacity to develop and participate in global value chains.

The continual development of e-commerce has prompted the Commission to draft a new chapter in free trade agreements in order to enable electronic contracts and transactions, including enhanced consumer protection, in future talks. This matter has already been brought up with Mexico, and the EU is requesting that the WTO look into it further. The Commission will continue to investigate the implications of digitalization on the European economy and determine how trade policy can effectively reflect these changes.

Despite rising Internet penetration, many developing and emerging economies are falling behind in terms of digitization, with many people still lacking access to ICT and considerable inequalities across nations and urban and rural regions (Cameron & Quinn, 2011).

We must remember that digital technology is a tool, not a goal, and that the most effective means of ensuring that people's basic needs are met, particularly in terms of access to food, energy, water, and health, education, and health, must take precedence, even if digitization can be beneficial to the knowledge economy. Any approach to the digitization of the economy must be incorporated from the stage of infrastructure design if effective development of the digital sector is to be accomplished (Kotler & Keller, 2015).

Less than half of developing nations have data protection legislation, according to the EU. As a result, the EU must give technical support to the appropriate authorities in the development of such law, drawing on its own expertise and legislation, which is widely regarded as a model in this field. Given the cross-border nature of digital technology, there should not be too many differences in data protection regulation, since this would lead to incompatibilities. Of course, we must remember that guaranteeing SMEs' compliance with these rules is extremely costly.

At the moment, at the EU level, there is a persisting digital gap between men and women, between various geographical locations, and between individuals of different ages, incomes, ethnicities, health or disabilities, among other discriminating characteristics (Tong & Arvey, 2015).

Member States must work to overcome this disadvantage, stepping up their efforts to address the challenges of digital exclusion through education and training for the acquisition of essential digital skills, as well as initiatives to facilitate the appropriate use of ICT and digital tools in the implementation of participatory methodologies, according to age, personal silliness, and other factors.

Given our country's educational challenges during the COVID-19 epidemic, it is critical to include digital literacy into curriculum at all levels of education, from basic to higher education, in order to develop the skills necessary to increase access to information and instruction. The EU, on the other hand, thinks that ICT tools and new technology should not be used to replace actual instructors and schools, but rather as a method of enhancing educational access and quality. For spreading information, educating instructors, and administering institutions, new technologies are critical.

It is important to build an appropriate infrastructure in terms of high quality, cheap, dependable, and secure coverage and to provide access to it in order to minimize the existing digital divide, particularly in rural and isolated regions (Tajeddini, 2015).

Poverty and a lack of essential services, as well as underdeveloped terrestrial networks, a lack of favourable public policies and regulatory frameworks in this area, high taxation of digital products and services, low market competition, and a lack of an energy network, are all factors that prevent connectivity in our country (Arsenault & Faerman, 2014). Another issue confronting our country is cyber-attacks, which have the potential to undermine economic, political, and democratic stability unless digital security is ensured.

IT WAS DIGITAL: PRESENT AND PERSPECTIVE

Because of the importance of information in the creation of wealth, the digital economy is also known as the information or information economy. Information, rather than tangible resources or money, is a considerably more essential element of production in the digital age. As a result, the new economy, in addition to labour and capital, handles information, either as a separate element or as a factor connected to one of the two previously stated variables (Hartnell, Ou & Kinicki, 2011)

The advent of the Internet and e-business, as well as the information economy, has resulted in significant changes in socio-economic systems. As a result, the digital economy has spawned new organizational and economic activity models (Taticchi, Tonelli & Cagnazzo, 2010).

Furthermore, the digital economy causes major reorientations in economic and social life. While all countries in the world are aware of the digital economy's defining characteristics, not all economies are structured and operate in accordance with its trends, or to the same extent. As a result, the European Commission's Market Strategy for the Digital Economy has been based on ensuring better access for consumers. In the EU, the digital economy is the bedrock of development and jobs, and it is critical for the modernisation of conventional industries. The EU is leading the fight to build the proper environment for the digital economy to thrive, give more choice for consumers, and promote social inclusion, with an estimated € 500 billion in additional development gains and a significant boost to job creation in Europe.

The ability of states to boost technological innovation, entrepreneurial relationships, education, specialized qualification, and the transition of all public and private organizations from bureaucratic hierarchy to type networks learning will increasingly determine their success in the digital economy. As a result, while the digital economy is projected to contribute to greater social and economic equality, there are no indications that this will occur anytime soon. Technology, on the other hand, will assist improve access to education, jobs, and financing, even if it will result in a decline in repetitious and low-value-added occupations in nearly all economic sectors, whether we're talking about manufacturing, agriculture, or services, in the short run.

As a result, the electronic economy refers to both new organizational structures and new technology, with information, information linkage, and communication serving as the cornerstones of the digital economy. Digitization has profoundly altered how businesses function, while also providing new chances for survival and growth. The EU emphasizes that allowing well-regulated cross-border e-commerce may directly improve livelihoods, raise living standards, and stimulate employment and economic development. Because a substantial percentage of digital businesses are held by women, digitization can help to achieve gender equality. Digitalization must be utilized to encourage entrepreneurial education and capacity building in poor nations, while also providing a conducive climate for start-ups and innovative societies (Hartnell, Ou, & Kinicki, 2011).

ICT tools may also be used to distribute information, which is important during natural, medical (COVID-19 pandemic), and technical catastrophes, as well as in sensitive and conflict-affected areas, as discovered. Low-income and other vulnerable populations can use digital technology to get access to essential services such as health, education, water, sanitation, and power, as well as humanitarian relief and other public and commercial services.

The Romania Partnership Agreement with the European Union 2014-2020 assumes the national strategy framework in the form of the Strategy for the Digital Agenda 2020 and other supporting initiatives. Romania's export plan till 2020, the Cyber Security Strategy, the National Intellectual Property Strategy 2012-2015, and the Next Generation Networks Plan for broadband communications are all part of the digital single market.

The set of legislation dedicated to ICT, internet, operations, and digital services, as well as normative actions that controlled electronic commerce, provide the national legal framework. The National Strategy on the Digital Agenda for Romania 2020 (SNADR), which identifies four action areas, was adopted in February 2015, however implementation has been slow.

Copyright, the complexities of value added tax (VAT), and the idea of access through the provision of high-speed, secure, and reliable infrastructure and services are all concerns that influence the entire European approach. The European Commission advocates for a level playing field for similar digital services, as well as national fairness and transparency.

The DESI indicator is the most visible indication of Romania's digital gaps (Index of the digital economy and society). This index has 5 chapters in total:

- Internet connectivity (fixed and mobile broadband services, as well as the speed and cost of a broadband connection);
- Human resources (internet access, basic and advanced digital skills);
- Internet use (citizens' access to online material, conversations, and transactions);
- Digital technology integration (digitalization of businesses and electronic commerce);
- Public services in the digital age (e-government).
- According to the European Commission's Digital Economy and Society Index (DESI) for 2019, Romania is ranked 27th out of 28 EU member nations.
- DESI is currently responsible for the following areas (ec.europa.eu, 2020):
    - a measure of how ready 5G networks is to be used;
    - a degree of digital proficiency above that of an elementary school student;
    - a working knowledge of software; at the very least, a working knowledge of software;
    - Specialists in information and communication technology (ICT);
    - Graduates in the field of information and communication technology (ICT);
    - those who have never used the Internet before;
    - a professional in social networks;
    - registering for an online course;
    - Consultations and voting through the internet;
    - Individual sales on the internet;
    - a huge amount of info;
    - Data interchange in the medical field;
    - Prescriptions that are written in an electronic format.

The fact that Romania is ranked 27th in the world raises serious concerns. The impact of the digital divide, as well as other structural flaws, should be discussed from the perspective of PUD (digital single market). Digital convergence must be a tool for Romania to boost productivity and encourage prosperity.

Romania has a mobile communications infrastructure with four major operators and many others offering internet services, high-speed broadband communications, and a large number of computer scientists and software solution developers, providing Romania with the necessary opportunities to join the single digital market. Romania faces a significant challenge in the digital single market.

At the same time, cross-border e-commerce rules will benefit the PUD by increasing trust in services, developing high-quality and affordable cross-border parcel services, eliminating unjustified geographical bottlenecks, strengthening trust in digital services and processing personal data, and ensuring the security of these services.

According to the Country Report for Romania on the Digital Economy and Society Index, Romania was last in the EU in terms of digitization of the economy and society in 2019, while it was in the second tier globally (DESI) (int.search.tb.ask.com, 2020) – Table 1.

According to the European Commission's (EC) report on the Digital Economy and Society Index - DESI 2018 and 2019, Romania ranks last among the 28 EU member states in terms of digitization. Bulgaria took the last place in 2020, with Romania reverting to position 27.

Despite minor improvements in virtually all measured DESI parameters, Romania's position in the rankings remained largely constant, given the country's sluggish overall growth.

Romania has made progress, but it has been sluggish and has fallen behind. According to the EC study on Romania's degree of digitalization, the economy's level of digitalization, as well as the population's

Table 1. The evolution of DESI for Romania, in the period 2018-2019

	Index Name	Romania		UE
		Place	Scores	Scores
1	DESI 2020	27	36,5	52,5
2	DESI 2019	28	35,4	49,8
3	DESI 2018	27	32,0	46,9

Source: European Commission Report on the Digital Economy and Society Index - DESI 2018, 2019 and 2020

digital skills, are both inadequate, preventing development in most DESI aspects. At the European level, there are significant disparities between the north and south, as well as the east and west. The EU, on the other hand, must recoup from Canada, Japan, Australia, the United States, and South Korea.

Due to the widespread availability of high and extremely high speed fixed broadband networks (particularly in metropolitan areas), Romania gets the greatest results in the "Connectivity" category – Table 2. However, Romania's economy has lagged behind in terms of digitization, with more than a fifth of Romanians having never accessed the Internet and fewer than a third possessing basic digital skills. There is a contradiction in our nation in that the Internet is really fast, yet the degree of digitalization is quite low.

Table 2. The evolution of "Connectivity" for Romania, in the period 2018-2020

	Index Name	Romania		UE
		Place	Scores	Scores
1	DESI 2020	22	53,5	59,3
2	DESI 2019	19	52,5	54,8
3	DESI 2018	23	45,2	51,2

Source: European Commission Report on the Digital Economy and Society Index - DESI 2019

In terms of connection, Romania is ranked 22nd. Romania did not maintain the same rate of progress in 2019 as it had in previous years. In instance, fixed broadband coverage has been stable, with about 87 percent of homes served, and nevertheless trails behind most Member States (26th in the EU). Fixed broadband service use remains unchanged in 66 percent of households, considerably below the EU average of 77 percent. Romania continues to outperform the EU average in terms of the adoption of ultra-high-speed broadband services (45 percent compared to 20 percent).

The Romanian Competitiveness Operational Program allocated EUR 100 million from the European Regional Development Fund (ERDF) to address the digital divide between urban and rural areas in the 2014-2020 financial framework, while the Operational Development Program Rural Development 2014-2020 initially provided an indicative amount of EUR 25 million from the Eur. The Ronette project, which aims to support the construction of backhaul networks in "white areas," received EUR 45 million in ERDF funding, out of a total of EUR 54 million, to finish the coverage provided for in the current funding period, providing broadband connection infrastructure for 721 localities.

Table 3. The evolution of "Human Capital" for Romania, in the period 2018-2020

	Index Name	Romania		UE
		Place	Scores	Scores
1	DESI 2020	27	31,1	48,0
2	DESI 2019	28	31,5	47,6
3	DESI 2018	27	30,2	45,4

Source: European Commission Report on the Digital Economy and Society Index - DESI 2020

Romania is ranked 27th among EU nations in terms of human capital size, significantly below the EU average. The lowest levels of basic and advanced digital skills are seen in EU Member States. Only 29% of persons aged 16 to 74 have basic digital abilities (compared to 57 percent across the EU) and 10% have advanced digital skills (compared to an EU average of 31 percent).

Despite a rise in the number of ICT experts last year, they still make up a smaller share of the workforce than in the rest of the EU (2.1 percent compared to the EU average of 3.7 percent). Romania performs well in the field of information and communication technologies, ranking sixth among EU member states with 49% of all graduates. Romania is ranked 16th in the world in terms of ICT specialists, with these professionals accounting for 1.3 percent of Romanian women working, just below the EU average of 1.4 percent. Romania is third among all ICT professionals in terms of the proportion of women (25.7 percent in 2018, compared to the EU average of 17.2 percent). Romania is ranked 11th in the world in terms of the wage disparity between men and women, with a pay difference of 16% (ec.europa.eu, 2020).

The Romanian government announced a tender in 2019 for a project called "Wireless Campus" - an integrated national platform that would give wireless internet connectivity in 4,500 public schools - in order to promote digital skills. The ERDF will provide RON 117 million (EUR 25 million) to the project, while the state budget will contribute RON 32.8 million (EUR 7 million). The private sector has taken a number of efforts. The Google Digital Workshop platform, which was created in October 2018 by the University of Bucharest and Google Romania, is an innovation hub for digital skills.

Table 4. The evolution of "Use of Internet services" for Romania, in the period 2018-2020

	Index Name	Romania		UE
		Place	Scores	Scores
1	DESI 2020	28	31,9	53,4
2	DESI 2019	28	28,5	50,7
3	DESI 2018	28	23,8	47,8

Source: European Commission Report on the Digital Economy and Society Index - DESI 2020

Romania continues to have the lowest rate of internet usage among EU member nations in general. The internet has never been utilized by 21% of persons aged 16 to 74. (Compared to the EU average of 11 percent).

People in Romania are keen to participate in a variety of online activities, particularly social networks and video chats. The usage of social networks is more prevalent than in any other EU country, with Romania leading the way with 86 percent of internet users using social networks (compared to 65 percent in the EU). Furthermore, Romanian residents utilized video calls at a rate of 51%, which is higher than the EU average (49 percent). However, due to a lack of confidence in digital technology, the usage of banking and shopping, music, video, and gaming (10 percent, 26 percent, and 63 percent, respectively) falls below the EU average.

Table 5. The evolution of "Use of Internet services" for Romania, in the period 2018-2020

	Index Name	Romania		UE
		Place	Scores	Scores
1	DESI 2020	27	20,5	41,1
2	DESI 2019	27	20,1	39,6
3	DESI 2018	27	20,3	37,6

Source: European Commission Report on the Digital Economy and Society Index - DESI 2020

Romania is ranked 27th among EU nations in terms of business digital technology integration, considerably behind the EU average. In terms of this component, Romania's position has been constant during the previous two years. Almost all of the indicators showed no change.

Romanian businesses are taking use of the opportunities given by big data analysis (11 percent vs. the EU average of 12 percent), placing them 14th out of 28 EU member states. In comparison to the European average of 21%, less than half of Romanian businesses (9%) utilize social media. Although there has been a modest increase in the use of cloud services from 6% in 2017 to 7% in 2019, Romania remains significantly behind the EU average of 18%. Only 8% of all SMEs conduct online sales (compared to the EU average of 17%), and only 2% of them make cross-border internet sales (compared to the EU average of 8 percent).

The country is a member of the EuroHPC Joint Undertaking and has signed the European Blockchain Technology Partnership Declaration and the Declaration on Artificial Intelligence Cooperation Declaration. Businesses' digitalization remains a significant problem. The "Start-up Nation" initiative is one of the strategies to help SMEs. The initiative targets around 10,000 businesses every year and offers a maximum funding of EUR 44,000 for the purchase of IT equipment, websites, software licenses, courses, and consultancy.

Table 6. The evolution of "Digital public services" for Romania, in the period 2018-2020

	Index Name	Romania		UE
		Place	Scores	Place
1	DESI 2020	28	43,2	62,9
2	DESI 2019	27	40,4	57,9
3	DESI 2018	26	36,5	54,0

Source: European Commission Report on the Digital Economy and Society Index - DESI 2020

The situation has deteriorated in terms of digital public services, with Romania now ranked last in the EU. However, several indications show that the country is doing well. Romania ranks eighth in terms of e-government users, accounting for 82 percent of internet users, compared to a European Union average of 64 percent. This contrasts with the poor results on pre-completed forms and services delivered fully online, which might suggest a systematic issue with the quality and accessibility of the services offered.

Romania's performance in terms of fully online services increased by 5 percentage points in 2019 compared to the previous year (the score increasing from 62 to 67). Furthermore, Romania's open data policy and national open data site are somewhat below the EU average (62 percent compared to 64 percent).

The administration may connect electronically with taxpayers and receive online tax returns thanks to the new National Centre for Financial Information, which was restructured in October 2017. In 2019, it was updated and streamlined, and it is now accessible via the Electronic Single Point of Contact (PCUE). The number of tax returns filed electronically grew to over 600,000 each month in the first three months, accounting for 96 percent of all tax filings. The Virtual Private Space (SPV) is a system for handling citizens' tax returns and responsibilities, in which payment obligations are defined but no payment mechanism is included. SPV uses Ghişeul.ro as a payment platform. In the first three months of 2019, enterprises adopted SPVs at a rate of over 200,000 new customers per month.

Despite having the highest percentage of e-government users, Romania has the lowest performance among Member States in terms of digital public services (ranked 7th in the EU). Romania, on the other hand, has 45 percent of homes subscribed to ultra-high-speed internet connections, placing it third in the EU. Romania is ranked 16th in the world for ICT professionals, with 1.3 percent of Romanian residents employed in the area (int.search.tb.ask.com, 2020).

The National Trade Register Office (ONRC) has launched an online registration system for new businesses, which includes revisions and amendments to the company register, as well as sales and transfers of ownership (share transfers) and insolvency procedures. The maximum response time for simplified online registration is three working days. Currently, the ONRC offers 30 digital public services.

Romania has a low level of digital education, with Romanians utilizing the Internet mostly for social networking and pleasure; moreover, Romania has a huge gap in broadband internet technological infrastructure between urban and rural regions (only 40 percent coverage in rural areas).

Although Romania has seen substantial economic growth over the previous 20 years, it is still 1.2-2.5 percent per year behind nations in Eastern Europe that have advanced in terms of government service digitalization (Estonia, Lithuania, Latvia). Romania should explore increasing digitalization policy and considering technology investments as a means of transforming the economy and accelerating growth.

Because there is a positive relationship between labour productivity and the degree of digitization for the countries studied, it is clear that productivity in Romania is over 50% lower than in the countries that rank first in terms of digitization, with productivity of over 55 USD/h versus 25 USD/h in Romania. By easing business contact, lowering transaction costs and expediting communication, and integrating markets into the value chain, digital infrastructure boosts productivity.

Digital technologies shorten the time it takes to deliver diverse services and allow for faster human capital development (a more competent workforce with better innovation capabilities), boosting labour productivity.

Online tax payments would streamline the procedure while also increasing revenue. In the following 7 years, the implementation of a set of policies to encourage electronic payments may create additional economic growth of 1-1.5 percentage points each year (percentage of GDP).

SOLUTIONS AND RECOMMENDATIONS

The advancement of technology and the Internet has given rise to a new concept: e-business. It, in turn, encompasses two other concepts: e-commerce and e-payment, and assumes that all three phases of a business (negotiation, payment, and delivery of the good / provision of the service) are carried out through an electronic system incorporating a variety of technologies, specific techniques, services, and concepts. The following are the key categories of e-commerce that have a worldwide impact:

- B2C (Business-to-Consumer) refers to e-commerce transactions between a firm and a customer.
- Business-to-Business (B2B): This category comprises Internet-based e-commerce between businesses.

Because of the globalization of commerce, manufacturing, and consumption, it is now necessary to conduct business transactions in real time, regardless of geographical boundaries, time zone variations, currency, or other factors. All that counts is boosting the company's profitability by achieving the highest possible earnings at the lowest possible cost, practically instantly.

In the context of the usage of electronic methods, product promotion and direct marketing have received new importance. Currently, the Internet provides limitless opportunities for action in order to attract clients, gain their loyalty, and, most importantly, create beneficial connections with worldwide players.

The digital economy, which is the consequence of the combination of the personal computer, telecommunications, the Internet, and electronics, has a number of characteristics that set it apart from traditional economies. First and foremost, it is about developing a new business model (e-business, e-commerce, e-banking, and so on) based on a business / business relationship (B2B), a business / buyer (B2C), a business / employee (B2E), a business / government (B2G), a government / business (G2B), and so on, that radically changes their efficiency, in the sense of reducing costs, including transaction Recent years have seen the fastest growth of e-commerce as a real way of conducting business, with the emergence of unique marketplaces for scientific knowledge, fuelled by the extraordinary rate of development of the research and development industry.

The field of computer-assisted business has grown in popularity for financial networks since the 1970s. Different organizations (banks) were linked together via private networks to conduct various transactions using computer technology. Various global information sharing formats are specified by the EDI (Electronic Data Interchange) standard. The scale of e-business has grown dramatically since the Internet's introduction (e-training.iatp.md, fără an).

IBM coined the term "e-business" in 1997, describing it as a "secure, flexible, and integrated access to conduct various companies by merging procedures and systems that perform fundamental business activities with those that allow users to locate information on the Internet" (Yadav & Sagar, 2013). The word e-commerce was initially used, but it soon became merely one (essential) part of the e-business idea. Another word, e-service, was used by Hewlett-Packard in 1999 to describe the provision of comprehensive e-business solutions, including hardware, software, and consultancy.

The global economy is increasingly transforming into a digital one. Information and communication technologies (ICT) are no longer a niche industry, but rather the bedrock of today's creative economic systems. The demand, the requirements of customers who are more active in the design, manufacture, and usage of goods and services, starting from the stage of research and development, are at the forefront of the digital economy.

Competition and collaboration are two essential components of the digital economy, and an organization's capacity to shift from hierarchical and individual to collaborative work will ultimately determine its competitiveness. To produce additional value utilizing new information technologies, both individuality and unity will be required at the organizational level.

The Internet's and new technology's potential is a critical instrument for creating and altering corporate processes. In its most basic form, E-Business (electronic commerce) is the conduct of business through the Internet. It was coined by IBM in 1997 as a more general word than e-Commerce, referring not just to sales and purchasing operations, but also to additional client services, such as cooperation with business partners.

FUTURE RESEARCH DIRECTIONS

Many businesses are rethinking their strategies in light of the Internet's potential today. Companies utilize the Internet to buy and sell portions of their supplies from other businesses, collaborate to boost sales, and meet and participate in research (Fan, Li & Zheng, 2016).

Many organizations, regardless of size, have learned how to use the Internet successfully in their operations by taking advantage of the opportunities, availability, and worldwide reach that the Internet provides. As a result, many businesses have moved to the virtual realm or enhanced their current infrastructure for online business, resulting in changes in work processes in connection to online e-business solutions or the new opportunities that these solutions provide.

E-Business, often known as electronic business, is the practice of conducting business using Internet-based technology. This will encompass the selling and purchase of products and services through the Internet (e-commerce), as well as the supply of technical information and customer support (Barnes, Dang, Leavitt, Guarana & Uhlmann, 2018).

E-Business is a phrase that is frequently used interchangeably with E-Commerce, although it encompasses a wide range of services connected to the selling of products and services. There has recently been a profusion of commercial apps that take use of the Internet's open operating principles. Internet connectivity is combined with trade, database, or business process automation technologies in these applications.

E-business is a word that refers to a larger idea than e-commerce. Internal commissions and procedures, as well as transactions and business processes that produce online sales, are all included by this phrase.

To put it another way, it combines a company's core business, IT infrastructure, and Internet services. Its applications include the whole company cycle, as well as third parties like banks and insurance organizations. E-commerce, according to experts, is a relatively new commercial technique.

Modern technology and methodologies are integrated to assist businesses in increasing their value, lowering their expenses, and attracting as many consumers as feasible. Despite its broad character, this definition describes e-commerce as a method and practice for conducting commercial transactions.

The distinction between e-commerce and other technologies and procedures is that it can be used to start new enterprises as well as expand current ones.

Many firms' initial step into e-commerce is to establish a presence on the Internet in order to post employment openings, products, or trade policies. Other corporate functions, such as order processing, are frequently integrated into websites.

In the virtual world, there are a variety of business models. There is currently a completely new organizational pattern based on Internet capabilities and the development of new information and communication technologies. The virtual model substitutes a virtual location and a network configuration for a physical location and a real organizational structure.

This new digital business model is a little erratic, which presents new problems. Physical work dematerializes and becomes digital, organizational decision-making provides new avenues for success, and communication takes on new meanings and forms.

A structure with a linearly functional function, characterized by predictable occurrences, replaces a well-defined, sometimes inflexible, organizational structure characterized by departments, compartments, and roles (Cumming & Groh, 2018). Events are created at random, and their outcomes are predicted using probabilistic thinking patterns. Because one interconnection produces additional connections, the digital business model's complexity refers to a large number of interconnections and a continual dynamic of their existence.

There are several ways for a company to establish a commercial presence on the Internet. The Presentation Store Model, the Auction Model, the Portal Model, and the Dynamic Pricing Model are all examples of extant e-business models shown in this section.

Storefront Model - The Storefront Model is by far the most popular. The retailer provides an online inventory of its items, allowing customers to place orders directly through the internet. It integrates security, transaction processing, and data storage in the online shop database.

It is the simplest type of e-commerce, in which the customer and seller communicate directly through the use of a product catalogue and a shopping cart. The shopping cart is an order processing system that allows customers to add goods to their shopping basket while visiting an online business.

The basket information, together with the customer's personal information, is saved in a database once the order is completed. Amazon, which began selling books over the internet in 1994, is one of the most prominent online businesses that uses the store model. Amazon's product line has grown to include electrical products, music CDs, video movies, DVDs, games, and more.

Customers' movements are tracked using a system called "customization," which is based on prior purchases and product searches. Shopping malls have lately arisen, offering a diverse range of products and services, as well as the ability for customers to purchase many items in one transaction.

The auction model functions as a forum in which internet users can play the role of either a seller or a bidder. Flea market, which allows sellers and buyers to automate individual transactions, is one of the most successful online businesses that uses the auction concept. The procedure of selling or buying an item is similar to putting tiny advertising, with the exception that the seller or buyer has total control over the ad or offer.

The seller may see the item or all of his products, as well as the description, photo, initial price, and availability time, while potential buyers can search by various categories, get an overview of items sold, and instantly bid on items.

Visitors may use the portal template to locate information on any topic they are interested in. The phrases portal and search engines are often used interchangeably. Search engines are horizontal portals that provide broad information on a wide variety of subjects. Vertical portals are the second type of portal, and they provide more extensive information on a certain topic. Furthermore, many internet portals contain both the auction and shop models, resulting in an integrated e-commerce ecosystem. Another intriguing and helpful feature is the ability to tailor the gateway to the preferences of each visitor. That is, based on personal interests and preferences, it is possible to personalize the user, presentation, and content of various web sites by adding or removing articles.

Users may utilize the dynamic pricing model to discover the best deals on the goods they want. There are three subcategories in this model:

- Your Name-Price model, which allows a consumer to set a product's price. If the price given is not advantageous to the firm, the client should make a new offer. The method works by having agents examine a variety of websites or databases in order to locate the best deal. Expedia is one of the most well-known firms that uses this e-business model. Airline tickets, hotel rooms, vehicle rentals, holiday packages, maps and attractions, and other items are frequently included in proposals.
- Customers may use the comparative pricing model to find the best deal on a product or service from a group of vendors are two well-known firms that use this approach.
- The demand-sensitive pricing model is founded on the idea that the more consumers a product has, the lower the price it will sell for. Purchasing a thing from a group of people is more cost-effective, and the price achieved is generally cheaper than if the goods were purchased individually. Mecate is a well-known corporation that uses this e-business strategy.

One of the most significant discoveries arising from the development and widespread usage of the Internet as a new form of entrepreneurship is online business markets. In order to have a better understanding of what an online marketplace is, we can state that it is described as a website where several buyers and sellers interact online.

CONCLUSION

Despite the fact that the Internet has permeated all sectors of activity, many developing and rising economies are trailing behind in terms of digitization, many people still lack access to ICT, and there are substantial inequalities across nations and urban and rural regions. It is obvious that a country's digital economy performance is defined by its ability to increase technical innovation, entrepreneurship, education, specialized skills, and the transfer of all public and commercial organizations from bureaucratic hierarchy to learning networks.

However, we must remember that human resources are the most essential resource, and that digital technology remains a valuable instrument. The value of ICT tools was shown during the pandemic emergency, when they were utilized to transmit critical information. Low-income and other vulnerable populations can also benefit from digital technology, which can provide access to excellent essential services (health, education, water, sanitation, and power), as well as humanitarian relief and other public and commercial services.

In terms of digitalization, our nation falls into the category of EU member states that are trailing behind. The Digital Economy and Society Index demonstrates these differences from the European average (DESI).

According to the European Commission's Digital Economy and Society Index (DESI) for 2019, Romania is ranked 27th out of 28 EU Member States. Romania has progressed, albeit at a glacial pace, and has failed to close the gap that has persisted for years. According to the EC study on Romania's degree of digitalization, the economy's level of digitalization, as well as the population's digital skills, are both inadequate, preventing development in most DESI aspects.

Romania continues to have the lowest rate of internet use among EU member countries. The internet has never been utilized by 21% of persons aged 16 to 74. (Compared to the EU average of 11 percent). Romania also ranks 27th among EU nations in terms of business digital technology integration, considerably behind the EU average.

Romanian businesses are the ones who are taking use of the opportunities given by big data analysis (11 percent vs. the EU average of 12 percent), ranking 14th out of 28 EU member states.

However, compared to the European average of 21%, fewer than half of Romanian businesses (9%) utilize social media. Although the adoption of cloud services has increased somewhat from 6% in 2017 to 7% in 2018, Romania remains significantly behind the EU average of 18%. Only 8% of all SMEs conduct online sales (compared to the EU average of 17%), and only 2% of them make cross-border internet sales (compared to the EU average of 8 percent).

Because of the poor level of digital education in Romania, the Internet is mostly utilized for accessing social networks and entertainment. In terms of broadband internet technology infrastructure, Romania has a significant divide between urban and rural regions (only 40 percent coverage in rural areas).

The EuroHPC Joint Undertaking includes our nation. It also agreed to sign the Declaration on the Establishment of the European Blockchain Technology Partnership as well as the Declaration on Artificial Intelligence Cooperation. However, despite the fact that more and more firms are active in the online world through websites, digitization of Romanian businesses remains a significant problem.

New methods of company development and information transmission have emerged as a result of the digital era. The interface through which a company connects with consumers is represented by the firm's website. Websites have also evolved into strong advertising and business tools, with applications in a wide range of fields.

In addition, the technology used to design and construct websites have evolved and grown increasingly sophisticated. It is well recognized that a website provides a firm with a plethora of additional options. Sites are being utilized to promote not only businesses, but also periodicals, personalities, and goods.

The majority of the time, these websites serve as promotional tools. It's also true that a firm or organization doesn't have to rely entirely on a website to publish, store, and distribute its material. Any site may be marketed, with a variety of methods available in the literature, but the effectiveness of any online project marketing is always measured in relation to its goals. These serve as a baseline for the first several months after the site's inception.

According to the literature, a website might mature in 6 months or even a year, depending on the sector of activity and its character. High-performance search engine optimization or an internet advertising campaign can help speed up the process.

The site's general arrangement is simple, and the visitors like the high quality of the labels. The site's interface is user-friendly and has a pleasing visual appeal. The content is well-organized, the design is consistent, and the site's predominant colour is white, which provides a sense of peace and comfort when perusing the information.

REFERENCES

Agha, S., Alrubaiee, L., & Jamhour, M. (2012). Effect of core competence on competitive advantage and organizational performance. *International Journal of Business and Management*, *7*(1), 192–204.

Ahearne, M., Lam, S. K., Mathieu, J. E., & Bolander, W. (2010). Why are some sales people better at adapting to organizational change? *Journal of Marketing*, *74*(3), 65–79. doi:10.1509/jmkg.74.3.065

Akgün, A. E., Keskin, H., & Byrne, J. (2009). Organizational emotional capability, product and process innovation, and firm performance: An empirical analysis. *Journal of Engineering and Technology Management*, *26*(3), 103–130. doi:10.1016/j.jengtecman.2009.06.008

Alhyari, S., Alazab, M., Venkatraman, S., Alazab, M., & Alazab, A. (2013). Performance evaluation of e-government services using balanced scorecard. *Benchmarking*, *20*(4), 512–536. doi:10.1108/BIJ-08-2011-0063

Alstete, J. W., & Beutell, N. J. (2018). Designing learning spaces for management education: A mixed methods research approach. *Journal of Management Development*, *37*(2), 201–211. doi:10.1108/JMD-08-2017-0247

Arsenault, P., & Faerman, S. R. (2014). Embracing paradox in management: The value of the competing values framework. *Organizational Management Journal*, *11*(3), 147–158. doi:10.1080/15416518.2014.949614

Ashkanasy, N. (2011). International happiness; a multilevel perspective. *The Academy of Management Perspectives*, (February), 23–29.

Ben-Asher, N., & Gonzalez, C. (2015). Effects of cyber security knowledge on attack detection. *Computers in Human Behavior*, *48*, 51–61. doi:10.1016/j.chb.2015.01.039

Cameron, K. S., & Quinn, R. E. (2011). *Diagnosing and Changing Organizational Culture: Based on the Competing Values Framework*. Jossey-Bass.

Davila, A. (2012). New trends in performance measurement and management control. *In Performance Measurement and Management Control. Global Issues (Washington, D.C.)*, *25*, 65–87.

de Waal, A. A., & Kourtit, K. (2013). Performance measurement and management in practice. *International Journal of Productivity and Performance Management*, *62*(5), 446–473. doi:10.1108/IJPPM-10-2012-0118

Hartnell, C. A., Ou, A. Y., & Kinicki, A. (2011). Organizational culture and organizational effectiveness: A meta-analytic investigation of the competing values framework's theoretical suppositions. *The Journal of Applied Psychology*, *96*(4), 677–694. doi:10.1037/a0021987 PMID:21244127

Kotler, Ph. T., & Keller, K. L. (2015). *Marketing Management* (15th ed.). Pearson.

Li, Sh., Xu, L. D., & Zhao, S. (2018). 5G Internet of Things: A survey. *Journal of Industrial Information Integration*, *10*, 1–9. doi:10.1016/j.jii.2018.01.005

Orzan, Gh. (2001). *Cyber marketing*. Uranus Publishing House.

Tajeddini, K. (2015). Exploring the antecedents of effectiveness and efficiency. *International Journal of Hospitality Management*, *49*(7), 125–135. doi:10.1016/j.ijhm.2015.06.007

Taticchi, P., Tonelli, F., & Cagnazzo, L. (2010). Performance measurement and management: A literature review and a research agenda. *Measuring Business Excellence*, *14*(1), 4–18. doi:10.1108/13683041011027418

Tong, Y. K., & Arvey, R. D. (2015). Managing complexity via the Competing Values Framework. *Journal of Management Development*, *34*(6), 653–673. doi:10.1108/JMD-04-2014-0029

Yadav, N., & Sagar, M. (2013). Performance measurement and management frameworks. *Business Process Management Journal*, *19*(6), 947–971. doi:10.1108/BPMJ-01-2013-0003

ADDITIONAL READING

Barnes, C. M., Dang, C., Leavitt, K., Guarana, C., & Uhlmann, E. L. (2018). Archival data in micro organizational research: A toolkit for moving to a broader set of topics. *Journal of Management*, *44*(4), 1453–1478. doi:10.1177/0149206315604188

Cumming, D., & Groh, A. P. (2018). Entrepreneurial finance: Unifying themes and future directions. *Journal of Corporate Finance*, *50*, 538–555. doi:10.1016/j.jcorpfin.2018.01.011

Fan, J. P. H., Li, J., & Zheng, G. (2016). Revisiting the bright and dark sides of capital flows in business groups. *Journal of Business Ethics*, *134*(4), 509–528. doi:10.100710551-014-2382-6

Chapter 9
Top Seven Trends in Management Accounting

Gary Cokins
https://orcid.org/0000-0001-9832-0114
Analytics-Based Performance Management LLC, USA

ABSTRACT

Ultimately, costing principles, such as the causality principle, must be converted into practical practices with supporting tools. This chapter describes how cost modeling has evolved over the last century. It describes the trends and obstacles that have helped or delayed developments. These evolving areas and trends include (1) the expansion from product costing to include channel and customer profitability reporting and analysis, (2) the integration of managerial accounting with other enterprise and corporate performance management (EPM/CPM) methods, (3) the shift from historical reporting to predictive accounting (e.g., marginal/incremental costing, (4) driver-based budgeting and rolling financial forecasts, (5) customer lifetime value (CLV), (6) imbedding analytics into managerial accounting (e.g., correlation and regression analysis), (7) acceptance of two or more co-existing managerial accounting methods, and (8) chargebacks to internal users and service-level agreements of information technology (IT) and shared services.

INTRODUCTION

The field of management accounting is experiencing a punctuated shift toward more progressive methods and practices. The cause is reaction (1) to business marketing and sales techniques that are increasingly customer centric and require predictive planning and (2) to operational manager needs to improve productivity by removing waste, shortening cycle times, and increasing efficiency and effectiveness. *What are the major trends involved?*

Throughout my career I've observed numerous management fads appear and then fade away as a temporary craze. I've also watched managers excitedly jump onto these new bandwagons only to be disappointed when they haven't lasted. In some cases, though, what begins as a good idea actually sticks and becomes a trend, which is what I'll describe here for management accounting.

DOI: 10.4018/978-1-7998-8069-1.ch009

Before I share my observations, imagine if you reviewed the titles and content of The New York Times best-selling business books or of Harvard Business Review articles from the last 25 years. How many of them might cause you to react with a chuckle and say, "Oh, that one"? Do you remember any of the items in the following list? (Warning: Some advocates or book authors may be offended.)

Quality circles (for total quality management, or TQM), One minute manager, Business process reengineering (BPR), Management by objectives (MBOs), Six Sigma, Matrix management, Core competency, Intrapreneuring, Search for excellence, Best practices, Management by walking around (MBWA).

I'm not saying those practices served no purpose. They did introduce useful ideas, but they didn't live up to their promises as they ascended. Many organizations jump from one improvement program to another, hoping that each new one will provide that big competitive edge, only to discover with hindsight that it was just a method du jour. Most managers would acknowledge that pulling one lever for improvement rarely results in a substantial change--particularly a long-term sustained change. And the business media haven't helped. They hype what's fashionable at the time, mostly because that's their role.

Will the management accounting trends that I describe here take root or be just another fad or fashion?

MANAGEMENT ACCOUNTING ERAS

First let's look at some history. Figure 1 illustrates a humorous but valid timeline of the shifts in accounting:

1. Ancient Era--Rocks and stone piles.
2. Medieval Era--Piles of precious metal and paper money. This situation ultimately led to the book published in 1494 by Luca Pacioli, an Italian mathematician and Franciscan friar, titled Summa de arithmetica, geometria, proportioni et proportionalità. It dealt with Hindu-Arabic arithmetic and its offshoot, algebra, and contained Pacioli's 27-page treatise on Venetian accounting that described double-entry bookkeeping.
3. Industrial Age Era--Standard cost accounting. In the 1860s, Albert Fink, a German-born civil engineer who worked in the United States, developed cost per ton/mile rates for the railroad industry using cost allocations. In the 1890s, to reflect Frederick Winslow Taylor's manufacturing scientific methods, Alexander Hamilton Church developed standard costing methods.
4. Regulatory Compliance Era--The Great Depression in the U.S. resulted in regulatory reforms to protect investors from shady financial reporting practices (1930s). In one sense, they were a setback to management accounting because the reforms established simplified rules that calculated inventory values and costs of goods sold (COGS), yet the overhead cost allocation methods were misleading because they were based on cost factors that violated costing's causality principle (the need for cause-and-effect insights).
5. Consumer Era--The emergence of activity-based costing (ABC). This next era arguably led to a transition from management accounting to managerial economics. ABC reflected "causal" cost tracing of increasingly diverse types of products, services, channels, and customers that resulted in an organization's relatively greater indirect-to-direct expense structure to manage the increase in complexity. In 1987, the book Relevance Lost: The Rise and Fall of Management Accounting by H. Thomas Johnson and Robert S. Kaplan, documented the need for and benefits of upgrading

costing practices from a highly aggregated "cost pool" with a single, noncausal cost allocation factor to using multiple disaggregated cost pools with causally related factors.

6. Predictive Analytics Era--Predictive accounting. Today and moving forward, there's a shift in emphasis from an historical to a predictive view of strategy and operations. With cost projections, organizations can translate their plans and actions into monetary terms for decision evaluation and/or validation.

Where are the emerging practices in management accounting that may likely evolve into lasting trends? They are in steps 5 and 6 in Figure 1.

Figure 1.

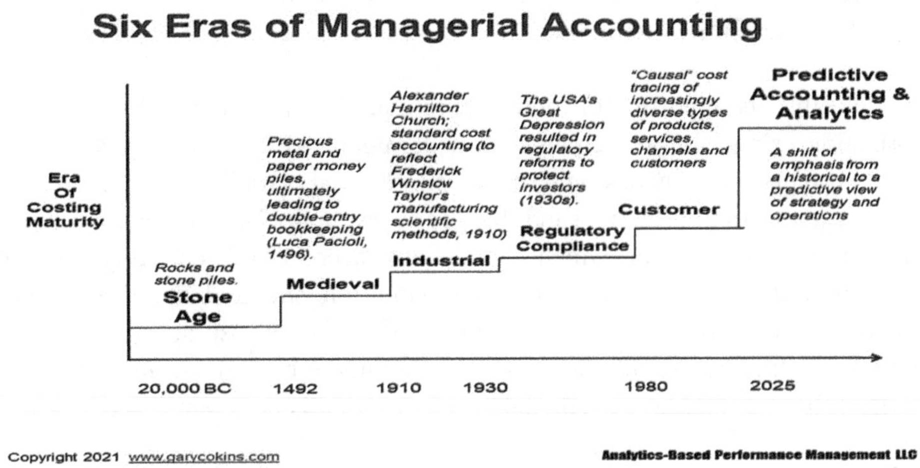

Before moving on to the trends, let's look at the role of management accounting. Contrary to beliefs that the only purpose of management accounting is to collect, transform, and report data, its primary purpose is first and foremost to influence behavior at all levels from the desk of the CEO down to each employee. It should do this by supporting decisions. A secondary purpose is to stimulate investigation and discovery by signaling relevant information (and, consequently, bringing focus) and by generating questions.

Here is the IMA® formal definition of management accounting: Management accounting is a profession that involves partnering in management decision making, devising planning and performance management systems, and providing expertise in financial reporting and control to assist management in the formulation and implementation of an organization's strategy.

My intent isn't to debate or replace IMA's definition but to emphasize the importance of its need to support decision making.

THE SEVEN MAJOR TRENDS IN MANAGEMENT ACCOUNTING

The seven major trends in management accounting are:

1. Expansion from product to channel and customer profitability analysis,
2. Management accounting's expanding role with enterprise performance management (EPM),
3. The shift to predictive accounting,
4. Business analytics imbedded in EPM methods,
5. Coexisting and improved management accounting methods,
6. Managing information technology and shared services as a business, and
7. The need for better skills and competency with behavioral cost management

Trend Number 1: Expansion From Product to Channel and Customer Profitability Analysis

I would like to believe that the reporting of more accurate product and standard service-line cost and profitability information using ABC principles is now common. ABC traces expenses into cost with resource and activity drivers and provides much cost visibility that is traditionally hidden. Sadly, many organizations continue to use a single indirect and shared expense "pool" that allocates resource expenses into costs based on a single cost factor, which violates cost accounting's causality principle. Hence, compared to ABC's disaggregating a single cost pool into multiple ones and tracing each pool's with an activity cost driver based on a cause-and-effect relationship, the existing costs are flawed and misleading. The products and service-lines are simultaneously over- and under-costing because allocations always have a zero-sum error. It's baffling how accountants can accept this deficient practice when ABC is a better alternative.

But let's put that observation aside and focus on an increasingly more relevant information need: channel and customer profitability reporting. Figure 2 illustrates that the expenses of a company are more than just product-related ones. The white spaces are "costs to serve" incurred through sales and distribution channels and by customers.

In the past, companies focused on developing standard products and standard service lines and then incenting their sales force to push and sell them to existing customers and prospects. But many products or service lines are one-size-fits-all and have become commodity-like. For example, most banks offer similar checking and deposit services. In addition, competitors can quickly replicate a company's standard products and services. Consequently, the importance of services rises, which results in a shift from product-driven differentiation toward service-driven differentiation to differentiated customer microsegments in order to gain a competitive advantage. That is, as the competitive edge from product advantages is reduced or neutralized, the customer relationship grows in importance.

To complicate matters, suppliers are aware that they have a broad range of high- and low-demand customers. For example, high-demand customers might regularly change delivery schedules, require special treatments, return goods, or phone the customer service help desk. Low-demand ones do none of these things. The extra consumption of expenses from high-demand customers means they are relatively less profitable than you might assume from the sales volume of their purchases. What this means for the marketing and sales functions is that their objective is no longer solely about increasing market share and

Figure 2.

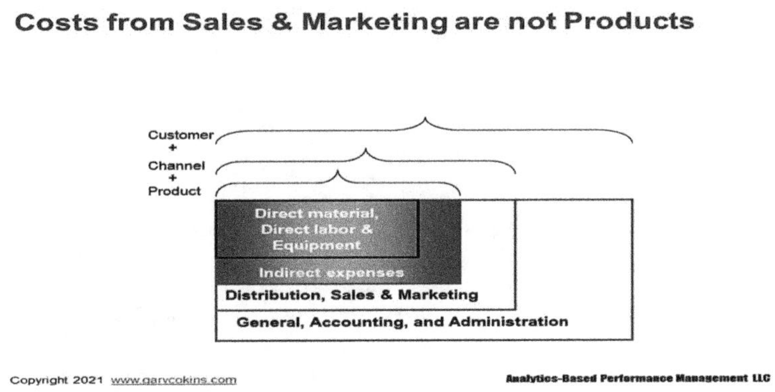

growing sales but about growing profitable sales. That requires tracing expenses below the product gross profit margin line, including channel distribution, selling, marketing, and customer service costs to serve.

The crucial challenge is to use ABC beyond calculating valid customer profitability data. The benefit comes from identifying the profit-lift potential and then realizing the potential and fulfilling it with smart decisions and actions. Marketing and sales need to view customers as an investment, such as in an individual's portfolio, rather than as someone to spend money on.

Customer profit and loss (P&L) information quantifies what everyone already may have suspected: Customers who purchase roughly the same volume and mix at similar prices aren't nearly the same when it comes to profit. As I just described, some customers may be more or less profitable based strictly on how demanding their behavior is. The information also provides cost visibility and transparency when it comes to the business processes and work activities that cause the higher or lower costs.

Although customer satisfaction and loyalty are important, a longer-term goal is to increase customer and corporate profitability. There must always be a balance between managing the level of customer service to earn customer loyalty and the impact it will have on increasing owner and shareholder wealth.

There are two major "layers" of profit margin in a company's P&L:

1. The mix of products and service lines purchased.
2. The nonproduct "costs to serve" apart from the unique mix of products and service lines purchased.

Figure 3 combines these two layers in a two-axis grid: the composite product gross profit margin of the product mix each customer purchases (reflecting net prices to the customer) and their cost to serve. Any individual customer (or grouped cluster) can be located at an intersection where the circle's diameter size reflects each customer's revenues. The figure debunks the myth that customers with the highest sales volume are also generating the highest profits.

The objective is to drive customers with profit-increase potential to the upper-left corner of the grid through a host of actions, such as surcharge pricing, upselling, and cross-selling. For example, if a customer purchases a set of golf clubs, can they also be sold a golf shirt? And if they purchase the shirt, can they be sold a second shirt at a discounted price? The data could also help suppliers identify customers who are substantially unprofitable: those who reside deep in the bottom-right of the grid. These relationships

Figure 3.

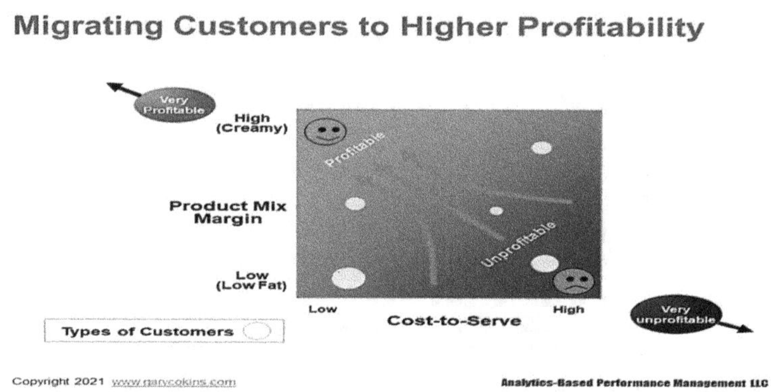

can be terminated through actions such as increased pricing or reduced service-level tactical actions that might encourage customers to "de-select" themselves ("firing" the customer).

One critical reason for knowing where each customer is located on the profit matrix is to protect your most profitable customers from your competitors.

Again, trend No. 1 is that management accounting must help the sales and marketing functions. A company needs to know the best types of customers to retain, grow, win back, and acquire--and those who aren't. To maximize shareholder wealth, a company also needs to know how much to optimally spend retaining, growing, winning back, and acquiring each type of customer. It can unnecessarily spend excessively on loyal customers and therefore destroy shareholder wealth. Or it can spend too little on marginally loyal customers and risk their defection to a competitor. Without this information, financial performance falls short of its full potential.

Trend Number 2. Management Accounting's Expanding Role With Enterprise Performance Management (EPM)

Enterprise performance management can be defined as the integration of multiple methods (such as strategy maps, balanced scorecard, performance measures, driver-based budgeting, lean management, and customer relationship management) to achieve the executive team's strategy, improve control, and increase financial profits--all through making better decisions. A major part of this is that each method is embedded with business analytics, such as segmentation and correlation analysis, and especially predictive analytics. The output of a management accounting system is always the input to use in gaining insights and managing activities and operations.

A key example of applying management accounting to EPM is strategy execution. In this area the popular method is a strategy map used to document and visualize the linkages of strategic objectives that realize the strategy and the strategy map's companion balanced scorecard. The scorecard's key performance indicators (KPIs) and its cascaded operational performance measures (often displayed in dashboards) have become the accepted technique for strategy execution. As we've heard many times, if you can't measure it, you can't easily manage it. And if you can't manage it, you can't improve it. A definition of a strategic KPI is to monitor the progress of accomplishing the strategy map's strategic objectives. Management accounting information provides a subset of KPIs. It translates performance into the language of money, such as unit cost of outputs to monitor favorable improvements or as product and customer profits – with both examples against target amounts.

A second example of applying management accounting to EPM was in trend No. 1: supporting the marketing and sales functions to view customers as an investment rather than as someone to spend money on.

Other examples will be evident as I describe the remaining trends. The key point in trend No. 2 is integration. The various components of EPM are like gears in a machine--interconnected. Commercial software increasingly provides integration, so, for example, when profitability information is calculated, it is reflected directly in the performance measures of a balanced scorecard or operational dashboards.

Trend Number 3. The Shift to Predictive Accounting

A gap is widening between what management accountants report and what managers and employee teams want. This doesn't mean that information produced by management accountants is of little value. In the last few decades, accountants have made significant strides in improving the utility and accuracy of the costs they calculate and report (such as with ABC). The gap is being caused by a shift in managers' needs--from just needing to know what things cost (such as a product cost) and what happened to a need for detailed information about what their future costs will be and why.

Many presentations from consultants and software vendors display an automobile's rearview mirror and humorously proclaim you can't drive the car by looking backward in time and that you should drive looking through the front window. I can make an argument that there's value from historical information. For example, in costing you can calculate highly relevant calibrated cost rates that are essential for projecting future resource requirements expenses.

This example shifts our focus to the future. The past reflects decisions already made. Decisions that will be made are the ones that impact the future. We once lived in a more stable world. Today there are increased volatility and uncertainty for a host of reasons, including the dropping of competitive barriers from globalization as well as more rapid changes in customer preferences, technologies, and competitor tactics. Business analytics—especially predictive analytics--and Big Data are popular buzzwords in the media today.

Figure 4 illustrates the large domain of accounting with three components: tax accounting, financial accounting, and management accounting. Two types of data sources are displayed in the upper right. The upper source is from financial transactions and bookkeeping, such as purchases and payroll. The lower source is nonfinancial measures, such as payroll hours worked, retail items sold, or gallons of liquid produced.

The financial accounting component is intended for external reporting, such as for regulatory agencies, banks, stockholders, and the investment community. Financial accounting follows compliance rules aimed at economic valuation, so it typically isn't adequate or sufficient for decision making. And the tax accounting component is its own world of legislated rules.

Our area of concern--the management accounting component--can be subdivided into three categories: (1) cost accounting, (2) cost reporting and analysis, and (3) decision support with cost planning. To oversimplify a distinction between financial and management accounting, financial accounting is about valuation, and management accounting is about value creation through good decision making.

The three management accounting subcomponents in Figure 4 are recipients of inputs from the "cost measurement" procedure of transforming incurred expenses (or their obligations) into calculated costs:

Figure 4.

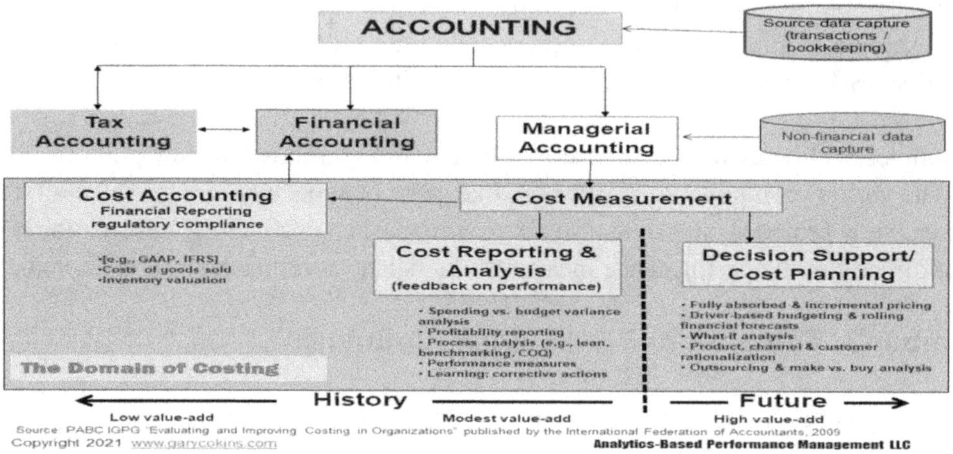

- Cost accounting represents the assignment of expenses into outputs, such as the cost of goods sold and the value of inventories. This box primarily provides external reporting to comply with regulatory agencies.
- Cost reporting and analysis represents the insights, inferences, and analysis of what has already taken place in the business in order to track performance.
- Decision support with cost planning involves decision making. It also represents using the historical cost reporting information in combination with other economic information, including forecasts and planned changes (such as processes, products, services, channels) in order to make the types of decisions that lead to a financially successful future.

It will be apparent that the key differentiator between cost accounting and the other two uses of the "Cost Measurement" box is that cost accounting is deeply constrained by regulatory practices and by describing the past in accordance with principles of financial accounting. The other two categories offer diagnostic support to interpret and draw inferences from what has already taken place and what can happen in the future. Cost reporting and analysis is about explanation. Decision support with cost planning is about possibilities. The message at the bottom of the figure is that the value-add, utility, and usefulness of the information increase, arguably at an exponential rate, from the left side to the right side of the diagram.

When the cost reporting and analysis component shifts right to the decision support with cost planning box in Figure 4, analysis shifts to the realm of decision support via economic analysis. For example, we need to understand the impact that changes will have on future expenses, so the focus shifts to resources and their capacities. This involves classifying the behavior of resource expenses as sunk, fixed, step-fixed, semivariable, variable, and discretionary with changes in service offerings, volumes, mix, processes, and the like. The classification is tricky. Here's a key concept: The "adjustability of capacity" of any individual resource expense depends on both the planning time horizon and the ease or difficulty of adjusting the individual resource's capacity (its "stickability"). This wanders into the messy area of marginal/incremental cost analysis that textbooks oversimplify but that is complicated to calculate accurately in the real world.

Figure 5 illustrates how a company's view of its profit and expense structure changes as analysis shifts from the historical cost reporting view to a predictive cost planning view. The latter is the context from which decisions are considered and evaluated.

Figure 5.

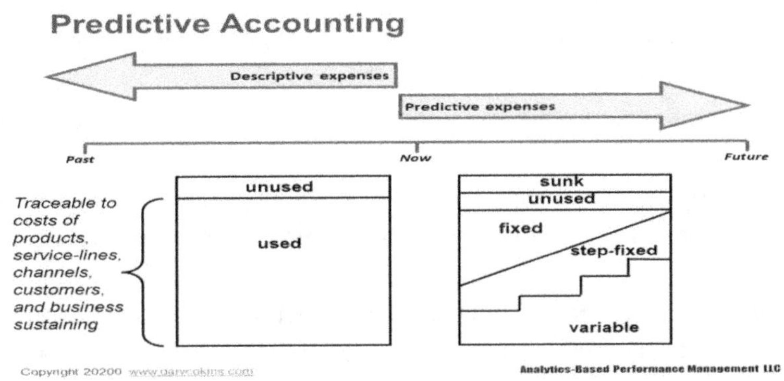

The resource expenses in the figure's left-hand side were incurred during the historical time period. The capacity for which these expenses were incurred was supplied. Then it was either (1) unused as idle or protective capacity, or (2) the expenses were used to make products, to deliver customer services, or to sustain the organization internally. This is the cost reporting and analysis component from Figure 4 that calculates output costs. The money was spent, and costing tells where it was used. This is the descriptive view of costs. Accountants refer to it as full absorption costing when all the expenses for a past time period are traced to outputs. It traces expenses (and, I hope, doesn't allocate indirect expenses with causal-insensitive, broadly averaged cost allocation factors like the number of direct labor input hours, units produced, head count, or square feet/meters) to measure which outputs uniquely consumed the resources, including individual output costs. The full absorption costing method uses direct costing methods and supplements the reporting with ABC techniques for the indirect and shared expenses.

In contrast, Figure 5's right-hand side is the predictive view of costs--the decision support with cost planning component from Figure 4. Capacity levels and types of resources can be adjusted in the future. Capacity exists only as a resource, not as a process or work activity. The classification of an expense as sunk, fixed, step-fixed, semivariable, or variable depends on the planning time horizon. The diagonal line reveals that most expenses aren't easily changed in the very short term; hence, they are classified as fixed. As the time horizon extends into the future, capacity becomes adjustable. For example, assets can be leased, not purchased, and future workers can be contracted from a temporary employment agency, not hired as full-time employees. Therefore, these expenses are classified as variable.

The broad decision-making categories for applying management accounting are:

- Product, channel, and customer rationalization--Which products, stock keeping units (SKUs), services, channels, routes, customers, and the like are best to retain or improve? And which ones aren't and should potentially be abandoned or terminated?

- Customer lifetime value (CLV)--It's useful to know how profitable a customer has been, but in some cases the future potential profit levels, especially in business-to-consumer (B2C) relationships, is more relevant because customers go through life cycles.
- Planning, budgeting, and rolling financial forecasts--Based on forecasts of future demand volume and mix for types of services or products, combined with assumptions of other proposed changes, how much will it cost to match demand with our supplied resources (for example, workforce staffing levels, purchased materials)?
- Capital expense justification--Is the return on investment (ROI) of a proposed asset purchase, such as equipment or an information system, justified?
- Make vs. buy and general outsourcing decisions--Should we continue to do it ourselves or contract with a third party?
- Process and productivity improvement--What can be changed? How can we identify opportunities? How should we compare and differentiate high-impact opportunities from nominal ones?

The term "cost estimating" is a general one and applies in all the previous decision-making categories. You might conclude that the first category, rationalization, focuses only on historical costs so doesn't require cost estimates, but the impact on resource expenses from adding or dropping various work-consuming outputs also requires cost estimates to validate the merit of a proposed rationalization decision.

Trend No. 3 is revealing a major transition from management accounting for reporting costs and profits to managerial economics for decision support and analysis that impact the future.

As you can see, management accounting is experiencing some interesting shifts. As management accountants, we need to lead the way in helping our organizations understand these changes and how we can help with strategic decision making.

Trend Number 4. Business Analytics Imbedded in EPM Methods

Business analytics and Big Data are hot topics. They are here to stay because complexity, uncertainty, and volatility are on the rise. When some managers hear these terms, they react with some trepidation and think, "I took a statistics course in school and just wanted a 'D' and be done with it!" Today the need for analytics may be the only sustainable long term competitive advantage. This is because the traditional generic strategies, like being the lowest cost supplier or product or customer differentiation, are vulnerable to agile competitors who can quickly match a supplier's price or invade your customer base.

Analytics is about investigation and discovery. Queries, like drill-downs, simply answer questions. Business analytics creates questions. Further, analytics then stimulate more questions, more complex questions, and more interesting questions. Most importantly, business analytics also has the power to answer the questions.

There are several examples of emerging applications to get more and deeper insights from EPM methods. Here are a few:

- Strategy maps typically have arrows that causally connect the strategic objectives in the traditional four perspectives of a strategy map (i.e., (1) learning, growth and innovation; (2) processes; (3) customer satisfaction and loyalty; and (4) financial). The arrows represent the selected key performance indicators (KPIs), and they are typically displayed in a PowerPoint diagram. With analytics, correlation analysis can be applied where the thickness of the arrows reflects the explanatory value that a KPI has on the dependent KPIs that it is presumed to influence. The thickness validates the quality of the selected KPIs. With higher correlation there is insight to where spending provides a higher ROI.

- The activity drivers in activity-based cost (ABC) system assign the activity costs to their final cost objects (e.g., products, services, channels, customers, and business sustaining). They should ideally be exactly proportional. That is, if the quantity of an activity driver increases 20%, so should its activity cost increase 20%. In poorly designed ABC systems this is not the case. Again, with correlation analysis, the quality of the activity driver can be validated. If there is low correlation, then a new activity driver can replace it and thus increase the cost accuracy of the final cost object. This also provides better insight as to what is driving the costs.
- As described in trend number 1 there is an expansion to calculating channel and customer profitability using ABC principles. This results in ranking the most to least profitable customers. Some of the reasons that differentiate high from low profit customers can jump off the report's pages. For example, excessively frequent orders rather than bundled. The "what do things cost?" is amplified with the "why do things cost?". However, the "why" question that differentiates high from low profit customers is not always is not always easily answered. With analytics' recursive partitioning and decision trees method, the computer can answer why. The customer profit level is a dependent variable. In the customer master file are dozens of other independent variables (e.g., number of sales orders) that can be compared and interpreted as the key differentiators. From that information, profit-lifting actions can be taken.
- Trend number 3 described the shift from the annual budget to rolling financial forecasts using driver-based resources expense modeling methods. It calculates a single point profit forecast. In some cases, three scenarios may be projected with best case, baseline, and lowest case assumptions for a few variables such as sales volume. Why stop with three and just a few variables? Why not estimate on a range of seven estimates for a dozen variables assumptions (e.g., material prices, labor wages). With 7 x 12, then 84 projections can be displayed and rank-order displayed in a profit distribution graph. An example is in Figure X. This moves understanding from possibilities to probabilities. And with such a curve, analysts can better understand what factors most lead to higher profits (other than the obvious sales volume and product mix) and apply sensitivity analysis.

Figure 6.

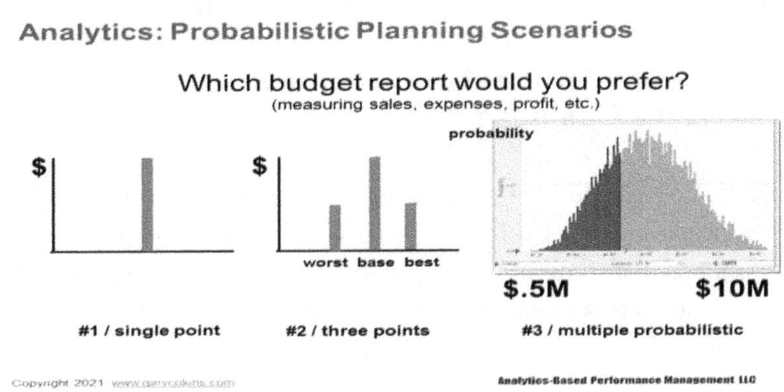

There are dozens of other examples where analytics can support the management accounting function well beyond simple and primitive ratio analysis like sales expense as a percentage of sales. Analytics is here to stay. The buzz about "data scientists" is not hype. Trend number 4 recognizes that progressive accounting functions now realize that competency and capabilities with analytics provides a competitive edge.

Trend Number 5. Co-Existing and Improved Management Accounting Methods

There are debates in the management accounting community about what is the most appropriate costing method. There are rival camps. For example, some lean accounting advocates who create "value stream maps" criticize activity-based costing (ABC) that has passionate advocates because it provides much greater cost accuracy and visibility to cost drivers compared to the flawed and misleading costs from traditional and grotesquely cost distorting cost allocation methods. Who is right?

The trend is to ask a different question that resolves this dilemma. That question is about how to support two or more co-existing management accounting methods. There can be different costs for different purposes used by different types of managers and employee teams. Lean accounting can be used by operational managers to focus on removing waste and increasing profitability. ABC can be used strategically to better understand the sources of what drives enterprise profitability and the linkages of resource expenses to customers.

As described in trend number 3 and Figure x, there are already three broad categories of accounting: (1) tax accounting; (2) external financial accounting (e.g., GAAP) for regulatory compliance and investors; and (3) management accounting. They each calculate different costs of outputs or products. Progressive accounting functions recognize that there can be two or more management accounting methods.

Another trend is a more intelligent way of evaluating which level and type of costing sophistication is required. Under some conditions an organization may not even need to aspire to advanced methods like resource consumption accounting (RCA) or the costing method, throughput accounting, that is a companion to theory of constraints (TOC) advocates. A useful document to assess the question of "Is the climb worth the higher view?" is a report published by the International Federation of Accountants (www.ifac.org) titled "Evaluating the Costing Journey: A Costing Levels Continuum Maturity Framework." Figure 7 displays a multiple stages maturity staircase that organizations can judge if the extra benefits from better accuracy and visibility of costs exceeds the incremental administrative effort to collect, validate, and report the information.

Trend number 5 demonstrates that the more progressive CFOs and their management accounting staff are considering the various needs of different types of managers in their organization.

Trend Number 6. Managing Information Technology and Shared Services as a Business

There is a trend toward using management accounting for internal chargebacks (like an invoice) from service providers to service users. This information also serves for establishing what are effectively "transfer prices" based on cost consumption rates for service level agreements (SLAs).

As background to understand this trend consider these questions. What do some diners do at an "all you can eat" restaurant buffet? They gorge out. What might you do if there are free items at an exhibitor

Figure 7.

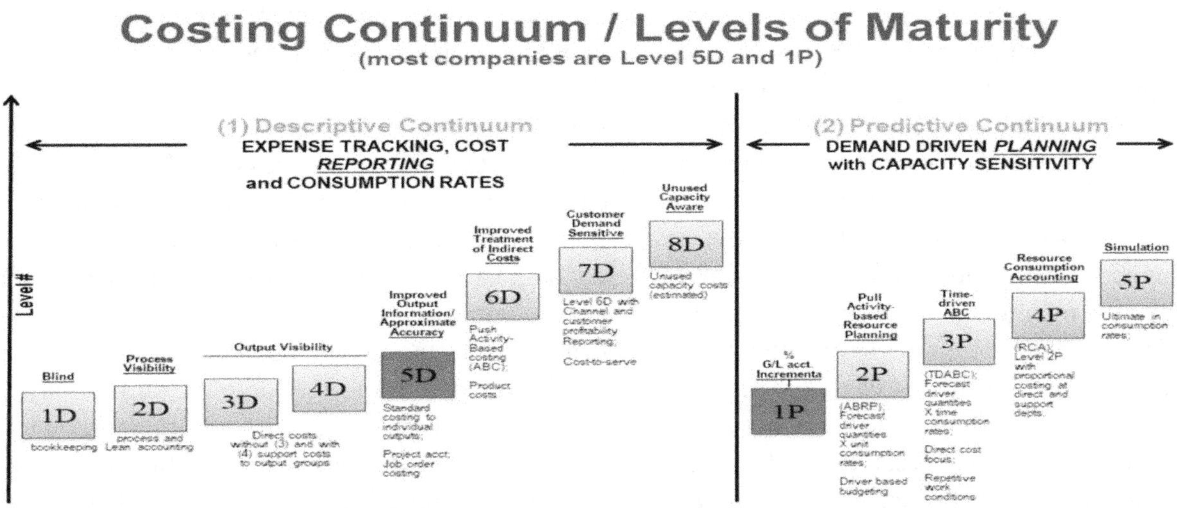

Source: "A Costing Levels Continuum Maturity Model" by Gary Cokins published by the International Federation of Accountants, 2015

booth at a conference? You might take more than one. It is human nature that when something is free one doesn't care how much one consumes whatever the item or service may be.

How is this different when an organization's information technology (IT) or shared services are also free to internal departments? The substantial growth in IT over the past decade has moved IT from being a back-office support function to a critical and strategic function. User demands for faster response times; more information and sophisticated equipment is driving IT spending upwards at an ever increasing rate so that IT now ranks among the top category of expenditures for many organizations. If IT does not in some way internally "charge back" of its expenses or provide "show back" to its users for its services, then expenses will get out of control.

Not surprisingly IT spending has been accelerating and, in some industries, has reached 10% of revenue. After Y2K the increase in IT spending forced increasingly more organizations to focus cost management and performance improvement efforts on their information technology groups. Many of the techniques used in commercial manufacturing and the service industries are now being applied specifically to the IT function. Activity-based cost management (ABC/M) and IT capacity usage reporting systems are being used to develop cost information that is used in both cost management and performance improvement efforts. The use of ABC/M and capacity usage information are supporting multidimensional cost analysis, performance measurement and monitoring, creation of internal IT markets, user/customer cost visibility, driver-based planning, and capacity management. Clearly IT spending can no longer be managed on the back of an envelope."

Having an "internal IT market" is important. When internal shared service providers and their users interact with an understanding of their mutual relationship using fact-based data, then everyone benefits – IT, the user, and the entire organization. Line-item IT charge back invoices not only create a service provider-user market for pricing; but the cost calculations also provide the basis, including service-level rates, for service level agreements (SLAs). SLAs formally document what a user should expect from IT.

With increasing spending and investment in IT comes increased scrutiny, and CIOs are having to demonstrate greater maturity and expertise in IT performance and financial management to reveal how IT money is being spent, the returns their organization are getting for their spending and investments, and how IT is contributing to overall enterprise performance.

IT users who care about their organization's financial health are demanding greater IT cost transparency, visibility, and financial analysis in order for everyone to understand the true costs of IT. CIOs often have difficulty in responding to these demands, and they struggle to easily and clearly communicate the cost of services provided and demonstrate the substantial value that IT brings to their organization. To complicate matters for CIOs chief financial officers (CFOs) are becoming increasingly influential and vigilant in monitoring and even approving IT budgets and purchases.

In the 1990's there were never enough resources, and organizations could not add them fast enough. The needs for IT seemed insatiable. Then shortly after the turn of the century a dramatic shift occurred, and the hungry demand for IT services began to be questioned and challenged. Organizations seemingly had too many IT resources, and they began questioning the value of the money spent in the 1990's. The IT model of the 1990's, 'spend first, ask questions later' is gone and is being replaced by 'ask questions first, spend later'.

An additional problem is CIOs toil when they attempt to track and measure the benefits of the technology after it is implemented. They often lack the insight and information needed to understand the implications of investments, accurately forecast demand and costs, and ensure that any investment provides maximum benefit to the business.

The consequences of failing to implement IT business performance management methods, like ABC/M and KPI scorecard metrics, are often hidden, yet they are substantial. Without performance management methods IT is stumbling in the dark. IT struggles to control its budget, cannot maximize its returns on investment, suffers from increased complexity and cost, and is unable to make sustainable cost reductions. The result is organizations make decisions to implement infrastructure or outsource capabilities with inadequate service cost information that does not support or may even negatively impact strategic goals with suboptimal results. Outsourcers prey on IT organization that do not know their costs and especially those that do not understand the fixed and variable nature of costs.

These pressures are creating a changing role for the CIO to manage IT as a business, to prove the value of IT across its organization, to ensure user-customer satisfaction, and to maximize value from new and existing investments.

IT can no longer be viewed as just a technology supplier. IT must be seen to be adding value to the organization and providing strategic capability. As such, the cost to provide services must be understood and become part of the decision-making process. IT performance management methods allow IT to change the focus from technology and daily "keep the lights on" operations to a focus on its user-customers and services. It enables IT to become service oriented, aligning itself with the organization to provide customer-driven solutions to user problems and opportunities.

These are all reasons why there is this trend number 6 for management accounting to support internal IT and shared services to be managed as a business.

Trend Number 7. The Need for Better Skills and Competency With Behavioral Cost Management

An evolving trend is that activist management accountants, those who are promoting progressive methods as described in the trends already mentioned, are encountering obstacles to get buy-in and acceptance of their ideas. They are realizing they need to improve their behavioral change management skills and capabilities.

As background, a few years ago as I concluded my presentations at seminars, I began asking this question: "Since these management methodologies are so logical, proven and beneficial, why is their adoption rate by organizations so gradual and slow?" Eureka! A flood of replies gushed from people, describing many diverse barriers and obstacles. I found myself personally and increasingly attracted to these "why-not and why-to" discussions in contrast to my "how-to" lectures. They filled an emerging void for me – explaining my frustration with why more organizations were not advancing to a higher level of maturity with management methods.

With hindsight, we now realize that past barriers impeding adoption are easily removable. That is, technical barriers such as disparate data sources or "dirty" data now have software solutions like ETL. EPM component design deficiency barriers, such as how to properly construct a strategy map and select its appropriate KPIs, are broken down with experienced consultants and better training courses.

What type of barrier continues to primarily obstruct the adoption rate of management accounting and EPM methodologies? That barrier category is social, behavioral and cultural. There are many examples of this type obstacle, including people's natural resistance to change; not wanting to be measured or held accountable; fear of knowing the truth (or of someone else knowing it); reluctance to share data or information; and "we don't do that here." When you mention these social, behavioral and cultural examples to project teams or internal champions tasked to explore, evaluate, implement or operate PM solutions, their heads all nod with a "yes! Figure 8 lists the three barriers described here.

Figure 8.

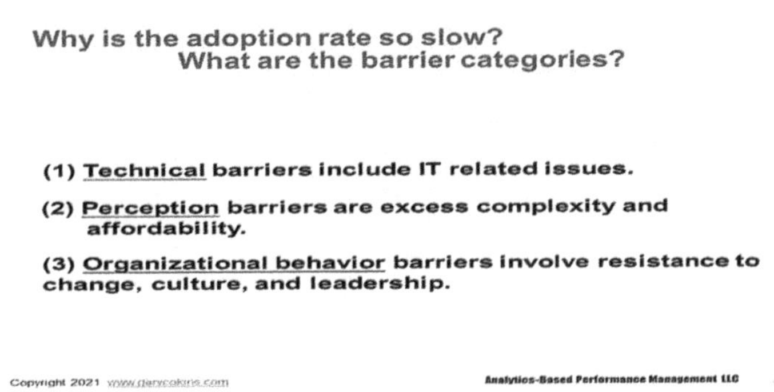

The problem with the final barrier described has been that few management accountants have had adequate training or experience as organizational change management specialists. We are not sociologists. We are not psychologists. However, the trend is that effective management accountants are learning to become like them. They are learning about motivational theory and how to apply it.

During my seminars and discussions with customers, I am more routinely citing the need for executive team leadership with vision and inspiration to drive organizational transformation, not to manage more intensely. This trend number 7 requires change agent management accountants to motivate mid-level managers and other "champions" to demonstrate to their co-workers that progressive management accounting and EPM methodologies make sense to implement. There are personal rewards and satisfaction in explaining the importance of overcoming social, behavioral and cultural barriers for organizations to take next steps.

CONCLUDING REMARKS

This article has been a journey describing seven (7) current trends. Few organizations are pursuing all seven, but years from now the successful organizations will be well along the way with all of them. Will there be future new trends? Of course. If you care to know what my crystal ball is showing me, keep your eye on the role that technology, such as in-memory chip technology with analytics at the "speed of thought," will bring.

PERMISSION STATEMENT

Chapter 10
A Qualitative Research on Sectoral Problems and Expectations

Fahri Özsungur
https://orcid.org/0000-0001-6567-766X
Mersin University, Turkey

Himmet Karadal
Bolu Abant İzzet Baysal University, Turkey

ABSTRACT

This research aims to investigate the sectoral market share of the professional committees, their current status, and expectations in the context of employment. It was determined that the market share of the sectors of 58.55% of the participants decreased in 2019. 46.71% of participants had the prediction that there would be no change in their market share in 2020. 45.39% of the participants anticipated a decrease in employment in 2019, and 58.55% anticipated that there would be no change in employment in 2020. 69.74% of the members of the professional committees participating in the research stated that there was a qualified employee shortage in the sector. The agriculture sector comes to the fore in the required employment areas. Participants stated that qualified employees trained according to the sector should be increased. According to the results, it was determined that there was a need for employment in agricultural products sales, textile, medical equipment, restaurants and cafes, insurance, private health services, advertising and media, paper, and packaging sectors.

INTRODUCTION

Chambers of commerce and industry have an important place in increasing, supporting, and promoting entrepreneurship in today's commercial life (Dawley, Stephens, & Stephens, 2005). Chambers of commerce and industry, which adopt the membership system, enable businesses to gain sustainable competitive advantage (Brown, 1997; Ruder, 2005; Swenson, 1935). These professional organizations, which

DOI: 10.4018/978-1-7998-8069-1.ch010

have key functions such as providing solutions to the sectoral problems of their members, providing the necessary information about investment and incentives, helping to enter new markets by developing the business network, enable enterprises to make self-evaluation by providing services in terms of capacity and performance (Giurgiu, Manciu, & Lese, 2016 Laffey, 1975). These organizations, which provide the promotion of markets and business networks through fairs, help to communicate current issues of legal developments to policymakers (Lacho & Brockmann, 2012; Hong, 2000).

Professional organizations are national and international actors serving their members in today's commercial life (Brown, 1922; Elkins, 1995). The services that organizations provide to their members contribute to the development of commercial life (Ju-zhang, 2006; Kelly, 2005). The strategic structuring of enterprises, the functions of the organs, the service and production sector, and their contribution to employment increase the importance of organizations functioning as chambers of commerce and industry (Curtis & McKenzie, 2002). The professional groups of these professional organizations, which contribute to the development of the local economy with the services they provide to their members, come to the fore (Noel & Luckett, 2014; Wilk, 1940). The professional groups formed by the members and differing according to the sectors play an active role in the formation of the organizational structure of the chambers of commerce and industry. On the other hand, professional groups play an important role in the formation of the vision of this organization (Fox, 2000; Ridgeway, 1938; Min, 2003). It is the duty of these groups to reveal sectoral problems and provide information on economic difficulties (Libbey, 1985; Friedman, 1947; Eisenberg, 2009). For this reason, issues related to entrepreneurship, sectoral problems, lack of incentives and support, production and service-based problems, tax, and legal obligations are brought to the agenda by professional groups (Lacho & Brockmann, 2011; Werking, 1978). For this reason, examining occupational groups in chambers of commerce and industry in the context of sectoral problems will provide employment, market share, professional problems, and solution suggestions.

The aim of this chapter is to reveal the functions of occupational groups in trade and industry chambers and to reveal sectoral problems. The target audience of the chapter is academicians, policymakers, business, and professional organizations study on business, organization, law, policy, management, and strategy. It is thought that the chapter will contribute to the fields of management and strategy, including sectoral studies.

This research aims to investigate the sectoral market share of professional committees (occupational groups), the current situation, and expectations in terms of employment. With the findings to be revealed, recommendations will be made to policymakers, academicians and industry groups. The readership of the chapter includes business, management and organization, sector studies, and law.

BACKGROUND

Sectoral Problems in the Global Crisis

The global economy significantly affects the sustainability of businesses and organizations thanks to new competitive strategies and economic policies (Paunov, 2012). Seeking new markets, the growth rate of businesses and the changing needs of consumers affect the economies of countries (Chowdhury, 2011; Hasan & Dridi, 2011). Especially due to the pandemic that has emerged recently and is a global problem, the economies of many countries have been negatively affected and the economy has come to a decline (Rebmann et al., 2013; Babalola & Babalola, 2013; Sikich, 2008). This problem has turned into a global crisis by negatively affecting the internationalization of businesses (Dalton, 2006; Hanson, Stein, Sunderman, & Zwick, 2020; Cajner et al., 2020; Obal & Gao, 2020). Especially the manufacturing sector is affected by this crisis (Abdallah, 2020; Lenzen et al., 2020).

From a sectoral perspective, the effects of the global crisis lead to a decline in entrepreneurship in the context of developing countries (Colombo et al., 2016; Năstase & Kajanus, 2009). On the other hand, the opportunity to benefit from digital innovations has opened the way for new entrepreneurship ideas (Wiesböck & Hess, 2020; Simmons, Palmer, & Truong, 2013). Businesses try to eliminate the negative effects of the global crisis with innovative ideas about product delivery and supply to consumers (Meristö & Laitinen, 2018). The need for hygiene that emerged due to curfews and the pandemic has led to the emergence of new business areas in the sectoral context. While the healthcare and retail industry benefits from the effects of this global crisis, the service industry is experiencing a significant loss (Laperche, Lefebvre, & Langlet, 2011; Talwar et al., 2020).

The global crisis affects the sectoral management strategies of businesses (De Sausmarez, 2004). Managerially, many stages in the process of the value chain such as supply, logistics, distribution, after-sales services have changed (Fromhold-Eisebith, 2015). Small and medium-sized companies can survive thanks to digital innovations and crisis-oriented management strategies in this process (Shafi, Liu, & Ren, 2020; Verbeke,2020). Hygiene, health, timely delivery to the customer, digital information, environmentally friendly products are becoming more and more important. The supply chain, inspired by these factors and the effects of the global crisis, has changed its management strategies (Zemtsov & Tsareva, 2020). The factors that contribute to the management process from the processing of the raw material to its delivery to the customer have an important function in crisis management (Lee & Harrald, 1999). The sectoral effects that emerged with the effects of the crisis shaped management strategies (Elliott, Swartz, & Herbane, 2010).

Economic recession causes many businesses to change their sectoral status (Powell et al., 2016; Luo, 2013). Adaptation to changing conditions and needs reveals the need for efficient use of resources. Pandemic, war, extreme natural events, migration, economic recession, fluctuations in the exchange rate affect imports and exports negatively in the sector (O'Riordan & Fitzpatrick, 2015). Adaptation to these conditions requires new resources and sustainable management of existing resources. Professional organizations provide an important support service in this regard (Knoke, 2018; Gaumnitz & Lere, 2002). Organizations such as chambers of commerce and chambers of industry play important roles such as identifying the managerial deficiencies of the enterprises and providing resources in meeting the current needs in the global crisis (Tordoir, 2012; Hitt, 1998).

The Relation of Sectoral Problems With Professional Organizations

Sectoral problems are the problems that are among the manufacturing and service main activities of the enterprises and vary regionally (Bucher & Stelling, 1969). These problems are tried to be solved in the management units of the enterprises (Montagna, 1968). However, businesses need a strong network to solve these problems and organizations that will professionally support sectoral issues (Wallace, 1995). These organizations are professional organizations that qualify as public or private law institutions (Abernethy & Stoelwinder, 1995; Hinings,2005).

Professional organizations provide important contributions to many issues such as solving sectoral problems, identifying business problems, eliminating the problems encountered in enterprises entering new markets, promotion, and strategy. In particular, professional organizations where public law is effective to have important support functions in terms of sustainability of enterprises in issues such as providing financial resources, benefiting from incentives, entrepreneurship (Bleiklie, Enders, & Lepori, 2015). These functions enable businesses to gain a sustainable competitive advantage, the development of the regional economy, and the internationalization of businesses (Strauss, 2013; Montagna, 1968). Chambers of commerce are among these professional organizations.

Organizational Structure of Chambers of Commerce and Industry

Chambers of commerce and industry are professional organizations that support their members in the context of professional, commercial, and entrepreneurship (Zainol et al., 2014). These organizations are formed according to the membership system. These organizations, which are organized as companies in England and the USA, have legal structures that differ according to private and public law (Willard, 1899). Membership in the chambers of commerce and industry subject to private law is not compulsory (Minja, 2011). These organizations do not earn a mandatory income for the professional service they provide to their members (Cargill, 1840). Therefore, the principle of volunteerism is essential in such organizations. On the other hand, there is a compulsory membership system for chambers of commerce and industry subject to public law. These organizations collect compulsory service fees for the service they provide to their members. However, regardless of the law, they support businesses and companies, which are members of the common features of chambers of commerce and industry, in matters of law, commerce, financial, promotion, marketing, sustainability, and networking (Xiao-cai, 2006). In addition, these professional organizations are pioneers in the development of the local economy, internationalization, import, and export.

Chambers of commerce and industry mediate relations with the state in solving the problems of their members operating in different sectors (Katz, 2015). Professional problems, financial and employment-related problems are communicated to government and policymakers through these professional organizations. Policymakers can seek opinions on the economy, trade, and many other issues from chambers of commerce and industry subject to public law. On the other hand, courts can get information from these professional organizations about employment-related workers' precedent wages.

The organizational structure of chambers of commerce and industry subject to private or public law varies (Newmark, 1945). Private law professional organizations consist of the general assembly or executive board, supervisory board, and administrative body (Ritchie, 1912). The organizational structure of chambers of commerce and industry subject to public law consists of the chamber council and the board of directors. However, the administrative body of the chamber has a different structure than these two organs. The administrative body consists of the general secretariat, financial affairs, chamber registry, trade registry, foreign trade, and human resources units. The general secretariat is the superior of these units. The board of directors is the chief of the general secretariat.

Chambers of commerce and industry consist of the chamber council (general assembly), the management board, and the general secretary in Turkey. The General Secretariat ensures that the units decided to be established by the chamber council are managed. The chamber council is represented by professional groups formed by the members of the chamber. The chamber council ensures that the board of directors and professional groups are formed. Thus, the representation of members operating according to the sector through professional groups is provided.

Occupational Groups (Professional Committees) in Chambers of Commerce and Industry

Professional committees of chambers of commerce are the people selected for four years by professional groups that deal with sectoral problems and work to produce solutions. Professional committees make proposals to the board of directors to make examinations on their professions, to discuss and resolve the necessary measures, the report by carrying out researches on the information requested by the assembly or the board of directors regarding the practice of their profession (Smith, 1982).

Thus, it enables the chamber to develop itself in a sectoral and professional sense and to become a learning organization (Brockmann & Lacho, 2015). Changing technological infrastructures, developing economy, competitive power in the external environment, sectoral disagreements, and problems, occupational problems are instantly perceived by professional groups and in-chamber information flow is provided by these groups. In terms of ensuring the formation of the council, it ensures that the chamber specializes in terms of professions and sectors and that the management is carried out within the framework of this expertise (Hall, 1969).

The opinions of professional groups are taken to solve many issues such as unemployment, economic turndown, glass ceiling, product and service prices, quality, marketing, advertising, unfair competition among the sectoral problems (Sakchutchawan, 2009; Lacho, 2008). If technical information from the court and official institutions is requested from the chamber, the expert opinion of the professional groups is obtained (Arthur, 2016).

RESEARCH METHODOLOGY

Sample Selection

The research was carried out in February 2020. There was 12 Chamber of Industry, 56 Chamber of Commerce, 182 chamber of commerce and Industry. The sample was determined by choosing Adana province from among the chambers of commerce. According to the Adana Chamber of Commerce data, there are 265 members registered in 46 professions. The study was carried out with 152 professional committee members registered with the Adana Chamber of Commerce. Professional committee meetings are held once a week. For this reason, the study took two weeks and pre-determined research questions were asked to the participants by face-to-face interviews at the profession committee meetings. The research tool consisted of five open-ended questions and demographic information.

Measures and Data Analysis

The phenomenological research method, one of the qualitative research methods, was adopted in the study. This method enables us to reveal information that cannot be obtained with quantitative research instruments. Because the results that are tried to be obtained with pre-determined instruments are limited to the framework determined by the researcher. Phenomenological research provides information about the causes and consequences of the subject under investigation. The research subject can be examined in-depth, especially with open-ended questions. The interpretive phenomenology method, which reveals experiences and perceptions, was applied in this research. This method helps to reveal individual experiences, thoughts, and perceptions about the research subject. In accordance with the research method, the following steps were applied in order:

- Determining the research question with a literature review
- Presenting the theoretical basis and determining the reality of the research question
- Determining the target sample group
- Creation of research instrument
- Recording, compiling, extracting data
- Coding of data and determination of relationships
- Mapping the concepts and creating themes
- Interpretation and reporting

The research questions consist of the following five questions with demographic information:

Research Questions

1. What kind of a change occurred in the market share of your sector in general in 2019? Please explain.
2. What kind of change do you expect in the market share of your sector in 2020? Please explain.
3. How did the employment change in your sector in 2019? Please explain.
4. How will the employment change in your sector in 2020? Please explain.
5. Is there a qualified employee shortage in your sector? Please explain.

Limitations of the Study

The fact that the data of chambers of commerce and industry and chambers of the industry are out of the scope of the research limits the generalizability of the results. Because each province and region may have different sectoral problems. For this reason, it is recommended to conduct the same study in different regions of commerce and industry and to compare the results. In qualitative research, the similarities in the researcher's field of expertise related to the sample may cause bias in determining the research questions and the results to be obtained. In order to eliminate this bias, the data should be analyzed by a researcher from a different field of expertise in addition to the researcher. For this reason, the research data were analyzed by a researcher who is not an expert on chambers of commerce and industry and both results were compared.

Results

Demographic Variables

When the demographic data of the sample population of the study were examined, it was determined that the manufacturing sector (61.8%), high school graduates (69.1%), 36 and over age group (75%), and men (100%) were found to be in majority (Table 1). Women members are limited in chambers of commerce and industry.

Table 1. Demographic information

Variables	Data		Variables	Data	
Basic Sector Type	n	%	*Education Status*	n	%
Service industry	58	38,2	High school graduat	105	69,1
Manufacturing sector	94	61,8	Bachelor's degree	33	21,7
Age range			Master's degree	14	9,2
25-35	38	25,0	*Gender*		
36-46	67	44,1	Woman	0	0
47 and over	47	30,9	Man	152	100

Qualitative Findings

According to the results of the research, it was determined that the market share of the sectors of 58.55% of participants, in general, decreased in 2019, and the market share of 46.71% participants was predicted to not change in 2020 (Table 2).

Table 2. Sectoral market share changes

Changes in the Sectoral Market Share in 2019							
Sector Type	**Growth**		**Stabile**		**Downsizing**		**Total**
	n	%	n	%	n	%	n
All Sectors	18	11,84	45	29,61	89	58,55	152
Service industry	5	8,62	16	27,58	36	63,80	58
Manufacturing industry	13	13,83	29	30,85	53	55,32	94
Expected Change in the Sectoral Market Share for 2020							
Sector Type	**Growth**		**Stabile**		**Downsizing**		**Total**
	n	%	n	%	n	%	n
All Sectors	39	25,66	71	46,71	42	27,63	152
Service industry	17	29,31	27	46,55	15	24,14	58
Manufacturing industry	22	23,40	46	48,93	27	27,67	94

63.80% of the committee members operating in the service sector and 55.32% of the participants operating in the production sector stated that the market share in the sector decreased in 2019. The changes in market share in all sectors in 2019 are shown in Figure 1.

The participants who thought that the expectation of change in the sectoral market share for 2020 would maintain the current situation was 46.71%. 46.55% of the participants operating in the service sector and 48.93% of the members operating in the manufacturing sector stated that there would be no change in the market share for 2020. The expectation of change in all sectors in the market share in 2020 is shown in figure 2.

Figure 1. Sectoral market share change chart in 2019

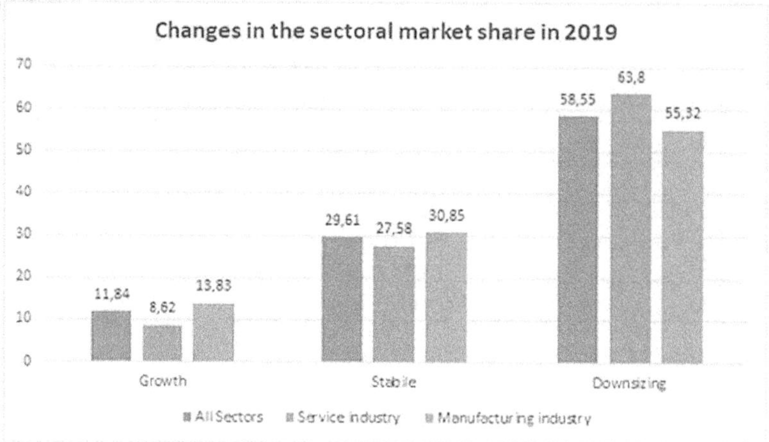

Figure 2. Sectoral market share change expectation chart

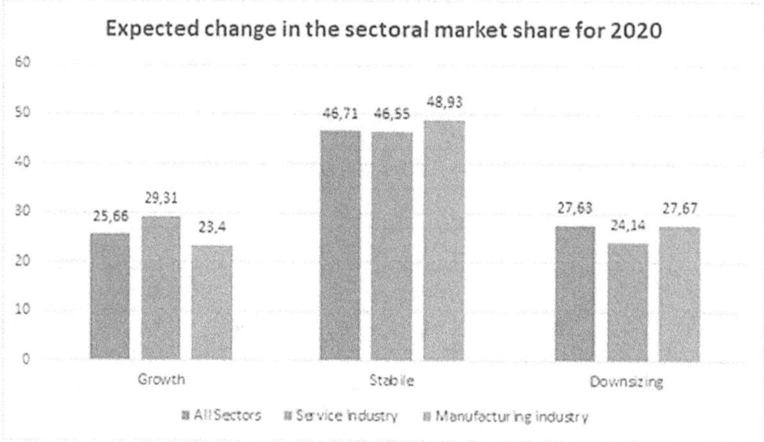

45.39% of the participants anticipated a decrease in employment in 2019 and 58.55% of them that there would be no change in employment in 2020 (Table 3).

Half of the participants operating in the service sector in 2019 and 42.55% of the participants operating in the production sector stated that employment decreased. The changes in all sectors in employment in 2019 are shown in Figure 3.

In the context of the employment expectation for 2020, 60.34% of the service sector and 57.44% of the manufacturing sector participants stated that the decrease in employment would remain. The expectation of change in employment in all sectors in 2020 is shown in Figure 4.

69.74% of the members of the profession committees participating in the research stated that there was a qualified personnel shortage in the sector. Those who stated that there was no qualified personnel shortage in the sector were 30.26% (Figure 5). In the interviews with the participants, it was stated that the vocational training given to the employees was insufficient. On the other hand, the low demand for the employees for the manufacturing sector was emphasized.

Table 3. Employment changes

Changes in Employment in 2019							
Sector Type	Increase		Stabile		Decrease		Total
	n	%	n	%	n	%	n
All Sectors	15	9,87	68	44,74	69	45,39	152
Service industry	4	6,90	25	43,10	29	50,00	58
Manufacturing industry	11	11,70	43	45,75	40	42,55	94
Employment-related Change Forecast for 2020							
Sector Type	Increase		Stabile		Decrease		Total
	n	%	n	%	n	%	n
All Sectors	29	19,08	89	58,55	34	22,37	152
Service industry	12	20,69	35	60,34	11	18,97	58
Manufacturing industry	17	18,08	54	57,44	23	24,48	94

Figure 3. 2019 employment change chart

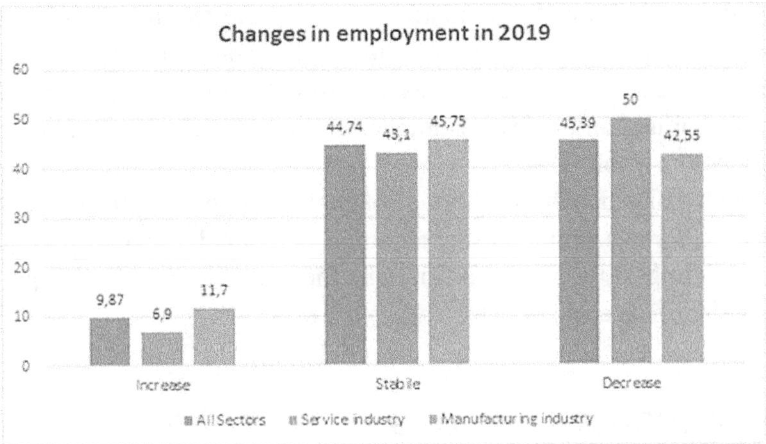

Figure 4. 2019 employment change expectation chart

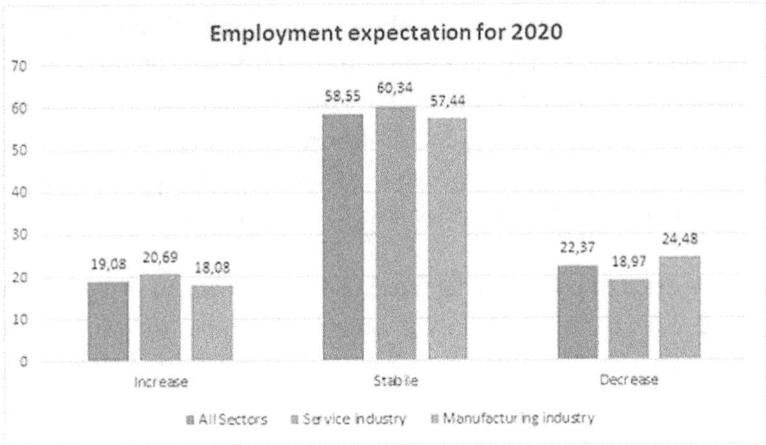

Figure 5. Qualified employee deficit chart

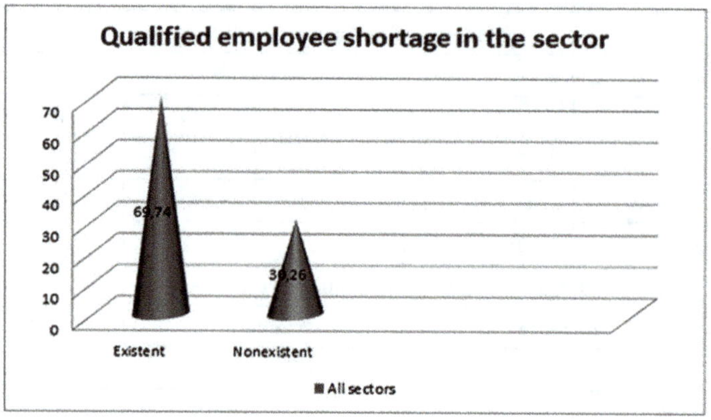

Required Employment Fields

Participants were asked about the fields of employment needed. According to the codes obtained as a result of the analysis, the agriculture sector stands out among the required employment fields. Participants stated that qualified employees trained according to the sector should be increased. According to the results, it was determined that employment was needed in the sales of agricultural products, textiles, medical equipment, restaurants and cafes, insurance, private health services, advertising and media, paper, and packaging sectors (table 4).

Research results showed that there was a shortage of qualified personnel to be employed in production. Participants expressed their views on increasing technical personnel, especially for product production. On the other hand, according to the research findings, there was a shortage of qualified personnel in sales and marketing in the service sector.

SOLUTIONS AND RECOMMENDATIONS

Economic problems, which are shown as the reasons for the contraction in market share in all sectors, need to be improved in terms of businesses. Measures should be taken to prevent a decrease in equity in enterprises by adopting a balanced exchange rate policy. Unfair competition control should be increased, and the factors preventing entrepreneurship should be removed from the sectoral point of view. Especially in the service sector, it is necessary to identify the enterprises with resource problems for new enterprises due to the lack of liquidity and to provide the necessary resources/support.

Measures should be taken to eliminate imbalances in expenditures related to basic activities that arise in operating expenses in the manufacturing sector. Necessary consultancy services can be provided by the chambers and the state.

Policies should be developed to prevent a decrease in employment. It is recommended to implement policies that will increase and develop the equity of enterprises rather than incentives in employment.

Table 4. Employment shortage fields by occupational groups

Sector	Occupational Group	Employment Shortage
Manufacturing	Cereals, legumes, grains, seeds, etc.	The agricultural sector, production planning, quality control, pattern preparation operator
Manufacturing	Shoemakers, bag sellers	Qualified personnel in production
Manufacturing	Machinery and hardware	Intermediate personnel, mechanical machine operator, machine operator
Manufacturing	Agricultural pesticides and fertilizers	Pruning, spraying
Manufacturing and Service	Elevator and air conditioning	Elevator maintenance master, Turkey Natural Gas Distributors Association certified gas workers, combi boiler, and natural gas appliances, air conditioning
Manufacturing and Service	Auto spare parts	Masters who know the business with ethical principles
Manufacturing	Furniture, furnishings, carpet	R&D, design, machinist, assembly staff
Manufacturing and Service	Stationery, paper, packaging	Packaging, sales marketing, technical machinist
Manufacturing and Service	Medical equipment, medical, pharmaceutical warehouses	sales and marketing, technical service personnel, personnel with biomedical technical knowledge
Manufacturing and Service	Fabric, textiles	Home textile sales staff
Manufacturing and Service	Garments, haberdashery	pattern operator, garment machine operator, sales and marketing, cutting operator, machine operator
Service	Food and beverage service providers	Qualified personnel in production
Service	Advertising and media activities	Shipping, marketing
Service	Insurance	Insurance personnel, qualified technical personnel
Service	Private health institutions	Qualified health personnel

FUTURE RESEARCH DIRECTIONS

For future studies, it is recommended to work with professional groups in other provinces and regions. Renewing this study, which was carried out especially before the impact of the COVID 19 pandemic, to reveal the situation after the pandemic, and making recommendations by making necessary comparisons will contribute to the literature and practice. It is recommended that awareness and studies in this direction should be increased since the occupational groups represent the sectors they are affiliated with.

CONCLUSION

Chambers are professional non-profit organizations and they take the necessary initiatives for the development of the economy. Chambers of public or private law entities play an important role in communicating economic or social problems to government officials (Loi, 2010). The fact that a member of the professional groups is the head of the chamber reflects the image of the chamber as a leader and provides the necessary initiatives to solve problems effectively and efficiently through social relations.

Businesses need credit and financial support for sustainable competition and the necessary financing source. Chambers of commerce and industry provide the necessary opportunities to access these financing sources. Chambers balance the risks of trust related to cooperation and prevent the negative impact of competition on cooperation (Bunger, 2013). Gaining competitive advantage for small businesses and providing access to national and international markets through fairs and events provide significant improvements in terms of economy and development (Newton, 1977).

The transparent presentation of the social and business network of the chambers of commerce provides assistance to individuals and non-governmental organizations that will provide the expected benefit from the network. In addition to social benefit communication networks, interaction, psychological benefits, chambers provide strategic innovations, new initiatives, business opportunities, and various opportunities for small businesses and individuals (Faems, Van Looy, & Debackere, 2005; Newton, 1977).

Crawford and Branch (2015) demonstrated in their qualitative study that rural chambers of commerce represent a unique example of emerging public-private partnerships that challenge the traditional commercial logic of chambers of commerce. Fallon and Brown (1999) discussed and compared various aspects of the British, French, and German Chambers of Commerce to assess whether the transition to public law status for the British Chambers of Commerce would be in the interests of the UK.

This study reveals the problems of sector representatives within the chamber of commerce. In the overall evaluation of the sectors in 2019, It was determined that there was a large downsizing (58.55%) in the market share; the service sector (63.80%) was more downsized than the manufacturing sector (55.32%); the manufacturing sector (13.83%) was grown more than the service sector (8.62%).

In the sectoral market share expectations for the year 2020, it was expected to maintain the current situation at a rate of almost 50% in all sectors. According to qualitative research results regarding the downsizing in market share and maintain the current situation for 2020, the sector representatives were asked the reasons for these results. According to the responses of the sector representatives, fluctuations in the exchange rate decreases in the value of the Turkish Lira, sudden changes in loan interest rates affected the raw material and labor market negatively. It was stated that product and service pricing could not be increased on time in proportion to these sudden changes.

Unfair competition is increasing gradually. It was stated that the sectoral control of competition should be increased by the state. According to the results regarding the employment changes in 2019, a decrease of almost 50% occurred in all sectors. In this decrease, the service sector (50%) had a higher share than the production sector (42.55%). In 2019, employment increased more in the production sector (11.70%) compared to the service sector (6.90%).

For the year 2020, an increase or decrease in employment is not expected in all sectors. In this expectation, the service (60.34%) and production (57.44%) sectors are close to each other. According to the data obtained from sector representatives, this decrease in employment is associated with capital decreases and losses of enterprises. Insufficiency of existing resources of enterprises and a decrease in equity constitute an important problem in meeting the expenses. Especially the service sector faces a resource problem for new enterprises due to the lack of assets (liquidity) that can be easily converted into money.

In the manufacturing sector, investment expenditures made for functions that include the service element do not cover the expenses arising from this factor. The increase in customer expectations towards the service sector increases the expenditures made on the units of this sector.

On the other hand, promotion expenses have become a necessity in the face of increasing competition. Thus, in operating expenses, the expenses of marketing, sales, and service basic activities prevent procurement, operation, and shipment. Due to these spending and expense imbalances, spending on support activities such as procurement, human resources, and business infrastructure development is restricted.

ACKNOWLEDGMENT

This research received no specific grant from any funding agency in the public, commercial, or not-for-profit sectors.

REFERENCES

Abdallah, A. (2020). The Effect Of Corona Pandemic On Workers' Psychology And Performance In The Manufacturing Sector. *Systematic Reviews in Pharmacy*, *11*(12), 1593–1599.

Abernethy, M. A., & Stoelwinder, J. U. (1995). The role of professional control in the management of complex organizations. *Accounting, Organizations and Society*, *20*(1), 1–17. doi:10.1016/0361-3682(94)E0017-O

Arthur, J. W. (2016). *The Seventeenth Highland Light Infantry (Glasgow Chamber of Commerce Battalion) (WWI Centenary Series)*. Read Books Ltd.

Babalola, D., & Babalola, Y. (2013). Economic effects of media campaign against pandemic diseases: The case of bird flu (H5N1) on poultry business in Ogun state, Nigeria. *Oman Chapter of Arabian Journal of Business and Management Review*, *34*(982), 1–9. doi:10.12816/0002364

Bleiklie, I., Enders, J., & Lepori, B. (2015). Organizations as penetrated hierarchies: Environmental pressures and control in professional organizations. *Organization Studies*, *36*(7), 873–896. doi:10.1177/0170840615571960

Brockmann, E. N., & Lacho, K. J. (2015). Benefits of chamber of commerce membership: Large vs. small population centers. *The Entrepreneurial Executive*, *20*, 31–38.

Brown, A. C. (1922). What the Chamber of Commerce Can Do in Promoting Better Industrial Relations in a Community. *Proceedings of the Academy of Political Science in the City of New York*, *9*(4), 210–217. doi:10.2307/1172300

Brown, D. R. (1997). Sustainability is not about money!: The case of the belize chamber of commerce and industry. *Development in Practice*, 185–189.

Bucher, R., & Stelling, J. (1969). Characteristics of professional organizations. *Journal of Health and Social Behavior*, *10*(1), 3–15. doi:10.2307/2948501 PMID:5776946

Bunger, A. (2013). Administrative coordination in nonprofit human service delivery networks: The role of competition and trust. *Nonprofit and Voluntary Sector Quarterly*, *42*(6), 1155–1175. doi:10.1177/0899764012451369 PMID:25349468

Cajner, T., Crane, L. D., Decker, R. A., Grigsby, J., Hamins-Puertolas, A., Hurst, E., . . . Yildirmaz, A. (2020). The US labor market during the beginning of the pandemic recession (No. w27159). National Bureau of Economic Research.

Cargill, W. (1840). *Address of William Cargill, Esq. to the South Shields Chamber of Commerce, May 4, 1840, on the foreign policy of England*. T. Brettell.

Chowdhury, S. R. (2011). Impact of global crisis on small and medium enterprises. *Global Business Review*, *12*(3), 377–399. doi:10.1177/097215091101200303

Colombo, M. G., Piva, E., Quas, A., & Rossi-Lamastra, C. (2016). How high-tech entrepreneurial ventures cope with the global crisis: Changes in product innovation and internationalization strategies. *Industry and Innovation*, *23*(7), 647–671. doi:10.1080/13662716.2016.1196438

Crawford, B., & Branch, J. (2015). Interest plurality and institutional work: An ethnography of rural community organizing. *Journal of Organizational Ethnography*, *4*(1), 98–116. doi:10.1108/JOE-10-2013-0018

Curtis, D., & McKenzie, P. (2002). *Employability skills for Australian industry: literature review and framework development. Report to: Business Council of Australia; Australian Chamber of Commerce and Industry*. Science and Training.

Dalton, C. B. (2006). Business continuity management and pandemic influenza. *New South Wales Public Health Bulletin*, *17*(10), 138–141. doi:10.1071/NB06035 PMID:17293894

Dawley, D. D., Stephens, R. D., & Stephens, D. B. (2005). Dimensionality of organizational commitment in volunteer workers: Chamber of commerce board members and role fulfillment. *Journal of Vocational Behavior*, *67*(3), 511–525. doi:10.1016/j.jvb.2004.09.001

De Sausmarez, N. (2004). Malaysia's response to the Asian financial crisis: Implications for tourism and sectoral crisis management. *Journal of Travel & Tourism Marketing*, *15*(4), 217–231. doi:10.1300/J073v15n04_01

Eisenberg, T. (2009). US Chamber of Commerce liability survey: Inaccurate, unfair, and bad for business. *Journal of Empirical Legal Studies*, *6*(4), 969–1002. doi:10.1111/j.1740-1461.2009.01155.x

Elkins, D. R. (1995). The structure and context of the urban growth coalition: The view from the chamber of commerce. *Policy Studies Journal: the Journal of the Policy Studies Organization*, *23*(4), 583–600. doi:10.1111/j.1541-0072.1995.tb00536.x

Elliott, D., Swartz, E., & Herbane, B. (2010). *Business Continuity Management 2e: A Crisis Management Approach*. Routledge.

Faems, D., Van Looy, B., & Debackere, K. (2005). Interorganizational collaboration and innovation: Toward a portfolio approach. *Journal of Product Innovation Management*, *22*(3), 238–250. doi:10.1111/j.0737-6782.2005.00120.x

Fallon, G., & Brown, R. B. (2000). Does Britain need public law status Chambers of Commerce? *European Business Review*, *12*(1), 19–27. doi:10.1108/09555340010307521

Feng. (2006). Recent Research On The History Of The Chamber Of Commerce. *Journal of Huazhong Normal University (Humanities and Social Sciences), 5.*

Feng. (2006). The Limits of Enterprise Cooperative Network-Chamber of Commerce as an Example. *China Industrial Economy, 1.*

Fox, J. (2000). Common Sense in Shanghai: The General Chamber of Commerce and Political Legitimacy in Republican China. *History Workshop Journal*, *50*(1), 22–44. doi:10.1093/hwj/2000.50.22

Friedman, L. M. (1947). The first chamber of commerce in the United States. *Bulletin of the Business Historical Society*, *21*(5), 137–143. doi:10.2307/3111178

Fromhold-Eisebith, M. (2015). Sectoral resilience: Conceptualizing industry-specific spatial patterns of interactive crisis adjustment. *European Planning Studies*, *23*(9), 1675–1694. doi:10.1080/09654313.2015.1047329

Gaumnitz, B. R., & Lere, J. C. (2002). Contents of codes of ethics of professional business organizations in the United States. *Journal of Business Ethics*, *35*(1), 35–49. doi:10.1023/A:1012718103007

Giurgiu, A. M., Manciu, I., & Lese, I. (2016). Technological Development–A Tool for Social and Economic Impact of the Chamber of Commerce and Industry of Mures County. *Procedia Technology*, *22*, 1092–1099. doi:10.1016/j.protcy.2016.01.154

Hall, D. R. (1969). *Cooperative lobbying: The power of pressure*. University of Arizona Press.

Hanson, S., Stein, J., Sunderman, A., & Zwick, E. (2020). (forthcoming). Business Credit Programs in the Pandemic Era. *Brookings Papers on Economic Activity*.

Hasan, M., & Dridi, J. (2011). The effects of the global crisis on Islamic and conventional banks: A comparative study. *Journal of International Commerce. Economic Policy*, *2*(02), 163–200.

Hinings, B. (2005). The changing nature of professional organizations. The Oxford handbook of work and organization. doi:10.1093/oxfordhb/9780199299249.003.0021

Hitt, M. A. (1998). Twenty-first-century organizations: Business firms, business schools, and the academy. *Academy of Management Review*, *23*(2), 218–224. doi:10.5465/amr.1998.533223

Hong, L. (2000). The Singapore Chinese Chamber of Commerce and Industry And the Institutionalization of Chinese Business Networks in Asia. *Historical Recearch, 1.*

Katz, A. (2015). *The Influence Machine: The U.S. Chamber of Commerce and the Corporate Capture of American Life*. Random House Publishing Group.

Kelly, D. (2005). The international chamber of commerce. *New Political Economy*, *10*(2), 259–271. doi:10.1080/13563460500144868

Knoke, D. (2018). *Changing organizations: Business networks in the new political economy*. Routledge. doi:10.4324/9780429501753

Lacho, K. J. (2008). Government affairs activities of chambers of commerce. In *Allied Academies International Conference. Academy of Legal, Ethical and Regulatory Issues Proceedings*, *12*(1), 11.

Lacho, K. J., & Brockmann, E. N. (2011). Promoting a small business through the services of a chamber of commerce: One chamber's story. *The Entrepreneurial Executive*, *16*, 1.

Lacho, K. J., & Brockmann, E. N. (2012). Improving the business skills of the small business owner through the educational services of a chamber of commerce: One chamber's story. In *Allied Academies International Conference. Academy of Entrepreneurship Proceedings*, *18*(1), 55.

Laffey, J. F. (1975). Municipal Imperialism in France: The Lyon Chamber of Commerce, 1900-1914. *Proceedings of the American Philosophical Society*, *119*(1), 8–23.

Laperche, B., Lefebvre, G., & Langlet, D. (2011). Innovation strategies of industrial groups in the global crisis: Rationalization and new paths. *Technological Forecasting and Social Change*, *78*(8), 1319–1331. doi:10.1016/j.techfore.2011.03.005

Lee, Y. J., & Harrald, J. R. (1999). Critical issue for business area impact analysis in business crisis management: Analytical capability. *Disaster Prevention and Management: an International Journal*, *8*(3), 184–189. doi:10.1108/09653569910275382

Lenzen, M., Li, M., Malik, A., Pomponi, F., Sun, Y. Y., Wiedmann, T., ... Gómez-Paredes, J. (2020). Global socio-economic losses and environmental gains from the Coronavirus pandemic. *PLoS One*, *15*(7), e0235654. doi:10.1371/journal.pone.0235654 PMID:32645023

Libbey, J. K. (1985). The American-Russian Chamber of Commerce. *Diplomatic History*, *9*(3), 233–248. doi:10.1111/j.1467-7709.1985.tb00534.x

Loi, K. M. (2010). *The Perception of Ethics and Social Responsibility of Malaysian International Chamber of Commerce and Industry Corporate Members in Relation to ISO 26000-Social Responsibility Adoption* (Doctoral dissertation). Universiti Utara Malaysia.

Luo, J. (2013). Which industries to bail out first in economic recession? Ranking US industrial sectors by the power-of-pull. *Economic Systems Research*, *25*(2), 157–169. doi:10.1080/09535314.2013.775111

Maxwell, J. A. (1996). *Qualitative Research Design: An Interactive Approach*. SAGE Publications.

Meristö, T., & Laitinen, J. (2018). Digital Innovations: Opportunity to Elderly People? *Proceedings of the ISPIM Connects Fukuoka 2018*.

Min, M. A. (2003). The Study of Chamber of Commerce History and the Paradigm Change of New Historiography. *Journal of Central China Normal University (Humanities and Social Sciences), 5*.

Minja, U. S. (2011). *Factors Influencing Lab our Turnover In Private Sector Organizations In Tanzania: A Case Study Of Chamber Of Commerce, Industry And Agriculture* (Doctoral dissertation). Open University of Tanzania.

Montagna, P. D. (1968). Professionalization and bureaucratization in large professional organizations. *American Journal of Sociology*, *74*(2), 138–145. doi:10.1086/224616

Năstase, C., & Kajanus, M. (2009). The impact of the global crisis on SME and entrepreneurship behavior–Romania and Finland cases. *Amfiteatru Economic*, *3*, 752–753.

Newmark, M. R. (1945). A Short History of The Los Angeles Chamber of Commerce. *The Quarterly: Historical Society of Southern California*, *27*(2-3), 56–79. doi:10.2307/41169698

Newton, R. C. (1977). *German Buenos Aires, 1900–1933: Social Change and Cultural Crisis*. University of Texas Press.

Noel, N. M., & Luckett, M. (2014). The benefits, satisfaction, and perceived value of small business membership in a chamber of commerce. *International Journal of Nonprofit and Voluntary Sector Marketing*, *19*(1), 27–39. doi:10.1002/nvsm.1485

O'Riordan, M., & Fitzpatrick, F. (2015). The impact of economic recession on infection prevention and control. *The Journal of Hospital Infection*, *89*(4), 340–345. doi:10.1016/j.jhin.2014.11.020 PMID:25639208

Obal, M., & Gao, T. (2020). Managing business relationships during a pandemic: Conducting a relationship audit and developing a path forward. *Industrial Marketing Management*, *88*, 247–254. doi:10.1016/j.indmarman.2020.05.025

Orgill, M. (2012). *Phenomenography. Encyclopedia of the Sciences of Learning*. Springer.

Paunov, C. (2012). The global crisis and firms' investments in innovation. *Research Policy*, *41*(1), 24–35. doi:10.1016/j.respol.2011.07.007

Powell, J. L., Chen, S., Pape, U., Chaves-Ávila, R., Pahl, J. B., Petrella, F., ... Savall-Morera, T. (2016). Working under pressure: Economic recession and third sector development in Europe. *The International Journal of Sociology and Social Policy*, *36*(7/8), 547–566. doi:10.1108/IJSSP-05-2016-0061

Rebmann, T., Wang, J., Swick, Z., Reddick, D., & delRosario, J. L. Jr. (2013). Business continuity and pandemic preparedness: US health care versus non-health care agencies. *American Journal of Infection Control*, *41*(4), e27–e33. doi:10.1016/j.ajic.2012.09.010 PMID:23337305

Ridgeway, G. L. (1938). Merchants of Peace. Twenty Years of Business Diplomacy through the International Chamber of Commerce, 1919–1938. *American Journal of Physical Medicine & Rehabilitation*, *17*(5), 350.

Ritchie, R. (1912). The modern chamber of commerce. *National Municipal Review*, *1*(2), 161–169. doi:10.1002/ncr.4110010201

Ruder, D. S. (2005). Balancing Investor Protection with Capital Formation Needs After the SEC Chamber of Commerce Case. *Pace Law Review*, *26*, 39.

Sakchutchawan, S. (2009). An inquiry into the strict compliance of the international chamber of commerce trade rules in financing process. *Global Journal of International Business Research*, *2*(2), 1.

Shafi, M., Liu, J., & Ren, W. (2020). Impact of COVID-19 pandemic on micro, small, and medium-sized Enterprises operating in Pakistan. *Research in Globalization*, *2*, 100018. doi:10.1016/j.resglo.2020.100018

Sikich, G. W. (2008). *Protecting Your Business in a Pandemic: Plans, Tools, and Advice for Maintaining Business Continuity*. Greenwood Publishing Group.

Simmons, G., Palmer, M., & Truong, Y. (2013). Inscribing value on business model innovations: Insights from industrial projects commercializing disruptive digital innovations. *Industrial Marketing Management*, *42*(5), 744–754. doi:10.1016/j.indmarman.2013.05.010

Smith, J. A. (2004). Reflecting on the development of interpretative phenomenological analysis and its contribution to qualitative research in psychology. *Qualitative Research in Psychology*, *1*(1), 39–54.

Smith, J. A., Flowers, P., & Larkin, M. (2009). *Interpretative Phenomenological Analysis: Theory, Method and Research*. Sage.

Smith, S. R. (1982). The centenary of the London Chamber of Commerce: Its origins and early policy. *The London Journal*, *8*(2), 156–170. doi:10.1179/ldn.1982.8.2.156

Strauss, P. L. (2013). Private Standards Organizations and Public Law. *Wm. & Mary Bill Rts. J.*, *22*, 497.

Swenson, R. J. (1935). The Chamber of Commerce and the New Deal. *The Annals of the American Academy of Political and Social Science*, *179*(1), 136–143. doi:10.1177/000271623517900118

Talwar, M., Talwar, S., Kaur, P., Tripathy, N., & Dhir, A. (2020). Has financial attitude impacted the trading activity of retail investors during the COVID-19 pandemic? *Journal of Retailing and Consumer Services*, *58*, 102341. doi:10.1016/j.jretconser.2020.102341

Tordoir, P. (2012). *The professional knowledge economy: The management and integration of professional services in business organizations*. Springer Science & Business Media.

Verbeke, A. (2020). Will the COVID-19 pandemic really change the governance of global value chains? *British Journal of Management*, *31*(3), 444–446. doi:10.1111/1467-8551.12422

Walcott, H. F. (1994). *Transforming Qualitative Data: Description, Analysis and Interpretation*. SAGE Publications.

Wallace, J. E. (1995). Organizational and professional commitment in professional and nonprofessional organizations. *Administrative Science Quarterly*, *40*(2), 228–255. doi:10.2307/2393637

Werking, R. H. (1978). Bureaucrats, Businessmen, and Foreign Trade: The Origins of the United States Chamber of Commerce. *Business History Review*, *52*(3), 321–341. doi:10.2307/3113734

Wiesböck, F., & Hess, T. (2020). Digital innovations. *Electronic Markets*, *30*(1), 75–86. doi:10.100712525-019-00364-9

Wilk, K. (1940). International organization and the international chamber of commerce. *Political Science Quarterly*, *55*(2), 231–248. doi:10.2307/2143913

Willard, C. D. (1899). *A History of the Chamber of Commerce of Los Angeles, California: From Its Foundation, September, 1888, to the Year 1900*. Kingsley-Barnes & Neuner.

Zainol, F. A., Wan Daud, W. N., Abdullah, Z., & Yaacob, M. R. (2014). Social entrepreneurship via corporate waqf: A case of Islamic chamber of commerce (ICC) in Malaysia. *Global Journal of Commerce & Management Perspective*, *3*(5), 50–53.

Zemtsov, S., & Tsareva, Y. (2020). Development trends of small and medium-sized enterprises amid pandemic-induced crisis. *IEP*, (9), 16–26.

ADDITIONAL READING

Craig, W. L., Park, W. W., & Paulsson, J. (2001). *International chamber of commerce arbitration*. Oxford University Press.

Dawley, D. D., Stephens, R. D., & Stephens, D. B. (2005). Dimensionality of organizational commitment in volunteer workers: Chamber of commerce board members and role fulfillment. *Journal of Vocational Behavior*, *67*(3), 511–525. doi:10.1016/j.jvb.2004.09.001

Kelly, D. (2005). The international chamber of commerce. *New Political Economy*, *10*(2), 259–271. doi:10.1080/13563460500144868

Özsungur, F. (2019). A research on women's entrepreneurship motivation: Sample of Adana Province. *Women's Studies International Forum*, *74*, 114–126. doi:10.1016/j.wsif.2019.03.006

Özsungur, F., & Karadal, H. (2020). Chambers of Commerce and Industry. *Sci J Research & Rev.*, *2*(3), 1–8.

KEY TERMS AND DEFINITIONS

Chamber of Commerce: Professional organizations that provide their members to share professional knowledge, provide financial and consultancy support to their members by closely following commercial developments, contribute to the development of the economy on a micro and macro scale by helping their members enter new markets, and whose legal structure differs from country to country in the context of public and private law legal entities.

Chamber of Industry: Professional organizations whose legal structure differs from country to country in the context of public and private law legal entities that contribute to the sectoral and financial development of manufacturing-oriented member enterprises and contribute to the development of their members in the context of entrepreneurship and management strategies.

Employment-Related Change: Percentage change in employment in one year.

Global Crisis: Events such as war, economic decline, pandemic, extreme natural events that affect all countries in economic, social, cultural, political, and many other issues.

Occupational Groups (Professional Committees): The people selected for four years by professional groups that deal with sectoral problems and work to produce solutions in chambers of commerce.

Qualified Employee Deficit: The low number of employees with professional qualifications in a particular sector.

Sectoral Market Share: The share of businesses in national and international markets by sectors.

Sectoral Problems: Problems related to factors such as economic, political, management, production, and service that arise in the predominant activity areas of enterprises.

Chapter 11
A Vision Regarding the Role of Financial-Accounting Practices in Tourism

Traian Ovidiu Calotă
Titu Maiorescu University, Romania

ABSTRACT

The primary role of general management's professionalism depends, to a large extent, on the correct assessment of the value of using the accounting information provided by the accounting management and, respectively, the efficient use in the decision-making process. What is extremely important is the fact that this process must be seen as in a continuously dynamic, as well as the fact that the options used must be in line with the permanent flow of opportunities that must be notified in time and exploited in the interest of economic entities. In the author's opinion, this aspect is predilection specific to tourism activities, with an important impact on success in this type of business. Thus, the opportunities are manifested and often start from them, from the start-up phase of a business, when the capital contribution will be made according to the perspectives opened by these opportunities, and then the construction of the tourist entity itself (including the system information-accounting) will be influenced by this.

INTRODUCTION

The existence and adopting various options in the organization and functioning accounting information system of tourist establishments as a benchmark requirement must fulfill three basic functions: decision-making and operational documentation. This opinion is based on two major considerations. So first, "information is the result of a complex process by which certain data are given meaning state or dynamics of an object, phenomenon or event in the formal procedures for processing" (Ahrens, 2008). Second, in tourism, information must respond to changing competitive conditions to be eliminated vulnerable points competition and increase efficiency of operations in general and especially those generating profit (Andon, Baxter & Chua, 2007).

DOI: 10.4018/978-1-7998-8069-1.ch011

Based on these considerations, but also by the definition, in practical terms, accounting as "an integrated system of techniques and tools for the collection, processing, transmission, use and storage of information on the financial position and performance of the organization strictly necessary managerial decision "(Baker & Bettner, 1997; Barth, M., Landsman, W., & Lang, 2008), we come to the obvious fact that for each type of transaction opens the possibility to configure and use different policies for the organization and functioning accounting information system. Also, the objective of continuously increasing the efficiency of organization and functioning accounting information may follow different paths and different ways depending on the achievement of feed-back (Byard, Li & Yu, 2011; Damayant, T. (2013; Florou & Pope, 2012; Jackson, S. B., & Liu, 2010; Ramanna, 2008; Vladu, Amat & Cuzdriorean, 2016).

The elements mentioned are of great importance and indicates that tourism operators "must cope with strong influences of the internal environment and the external complexity of the relationship established with clients" (Richardson, 2011; Lukka, 2010; He, Pan & Tian, 2017; Cahan & Sun, 2015). Therefore, the information system components accounting must target the internal environment and the external entity, the main sources of data and information, which are processed by a computer system properly (hard and soft), to be made available to users (internal and external), through whose feedback will be done at the end, closing the cycle of information flows (Arsenault & Faerman, 2014; Barth, 2013; Caylor, 2010; Hou, Jin, Yang, Yuan & Zhang, 2015; Parker, 2012).

Competitive advantage in tourism resulting from fundamental value that a company is able to create for its buyers so as to be greater than the costs incurred by the firm for its creation. Value is what buyers are willing to pay and the higher value is derived from offering lower prices than competitors for equivalent benefits, or providing unique benefits which more than offset a higher price (Dennis, 2014; Ball, 2013; Brown, 2010; Fan, Li & Zheng, 2016).

There were obtained representation sufficiently objective and detailed their company's competitive position compared with that of competitors, and the factors that determine a positive or negative competitive strength of the company and thus its position (Schleicher, Tahoun & Walker, 2010; Doukakis, 2014; Allen & Ramanna, 2013).

Coordination requires the harmonization of decision-making at all hierarchical levels (where tourism and the entire flow, from receiving guests until the end of your stay). This means preventing any action that may lead to disturbances and disruption, with a negative impact on business activity (Barth, Landsman, Young & Zhuang, 2014). As a result, management should be an ongoing concern to implement measures contributing to driving, respectively, motivating all staff for meeting quality targets. Also, last but not least, control through appropriate laws and internal regulations, it has a major role in monitoring implementation of gradual (during the operating cycle) performance and meeting the targets (Bettner & Kate, 2013).

Based on these considerations, we think that a decisive factor in the performance management, respectively entity's objectives all tourist information system must address three main issues: ensuring complete documentation and detailed, providing information needed to run the operating structures and ensuring all information necessary for decision-making structures.

On the other hand, the central role of management in the process of achieving performance has a special significance as the services and tourism products offered are subject to constant criticism from tourists, being the period of relaxation and recovery, exhibit maximum sensitivity. The management should be practically ubiquitous (through clear and precise or permanent control). Therefore, in practice, in a company tour, the performance depends not only on the proper functioning and permanent operational structures but heavily, opportunity, fairness and firmness making the whole hierarchy management (from the office reception up to upper management). In particular, it is that by these decisions to ensure that environment so cherished tourist resorts top, and so criticized in some resorts in Romania. Based on all the above, it can be said that, in its specifics, tourism, management decisions have a more important impact on the completion of performance.

In conclusion, we can say that the adoption of options for organization and operation of accounting information system in a tourism is dependent on two categories of factors: objective and subjective. The objective aimed mainly external environment and the financing capacity of the business and the subjective - the internal environment, namely, managerial capacity at all levels and the acting from the structures, to operate efficiently with a large number of variables generated market demand and resources available.

BACKGROUND

It is worth stressing that each component of this circuit may be bearing risks impacting the configuration and quality of accounting information (Chen, Tang, Jiang & Lin, 2010). Thus, particularly in tourism, characterized by a dynamic excessive customer relationship, supporting documents configurations and specific circuits, frequent changes caused by options common customer by adding and / or waiver of certain products and services, the risk omission and / or errors in drafting and supporting documents circuit is much higher. Therefore, rigor and order must be imposed since the drafting and enforcement of the organization and functioning of the internal regulation and how their provisions can be found in the job description of each employee (Holthausen & Watts, 2001).

The second moment is the risk generating data processing in accounting (Ozkan, Singer & You, 2012). Thus, if we assume that, for accounting, used a computer system able to collect, process, systematize and edit accurate and complete financial reports, however, cannot eliminate the risk of introducing errors dual origin. First, the risk of error may come from the supporting information and, secondly, from human error in data processing and accounting information system. Not least, the risk of errors can result from malfunctions that may occur in the connections of the three basic subsystems: accounting, operational and decision-making (Alstete & Beutell, 2018).

That is why, in our view, a system accounting will be performing and since they eliminate the risk of errors through an interconnection reliable with other subsystems mentioned, which cannot be achieved only through their design and delivery in a conception unit (Chen, Qu & Sun, 2017).

However, the most important aspect to be noted is that reports and information resulting from the accounting statements will bear the mark all errors may be induced in the two previous stages of the circuit. Thus, any previous error will affect the quality of accounting information in these reports will affect practically truth accountant. The consequences can be discerned. First, fiscal impact, or even criminal contravention. In lighter cases can only lead to the recovery of financial damages and tourist enterprise products to internal disciplinary measures. However, it is a very serious negative impact on the quality of decision-making both domestic and external users (investors, customers, suppliers, creditors)

Therefore, from this perspective, we can talk about two categories of risks for economic entities from tourism accounting related configuration information (reports and financial statements) and respectively its impact on decision making external users.

The configuration of accounting information in tourism is to a large extent, dependent on the specifics of this type of activity on "measurement, assessment, knowledge and control of assets, liabilities and equity, as well as the results of work carried out by legal or natural persons"(Englund & Gerdin,

J2018). In this case, the risk factors and quality of the resulting tax and accounting policies adopted by the tourism entities, namely, the achievement of their professional capacity. It also plays a crucial role, especially in tourism, financial accounting interconnection with the managerial process more complex configuration statements and financial reports. From this perspective, "management information systems aimed at aggregating and selecting data from files and databases of information systems in the enterprise, to give meaning to the information output by decision factor. Typically, these systems are characterized by outstanding reports by management and meet modern management methods".

On top of that avoiding risks in setting accounting information is done by the joint action of several factors. It's about professionalism and rigor in the writing, recording and centralize documents, ensuring the realization of feed-back on the quality of information resulting from data processing, networks and enterprise systems that enable timely identification and correction of errors.

THE SPECIFIC ASPECTS OF THE IMPACT OF ACCOUNTING INFORMATION ON THE MANAGERIAL DECISION

Management decisions within specific tourism operators bear the imprint of such activities. Thus, accounting information is configuration dependent, as we pointed out earlier, the type of activities, how to measure the value of products and / or tourist services, as well as a sum of other factors involved. Tourism is also a type of activity with some specific dynamics, reflected by its computer interaction subsystems (accounting, front office, reservations, leisure, catering, sports, spa), it is characterized by a special intensity, virtually continuous managerial processes involving, among others, common shares of diagnosis, whose raw material is accounting information.

Specifics of tourism activities given the ongoing process of coming out to customers, the major impact on their satisfaction achieved within the stay will cause continuous metamorphosis default accounting information, determinant of business development decisions. Accounting information will constantly measure central to achieving the objective of the entity tourism respectively profit maximization.

This is specifically because of tourism and tourism functional cycle is much faster than in other types of activities and the impact of customer satisfaction is crucial for success. Also, the specific tourism is given and the place and role of accounting in a structure strongly hierarchical management of each hierarchy in side needing to provide rapid and complex accounting information for making decisions for the entire hierarchy, to general management, while realization feed-back.

Addressing this issue is based on the specifics of tourism activities, many factors related to financial risk, due mainly vulnerability tourist entity-relationship customers. It is the fact that tourist services required by the customer (tourists) must satisfy appropriate and best quality, the most diverse expectations of them. Therefore, management must know tourism entities heritage permanent situation, in particular the financial resources and potential accounting process that plays a crucial role.

Using the principles of fiscal accounting is widely discussed in academia, especially in business. Thus, accounts, taken as a science, but also in relation to its legal basis, aims central highlighting accurate, complete and timely position of the assets, the financial position and performance, cash flows or the true image of the result sheet. But accounting principles are not always aligned with those tax, having as objective the collection, an amount always heightened state revenues while carrying out a complex process of influencing the evolution of economic stimulation and / or inhibition, as appropriate, trends. Therefore, it requires management companies to plan and carry out detailed analysis of the effects arising from differences between accounting rules and tax and, on this basis, to design and apply it to their character most suitable accounting policies and tax whilst ensuring respect full law. It was found that in hotels distortion occurs turnover and recurrent costs, if the period of accommodation includes late and early next month and the bill is drawn at the end of accommodation.

Tourism is characteristic that there is a wide variety of transactions corresponding to the plurality of services required by tourists which raises issues concerning models optimum measurement, recognition, depreciation and counter risks, in terms of taxation, not converge always with the accounting. Therefore, the interest entity tourism is often at the intersection with the tax accounting law. Therefore, a fundamental obligation of tourism management is to always have the effects of fiscal impact on the business. From this perspective, we consider that the so-called "size tax" that subject to extensive reviews of the literature, should be a central element analysis yet of the design and setting up a business in tourism, being then a permanent attitudinal of during the running business management in a process that we encounter in everyday language as the fiscal management. From this perspective, "the objectives of the enterprise tax management should aim to provide safety and efficacy through prescriptions correction of form and substance: delays, rescheduling exemptions imposed by tax law. Avoids tax penalties and sanctions and proceed to a better allocation of its financial resources" (Stoian, 2001, p.17).

In tourism, tax aspects of business are determined by a number of factors such as: the diversity of transactions subject to the fiscal impact, dislocation across extended geographical areas, each with the specific local tax possibilities (facilities) provided by the state to encourage tourism activities of some kind or / and certain tourist areas, the advantages of outsourcing services etc. For example, recently the state has redefined travel package "all-inclusive" and set some encouraging tourism facilities, the ultimate goal being to increase the supply this economic branch in GDP. It remains to be seen how tourism businesses will be able to capitalize on the new legal provisions.

We note that the effectiveness of management tax entities tourism focuses on two main aspects: firstly, to identify and correct application of all tax regulations (including all facilities, exemptions, deferrals) so that, together with the payment of all obligations to the state, to obtain all possible legal advantages. In the second, but not least, it is about ensuring the security tax, which is decisive edge coercive taxation due to the very existence of the entity and / or those responsible.

Meanwhile, the management, under the impact of fiscal rules, makes decisions and establishes accounting and tax policies of undertaking, in turn, have an impact on accounting operations. Also, by counting the resulting accounting information, grouped into two main categories, namely the annual financial statements for third parties and domestic needs, to be published and reports for internal use only. After validation of financial statements (audited or, where appropriate, acceptance), published, shall be transmitted to the competent tax authorities. If not validated, the process is resumed by supplementing and / or correction data and information provided by the operating structures.

To conclude that the management of tourism activities is permanently connected to the integrated information system that includes accounting as entrances and exits are made throughout the 24 hours. Also, the accounts should take into account the myriad tax rules relating to specific tourist activities and state interest to encourage the development of this important economic sectors are tourism. In addition, management is the one who watches over compliance with fiscal rules and also performed the correct and legal deadlines for the declaration and payment of tax obligations.

Corroborating elements set with different options offered by accounting regulations and tax law creates prerequisites for professional accountants opt for various models accounting targeting specific evaluation procedures, depreciation and establishing risk provisions, and for those responsible at best interest to present the true image of the result, the financial position and performance. From this point of view, there is some flexibility in setting accounting information, but with the understanding that freedom of choice is still limited by the requirement compliance. This is said and International Standards. Thus, the "financial statements present fairly the financial position must, financial performance and cash flows of an entity. Fair presentation allows representation of the effects of transactions, other events and conditions in accordance with the definitions and recognition criteria for assets, liabilities, income and expenses set out in the General Framework "(IFRS, 2013 P.A. p.549).

From this perspective, correct accounting of economic and financial transactions in the tourism involves the development of policies based accounting and tax regulations, and the specific accounting theory and practice. They must pursue the goals of the configuration of accounting information, and counteracting risks and uncertainties. To this end, the choice of accounting method must be reconciled with accounting principles applicable to specific transactions, which will allow the appropriate configuration of accounting information both qualitatively and volume and in scope. But this process is very complex, requiring more professionalism while respecting professional ethics so as to prevent any interpretation.

The tourist entities, by their specificity, present a series of particularities of the accounting and fiscal management. These are related to the diversity, both as a typology and as a specific one, of the rules and procedures used to achieve the central objective - profit maximization. It is also about the multitude of financial risk factors generated by the vulnerability of the tourist entity-customer relationship. Therefore, it is necessary that the highlighting of tourist transactions express the exact situation in order to be able to take the necessary measures.

The special complexity and dynamics of tourism transactions also require the general management to approach the tourism entity as a set of systems: informational, operational and decision-making. Moreover, the pursuit of the performance criteria conditions the use of a complex system of procedures strictly necessary for the correct management of resources of all types. Starting from the permanent need of convergence of the accounting principles with the fiscal ones, the efficiency of the fiscal management in a tourist entity becomes an important objective.

This also creates the necessary conditions for fiscal security, while accurately expressing the accounting result. It also provides management with basic elements for configuring the accounting and fiscal policies of enterprises.

The specificity of the tourist activities presupposes a permanent interconnection of the management, both sequentially and totally, to all the computer systems of the entity, within a wider integrated system of which, necessarily, a fiscal information system must be part. The existence of the latter system, which includes all the legislation with fiscal impact with up-to-date additions and modifications, is essential for creating the premises for achieving fiscal security. Accounting information and tourism information sources are permanently under the impact of the accounting-taxation relationship, which determines both their configuration and the efficiency of the ways of use.

An important aspect in the setup and establishment of accounting policies in tourism is related entities and other specific considerations. For example, in the hospitality industry, the commissioning of objects of little value or duration of low use, they can be treated as a material inventory objects, either as assets. The difference is that in the first case the recognition in profit or loss is due wholly to put into use, and in the second case, the recognition of depreciation is done throughout life. This has an important impact because the outcome is different configuration.

Another issue concerns the practice of some travel agencies using the method of division into several components of a tourism product or service, leading to separate invoices at different times. In this way reaching change in the pattern of income and hence the result.

SOLUTIONS AND RECOMMENDATIONS

Given these considerations, it is clear that the organization and management must be viewed from two perspectives. Thus, first of all, we talk about general management, which addresses accounting in terms of its role and place within the organization established by the Rules of organization and functioning, the composition of which we distinguish in particular flowchart, diagram functions and relationships.

From this point of view, from the fact that "the purpose of initiating the conduct of tourism activities is meeting needs with social and cultural, educational and scientific and delivering results that, in addition to expenses incurred must to ensure maximum profit, the need that in the management process to determine how to use the resources, when will trigger certain actions (operations) and will be carried out and who will be responsible for various tasks imposed by desire success business".

Also given a specific economic, tourism entities will have as its main information system - accounting information subsystem which, in our view, gain valence enhanced substantiation and decision making at all hierarchical levels. In this respect, we give an example serving as forecast management to which I referred in the thesis to fulfil the performance criteria of the new tourism products.

The approach of this perspective allows tourism entities carrying optimize those processes that ensure rational financial decisions and therefore, actions and processes that depend on efficient allocation of resources, respectively, to maximize profits. In other words, management is projecting and implementation of the necessary organizational setup provides clear objectives permanent knowledge of the situation heritage, identification and effective use of all the tools necessary to make and execute decisions.

In practical terms, a tourist entity will build an information system in which accounting and accounting will be crucial on information management and decision support. Accounting through its two complementary sides, should be permanently connected structures, supply of inputs, which by processing allows configuring accounting information necessary to make decisions. From this perspective, it is mandatory approach and in terms of current activity, in which the firm must honour its payment obligations, thus facing liquidity problem. In tourism, the cash flow is more dynamic and comes from multiple sources (the accommodation, food, entertainment). Only such an entity can achieve Tourist desire to ensure customer satisfaction as one of the essential conditions for the realization of performance, respectively, to be truly competitive.

FUTURE RESEARCH DIRECTIONS

Performing Romanian tourism and thereby increase the capacity of the economic sectors to contribute to GDP growth in Romania, is an important part of achieving the national interest and, therefore, achieving this goal must be the result of joint efforts of investors (interested in maximizing profit) and the State (interested in increasing budget revenues).

Analysis from the perspective of what happens in reality, points out that the performance of Romanian tourism is burdened still by a multitude of factors with negative impact from the inefficiency of rules for structuring tourism activities, the negative impact of policies financial tax failure insurance and upgrading of strategic infrastructure and other aspects that create vulnerabilities in the functioning tourist entities that depend exclusively on the configuration and the opportunity for economic and social development policies.

Secondly, maintaining gaps in tourism due to the still modest investment, something that was manifested early stage of privatization that allowed access to the system without sufficient capacity of entrepreneurs to invest. In this way, an important part of the ancient heritage tourism was exploited intensively without her improvement, which led to degradation, and reduce competitiveness, namely diversion of tourists to other destinations.

Meanwhile, an important finding is the fact that looming growing need generalization professional management capable of building effective strategies that to materialize through increased capacity for collecting, processing and use of information of all kinds, obviously with the contribution of staff sufficiently trained and motivated, as shown in the flowchart of the process variants described in this research. Thus, given that the objective elements relating to capital, infrastructure, regulatory, economic and fiscal policy are provided respectively favorable, remains essential element organizing information and management's capacity to exploit them more effectively. Only such an approach will lead, in our opinion, to achieve the national interest in ensuring security Romanian tourism.

In the future, the contribution to the development of scientific research into the tourism economy through an original approach to the methods of organizing and conducting activities and configuration for a pragmatic vision of the tourist circuit (production, tendering, distribution and consumption), and by identifying the elements vulnerability management generators and performing other issues affecting Romanian tourism.

CONCLUSION

Resumption and deepening of managerial perspective, the issue of treatment of accounting information have highlighted the importance of correct choice of options for organizing and ensuring the functioning of accounting information, as information is the result of a complex process faced the impact of an intense flow of diverse data to be retrieved and processed. From this perspective, it is clear the primary role of general management and accounting of the correct configuration and efficient use of information system ever to be seen in its dynamics.

Starting from the configuration and dynamics of the operating cycle of the entity tourism is evident that the options used in data processing and configuration information to accounting, taken as information system must be consistent with the permanent flow of opportunities to be seized and used lawfully interest entity.

In an effort to achieve competitiveness, tour operators are constantly under the influence impact of the external and internal environment, constituted the main sources of information to be processed. From this perspective, a wider variety of options in organizing information system to adopt the most favourable circuit "data-information-decision". In this way, it creates favourable conditions to avoid or / and address risks in setting accounting information and ensure that it expresses the truth of accountants.

Tourism management decisions bear the imprint of specific activities such as product information is used interrelation of computing subsystems (accounting, front office, reservations, catering) as well as diagnostic tests whose succession to keep its transactions.

Organizing thorough and efficient use of accounting as information system and decision support management, proper evaluation of the role and place of sources of information and diagnostic analysis in management activities together with identifying and responding to risks, are effective ways of ensuring a high throughput the use of accounting information process.

REFERENCES

Ahmed, A., Neel, M., & Wang, D. (2013). Does mandatory adoption of IFRS improve accounting quality? Preliminary evidence. *Contemporary Accounting Research*, *30*(4), 388–423. doi:10.1111/j.1911-3846.2012.01193.x

Ahrens, T. (2008). Overcoming the subjective–objective divide in interpretive management accounting research. *Accounting, Organizations and Society*, *33*(2), 292–297. doi:10.1016/j.aos.2007.03.002

Allen, A., & Ramanna, K. (2013). Towards an understanding of the role of standard setters in standard setting. *Journal of Accounting and Economics*, *55*(1), 1–66. doi:10.1016/j.jacceco.2012.05.003

Andon, P., Baxter, J., & Chua, W. F. (2007). Accounting change as relational drifting: A field study of experiments with performance measurement. *Management Accounting Research*, *18*(2), 273–308. doi:10.1016/j.mar.2006.06.007

Arsenault, P., & Faerman, S. R. (2014). Embracing paradox in management: The value of the competing values framework. *Organizational Management Journal*, *11*(3), 147–158. doi:10.1080/15416518.2014.949614

Baker, C., & Bettner, M. (1997). Interpretive and Critical Research in Accounting: A Commentary on its Absence from Mainstream Research||. *Critical Perspectives on Accounting*, *8*(4), 293–310. doi:10.1006/cpac.1996.0116

Ball, R. (2013). Accounting informs investors and earnings management is rife: Two questionable beliefs. *Accounting Horizons*, *27*(4), 847–853. doi:10.2308/acch-10366

Barth, M., Landsman, W., & Lang, M. (2008). International accounting standards and accounting quality. *Journal of Accounting Research*, *46*(3), 467–498. doi:10.1111/j.1475-679X.2008.00287.x

Barth, M. E. (2013). Global comparability in financial reporting: What, why, how, and when? *China Journal of Accounting Studies*, *1*(1), 2–12. doi:10.1080/21697221.2013.781765

Barth, M. E., Landsman, W. R., Young, D., & Zhuang, Z. (2014). Relevance of Differences between Net Income based on IFRS and Domestic Standards for European Firms. *Journal of Business Finance & Accounting*, *41*(3-4), 297–506. doi:10.1111/jbfa.12067

Bettner, M., & Kate, K. (2013). Changes in annual reporting rituals of financial services firms in periods of market crisis. *International Journal of Critical Accounting*, *5*(6), 577–593. doi:10.1504/IJCA.2013.059027

Brown, J. (2010). Accounting and visual cultural studies: Potentialities, challenges and prospects. *Accounting, Auditing & Accountability Journal*, *23*(4), 482–505. doi:10.1108/09513571011041598

Byard, D., Li, Y., & Yu, Y. (2011). The effect of mandatory IFRS adoption on financial analysts' information environment. *Journal of Accounting Research, 49*(1), 69–96. doi:10.1111/j.1475-679X.2010.00390.x

Cahan, S. F., & Sun, J. (2015). The effect of audit experience on audit fees and audit quality. *Journal of Accounting, Auditing & Finance, 30*(1), 78–100. doi:10.1177/0148558X14544503

Caylor, M. L. (2010). Strategic revenue recognition to achieve earnings benchmarks. *Journal of Accounting and Public Policy, 29*(1), 82–95. doi:10.1016/j.jaccpubpol.2009.10.008

Chen, H., Tang, Q., Jiang, Y., & Lin, Z. (2010). The role of international financial reporting standards in accounting quality: Evidence from the European Union. *Journal of International Financial Management & Accounting, 21*(3), 220–278. doi:10.1111/j.1467-646X.2010.01041.x

Damayant, T. (2013). Who is afraid of Qualitative Research? A Compromise Accounting Research Failure in Improving Accounting Practices. *International Journal of Advances in Management and Economics, 2*(2), 89-94.

Dennis, I. (2014). *The Nature of Accounting Regulation*. Routledge.

Doukakis, L. C. (2014). The effect of mandatory IFRS adoption on real and accrual-based earnings management activities. *Journal of Accounting and Public Policy, 33*(6), 551–572. doi:10.1016/j.jaccpubpol.2014.08.006

Fan, J. P. H., Li, J., & Zheng, G. (2016). Revisiting the bright and dark sides of capital flows in business groups. *Journal of Business Ethics, 134*(4), 509–528. doi:10.100710551-014-2382-6

Florou, A., & Pope, P. (2012). Mandatory IFRS adoption and institutional investment decisions. *The Accounting Review, 87*(6), 1993–2025. doi:10.2308/accr-50225

He, K., Pan, X., & Tian, G. (2017). Legal liability, government intervention, and auditor behavior: Evidence from structural reform of audit firms in China. *European Accounting Review, 26*(1), 61–95. doi: 10.1080/09638180.2015.1100547

Holthausen, R. W., & Watts, R. L. (2001). The relevance of the value-relevance literature for financial accounting standard setting. *Journal of Accounting and Economics, 31*(1-3), 3–75. doi:10.1016/S0165-4101(01)00029-5

Hou, Q., Jin, Q., Yang, R., Yuan, H., & Zhang, G. (2015). Performance commitments of controlling shareholders and earnings management. *Contemporary Accounting Research, 32*(3), 1099–1127. doi:10.1111/1911-3846.12111

Jackson, S. B., & Liu, X. K. (2010). The allowance for uncollectible accounts, conservatism, and earnings management. *Journal of Accounting Research, 48*(3), 565–601. doi:10.1111/j.1475-679X.2009.00364.x

Li, S. (2010). Does mandatory adoption of international accounting standards in the European Union reduce the cost of equity capital? *The Accounting Review, 85*(2), 607–636. doi:10.2308/accr.2010.85.2.607

Lukka, K. (2010). The roles and effects of paradigms in accounting research. *Management Accounting Research, 21*(2), 110–115. doi:10.1016/j.mar.2010.02.002

Ozkan, N., Singer, Z., & You, H. (2012). Mandatory IFRS adoption and the contractual usefulness of accounting information in executive compensation. *Journal of Accounting Research, 50*(4), 1077–1107. doi:10.1111/j.1475-679X.2012.00453.x

Parker, L. (2012). Qualitative management accounting research: Assessing deliverables and relevance. *Critical Perspectives on Accounting, 23*(1), 54–70. doi:10.1016/j.cpa.2011.06.002

Ramanna, K. (2008). The implications of unverifiable fair-value accounting: Evidence from the political economy of goodwill accounting. *Journal of Accounting and Economics, 45*(2-3), 253–281. doi:10.1016/j.jacceco.2007.11.006

Richardson, A. (2011). Myth, Paradigms and Academic Accounting Research: A Comment on Reading and Understanding Academic Research in Accounting. *Global Perspectives on Accounting Education, 8*, 67–77.

Schleicher, T., Tahoun, A., & Walker, M. (2010). IFRS adoption in Europe and investment-cash flow sensitivity: Outsider versus insider economies. *The International Journal of Accounting, 45*(2), 143–168. doi:10.1016/j.intacc.2010.04.007

Vladu, A. B., Amat, O., & Cuzdriorean, D. D. (2016). Truthfulness in accounting: How to discriminate accounting manipulators from non-manipulators. *Journal of Business Ethics, 140*(4), 633–648. doi:10.100710551-016-3048-3

ADDITIONAL READING

Alstete, J. W., & Beutell, N. J. (2018). Designing learning spaces for management education: A mixed methods research approach. *Journal of Management Development, 37*(2), 201–211. doi:10.1108/JMD-08-2017-0247

Ball, R., Li, X., & Shivakumar, L. (2015). Contractibility and transparency of financial statement information prepared under IFRS: Evidence from debt contracts around IFRS adoption. *Journal of Accounting Research, 53*(5), 915–963. doi:10.1111/1475-679X.12095

Chen, M., Qu, X., & Sun, X. (2017). Whose cost of equity capital reduces after IFRS convergence and why? Heterogeneity evidence from Chinese stock market. *China Journal of Accounting Studies, 5*(1), 1–27. doi:10.1080/21697213.2017.1304539

Englund, H., & Gerdin, J. (2018). Management accounting and the paradox of embedded agency: A framework for analyzing sources of structural change. *Management Accounting Research, 38*(1), 1–11. doi:10.1016/j.mar.2017.12.001

Li, L., Qi, B., Tian, G., & Zhang, G. (2017). The contagion effect of low-quality audits at the level of individual auditors. *The Accounting Review, 92*(1), 137–163. doi:10.2308/accr-51407

Chapter 12
The Budget:
The Basic Element of Management Accounting

Alin Eliodor Tănase
Titu Maiorescu University, Romania

ABSTRACT

Knowing precisely the costs by sectors, products, activities, and functions helps locate in time and space the sub-units contributing to the improvement or, on the contrary, the depreciation of the results obtained by the company. Breaking down the costs by each function is another way to acquire knowledge about the internal accounting management conditions. A comparative analysis of expenditure by functions related to certain forecasts is the main way of identifying performance, efficient responsibility centers, as well as those whose functioning is deficient. On the other hand, the budget may be seen as a correlation and streamlining instrument for the relation between expenditures and income. Budgeting can also be seen as a systematic economic practice involving a formal process of allocating financial resources to achieve the objectives set for the following period of time. The revenue and cost budget are the objects of managerial accounting and the instruments to control the costs and the income by comparing the forecasts with the achievements.

INTRODUCTION

The term "budget" comes from Old French where the word" bougette" meant a small bag or purse of money (Jones & Smith, 2012). The term has been adopted in the Anglo-Saxon countries during the Norman Conquest and from there it spread throughout the world with its financial meaning.

The activity of any company is carried out based on a development strategy prepared within a competitive environment for the purpose of achieving the set objectives, some of its priorities being efficiency and effectiveness, as well as profit maximization (Landsman, Maydew & Thornock, 2012; Mechelli & Cimini, 2014; Tendeloo & Vanstrelen, 2005; Xiong, 2006). The budget is a plan establishing the consumption, the needs forecasted for a specific action, providing the funds required to cover all of these needs.

DOI: 10.4018/978-1-7998-8069-1.ch012

The production budget therefore presents in detail "the analysis of the investment in raw materials, materials, labor and production equipment required to achieve the forecasted sales level (namely the implicit production level)"(Watts & Zimmerman, 1978; Messier, Glover & Prawitt, 2008). Each of the major elements forming the production budget can be subdivided into sub budgets: a budget for the raw materials and materials, a budget for the administrative personnel, a budget for each utility.

The process of cost budgeting as well as the organization of management accounting and cost calculation, require strict observance of theoretical and methodological principles to ensure a real and accurate content of the cost of production (Louwers, Ramsay, Sinason & Strawser, 2007; Klein, 2002).

For this purpose, it is necessary that before calculating the costs, regardless of the type of calculation (forecast or effective), to proceed to a complex analysis of production costs in order to select and delimit them on the main activities of the company, on the cost centers (Ghosh & Olsen, 2008; Beasley, Buckless, Glover & Prawitt, 2009; Alzola, 2017). They have occurred, according to the opportunity and the degree of finishing of the production, as well as according to the period of time in which the production is made that causes the respective expenses, so that, for each calculation period (month, quarter, year), in the production cost to include only those expenses which are directly or indirectly related to the manufacture of the products obtained during that period, regardless of when they were made (Balachandran & Faff, 2015; Barth, Landsman & Lang, 2008; Cairns, Massoudi, Taplin & Tarca, 2011).

Carrying out budgetary control over production costs is also conditioned by the application in both the budgeting and the accounting activity, of rigorous procedures regarding the budgeting, accounting and calculation of production costs that combine the specific elements of the enterprise with the general ones (Chen, Tang, Jiang & Lin, 2010; DeFond, 2010; Iatridis, 2012; Leuz, Nanda & Wysocki, 2003; Zéghal, Chtourou & Mnif, 2011).

Therefore, in order to calculate as accurately as possible the cost of manufactured production, as well as to carry out budgetary control of costs in enterprises belonging to the steel industry, the following theoretical and methodological principles must be taken into account: determining the object of calculation, choosing the costing method, organization of accounting calculation in accordance with other forms of economic calculation, delimitation by types of activities of economic and financial indicators that are subject to cost calculation, delimitation in time of data and information based on which costs are calculated, delimitation in space or places (expenditure) of the data and information underlying the cost calculation, the principle of delimiting the costs related to the finished production from those related to the current production, the principle of delimiting the productive expenses from the non-productive ones, the principle of substantiating the cost calculation on justifying documents (Zeghal, Chtourou & Fourati, 2012; Schleicher, Tahoun & Walker, 2010; Pope & McLeay, 2011; Houque, Zijl, Dunstan & Karim, 2012; Brüggemann, Hitz & Sellhorn, 2013).

The expenditure budget does not include non-productive ones, as it would legally create possibilities for the company to carry out an inappropriate activity in certain respects, which is not allowed (Allen & Ramanna, 2013; Barth, Landsman & Lang, 2008; Chebaane & Othman, 2014; Daske & Gebhardt, 2006; Fu, Kraft & Zhang, 2012).

Because such non-productive expenses occur, however, the accounting groups them into the general expenses of the non-productive section and records them separately according to the place where they appeared (sections, sectors, services) and the causes that determined them (Jeanjean & Stolowy, 2008; Lang, Raedy & Wilson, 2006; Richardson, 2011).

An appropriate budgetary system must have as its objectives the obtaining of reliable information at low cost and operatively on the important activities of the enterprise, so that on the basis of budgetary control the necessary corrective measures can be taken and allow the assessment of the activity of managers at different stages (Whittington & Pany, 2008).

BACKGROUND

The operational budgets preparation procedure is based on the calculation of the production results related to forecasts for a longer or shorter period of time (Thong, Ding & Lim, 2008; Doukakis, 2010; Horton, Serafeim & Serafeim, 2013; Iatridis, 2010).

The budget serves as reference to guide action and assess performance. It is reviewed when new information reopens the issue of the budget structure and the possibilities for its execution. If radical environment changes because the hypotheses that formed the basis for the drawing up of the budget disappear, then the budget will be reviewed in order to recover its logic as an accounting instrument (Kothari, Leone & Wasley, 2005).

Production activity budgets or, in a different formulation, production cost budgets, are prepared in more complex industrial companies and involve the preparation of the production budget as such, the stocks and work in progress budget, the raw materials budget, the personnel, supply, indirect production expense budgets (Lobo & Zhou, 2001).

It is practical to determine the necessary steps for the preparation of a budget, for it to be the result of the conjoint activity of the entire managerial team (Lin, S., Riccardi & Wang, 2012; Rittenberg & Schwieger, 2005). The steps are:

1. Informing about the main directions of the strategic policy. Since the annual budget represents a component of the long-range plan and reflects a certain stage in view of reaching the set objective, it is first of all necessary to inform all the experts who draw up budgets about the company's policy during the budgeted period.

This information usually refers to the volume and type of production, the price policy, the outlet. In addition, other important conditions bearing on the budget preparation must be determined, such as the corrections introduced considering the forecasted inflation, salary increase or the modification of labor productivity (Marra, Mazzola & Prencipe, 2011).

2. Determine the restrictive factors. For most of the companies, the restrictive factor is the buyers' demand. But there are also cases when production is stopped because of the productive capacities and the buyers' demand exceeds the companies' possibilities. This is why, at the beginning of the budget preparation activity, the top management must determine and communicate such restrictions to the people directly involved in the preparation of the budget. Only afterwards will the preliminary budgets be drawn up.
3. Preparation of preliminary budgets. The preparation of the company's general budget begins from the lower management level. In the beginning, the managers of the various subdivisions prepare the preliminary budgets for the activities under their responsibility that is for their centers of responsibility. For example, the marketing section elaborates the sales budget and the sales revenue

budget, the supply section – the budget for the purchase of raw materials and materials, and, in addition to that, each of them also draws up the general and administrative expense budget for the respective subdivision.

4. Discussing budgets with the company's management. When the preliminary budgets of the functional subdivisions have been prepared, the managers at this level submit them for approval to the hierarchically superior managers who, in turn, must unify all budgets into one and submit it for approval to their manager who will subsequently become responsible for the drawing up of the budget at his level of activity.
5. Coordinate and analyses the budgets and their possible modifications. As the budgets are being prepared upwardly, the relation between the indicators included in the budget and their correspondence with the main indicators in the long-term program is analyzed. This analysis reveals the imbalance of some budgets, their inconsistency with the restrictive factors and the plans which may have been unknown to the one who prepared the budget, or it has no bearing on them. For example, the manager of a certain section may plan to replace a piece of equipment at a time when he has no funds available for such an action. In such a case, the financial manager must remove from the records such inconsistencies and the respective modifications must be introduced in the budget.

Only the expert charged with the preparation of the budget may introduce such modifications into the budget. It may request that the budget be reviewed a second or a third time, until the budget is fully coordinated and acceptable for the entire company (Choi, Peasnell & Toniato, 2013). The coordination stage requires a forecast of the financial results, of the money flows and of the balance sheet to make sure that all budgets correlate with each other and form a single document that is acceptable for the company.

6. Final approval of the budgets. When the general budget comprising all the operational and financial budgets has been prepared, the budget commission approves this generalizing document and submits it for approval to all the responsibility center managers in the company. When the general budget has been approved by all the responsibility center managers, this constitutes the ground for its execution.
7. Subsequent budget analysis. Budget preparation does not end with their approval. The company's results must be compared with those in the budget on a monthly (or weekly) basis. This will reveal the budget indicators that have not been fulfilled and the cause of such deviations. When the cause of the deviations lies with the competence of the management, measures can be taken immediately to prevent such deviations in the future (Barth & Konchitchki, 2013). But deviations can also be caused by the fact that the budget was initially drawn up based on unreal conditions or the fact that the real conditions differ a lot from the ones forecasted for the preparation of the budget. In this case, the budget commission must review the company's budgets for the remaining budget period and make a forecast for the following budget period (Barth, Landsman, Young & Zhuang, 2014).

If properly drawn up and managed, the budgeting process has some advantages, namely it provides clear activity coordinates for the managers and the entire administration, being the main way to transform general objectives into specific tasks and individual objectives for the managers; it provides an important means of communication and coordination both horizontally and vertically; due to the fact that budget control is based on the exception principle, the organization time is cut down because the attention is focused on the aspects of maximum interest; budget integration enables better control over the cash flow and the capital management; more effective control can be exerted through regular and systematic monitoring and reporting of activities; adequate participation encourages congruent interests and increases motivation (Barth, 2013).

BUDGETED REVENUE AND EXPENDITURE SIZING CHARACTERISTICS

The budget preparation procedure also has some disadvantages no matter how well it is applied (Ball, Li & Shivakumar, 2015). For example, deviations frequently appear because the situation has changed, because of poor forecasts or a poor managerial performance; budgets are drawn up according to the existing structures of the industrial company, which may be inadequate for the situation at a given moment in time; well documented programs may lead to inertia and lack of flexibility to change; wrongly approached budget systems, with excessive pressure or lack of interest towards behavioural factors may create antagonism and cause low morale on the part of the executants (Guthrie & Parker, 2016).

A study of budget typology recommends three basic criteria, namely:

1. ***Time criterion*** - The period of time for which they are prepared, according to which there are three types of budgets:
    a. *Provisional budgets* show the estimates for a longer period of time (5 years) to achieve the strategic objectives.
    b. *Execution budgets*. The annual provisions for the provisional budgets.
    c. *Operational budgets* break down for shorter periods the execution budgets.
2. ***Budget activity object criterion*** – according to which there are the following types of budgets:
    a. *Commercial budgets* estimate the forecasts regarding the company's sales and its supply activities.
    b. *Production activity budgets* forecast the annual physical and value volume of the main and auxiliary production sections.
    c. *Costs budgets* pre-calculate the direct and indirect production costs by cost-generating places and cost bearers.
    d. *Results budgets* – based on the activities and costs budgets, they estimate the whole patrimonial and monetary situation, under the form of a results account and a provisional balance sheet, and the cash budget.
3. ***Functional criterion*** - The budgets' functions in the management of the company, according to which there are:
    a. *Determined budgets* deal with the activities involved by the basic functions of the company, forming the basis for its results (sales budget, production budget).
    b. *Resulting budgets* estimate the economic and financial results, free from the basic activities projected by the *determined* budgets (commercial expenses budget, costs budget, supply budget, synthesis budgets comprising the cash budget, the results account and the provisional balance sheet, and the provisional financing table).

Control is the essence of budgeting because the preparation and use of budgets cannot be imagined in the absence of a budget control. It enables a comparison between the real situation and the situation provided in the budget (Pieper, Trevor, Weller & Duchon, 2017).

When the level of effective achievements is known, it must be seen in terms of the budget allocated for that purpose. This is done by comparing and deciding which actions should be taken based on the conclusions revealed by the respective comparisons.

The use of budgets in the company's management has the following advantages:

- Requires the use of planning in the management of the respective business;
- It provides the framework for measuring performance because it reveals the parameters the company must fulfil in time in order to achieve the set objectives: the sales, production, and costs levels to be achieved in order to reach the forecasted benefits;
- Promotes communication and coordination in order to engage and balance all company departments and functions to achieve the forecasted objectives;
- Forces those responsible for the responsibility centres to foresee the consequences of the decisions already taken or to be taken, budgets being a reference instrument in the decision-making process.
- Grants the existence of an effective accounting system;
- Ensures management by exception;
- Participation in the planning activity of both the management and the executants.

The activities carried out by a patrimonial unit in order to achieve the objectives of managerial accounting can be structured according to its three main functions, namely:

1. The function to determine costs by products, works, services, and activity sectors;
2. The function to determine profitability by products, works, services, and activity;
3. The function to produce and supply the information needed to draw up, standardize, monitor and control the revenue and cost budgets, and to update the indicators of the patrimonial unit managers' "dashboard".

The expenditures – according to the generally accepted definition by various national accounting regulations – are decreases in the economic benefits registered during the accounting period, under the form of asset exits or diminished asset values or increased debts resulting in decreases in the owner's equity other than those resulting from their distribution to the shareholders.

The revenues are increases in the economic benefits registered during the accounting period, under the form of asset entries or increased asset values or decreased debts resulting in increases in the owner's equity other than those resulting from the shareholders' contributions.

The revenue and expenditure definitions are focused on their main characteristics but do not specify the criteria that must be fulfilled for them to be recorded in the profit and loss account.

Expenditures are recognized in the profit and loss account when future economic benefits have decreased because of diminished asset values or increased debts, a modification which can be assessed in a credible manner. Expenditures are therefore recognized simultaneously with the increased debts or the decreased asset values.

Revenues are recognized in the profit and loss account when future economic benefits have increased because of increased asset value or diminished debts, a modification which can be assessed in a credible manner.

Expenditures are recognized in the profit and loss account based on a direct association between the criteria involved in obtaining the specific income elements, a process known as connecting expenses to revenues.

Therefore, to be aggregated with the costs of products, works, and services, the expenditures recorded in the financial accounting according to their nature must be regrouped in the managerial accounting according to other essential and logical criteria that fulfil the costs recording and calculation requirements.

Apart from these general classifications of expenditures, costs, and revenues, the managerial accounting also operates, depending on the specific activity, with the deciders' information needs and specific classification criteria either for the expenses or for the costs, namely:

1. The production activities that generate them, based on which we have:
    a. Direct expenditures from the basic production – generated in the main production sections.
    b. Direct expenditures from the auxiliary production – made to maintain production at normal levels.
    c. Indirect expenditures from the organization, management and administration of various places or expenditure sectors, namely:
        i. Indirect expenditures from the basic and auxiliary production – because two or more products are manufactured concurrently or because there are several sections and manufacturing locations common for different products or works;
        ii. General administration expenditures – pertaining to the entire activity of the production unit;
        iii. Sale or marketing expenditures – from the storage, packaging, handling, and transport of manufactured products. It is an extension of the production process towards the goods circulation sector.
2. The economic contents and nature of expenses, irrespective of the bearer and the expenditure area or the place generating them, depending on which expenditures are structured according to primary expense elements. The primary expense elements structure, be they direct or indirect, includes:
    a. Expenses for raw materials and materials, representing consumption to be found in the contents of the finished product either in its initial form or in a transformed one;
    b. Fuel, power, and water expenses for the production process but also for administrative and purposes;
    c. Expenses generated by the depreciation of intangible assets calculated according to economic criteria;
    d. Expenses for works and services performed by third parties, such as maintenance and repair expenses, royalty expenses, commercial leasing and rent, insurance premium expenses, study and research expenses, etc.
    e. Expenditure for salaries paid to employees according to the work performed and to the negotiated salary level set in collective and individual work contracts;
    f. Social security and protection expenditures generated by the employer's contributions to the state social security fund and the unemployment and professional reorientation funds for the unemployed;
    g. Other expenditures (costs), such as the depreciation of intangible assets, losses caused by debts, other production and extraordinary expenses primarily included in the effective costs.

3. The relation between the moment when the expenditure is made and that when it is included in the costs of a product or of an expenditure area or sector, based on which we have:
    a. Current expenditures, included in the costs of the bearers or of the expenditure area or sector in the period when they are made;
    b. Anticipated or predetermined expenditures made during the current calculation period but pertaining to future production calculation periods;
    c. Estimated expenditures or reserves, included in the costs of the current calculation period but to be made during future calculation periods.

An important issue related to cost allocation is the allocation of service department's costs (e.g. maintenance, receiving, handling, etc.). Generally large companies have several production departments. Each of these departments may calculate a separate predetermined overhead rate. Costs of these service departments should be allocated to production departments.

All the manufacturing costs must ultimately be traced to products. If we talk, for instance, about the materials – handling cost center the costs of this center will be allocated to the production departments (the entire value of these costs or – at least-the largest part of them) and possibly other service departments. Apportionment of service department costs should be based on meaningful criteria such as: services provided services available, benefits received or equity.

SOLUTIONS AND RECOMMENDATIONS

The sizing of budgeted revenue and expenditures is based on the principle of locating them based on two distinct criteria, namely:

1. Locating revenues and expenditures according to the *operational criterion*, namely by manufactured products, works and services performed that are at the same time income generators, on the one side, and expenditure bearers, on the other. Revenues can generally be fully identified under the "income generators" item when they are achieved, whereas expenditures can be identified under the "expenditure bearers" item when they are made only as direct expenditures.
2. Locating revenues and expenditures according to the *structural criterion*, that is by sectors of activity, basic and auxiliary production sections, agencies, operative unite, etc.

According to the specialized literature, the sizing of budgeted revenues and expenditures involves:

- Determine the revenue generators and the expenditure bearers;
- Determine the revenue and expenditure locations or sectors;
- Selecting the revenue and expenditure reference sizes and the sizing periods.

By revenue generators and expenditure bearers we mean the manufactured products, the works performed, and the services performed as material, concrete results of the production process. The revenue generators and the expenditure bearers fulfil, together or separately, several functions, such as:

- Identification of total revenues and direct expenditures for each product, work or tourist or commercial service;
- Taking over and distributing, at the end of the accounting period, the indirect expenses initially sized and identified according to expenditure areas or sectors, in order to determine the effective cost of products, works, and tourist and/or commercial services;
- Monitoring the profitability of each product, work or tourist or commercial service forming the object of activity of a patrimonial unit.

The most representative reference value of the revenue generators and the expenditure bearers is the manufactured production for each product, work, service, or order.

The process of determining, for each and every concrete case, the revenue generators and the expenditure bearers is influenced by the manufactured production nomenclature, by its complexity, by the manufacturing technology, by the organization of production and work. Depending on the preparation, monitoring, and control stages of the revenue and expenditure budgets, or just of the revenue ones or of the expenditure ones, we can identify:

- Intermediary revenue generators or expenditure bearers used at various stages of the budget preparation or the cost calculation processes.
- Final revenue generators or expenditure bearers used for the preparation of the general budget and the calculation of the unit cost.

Besides, the practical application of these methods has revealed some difficulties related to the budget production, approval and execution. Most of the times, their application infringes upon the requirements of some budget principles such its annual production and the fact that budget revenues should not be affected.

FUTURE RESEARCH DIRECTIONS

Managerial accounting differentiates among the expenditure bearers according to their role at various moments of the production cost formation process, identifying final bearers and intermediary bearers.

The final expenditure bearers are represented by the unit of product, work or service for which the unit cost is calculated. It is present during the entire length of the production process and at all the cost formation stages, as is the case for the manufacturing of one-off products. In other cases, the final expenditure bearers act only at the end of the manufacturing process, namely at the last cost-formation stage.

This is the case when several units of product are manufactured, when the expenses are collected during the production process according to a structure, by product series or lots acting as intermediary bearers, the final cost being determined by comparing the total production expenditures to the quantity of products obtained.

The intermediary bearer may be formed of groups of products with similar functions to those of the series or the lots. In the case of sort-type-size production or coupled production, the intermediary expenditure bearer may be formed as a whole, according to the manufacturing stage.

CONCLUSION

In the context of the process of economic globalization and implicitly of the development of the competitive environment, the managerial exercise, at all levels, is of a special complexity as the decision-making act presupposes numerous information that must be elaborated, provided, interpreted and rigorously controlled.

The information needs of managers on costs, over time, have evolved considerably. Taking into account the intensification of competition that has the effect of shifting economic power from producer to consumer, the emergence of new management styles and accelerating technological evolution, methods of calculating costs, providing information, control and analysis have had to evolve.

The process of organizing budgeting, management accounting and costing is influenced, as is natural, by a set of factors, the most important of which can be mentioned: the size of the enterprise, the organizational structure of the enterprise, the type of production and the organization of its production technology, the degree of concentration, profiling and specialization of the enterprise, the degree of integration of the enterprise, the character of the production process and others.

Regarding the budgeting of production costs, it can be mentioned that the automatic manufacturing processes that take place in continuous flow, influence the number of cost calculations in the sense of reducing them, compared to the complex production, where their number is higher.

The process of cost budgeting as well as the organization of management accounting and cost calculation, require strict observance of theoretical and methodological principles to ensure a real and accurate content of the cost of production.

REFERENCES

Allen, A., & Ramanna, K. (2013). Towards an understanding of the role of standard setters in standard setting. *Journal of Accounting and Economics, 55*(1), 1–66. doi:10.1016/j.jacceco.2012.05.003

Alzola, M. A. (2017). Beware of the watchdog: Rethinking the normative justification of gatekeeper liability. *Journal of Business Ethics, 140*(4), 705–721. doi:10.100710551-017-3460-3

Balachandran, B., & Faff, R. (2015). Corporate governance, firm value and risk: Past, present, and future. *Pacific-Basin Finance Journal, 35*(A), 1-12.

Ball, R., Li, X., & Shivakumar, L. (2015). Contractibility and transparency of financial statement information prepared under IFRS: Evidence from debt contracts around IFRS adoption. *Journal of Accounting Research, 53*(5), 915–963. doi:10.1111/1475-679X.12095

Barth, M., Landsman, W., & Lang, M. (2008). International accounting standards and accounting quality. *Journal of Accounting Research, 46*(3), 467–498. doi:10.1111/j.1475-679X.2008.00287.x

Barth, M. E. (2013). Global comparability in financial reporting: What, why, how, and when? *China Journal of Accounting Studies, 1*(1), 2–12. doi:10.1080/21697221.2013.781765

Barth, M. E., Konchitchki, Y. L., & Landsman, W. R. (2013). Cost of capital and earnings transparency. *Journal of Accounting and Economics, 55*(2–3), 206–224. doi:10.1016/j.jacceco.2013.01.004

Barth, M. E., Landsman, W. R., & Lang, M. H. (2008). International accounting standards and accounting quality. *Journal of Accounting Research, 43*(3), 467–498. doi:10.1111/j.1475-679X.2008.00287.x

Barth, M. E., Landsman, W. R., Young, D., & Zhuang, Z. (2014). Relevance of Differences between Net Income based on IFRS and Domestic Standards for European Firms. *Journal of Business Finance & Accounting, 41*(3-4), 297–506. doi:10.1111/jbfa.12067

Beasley, M. S., Buckless, F. A., Glover, S. M., & Prawitt, D. F. (2009). *Auditing Cases. An Interactive Learning Approach* (4th ed.). Prentice Hall.

Brüggemann, U., Hitz, J.-M., & Sellhorn, T. (2013). Intended and unintended consequences of mandatory IFRS adoption: A review of extant evidence and suggestions for future research. *European Accounting Review, 22*(1), 1–37. doi:10.1080/09638180.2012.718487

Cairns, D., Massoudi, D., Taplin, R., & Tarca, A. (2011). IFRS fair value measurement and accounting policy choice in the United Kingdom and Australia. *The British Accounting Review, 43*(1), 1–21. doi:10.1016/j.bar.2010.10.003

Chebaane, S., & Othman, H. B. (2014). The Impact of IFRS Adoption on Value Relevance of Earnings and Book Value of Equity: The Case of Emerging Markets in African and Asian Regions. *Procedia: Social and Behavioral Sciences, 145*, 70–80. doi:10.1016/j.sbspro.2014.06.012

Chen, H., Tang, Q., Jiang, Y., & Lin, Z. (2010). The role of international financial reporting standards in accounting quality: Evidence from the European Union. *Journal of International Financial Management & Accounting, 21*(3), 220–278. doi:10.1111/j.1467-646X.2010.01041.x

Choi, Y.-S., Peasnell, K., & Toniato, J. (2013). Has the IASB been successful in making accounting earnings more useful for prediction and valuation? UK evidence. *Journal of Business Finance & Accounting, 40*(7–8), 741–768. doi:10.1111/jbfa.12025

Daske, H., & Gebhardt, G. (2006). International financial reporting standards and experts' perceptions of disclosure quality. *Abacus, 42*(3/4), 461–498. doi:10.1111/j.1467-6281.2006.00211.x

DeFond, M. L. (2010). Earnings quality research: Advances, challenges and future research. *Journal of Accounting and Economics, 50*(2-3), 402–409. doi:10.1016/j.jacceco.2010.10.004

Doukakis, L. C. (2010). The persistence of earnings and earnings components after the adoption of IFRS. *Managerial Finance, 36*(11), 969–980. doi:10.1108/03074351011081286

Fu, R., Kraft, A., & Zhang, H. (2012). Financial reporting frequency, information asymmetry, and the cost of equity. *Journal of Accounting and Economics, 54*(2–3), 132–149. doi:10.1016/j.jacceco.2012.07.003

Ghosh, A., & Olsen, L. (2008). Environmental uncertainty and managers' use of discretionary accruals. *Accounting, Organizations and Society, 34*(2), 188–205. doi:10.1016/j.aos.2008.07.001

Horton, J., Serafeim, G., & Serafeim, I. (2013). Does mandatory IFRS adoption improve the information environment? *Contemporary Accounting Research, 30*(1), 388–423. doi:10.1111/j.1911-3846.2012.01159.x

Houque, M. N. (2012). The effect of IFRS adoption and investor protection on earnings quality around the world. *The International Journal of Accounting, 47*(3), 333–355. doi:10.1016/j.intacc.2012.07.003

Iatridis, G. (2010). International Financial Reporting Standards and the quality of financial statement information. *International Review of Financial Analysis*, *19*(3), 193–204. doi:10.1016/j.irfa.2010.02.004

Iatridis, G. (2012). Hedging and earnings management in the light of IFRS implementation: Evidence from the UK stock market. *The British Accounting Review*, *44*(1), 21–35. doi:10.1016/j.bar.2011.12.002

Jeanjean, T., & Stolowy, H. (2008). Do accounting standards matter? An exploratory analysis of earnings management before and after IFRS adoption. *Journal of Accounting and Public Policy*, *27*(6), 480–490. doi:10.1016/j.jaccpubpol.2008.09.008

Jones, D. A., & Smith, K. J. (2012). Comparing the value relevance, predictive value, and persistence of other comprehensive income and special items. *The Accounting Review*, *86*(6), 2047–2073. doi:10.2308/accr-10133

Klein, A. (2002). Audit committee, board of director characteristics and earnings management. *Journal of Accounting and Economics*, *33*(3), 375–400. doi:10.1016/S0165-4101(02)00059-9

Kothari, S. P., Leone, A. J., & Wasley, C. E. (2005). Performance matched discretionary accrual measures. *Journal of Accounting and Economics*, *39*(1), 163–197. doi:10.1016/j.jacceco.2004.11.002

Landsman, W. R., Maydew, E. L., & Thornock, J. R. (2012). The information content of annual earnings announcements and mandatory adoption of IFRS. *Journal of Accounting and Economics*, *53*(1-2), 34–54. doi:10.1016/j.jacceco.2011.04.002

Lang, M., Raedy, J. S., & Wilson, W. (2006). Earnings management and cross listing: Are reconciled earnings comparable to US earnings? *Journal of Accounting and Economics*, *42*(1-2), 255–283. doi:10.1016/j.jacceco.2006.04.005

Leuz, C., Nanda, D., & Wysocki, P. D. (2003). Earnings management and investor protection: An international comparison. *Journal of Financial Economics*, *69*(3), 505–527. doi:10.1016/S0304-405X(03)00121-1

Lin, S., Riccardi, W., & Wang, C. (2012). Does accounting quality change following a switch from U.S.GAAP to IFRS? Evidence from Germany. *Journal of Accounting and Public Policy*, *31*(6), 641–657. doi:10.1016/j.jaccpubpol.2012.10.006

Lobo, G. L., & Zhou, J. (2001). Disclosure quality and earning management. *Asia-Pacific Journal of Accounting & Economics*, *8*(1), 1–20. doi:10.1080/16081625.2001.10510584

Louwers, T. J., Ramsay, R. J., Sinason, D. H., & Strawser, J. R. (2007). *Auditing and Assurance Services* (2nd ed.). McGraw-Hill Irwin.

Marra, A., Mazzola, P., & Prencipe, A. (2011). Board Monitoring and Earnings Management Pre- and Post-IFRS. *The International Journal of Accounting*, *46*(2), 205–230. doi:10.1016/j.intacc.2011.04.007

Mechelli, A., & Cimini, R. (2014). Is comprehensive income value relevant and does location matter? A European study. *Accounting in Europe*, *16*(25), 1–35. doi:10.1080/17449480.2014.890777

Messier, W. F., Glover, S. M., & Prawitt, D. F. (2008). *Auditing and Assurance Services. A Systematic Approach* (5th ed.). McGraw-Hill Irwin.

Pope, P., & McLeay, S. (2011). The European IFRS experiment: Objectives, research challenges and some early evidence. *Accounting and Business Research, 41*(3), 233–266. doi:10.1080/00014788.2011.575002

Richardson, A. (2011). Myth, Paradigms and Academic Accounting Research: A Comment on Reading and Understanding Academic Research in Accounting. *Global Perspectives on Accounting Education, 8*, 67–77.

Rittenberg, L. E., & Schwieger, B. J. (2005). *Auditing. Concepts for a Changing Environment* (5th ed.). Thomson South-Western.

Schleicher, T., Tahoun, A., & Walker, M. (2010). IFRS adoption in Europe and investment-cash flow sensitivity: Outsider versus insider economies. *The International Journal of Accounting, 45*(2), 143–168. doi:10.1016/j.intacc.2010.04.007

Tendeloo, B., & Vanstrelen, A. (2005). Earnings management under German GAAP versus IFRS. *European Accounting Review, 14*(1), 155–180. doi:10.1080/0963818042000338988

Thong, T. Y., Ding, D. K., & Lim, C. Y. (2008). Firm diversification and earning management: Evidence from seasoned equity offerings. *Review of Quantitative Finance and Accounting, 30*(1), 69–92. doi:10.100711156-007-0043-x

Watts, R., & Zimmerman, J. (1978). Towards a Positive Theory of the Determination of Accounting Standards. *The Accounting Review, 53*(1), 112–134.

Whittington, O. R., & Pany, K. (2008). *Principles of Auditing & Other Assurance Services* (16th ed.). McGraw-Hill Irwin.

Xiong, Y. (2006). Earning management and its measurement; a theoretical perspective. *The Journal of American Academy of Business, Cambridge, 9*(1), 214–219.

Zeghal, D., Chtourou, S., & Fourati, M. Y. (2012). Thc cffcct of mandatory adoption of IFRS on carning quality: Evidence from the European Union. *Journal of International Accounting Research, 11*(2), 1–25. doi:10.2308/jiar-10221

Zéghal, D., Chtourou, S., & Mnif, S. Y. (2011). An analysis of the effect of mandatory adoption of IAS/IFRS on earnings Management. *Journal of International Accounting, Auditing & Taxation, 20*(2), 61–72. doi:10.1016/j.intaccaudtax.2011.06.001

ADDITIONAL READING

Ahmed, A., Neel, M., & Wang, D. (2013). Does mandatory adoption of IFRS improve accounting quality? Preliminary evidence. *Contemporary Accounting Research, 30*(4), 388–423. doi:10.1111/j.1911-3846.2012.01193.x

Ball, R., Li, X., & Shivakumar, L. (2015). Contractibility and transparency of financial statement information prepared under IFRS: Evidence from debt contracts around IFRS adoption. *Journal of Accounting Research, 53*(5), 915–963. doi:10.1111/1475-679X.12095

Fan, J. P. H., Li, J., & Zheng, G. (2016). Revisiting the bright and dark sides of capital flows in business groups. *Journal of Business Ethics*, *134*(4), 509–528. doi:10.100710551-014-2382-6

Guthrie, J., & Parker, L. D. (2016). Whither the accounting profession, accountants and accounting researchers? Commentary and projections. *Accounting, Auditing & Accountability Journal*, *29*(1), 2–10. doi:10.1108/AAAJ-10-2015-2263

Pieper, J. R., Trevor, C. O., Weller, I., & Duchon, D. (2017). Referral Hire Presence Implications for Referrer Turnover and Job Performance. *Journal of Management*, *19*, 14–20.

Chapter 13

Managerial Accounting: An Integral Part of the Decision-Making Process

Traian Ovidiu Calotă
Titu Maiorescu University, Romania

ABSTRACT

The role of managerial accounting consists in detailing, analyzing, and interpreting the information provided by the general accounting, presenting it in a form that is accessible to the company management. Financial information is confidential, addressed to the internal environment of the company and presented as no standardized periodical reports adapted to the internal management needs. Costs play a determinant role in substantiating the decisions regarding the optimum production system and its adjustment in any competitive economic environment, as a special instrument determining the management of the company both as a whole and for each internal subdivision. But cost will only be able to play its true role if determined in a realistic and pertinent way. Consequently, the final objective of management from the point of view of forecasting, rational organization, information, analysis, prompt decision, and constant control is to obtain production at minimum cost.

INTRODUCTION

The complexity of the economic life under the market economy competitively requirements have determined an increased role of information in the process of decision making (Allen & Ramanna, 2013). The quality of current and long-term decisions and implicitly the results obtained depend on the quality of the information (Alzola, 2017; Baker & Bettner, 1997; Barth, Landsman, Young & Zhuang, 2014; Caylor, 2010).

Managers are generally preoccupied by constant issues: to understand the future, to manage the activity of others (Damayant, 2013). To understand the future, managerial accounting is built to identify the connections between the goals pursued and the resources engaged to obtain them (He, Pan & Tian, 2017; Li, 2010; Ramanna, 2008; Soltani, 2014).

DOI: 10.4018/978-1-7998-8069-1.ch013

The managerial accounting refers to an accounting system intended for managers, which does not mean that they do not use the information supplied by financial accounting as well (Schleicher, Tahoun & Walker, 2010). It must provide the manager with the information absolutely necessary to help him understand the phenomena and the processes taking place in the economic entity, the real information based on which he can make pertinent decisions, can foresee the consequences of his decisions and have at his disposal the levers needed to exert constant and efficient control (Lukka, 2010; Hou, Jin, Yang, Yuan & Zhang, 2015; Dennis, 2014).

BACKGROUND

The economic management as a process administrating the assets forming an economic entity's patrimony and managing the activity carried out based on that patrimony is conditioned by the way in which the entire economic potential is organized, turned to profit and made to act toward the fulfilment of the budgetary commitments with maximum efficiency (Florou & Pope, 2012).

Moreover, economic and financial management "is a tool in the decision-making relating to the collection and analysis of information in order to increase the performance level of the economic entity" (Barth, Landsman & Lang, 2008).

The foundation of the economic management – as management vehicle – is the achievement of the budget objectives with minimum costs so that when the activity is completed the revenue exceeds the costs, namely there is a profit that ensures a level of profitability as high as possible both at general level and by product, department or service performed (Ahmed, Neel & Wang, 2013; Andon, Baxter & Chua, 2007; Barth, 2013; Byard, Li & Yu, 2011; Chen, Qu & Sun, 2017).

The decision-making process is one of the manager's main functions:" a decision is a person or group of persons' social and deliberate act defining the purpose and the objectives of a certain action, the directions and the ways to achieve that action, all of them determined, according to a certain need, by a process of obtaining information, deliberation, and assessment of the means and consequences of carrying out that action" (Parker, 2012).

Managers are constantly faced with situations when they need to decide what products should be sold, what production method should be used, whether to produce or to buy certain product component parts, what the price should be, what distribution channels should be used (Richardson, 2011). This is why the decision-making process is a difficult and complex managerial task.

The difficulty of the task is increased by the various types of situations the company may be faced with at a given moment (Ahrens, 2008).

To be successful in their decision-making activity, managers must have at their disposal all the required instruments, to be able to distinguish between the relevant costs and the irrelevant ones and eliminate the latter from the decision-making process (Ball, 2013).

Costs may be relevant for one decision and irrelevant for another. In other words, a manager must have at his disposal different costs for different objectives. A group of costs may be relevant for a certain objective but if the company's objective changes, relevant costs may also change. For each decision, the manager must examine the data placed at his disposal and isolate the relevant costs. If not, the manager assumes the risk of using irrelevant data (Arsenault & Faerman, 2014).

Such an information system is not efficient unless the way in which it has been conceived responds to certain rules both in point of its operation and in point of its content (Bettner & Kate, 2013). The way in which the information is presented may vary but it must observe certain restrictions as to concision and pertinence. In this respect, the companies' dashboards for example incite to dialogue and motivate those responsible (Cahan & Sun, 2015).

Budget monitoring is formed of all the documents, such as dashboards, the analytical activity report, and the coercing actions plan (Chen, Tang, Jiang & Lin, 2010).

The dashboard is a control and comparison instrument but the information system incorporated in it makes it a dialogue and communication instrument and a helping hand in the decision-making process (Doukakis, 2014).

Knowing the weak points must always be accompanied by the analysis of the causes and followed by the adoption of coercing actions, while observing the set terms (Holthausen & Watts, 2001). The dashboard is therefore an efficient instrument in the decision-making process, with a primary role among the budget monitoring instruments (Li, Qi, Tian & Zhang, 2017).

ASSISTING THE DECISION-MAKING PROCESS IN PROFIT CENTRES BASED ON THE PERFORMANCE INDICATORS

The cost-production-profit analysis is one of the most important instruments made available to managers. This analysis helps them understand the connexions between costs, production volume, and profit in the company they are managing, based on the interactions between variable unit costs, fixed costs, product costs, and the volume of the activity (Ahmed, Neel & Wang, 2013).

This type of analysis represents a key factor for managers in the decision-making process (Brown, 2010). Such decisions may refer for example to the products to be manufactured or sold, to the types of production facilities required, to the price policy to be adopted, and to the marketing strategy to be applied. The presence of the cost-volume-profit concept in managerial accounting is so strong that it influences all the decisions adopted by managers (Jackson & Liu, 2010).

When producing goods and services, a company must constantly make decisions on the organization of incoming flows and on the ways in which the production factors should be combined. Irrespective of the company's option concerning the procurement and combination of production factors in the production process, such factors will be consumed, transformed, will change their initial physical form and utility, becoming goods and services with different values and uses.

Defined as the "all of the expenditures incurred to obtain a product, carry out a job or perform a service" (Ball, Li & Shivakumar, 2015), cost is a category specific to the production of goods, revealing the relations occurring when we compare the money form of the expenditure incurred for the production means with that of the labour employed to obtain a product or a service.

Being a fundamental category of a competitive economy, cost is the synthetic indicator used in the managerial decision-making process to assess quantitatively and qualitatively the company's efficiency in combining and consuming its production factors to become an economic player on a highly competitive market.

A company cannot act directly on prices, the decisive element when it comes to ensuring high profits, but the production cost represents for it the operational indicator constantly present on the dashboard of the current and projection management that can be acted upon as early as the designing stage to create a product similar to that of the competition.

A solid system of indicators to measure and analyse the economic efficiency of the consumption of resources cannot be obtained in the absence of adequate instruments to separate and monitor efforts made for each product, work executed or service performed. This is why we need to systematize consumption and properly calculate costs, to be able to make various generalizing comparisons in time and space of the positive results and cut wastes. Tailoring costs in order to create correlated analysis and decision instruments is a complex process that will only trigger favourable results if the qualitative side of the tailored phenomenon is not neglected. The modernization of production systems must therefore be accompanied by a general reconsideration of the way in which cost information and managerial accounting are approached and organized.

The cost-production-profit relation analysis is extremely important in real economic circumstances, showing certain particularities depending on the forms of competitively, the characteristics of the supply and the period it refers to.

In the short run, when the main way to increase the supply is to increase production capacities and, consequently, significantly increase costs, the individual offer of a rational producer will oscillate within certain limits determined by a certain cost the market price of the product. To reach his goal, namely to obtain maximum profit, the rational producer will first decide to minimize costs using the optimum combinations of production factors, then, based on the market prices, he will decide a certain production volume to ensure maximum profit. Maximizing profit in this situation means maximum increase of revenues alongside with minimum levels of total costs.

An important tool in assisting decisions is the budget (Ozkan, Singer, & You, 2012).). The budget management as a management technique relies on the profit estimations produced according to the company's internal and external conditions. Based on these estimations, the responsible factors are assigned tasks, programs, and means expressed as values, to be achieve during a limited period of time. Managerial practice constantly compares budgets and expenditures in order to determine the differences, which is in fact the internal accounting management control.

Budget accounting management is related not only to the accounting activity but is a true company administration technique, a company management philosophy involving three stages: estimation, budgeting, and control. These three stages provide the managers with the needed dashboard information – the main way to rationalize the microeconomic information subsystem at company level.

The first stage of the budget accounting management is the estimation. It may be defined as "a voluntarist, scientific, and collective attitude toward the future action" (Soltani, 2014). One of the foundations of estimation is the scientific method. Flair and intuition are not rejected a priori but must be exercised within a previously defined framework.

This operation can be performed by a company economist or it can be the result of the reflections of a company responsible factor who may issue three hypotheses (maximal, average, minimal) and then, based on them, determine the possible budgets for the future periods. As opposed to estimations, forecasts consist in advancing a possible future result not justified by any source or reasoning.

The budget relies on a concept quite spread in collectivises. This concept may be defined as "the estimation of a set of revenues and expenditures" which reveals from the start its financial character (Lukka, 2010). A company's internal budgets have many specific characteristics but they are all comparable, which makes it easy to regroup them in a general budget.

Advancing budget numbers and objectives requires immediate ascribing of responsibilities so that the targeted objectives are achieved without using more means than the ones provided.

Responsibility requires a close relationship between the budget and the company's general organization. The latter involves an organizational chart and a payroll which lists all the tasks the holder of the function has to perform. The budget is nothing more than a numerical version of the documents, considering that every activity has a monetary identification and value. This does not mean that the budget must by all means follow the shape of the existing organization form.

The constant influence exerted by the general economic development on the activity of the company determines a series of adjustments during the respective period of time. At company level, adjustment is achieved in two ways: a flexible budget and budget revision. Budget flexibility consists in the fact that any expenditure budget is defined according to the activity performed by the respective department.

Budget revision means that every budget can be modified when external circumstances request it or when other budgets it relies on are themselves being modified. Every company has an investment plan divided into annual tranches which provides the budget series. Any slow down or acceleration of the company's activity triggers a variation in the investment budget tranches commitment.

As economic model, a budget is the simplified representation of the way in which a unit functions. Economically speaking, it is more precisely a mathematical and accounting model, namely a schematic representation of a monetarily assessed reality. It consists of a series of equations, some of them accounting equations, others behavioural equations. The accounting equations allow certain positions to be interconnected.

The third stage of the budget accounting management is the control which may be defined as "a comparison between estimations and achievements" (Ahrens, 2008). Control application requires several stages: determine the differences, sort and communicate the differences, explain the differences.

The first work stage, namely determining the differences, concerns the following problems: comparability between estimations and achievements, and knowledge efficiency.

To compare them, these budget and accounting categories must be comparable, their accounting structure must be identical with the budget one. This means that the budget must be calculated according to the way in which the accounting system is organized. The implementation of a budget system may somehow confuse the company's accounting plan because each has its own particular view.

The difference resulting from this comparison may indicate an accounting error. To be useful to those interested, the information must be timely. If the estimations are known in advance, the achievements may be determined much later.

The managerial dashboard contains a set of actual information presented in a predetermined form, relating to the main results of the company's activities or to some of them and to the main factors conditioning their effective and efficient progress.

The accounting dashboard provides information indispensable for the short term control over the company's activity. It is determined for very short periods of time and on a frequent regular basis enabling the managers to perform rapid coercing actions or even anticipate events.

To create an accounting dashboard panel, in addition to the documents specific for the standard cost method, certain common documents used for gathering information are also used, such as individual or collective consumption tickets, individual or collective limit consumption cards, consumption and other stock exits registers, payrolls, salary and social contribution registers, production costs distribution and deduction registers, equipment items operation hours record charts, delivery, transfer, return tickets. Cost, time, and quality are the foundation of managerial accounting because of the accent placed on processes and their improvement. The accounting dashboard is therefore the instrument helping the cost-oriented management to monitor the processes taking place in the company and form an opinion on the way they are carried out.

Dashboards are created to enable rapid action. This means a short period of time (maximum 10 days) and rapid consultation (a single glance should enable proper consultation of a dashboard panel). The dashboard panel should therefore display only the strictly necessary information. It contains little information, namely just the selected and pertinent information.

If a plane cannot be piloted by means of a single instrument, neither can a company be managed only from the perspective of its financial indicators. An efficient and good manager, just like a pilot, must use and analyse the countless information around him in order to be able to take the best decisions and obtain commensurate results. The balanced scorecard provides managers with the entire range of instruments needed to align objectives with the organization's strategy.

The financial axis refers to the improvement of the company's financial performance. The objectives are set according to the level of development of the business, as follows: if it is a start-up, the financial objectives will be aggressive because the turnover must increase, if it is a mature company, maintaining the results would be preferred.

The balanced scorecard draws the attention to the importance of maintaining a long-run view of the activity because it is not enough for a company to purchase new and performant equipment items but also to invest in the human capital.

The implementation of the balanced scorecard system in various service and production companies has determined three main categories of the learning development perspective, namely the employees' capabilities, the efficiency of the information systems, and employee motivation. The success of these companies is the best example to evaluate the versatility of the BSC.

Each objective, the target of each of the four perspectives is selected based on the organization's view and strategy. The company's strategy is "an important lever to drive and maintain change, to emphasize the organization's creative management" (Alzola, 2017). Strategic planning is a determining factor for the creation, launching, and survival of a business.

Before starting a business, the entrepreneur must ask himself which direction he wants to follow in the world of business and assess the possibilities regarding the course of his actions. The company's strategy must not be mistaken for the concept of strategic management which is a dynamic process by means of which the company's managers take strategic decisions estimating and performing future organizational changes as a result of modifications in their business environment.

The balanced scorecard supplies a balanced set of objective or subjective, internal and external indicators relating to processes, innovation, education and growth, but also indicators relating to results as an effect of previous efforts and indicators anticipating future performance. The strategic objectives are established at the organization's top management level and are subsequently communicated in "cascade" to the operational levels. In this way, each employee will know his role in the success of the company and his particular contribution to the global performance.

When the employees are correctly informed about the managers' intentions and the decisions taken by them, they will be able to contribute actively to reaching those goals and implicitly fulfil the chosen strategy. This route followed by the information coming from the executive sectors, namely the managers, to the employees in the productive/operational sectors is also known as the "top-down" route.

Finally, the balanced scorecard is conceived and designed by the organization's managers (generally those in the economic and financial departments) but is driven by the company's employees, which explains why it is paramount for them to know the strategy, the mission, and the objectives. The balanced scorecard must be everybody's concern and must align the entire company to the respective strategy.

The next check list shows the points to be observed by the company and the design team when creating a balanced scorecard. Using a balanced scorecard starts with the top management's consensus on a common view and strategy.

Only after having reached such consensus can the activity of designing a balanced scorecard architecture begin. This will clarify the perspectives to be specifically illustrated for the company, transposing the manager's strategy.

The objective is to reduce complexity and to direct the top manager's attention toward the strategically important elements and a clear expression of the relationships among the objectives on the Strategy Map, even if in the beginning only statements regarding trends will be possible.

The expectation that a balanced scorecard could produce a determined image of business should be eliminated. Used correctly, the balanced scorecard provides the possibility to abandon the endless planning rounds and go back to efficient strategic discussions relating to the business issues decisive for the competition.

THE ROLE OF CONTROLLING IN MANAGERIAL PERFORMANCE

The concept of controlling has been constantly developed by companies in the last twenty years, becoming a management function indispensable to any modern company. However, outside the circle of experts, there are major differences of opinion both in theory and in practice concerning the term "controlling". Controlling is often mistakenly considered a synonym of exercising control. However, controlling means much more than that, namely a functional management concept with the role of coordinating the planning, the monitoring and the information aimed at obtaining the desired results. The *controller* is to a large extent the "economic conscience" of a company.

In principle, we must strictly differentiate between controlling as a function and controller as the person responsible. In fact, controlling is, in the sense of management, a central task of the management activity. Every manager also performs controlling functions among his other tasks. As a process and way of thinking, controlling is generated by the manager and the controller together as a team, representing a type of "interface" (Ball, 2013).

In its primary sense, controlling does not indicate a position or a person but a field of tasks achieved by various persons or even by the management, without someone in particular occupying the position of "controller". The controlling function is taken by the company management or the accounting department management, especially in small and medium-size companies. In companies with over two hundred employees, a controller is most often appointed to be responsible for the controlling tasks.

The controller's coordination job consists therefore in seeing that the management's planning and control activities are result-oriented and the information they need is always available. The controller's role within the planning activity consists in coordinating the partial plans and organizing the whole planning process. It is therefore not the controller the one who normally plans and coordinates but the manager. To be more precise, we should point out that in small or middle-sized companies the controller's task is often more than a purely coordinating job. Thus, a controller often also performs planning jobs relating to the content, jobs that should have been carried out by the specialized departments. This is especially the case with his contribution to the activity of organizing the company's business policy and of strategic planning. In recent years, an expansion of the job's significance has been noted globally. From a simple performer of services, the controller is turning into a management consultant.

On the other hand, the controller's responsibility results from the fact that, by organizing and monitoring the management process to ensure the achievement of the objectives, the planning and the management, he clearly supports the management in taking the right, objective-oriented decisions. The responsibility for the decisions taken and expressed in the plans developed still lies with the management.

In fact, controlling is not just a service helping the management with the supplied information. It is to the same extent an idea to be brought to the knowledge of all the company's employees. This idea includes both a success-oriented course of action with personalized responsibilities, but also a way of thinking beyond the individual area of activity, in the sense of interface management.

Controlling is carried out not only through the controller but best on the spot, through the directly involved employees. Thus, controlling is becoming more and more an integrated controlling, with the institution of controlling and controller playing increasingly the role of moderator in promoting the idea of controlling.

The current definition of controlling assigns to the controller planning, control, and information tasks. This concept will be further analysed and explained in the following paragraphs.

Every company follows its own strategy whose success is ensured through a proper structuring of the production processes and through an adequate organizational structure. The controlling system is anchored in this organization. Controlling must form a whole, a system as far as the tasks, the organization, and the instruments are concerned.

The task of controlling inside the company consists in sorting the usually existing individual component elements, check their usefulness, complete and organize them in the form of a system.

The most important source of information within the information system is the accounting department. The automatic data processing system has become an indispensable element. Budgeting would be worth mentioning as an important component of the planning and control system. However, the controller's job covers not only the short term actual planning area; strategic aspects are already increasingly marking the controller's job.

In principle, the controller has two different coordination tasks, both in relation to the planning system, and in relation to the information system. He deals with structuring and development, on the one hand, and with the daily operation, on the other hand (permanent coordination).

The structuring of the information system means determining the information needed, obtaining and processing it (through accounting operations) and transmitting it under the form of reports. This, for example, has to do with the type of cost calculation system to be employed or the investment calculation procedure to be used to cover the information requirements of the management. The questions regarding the structure of the planning and control system refer to the type and number of plans, for example, their content, the development in time of a planning period.

This also clarifies the following: the information system and the planning and control system cannot be structured independently. They depend on each other as regards the content because the accounting figures, for example, are processed within the planning activity. This defines the first coordination task of the controller: the coordinated organization in point of content and form of an information system as well as of a planning and control one.

The second coordination task, namely the permanent coordination of the two systems, is performed by the controller in the following manner: the information system determines on a regular basis, for example, the real values providing information on the actual achievement of the company's objectives (for example, the real turnover in the first semester). Comparing these real values with the estimated ones (real-estimated comparison), analysing the deviations and the resulting effects on the subsequent planning are an example of the controller's permanent coordination activity. Permanent coordination must therefore be understood as a reaction to the modified information from inside and outside the company "to overcome the disturbances".

The above-mentioned information enables a new approach of the activity of controllers who therefore coordinate an adjustment cycle.

Let us start with planning. Based on the information supplied when the planning was made, he tries to find and determine certain efficiency criteria adequate for the company. The planning system is based on a given level of information, unlike the information system which constantly improves the information level. The comparison between real and estimated finally leads to a comparison between the planned figures and those actually achieved. Therefore, we need to determine the cause, possibly correct the errors or establish some coercing measures. So, the adjustment cycle returns to the planning stage.

The most important principle of the controlling adjustment cycle is the following: deviations always occur as a result of modifications in the company and the company's environment. That is why such deviations must not be used justify penalties inflicted on employees for negligence, but only as basis to determine new measures. These measures will help achieve the planned objectives or – in serious individual cases – to adapt the objectives according to the modified conditions.

On the whole, the controlling system and its components help the management by using the management system to develop concrete plans and process for it the information made available by the controller through the information system. The managerial decisions are expressed through plans materialized in concrete actions.

The secondary systems – instruments, organization, and process – are structured and employed based on the controlling philosophy.

Controlling instruments are based on a flexible database system using the basic cost accounting information, product calculations, results account, etc. and are completed additionally with market and strategic information. Other important controlling instruments are the investments account as well as indicators and systems of indicators. The instruments are used in planning, management and control, and reporting.

Typical organization of controlling in a large, modern company. Besides central controlling (company controlling), a cross-sectional function performing general controlling tasks for various departments and functions, there are decentralized controlling departments for each area, department, and subsidiary. The organization of controlling follows the structure of the organization according to the dotted line principle. The most important thing is that the controller's way of thinking and know-how are always available on the spot, for example in functional areas, and that the employees are familiar with it. This is strictly connected with the current trends in integrated controlling dealt with previously. The responsible controlling specialist at central level ensures the unity and the integrity of all controlling systems.

The controlling process is characterized by the joint action of the information and the planning systems. The departments work out individual, detailed plans based on the objectives planned by the company management. The individual department plans are then gathered at a higher level and harmonized (the consolidated plan). The controlling activity is carried out in a coordinated manner based on the three-year planning detailed on a yearly basis. Plans and measures can be expressed in quantifiable management indicators.

The practical application and development of controlling are aimed at increasing the employees' level of acceptance toward it. The basic reasoning of the concept of controlling must in the end be implemented among the employees to enable it to become integrated even in the absence of a permanent department responsible for controlling.

SOLUTIONS AND RECOMMENDATIONS

The minimum requests a dashboard must fulfil are integrity, rigorousness, aggregations, accessibility, balance, explicitness, adaptability, and be economic.

These requirements ensure the fulfilment by the dashboard of its main functions, namely to alert, assess-diagnose, eliminate negative aspects and generalize positive elements.

A dashboard must observe the organizational structure of the economic unit so that the information provided corresponds to the action areas at every hierarchical level and cost centre. The indicators calculated at higher hierarchical levels are obtained from the consolidated indicators at lower hierarchical levels, on a pyramidal structure.

Common measurement units must therefore be used for the calculation of the indicators and publication should be set at regular intervals authorizing a coherent regrouping and simultaneous updating of the accounting information. The accounting management dashboard enables control over the delegated responsibilities and a synthetic evaluation of the results obtained by the subordinates.

To create an accounting dashboard panel, we have to select the indicators and define the information to be supplied by the lower hierarchical levels. Dashboard panels provide indicators regarding the current situation as well as historical indicators. This provides an image of the evolution of accounting indicators, alerting the responsible factors before the occurrence of critical results, anticipating future actions.

There are two types of dashboard panels: An independent one, with heterogeneous panels adapted to the precise requirements of the responsible factors at various levels, and one integrated in the general information system of the company based on adequate software. As part of the company's general information system, the dashboard panel becomes a very important internal communication instrument.

Automated dashboards require the existence of an information system to gather, process, and display the needed information. As far as the information sources are concerned, dashboards must be able to process a consistent amount of data and observe restrictions in point of confidentiality, differentiated user access, and provide evolution and development possibilities.

Knowledge of the company's achievements remains therefore one of the main pursuits of accounting management control. With or without budget management, the management and control of a company relies on all type of recent information concerning its performance.

FUTURE RESEARCH DIRECTIONS

The financial objectives of the divisions would therefore be subordinated to the corporation strategy. In the end, all the objectives and the targets of the other three fundamental axes should be tied to the achievement of one or more of the financial objectives.

The client axis refers to the way in which companies identify clients and the markets they have chosen to be active on. Managers must concentrate only on those markets where their products and services can be best sold and try to become the best on that market. It is useless and also risky for a company to try and diversify its activity on certain markets where other strong competitors are already active.

The organization must concentrate on maintaining and strengthening its position on those markets where it is active by increasing the client satisfaction level, the number of clients, and its market share. In addition to doing their best to satisfy their clients, division managers must also translate the mission and the strategy into client-market specific objectives. To be able to set such objectives, market surveys and questionnaires are needed regarding quality, brand, functionality, reputation, and price.

The axis of internal processes refers to those critical processes inside the organization that can be constantly improved to reach the clients and the shareholders' goals. From this point of view, objectives are set when the financial objectives and those of the clients have already been set.

Innovation is a major process because the development of new technologies can satisfy the clients' new needs securing a sure profit for the company, then the current needs of the clients but also their post-sale needs must be granted increased attention. The learning and development axis concerns in principle the company's capacity for adaptation and innovation in order to achieve its strategic objectives.

CONCLUSION

Considered for a long time the very objective of managerial accounting, is to have multi-criterial knowledge of the costs. Knowledge of product costs is crucial considering both the commercial reason and the reason provided by an efficient management or other reasons.

From the commercial reason point of view, one important reason for knowing the cost is the determination of the sale price. This reason will however remain valid only under certain circumstances, for a new product or a single order, because in a competitive economy it is not the price that determines the price formation. When prices are formed based on the demand and supply balance mechanism, the knowledge of costs has a different significance and importance for the management decision, helping to determine results by products, works or services, thus ensuring that pertinent decisions are taken concerning the optimization of the production and marketing structures.

This is why involving cost and works accounting information in the decisions regarding the product portfolio has also a strategic connotation. The knowledge of costs certainly has other reasons as well, such as determining the value of in-stock products, a comparative analysis in time and space of the production factors consumption efficiency.

REFERENCES

Ahmed, A., Neel, M., & Wang, D. (2013). Does mandatory adoption of IFRS improve accounting quality? Preliminary evidence. *Contemporary Accounting Research, 30*(4), 388–423. doi:10.1111/j.1911-3846.2012.01193.x

Ahrens, T. (2008). Overcoming the subjective–objective divide in interpretive management accounting research. *Accounting, Organizations and Society, 33*(2), 292–297. doi:10.1016/j.aos.2007.03.002

Allen, A., & Ramanna, K. (2013). Towards an understanding of the role of standard setters in standard setting. *Journal of Accounting and Economics, 55*(1), 1–66. doi:10.1016/j.jacceco.2012.05.003

Alzola, M. A. (2017). Beware of the watchdog: Rethinking the normative justification of gatekeeper liability. *Journal of Business Ethics*, *140*(4), 705–721. doi:10.100710551-017-3460-3

Andon, P., Baxter, J., & Chua, W. F. (2007). Accounting change as relational drifting: A field study of experiments with performance measurement. *Management Accounting Research*, *18*(2), 273–308. doi:10.1016/j.mar.2006.06.007

Arsenault, P., & Faerman, S. R. (2014). Embracing paradox in management: The value of the competing values framework. *Organizational Management Journal*, *11*(3), 147–158. doi:10.1080/15416518.2014.949614

Baker, C., & Bettner, M. (1997). Interpretive and Critical Research in Accounting: A Commentary on its Absence from Mainstream Research||. *Critical Perspectives on Accounting*, *8*(4), 293–310. doi:10.1006/cpac.1996.0116

Ball, R. (2013). Accounting informs investors and earnings management is rife: Two questionable beliefs. *Accounting Horizons*, *27*(4), 847–853. doi:10.2308/acch-10366

Barth, M., Landsman, W., & Lang, M. (2008). International accounting standards and accounting quality. *Journal of Accounting Research*, *46*(3), 467–498. doi:10.1111/j.1475-679X.2008.00287.x

Barth, M. E. (2013). Global comparability in financial reporting: What, why, how, and when? *China Journal of Accounting Studies*, *1*(1), 2–12. doi:10.1080/21697221.2013.781765

Barth, M. E., Landsman, W. R., Young, D., & Zhuang, Z. (2014). Relevance of Differences between Net Income based on IFRS and Domestic Standards for European Firms. *Journal of Business Finance & Accounting*, *41*(3-4), 297–506. doi:10.1111/jbfa.12067

Bettner, M., & Kate, K. (2013). Changes in annual reporting rituals of financial services firms in periods of market crisis. *International Journal of Critical Accounting*, *5*(6), 577–593. doi:10.1504/IJCA.2013.059027

Brown, J. (2010). Accounting and visual cultural studies: Potentialities, challenges and prospects. *Accounting, Auditing & Accountability Journal*, *23*(4), 482–505. doi:10.1108/09513571011041598

Byard, D., Li, Y., & Yu, Y. (2011). The effect of mandatory IFRS adoption on financial analysts' information environment. *Journal of Accounting Research*, *49*(1), 69–96. doi:10.1111/j.1475-679X.2010.00390.x

Cahan, S. F., & Sun, J. (2015). The effect of audit experience on audit fees and audit quality. *Journal of Accounting, Auditing & Finance*, *30*(1), 78–100. doi:10.1177/0148558X14544503

Caylor, M. L. (2010). Strategic revenue recognition to achieve earnings benchmarks. *Journal of Accounting and Public Policy*, *29*(1), 82–95. doi:10.1016/j.jaccpubpol.2009.10.008

Chen, H., Tang, Q., Jiang, Y., & Lin, Z. (2010). The role of international financial reporting standards in accounting quality: Evidence from the European Union. *Journal of International Financial Management & Accounting*, *21*(3), 220–278. doi:10.1111/j.1467-646X.2010.01041.x

Chen, M., Qu, X., & Sun, X. (2017). Whose cost of equity capital reduces after IFRS convergence and why? Heterogeneity evidence from Chinese stock market. *China Journal of Accounting Studies*, *5*(1), 1–27. doi:10.1080/21697213.2017.1304539

Damayant, T. (2013). Who is afraid of Qualitative Research? A Compromise Accounting Research Failure in Improving Accounting Practices. *International Journal of Advances in Management and Economics, 2*(2), 89-94.

Dennis, I. (2014). *The Nature of Accounting Regulation*. Routledge.

Doukakis, L. C. (2014). The effect of mandatory IFRS adoption on real and accrual-based earnings management activities. *Journal of Accounting and Public Policy, 33*(6), 551–572. doi:10.1016/j.jaccpubpol.2014.08.006

Florou, A., & Pope, P. (2012). Mandatory IFRS adoption and institutional investment decisions. *The Accounting Review, 87*(6), 1993–2025. doi:10.2308/accr-50225

He, K., Pan, X., & Tian, G. (2017). Legal liability, government intervention, and auditor behavior: Evidence from structural reform of audit firms in China. *European Accounting Review, 26*(1), 61–95. doi: 10.1080/09638180.2015.1100547

Holthausen, R. W., & Watts, R. L. (2001). The relevance of the value-relevance literature for financial accounting standard setting. *Journal of Accounting and Economics, 31*(1-3), 3–75. doi:10.1016/S0165-4101(01)00029-5

Hou, Q., Jin, Q., Yang, R., Yuan, H., & Zhang, G. (2015). Performance commitments of controlling shareholders and earnings management. *Contemporary Accounting Research, 32*(3), 1099–1127. doi:10.1111/1911-3846.12111

Jackson, S. B., & Liu, X. K. (2010). The allowance for uncollectible accounts, conservatism, and earnings management. *Journal of Accounting Research, 48*(3), 565–601. doi:10.1111/j.1475-679X.2009.00364.x

Li, L., Qi, B., Tian, G., & Zhang, G. (2017). The contagion effect of low-quality audits at the level of individual auditors. *The Accounting Review, 92*(1), 137–163. doi:10.2308/accr-51407

Li, S. (2010). Does mandatory adoption of international accounting standards in the European Union reduce the cost of equity capital? *The Accounting Review, 85*(2), 607–636. doi:10.2308/accr.2010.85.2.607

Lukka, K. (2010). The roles and effects of paradigms in accounting research. *Management Accounting Research, 21*(2), 110–115. doi:10.1016/j.mar.2010.02.002

Parker, L. (2012). Qualitative management accounting research: Assessing deliverables and relevance. *Critical Perspectives on Accounting, 23*(1), 54–70. doi:10.1016/j.cpa.2011.06.002

Ramanna, K. (2008). The implications of unverifiable fair-value accounting: Evidence from the political economy of goodwill accounting. *Journal of Accounting and Economics, 45*(2-3), 253–281. doi:10.1016/j.jacceco.2007.11.006

Richardson, A. (2011). Myth, Paradigms and Academic Accounting Research: A Comment on Reading and Understanding Academic Research in Accounting. *Global Perspectives on Accounting Education, 8*, 67–77.

Schleicher, T., Tahoun, A., & Walker, M. (2010). IFRS adoption in Europe and investment-cash flow sensitivity: Outsider versus insider economies. *The International Journal of Accounting, 45*(2), 143–168. doi:10.1016/j.intacc.2010.04.007

Soltani, B. (2014). The anatomy of corporate fraud: A comparative analysis of high profile American and European corporate scandals. *Journal of Business Ethics, 120*(2), 251–274. doi:10.100710551-013-1660-z

ADDITIONAL READING

Ahmed, A., Neel, M., & Wang, D. (2013). Does mandatory adoption of IFRS improve accounting quality? Preliminary evidence. *Contemporary Accounting Research, 30*(4), 388–423. doi:10.1111/j.1911-3846.2012.01193.x

Ball, R., Li, X., & Shivakumar, L. (2015). Contractibility and transparency of financial statement information prepared under IFRS: Evidence from debt contracts around IFRS adoption. *Journal of Accounting Research, 53*(5), 915–963. doi:10.1111/1475-679X.12095

Fan, J. P. H., Li, J., & Zheng, G. (2016). Revisiting the bright and dark sides of capital flows in business groups. *Journal of Business Ethics, 134*(4), 509–528. doi:10.100710551-014-2382-6

Ozkan, N., Singer, Z., & You, H. (2012). Mandatory IFRS adoption and the contractual usefulness of accounting information in executive compensation. *Journal of Accounting Research, 50*(4), 1077–1107. doi:10.1111/j.1475-679X.2012.00453.x

Compilation of References

Abdallah, A. (2020). The Effect Of Corona Pandemic On Workers' Psychology And Performance In The Manufacturing Sector. *Systematic Reviews in Pharmacy, 11*(12), 1593–1599.

Abernethy, M. A., & Stoelwinder, J. U. (1995). The role of professional control in the management of complex organizations. *Accounting, Organizations and Society, 20*(1), 1–17. doi:10.1016/0361-3682(94)E0017-O

Accor CSR & Performance. (2021). https://group.accor.com/en/commitment/sharing-our-knowledge/csr-and-performance

AccountAbility. (2018). *AA1000 AccountAbility principles*. Author.

Accounting, E. (2010). *Current Status and Options for SAIs*. INTOSAI. Working Group on Environmental Auditing.

Agha, S., Alrubaiee, L., & Jamhour, M. (2012). Effect of core competence on competitive advantage and organizational performance. *International Journal of Business and Management, 7*(1), 192–204.

Ahearne, M., Lam, S. K., Mathieu, J. E., & Bolander, W. (2010). Why are some sales people better at adapting to organizational change? *Journal of Marketing, 74*(3), 65–79. doi:10.1509/jmkg.74.3.065

Ahmed, A., Neel, M., & Wang, D. (2013). Does mandatory adoption of IFRS improve accounting quality? Preliminary evidence. *Contemporary Accounting Research, 30*(4), 388–423. doi:10.1111/j.1911-3846.2012.01193.x

Ahn, J. (2020). Role of hope and compulsion for CSR activities in hotel customers' engagement. *Current Issues in Tourism*, 1–7. doi:10.1080/13683500.2020.1839026

Ahn, J., & Kwon, J. (2020). CSR perception and revisit intention: The roles of trust and commitment. *Journal of Hospitality and Tourism Insights, 3*(5), 607–623. doi:10.1108/JHTI-02-2020-0022

Ahrens, T. (2008). Overcoming the subjective–objective divide in interpretive management accounting research. *Accounting, Organizations and Society, 33*(2), 292–297. doi:10.1016/j.aos.2007.03.002

Air Charity Network. (2021). https://aircharitynetwork.org/about-us/

Ak, F., & Sönmez, Z. (2007). *Fatura ve e-fatura*. Ak Denetim. Avalaible at: http://www.vergihesabi.com/ makaleler/2007/2007_06.htm

Akgül, M., & Gökçöl, O. (1997). Internet ve ilgili konularda çokça sorulan sorular: INET-TR.CSS. *Sürüm, 2*, 5.

Akgün, A. E., Keskin, H., & Byrne, J. (2009). Organizational emotional capability, product and process innovation, and firm performance: An empirical analysis. *Journal of Engineering and Technology Management, 26*(3), 103–130. doi:10.1016/j.jengtecman.2009.06.008

Alali, F., & Yeh, C. L. (2012). Cloud Computing: Overview and Risk Analysis. *Journal of Information Systems, 26*(2), 13–33. doi:10.2308/isys-50229

Alazard, C., & Sépari, S. (1998). *Management control. Manual & Applications* [Contrôle de gestion. Manuel&Applications] (4th ed.). Dunod.

Albu, N., & Albu, C. (2003). *Performance management tools. Management Control* [Instrumente de management al performantei. Control de gestiune]. Economica.

Alfsen, K. H., Bye, T., & Lorentsen, L. (1987). *Natural Resource Accounting and Analysis. The Norwegian Experience 1978-86*. Central Bureau of Statistics of Norway.

Algan, S. (1997). Bilgi yolunda bildik yeni bir durak: Ekstranet. *BT Haber, 111*, 54–55.

Alhyari, S., Alazab, M., Venkatraman, S., Alazab, M., & Alazab, A. (2013). Performance evaluation of e-government services using balanced scorecard. *Benchmarking, 20*(4), 512–536. doi:10.1108/BIJ-08-2011-0063

Allen, A., & Ramanna, K. (2013). Towards an understanding of the role of standard setters in standard setting. *Journal of Accounting and Economics, 55*(1), 1–66. doi:10.1016/j.jacceco.2012.05.003

Al-Majadi, M., & Mat, M. K. (2011). Modelling the antecedents on internet banking service adoption (IBSA) in Jordan: A strutural equation modelling (SEM) approach. *Journal of Internet Banking and Commerce, 16*(1), 1–15.

Alp, A. (2007). *Muhasebede kullanılan defter ve belgelerin elektronik ortamda izlenmesi* (Master's thesis).

Alstete, J. W., & Beutell, N. J. (2018). Designing learning spaces for management education: A mixed methods research approach. *Journal of Management Development, 37*(2), 201–211. doi:10.1108/JMD-08-2017-0247

Alzola, M. A. (2017). Beware of the watchdog: Rethinking the normative justification of gatekeeper liability. *Journal of Business Ethics, 140*(4), 705–721. doi:10.100710551-017-3460-3

Amidu, M., Effah, J., & Abor, J. (2011). e-Accounting practice in small and medium enterprise in Ghana. *Journal of Management Policy and Practice, 12*(4), 146–155.

Andon, P., Baxter, J., & Chua, W. F. (2007). Accounting change as relational drifting: A field study of experiments with performance measurement. *Management Accounting Research, 18*(2), 273–308. doi:10.1016/j.mar.2006.06.007

Angels of Flight Community Involvement. (2021). https://www.angelsofflightcanada.com/community-involvement/

Appiah, K., Agyemang, F., Agyei, Y., Nketiah, S., & Mensah, B. (2014). Computerised accounting information systems: Lesson in state owned enterprises in developing economies. *Journal of Finance and Management in Public Services, 12*(1).

Aras, G., & Crowther, D. (2009). Making sustainable development sustainable. *Management Decision, 47*(6), 975-988.

Arcega, C. K., Datinguinoo, E., Guerra, J., Guno, C., Mayuga, H. J., Villamena, E., & Manongsong, J. L. (2015). Computerized vs non-computerized accounting system of small and medium enterprises in Lipa City, Philippines: A comparative analysis. *Asia Pacific Journal of Academic Research in Business Administration, 1*(1), 48–55.

Argyris, C. (1976). Single-loop and double-loop models in research on decision making. *Administrative Science Quarterly, 21*(3), 363–375. doi:10.2307/2391848

Argyris, C., & Schon, D. (1978). *Organizational Learning: A theory of action approach*. Addision Wesley.

Arsenault, P., & Faerman, S. R. (2014). Embracing paradox in management: The value of the competing values framework. *Organizational Management Journal, 11*(3), 147–158. doi:10.1080/15416518.2014.949614

Arthur, J. W. (2016). *The Seventeenth Highland Light Infantry (Glasgow Chamber of Commerce Battalion) (WWI Centenary Series)*. Read Books Ltd.

Ashkanasy, N. (2011). International happiness; a multilevel perspective. *The Academy of Management Perspectives*, (February), 23–29.

Ashrafi, R., & Murtaza, M. (2013). ICT adoption in SME in an Arab GCC country: Oman. In Small and Medium Enterprises: Concepts, Methodologies, Tools, and Applications. IGI Global.

Aslău, T. (2001). *Management control beyond appearances* [Controlul de gestiune dincolo de aparenţe]. Economica.

Association of Chartered Certified Accountants - ACCA. (2016). *Mapping the sustainability reporting landscape. Lost in the right direction*. ACCA.

Aureli, S., Salvatori, F., & Magnaghi, E. (2020). A country-comparative analysis of the transposition of the EU non-financial Directive: An institutional approach. *Accounting, Economics, and Law: A Convivium, 10*(2), 20180047.

Babalola, D., & Babalola, Y. (2013). Economic effects of media campaign against pandemic diseases: The case of bird flu (H5N1) on poultry business in Ogun state, Nigeria. *Oman Chapter of Arabian Journal of Business and Management Review, 34*(982), 1–9. doi:10.12816/0002364

Badea, F., & Dobrin, C. (2006). *Budgetary management of production systems* [Gestiunea bugetară a sistemelor de productie] (2nd ed.). Economica.

Baker, G. (2014). Ledgers in the cloud. *The Owner Manager's Magazine*, 26-32.

Baker, C., & Bettner, M. (1997). Interpretive and Critical Research in Accounting: A Commentary on its Absence from Mainstream Research||. *Critical Perspectives on Accounting, 8*(4), 293–310. doi:10.1006/cpac.1996.0116

Baker, E. W., Al-Gahtani, S. S., & Hubona, G. S. (2010). Cultural impacts on acceptance and adoption of information technology in a developing country. *Journal of Global Information Management, 18*(3), 35–58. doi:10.4018/jgim.2010070102

Balachandran, B., & Faff, R. (2015). Corporate governance, firm value and risk: Past, present, and future. *Pacific-Basin Finance Journal, 35*(A), 1-12.

Ball, R. (2013). Accounting informs investors and earnings management is rife: Two questionable beliefs. *Accounting Horizons, 27*(4), 847–853. doi:10.2308/acch-10366

Ball, R., Li, X., & Shivakumar, L. (2015). Contractibility and transparency of financial statement information prepared under IFRS: Evidence from debt contracts around IFRS adoption. *Journal of Accounting Research, 53*(5), 915–963. doi:10.1111/1475-679X.12095

Banerjee, S. B. (2002). Corporate environmentalism: The construct and its measurement. *Journal of Business Research, 55*(3), 177–191. doi:10.1016/S0148-2963(00)00135-1

Bari, I. (2003). *Probleme globale contemporane*. Bucureşti: Editura economică.

Barth, M. E. (2013). Global comparability in financial reporting: What, why, how, and when? *China Journal of Accounting Studies, 1*(1), 2–12. doi:10.1080/21697221.2013.781765

Barth, M. E., Konchitchki, Y. L., & Landsman, W. R. (2013). Cost of capital and earnings transparency. *Journal of Accounting and Economics, 55*(2–3), 206–224. doi:10.1016/j.jacceco.2013.01.004

Barth, M. E., Landsman, W. R., Young, D., & Zhuang, Z. (2014). Relevance of Differences between Net Income based on IFRS and Domestic Standards for European Firms. *Journal of Business Finance & Accounting, 41*(3-4), 297–506. doi:10.1111/jbfa.12067

Barth, M., Landsman, W., & Lang, M. (2008). International accounting standards and accounting quality. *Journal of Accounting Research*, *46*(3), 467–498. doi:10.1111/j.1475-679X.2008.00287.x

Bass, S., Ahlroth, S., Ruijs, A., & Vardon, M. (2017, October). Natural capital accounting for policy–a global view of achievements, challenges and prospects. In Forum on Natural Capital Accounting for Better Policy Decisions: Taking Stock and Moving Forward (p. 17). World Bank WAVES.

Beasley, M. S., Buckless, F. A., Glover, S. M., & Prawitt, D. F. (2009). *Auditing Cases. An Interactive Learning Approach* (4th ed.). Prentice Hall.

Belfo, F., & Trigo, A. (2013). Accounting information systems: Traditions and future directions. *Procedia Technology*, *9*, 536–546. doi:10.1016/j.protcy.2013.12.060

Ben-Asher, N., & Gonzalez, C. (2015). Effects of cyber security knowledge on attack detection. *Computers in Human Behavior*, *48*, 51–61. doi:10.1016/j.chb.2015.01.039

Berland, N. (2009). *Measure and drive performance* [Mesurer et piloter la performance]. Retrieved from: http://www.crefige.dauphine.fr/publish/berland/performance.pdf

Berumen, S., & Arriaza, K. (2013). Medición de la intensidad en el uso de las tecnologías de la información y la comunicación en Escandinavia. *Contaduría y Administración*, *58*(1), 289–306. doi:10.1016/S0186-1042(13)71206-3

Bettner, M., & Kate, K. (2013). Changes in annual reporting rituals of financial services firms in periods of market crisis. *International Journal of Critical Accounting*, *5*(6), 577–593. doi:10.1504/IJCA.2013.059027

Birt, J., Chalmers, K., Maloney, S., Brooks, A., Oliver, J., & Bond, D. (2020). *Accounting: Business Reporting for Decision Making*. John Wiley & Sons.

Blei, D. M., Ng, A. Y., & Jordan, M. I. (2003). Latent Dirichlet Allocation. *Journal of Machine Learning Research*, *3*, 993–1022.

Bleiklie, I., Enders, J., & Lepori, B. (2015). Organizations as penetrated hierarchies: Environmental pressures and control in professional organizations. *Organization Studies*, *36*(7), 873–896. doi:10.1177/0170840615571960

Bloomberg & PwC. (2020). *Global Top 100 companies by market capitalization*. Author.

Boian, F. (2004). *Tehnologii fundamentale Java pentru aplicaţii Web*. Cluj: Editura Albastră.

Bouquin, H. (1994). *Fundamentals of management control* [Fondements du contrôle de gestion]. PressesUniversitaires de France.

Bowen, F., & Aragon-Correa, J. A. (2014). *Greenwashing in corporate environmentalism research and practice: The importance of what we say and do*. Academic Press.

Boyabatli, O., Leng, T., & Toktay, L. B. (2016). The Impact of Budget Constraints on Flexible vs. Dedicated Technology Choice. *Management Science*, *62*(1), 225–244.

Brandas, C., Megan, O., & Didraga, O. (2015). Global perspectives on accounting information systems: Mobile and cloud approach. *Procedia Economics and Finance*, *20*, 88–93. doi:10.1016/S2212-5671(15)00051-9

Branke, J., & Elomari, J. A. (2012, July). Meta-optimization for parametertuningwith a flexible computing budget. *Proceedings of the 14th annual conference on Genetic and evolutionary computation*, 1245-1252. 10.1145/2330163.2330336

Brault, R., & Giguère, P. (2003). *Management accounting* [Comptabilité de management] (5th ed.). Presses Université Laval.

British Airways Corporate Responsibility Report 2010/2011. (n.d.). https://www.britishairways.com/cms/global/pdfs/environment/ba_corporate_responsibility_report_2010-2011.pdf

Brockmann, E. N., & Lacho, K. J. (2015). Benefits of chamber of commerce membership: Large vs. small population centers. *The Entrepreneurial Executive*, *20*, 31–38.

Brown, A. C. (1922). What the Chamber of Commerce Can Do in Promoting Better Industrial Relations in a Community. *Proceedings of the Academy of Political Science in the City of New York*, *9*(4), 210–217. doi:10.2307/1172300

Brown, D. R. (1997). Sustainability is not about money!: The case of the belize chamber of commerce and industry. *Development in Practice*, 185–189.

Brown, J. (2010). Accounting and visual cultural studies: Potentialities, challenges and prospects. *Accounting, Auditing & Accountability Journal*, *23*(4), 482–505. doi:10.1108/09513571011041598

Brüggemann, U., Hitz, J.-M., & Sellhorn, T. (2013). Intended and unintended consequences of mandatory IFRS adoption: A review of extant evidence and suggestions for future research. *European Accounting Review*, *22*(1), 1–37. doi:10.1080/09638180.2012.718487

Bruque, S., & Moyano, J. (2007). Organisational determinants of information technology adoption and implementation in SMEs: The case of family and cooperative firms. *Technovation*, *27*(5), 241–253. doi:10.1016/j.technovation.2006.12.003

Bucher, R., & Stelling, J. (1969). Characteristics of professional organizations. *Journal of Health and Social Behavior*, *10*(1), 3–15. doi:10.2307/2948501 PMID:5776946

Buckley, R., & de Vasconcellos Pegas, F. (n.d.). *Tourism and CSR*. The Routledge Handbook of Tourism and the Environment., doi:10.4324/9780203121108.ch46

Bukamal, O., & Abu Wadi, R. (2016). Factors Influencing the Success of ERP System Implementation in the Public Sector in the Kingdom of Bahrain. *International Journal of Economics and Finance*, *8*(12), 21–36. doi:10.5539/ijef.v8n12p21

Bunger, A. (2013). Administrative coordination in nonprofit human service delivery networks: The role of competition and trust. *Nonprofit and Voluntary Sector Quarterly*, *42*(6), 1155–1175. doi:10.1177/0899764012451369 PMID:25349468

Burlaud, A., & Simon, C. (2003). *Management accounting. costs / control* [Comptabilité de gestion. coûts/contrôle] (3rd ed.). Vuibert.

Burlea-Schiopoiu, A., & Mihai, L. S. (2019). An integrated framework on the sustainability of SMEs. *Sustainability*, *11*(21), 6026. doi:10.3390u11216026

Busco, C., Consolandi, C., Eccles, R. G., & Sofra, E. (2020). A preliminary analysis of SASB reporting: Disclosure topics, financial relevance, and the financial intensity of ESG materiality. *Journal of Applied Corporate Finance*, *32*(2), 117–125. doi:10.1111/jacf.12411

Byard, D., Li, Y., & Yu, Y. (2011). The effect of mandatory IFRS adoption on financial analysts' information environment. *Journal of Accounting Research*, *49*(1), 69–96. doi:10.1111/j.1475-679X.2010.00390.x

Cadez, S., & Guilding, C. (2008). An exploratory investigation of an integrated contingency model of strategic management accounting. *Accounting, Organizations and Society*, *33*(7-8), 836–863. doi:10.1016/j.aos.2008.01.003

Cahan, S. F., & Sun, J. (2015). The effect of audit experience on audit fees and audit quality. *Journal of Accounting, Auditing & Finance*, *30*(1), 78–100. doi:10.1177/0148558X14544503

Cairns, D., Massoudi, D., Taplin, R., & Tarca, A. (2011). IFRS fair value measurement and accounting policy choice in the United Kingdom and Australia. *The British Accounting Review*, *43*(1), 1–21. doi:10.1016/j.bar.2010.10.003

Cajner, T., Crane, L. D., Decker, R. A., Grigsby, J., Hamins-Puertolas, A., Hurst, E., . . . Yildirmaz, A. (2020). The US labor market during the beginning of the pandemic recession (No. w27159). National Bureau of Economic Research.

Caldeira, M. M., & Ward, J. M. (2003). Using resource-based theory to interpret the successful adoption and use of information systems and technology in manufacturing small and medium-sized enterprises. *European Journal of Information Systems*, *12*(2), 127–141. doi:10.1057/palgrave.ejis.3000454

Cameron, K. S., & Quinn, R. E. (2011). *Diagnosing and Changing Organizational Culture: Based on the Competing Values Framework*. Jossey-Bass.

Cargill, W. (1840). *Address of William Cargill, Esq. to the South Shields Chamber of Commerce, May 4, 1840, on the foreign policy of England*. T. Brettell.

Carrots & Sticks. (2020). *Global trends in sustainability reporting regulation and policy*. Author.

Casanovas, A. (2013). Resistencia al cambio y conductas obstructivas. *Serie de Cuadernos Sobre Cumplimiento Legal*, 3-30.

Caylor, M. L. (2010). Strategic revenue recognition to achieve earnings benchmarks. *Journal of Accounting and Public Policy*, *29*(1), 82–95. doi:10.1016/j.jaccpubpol.2009.10.008

Center for Sustainability & Excellence – CSE. (2010). News, CSE managing director, Nikos Avlonas, speaks on carbon footprint strategy & CSR at the 7th CSR Summit, Dubai. Author.

Chao, C. A., & Chandra, A. (2012). Impact of owner's knowledge of information technology (IT) on strategic alignment and IT adoption in US small firms. *Journal of Small Business and Enterprise Development*, *19*(1), 114–131. doi:10.1108/14626001211196433

Chebaane, S., & Othman, H. B. (2014). The Impact of IFRS Adoption on Value Relevance of Earnings and Book Value of Equity: The Case of Emerging Markets in African and Asian Regions. *Procedia: Social and Behavioral Sciences*, *145*, 70–80. doi:10.1016/j.sbspro.2014.06.012

Chen, H., Tang, Q., Jiang, Y., & Lin, Z. (2010). The role of international financial reporting standards in accounting quality: Evidence from the European Union. *Journal of International Financial Management & Accounting*, *21*(3), 220–278. doi:10.1111/j.1467-646X.2010.01041.x

Chen, M., Qu, X., & Sun, X. (2017). Whose cost of equity capital reduces after IFRS convergence and why? Heterogeneity evidence from Chinese stock market. *China Journal of Accounting Studies*, *5*(1), 1–27. doi:10.1080/21697213.2017.1304539

Cho, C. H. (2020). CSR accounting 'new wave' researchers: 'step up to the plate'… or 'stay out of the game'. *Accounting and Management Information Systems*, *19*(4), 626–650.

Chod, J., & Zhou, J. (2014). Resourceflexibilityand capital structure. *Management Science*, *60*(3), 708–729. doi:10.1287/mnsc.2013.1777

Choi, Y.-S., Peasnell, K., & Toniato, J. (2013). Has the IASB been successful in making accounting earnings more useful for prediction and valuation? UK evidence. *Journal of Business Finance & Accounting*, *40*(7–8), 741–768. doi:10.1111/jbfa.12025

Chowdhury, S. R. (2011). Impact of global crisis on small and medium enterprises. *Global Business Review*, *12*(3), 377–399. doi:10.1177/097215091101200303

Christensen, H., Hail, L., & Leuz, C. (2019). *Adoption of CSR and sustainability reporting standards: economic analysis and review.* NBER Working Papers, 26169, National Bureau of Economic Research.

Climate Disclosure Standards Board - CDSB. (2019). *Cadrul general CDSB- pentru raportarea informatiilor cu privire la mediu si schimbarile climatic*. CDSB.

Colombo, M. G., Piva, E., Quas, A., & Rossi-Lamastra, C. (2016). How high-tech entrepreneurial ventures cope with the global crisis: Changes in product innovation and internationalization strategies. *Industry and Innovation*, *23*(7), 647–671. doi:10.1080/13662716.2016.1196438

Cosmulese, C. G., Socoliuc, M., Ciubotariu, M. S., Mihaila, S., & Grosu, V. (2019). An empirical analysis of stakeholders' expectations and integrated reporting quality. *Economic Research Journal*, *32*(1), 3963–3986. doi:10.1080/1331677X.2019.1680303

Costello, T. (2011). Better budget planning. *IT Professional*, *13*(5), 64–63. doi:10.1109/MITP.2011.78

Craig, P., & Glasser, H. (1994). Transfer models for 'green accounting': an approach to environmental policy analysis for sustainable development. *Assigning Economic Values to Natural Resources*, 67-110.

Crawford, B., & Branch, J. (2015). Interest plurality and institutional work: An ethnography of rural community organizing. *Journal of Organizational Ethnography*, *4*(1), 98–116. doi:10.1108/JOE-10-2013-0018

CSR Romania. (2021). *Forum for International Communications*. http://www.csr-romania.ro/

Cucui, I., Horga, V., & Radu, M. (2003). *Management Control* [Control de gestiune]. Niculescu.

Cunha, M. P. E., Rego, A., & Vieira da Cunha, J. (2008). Ecocentric management: An update. *Corporate Social Responsibility and Environmental Management*, *15*(6), 311–321. doi:10.1002/csr.169

Curtis, D., & McKenzie, P. (2002). *Employability skills for Australian industry: literature review and framework development. Report to: Business Council of Australia; Australian Chamber of Commerce and Industry*. Science and Training.

Dalton, C. B. (2006). Business continuity management and pandemic influenza. *New South Wales Public Health Bulletin*, *17*(10), 138–141. doi:10.1071/NB06035 PMID:17293894

Damayant, T. (2013). Who is afraid of Qualitative Research? A Compromise Accounting Research Failure in Improving Accounting Practices. *International Journal of Advances in Management and Economics*, *2*(2), 89-94.

Damerji, H. (2020). *Technology Readiness Impact on Artificial Intelligence Technology Adoption by Accounting Students* (Doctoral Dissertation). University of La Verne.

Daske, H., & Gebhardt, G. (2006). International financial reporting standards and experts' perceptions of disclosure quality. *Abacus*, *42*(3/4), 461–498. doi:10.1111/j.1467-6281.2006.00211.x

Davila, A. (2012). New trends in performance measurement and management control. *In Performance Measurement and Management Control. Global Issues (Washington, D.C.)*, *25*, 65–87.

Dawley, D. D., Stephens, R. D., & Stephens, D. B. (2005). Dimensionality of organizational commitment in volunteer workers: Chamber of commerce board members and role fulfillment. *Journal of Vocational Behavior*, *67*(3), 511–525. doi:10.1016/j.jvb.2004.09.001

de Guinea, A. O., Kelley, H., & Hunter, M. G. (2005). Information systems effectiveness in small business: Extending a Singaporean model in Canada. *Journal of Global Information Management*, *13*(3), 55–70. doi:10.4018/jgim.2005070104

De Nuccio, E. (2020). *Preparing future-ready professionals, from non-financial disclosure to integrated reporting*. Academic Press.

De Sausmarez, N. (2004). Malaysia's response to the Asian financial crisis: Implications for tourism and sectoral crisis management. *Journal of Travel & Tourism Marketing, 15*(4), 217–231. doi:10.1300/J073v15n04_01

de Waal, A. A., & Kourtit, K. (2013). Performance measurement and management in practice. *International Journal of Productivity and Performance Management, 62*(5), 446–473. doi:10.1108/IJPPM-10-2012-0118

DeFond, M. L. (2010). Earnings quality research: Advances, challenges and future research. *Journal of Accounting and Economics, 50*(2-3), 402–409. doi:10.1016/j.jacceco.2010.10.004

Deliu, D. (2020). The impact of a socio-economic crisis on corporate governance effectiveness and sustainable development. *Acumen: The current new Coronavirus (Covid-19) pandemic, 35th IBIMA (International Business Information Management Association) International Conference, 01-02.04.2020, Seville, Spain – Proceedings of the 35th International Business Information Management Association Conference.*

Delmas, M. A., & Burbano, V. C. (2011). The drivers of greenwashing. *California Management Review, 54*(1), 64–87. doi:10.1525/cmr.2011.54.1.64

DeLone, W., & McLean, E. (2003). The DeLone and McLean model of information systems success: A ten-year Update. *Journal of Management Information Systems, 19*(4), 9–30. doi:10.1080/07421222.2003.11045748

Dennis, I. (2014). *The Nature of Accounting Regulation.* Routledge.

DiPiazza, S. A., & Eccles, R. G. (2002). *Building public trust. The future of corporate reporting.* Wiley.

Directive 2014/95 / EU of the European Parliament and of the Council amending Directive 2013/34/EU as regards the submission of non-financial information and diversity information by certain undertakings and large groups.

Doukakis, L. C. (2010). The persistence of earnings and earnings components after the adoption of IFRS. *Managerial Finance, 36*(11), 969–980. doi:10.1108/03074351011081286

Doukakis, L. C. (2014). The effect of mandatory IFRS adoption on real and accrual-based earnings management activities. *Journal of Accounting and Public Policy, 33*(6), 551–572. doi:10.1016/j.jaccpubpol.2014.08.006

Duff, W., & McKemmish, S. (2000). Metadata and ISO compliance. *Information Management Journal, 34*(1), 4–15.

Dumitraşcu, M., & Feleaga, L. (2019). Mission, vision and organizational values, catalysts of social responsibility. *Financial Audit, 17*(153).

Dunk, A. S. (2011). Product innovation, budgetary control, and the financial performance of firms. *The British Accounting Review, 43*(2), 102–111. doi:10.1016/j.bar.2011.02.004

Dunning, J. (1997a). *The Advent of Alliance Capitalism, "The New Globalism and Developing Countries.* United Nations University Press.

Dunning, J. H. (1997). The New Globalism and Developing Countries. In *The Advent of Alliance Capitalism.* New York: United Nations University Press.

Dupuy, Y., & Rolland, G. (1991). *Management control* [Contrôle de gestion]. Dunod.

Dyer, T., Lang, M., & Stice-Lawrence, L. (2017). The evolution of 10-K textual disclosure: Evidence from Latent Dirichlet Allocation. *Journal of Accounting and Economics, 64*(2-3), 221–245. doi:10.1016/j.jacceco.2017.07.002

Eisenberg, T. (2009). US Chamber of Commerce liability survey: Inaccurate, unfair, and bad for business. *Journal of Empirical Legal Studies, 6*(4), 969–1002. doi:10.1111/j.1740-1461.2009.01155.x

Elkins, D. R. (1995). The structure and context of the urban growth coalition: The view from the chamber of commerce. *Policy Studies Journal: the Journal of the Policy Studies Organization*, *23*(4), 583–600. doi:10.1111/j.1541-0072.1995.tb00536.x

Elliott, D., Swartz, E., & Herbane, B. (2010). *Business Continuity Management 2e: A Crisis Management Approach*. Routledge.

Elmaghraby, A., & Lasavio, M. (2014). Cyber security challenge in smart cities: Safety, security and privacy. *Journal of Advanced Research*, *5*(4), 491–497. doi:10.1016/j.jare.2014.02.006 PMID:25685517

Emetumah, F. C. (2017). Modern perspectives on environmentalism: Ecocentrism and technocentrism in the Nigerian context. *Asian Research Journal of Arts & Social Sciences*, 1-9.

Epuran, M., Babaita, V., & Grosu, C. (1999). *Accounting and management control* [Contabilitate şi control de gestiune]. Economica.

Eriksson, P., & Kovalainen, A. (2015). Qualitative Methods in Business Research: A Practical Guide to Social Research. *Sage (Atlanta, Ga.)*.

EU. (2021). *Corporate social responsibility & Responsible business conduct*. https://ec.europa.eu/growth/industry/sustainability/corporate-social-responsibility_en

European Commission. (2017). *Information from European Union Institutions, bodies, offices and agencies. EU directive 2017/C215/01 for reporting its performance in relation to non-financial information*. https://ec.europa.eu/anti-trafficking/sites/antitrafficking/files/guidelines_on_non-financial_reporting.pdf

European Commission. (2020). *Summary report of the public consultation on the review of the Non-Financial Reporting Directive*. Author.

European Commission. (2021). *Screening of websites for 'greenwashing': Half of green claims lack evidence*. https://ec.europa.eu/commission/presscorner/detail/en/IP_21_269

European Reporting LAB – EFRAG. (2021). *Proposals for a relevant and dynamic eu sustainability reporting standard setting*. Author.

Eurostat. (2001b). *NAMEAs for air emissions. Results of pilot studies*. Detailed Tables. Eurostat.

Evans, M. H. (2005). *Financial planning and forecasting, excellence in financial management*. Retrieved from www.exinfm.com/training/pdfiles/course02.pdf

Faems, D., Van Looy, B., & Debackere, K. (2005). Interorganizational collaboration and innovation: Toward a portfolio approach. *Journal of Product Innovation Management*, *22*(3), 238–250. doi:10.1111/j.0737-6782.2005.00120.x

Fallon, G., & Brown, R. B. (2000). Does Britain need public law status Chambers of Commerce? *European Business Review*, *12*(1), 19–27. doi:10.1108/09555340010307521

Fan, J. P. H., Li, J., & Zheng, G. (2016). Revisiting the bright and dark sides of capital flows in business groups. *Journal of Business Ethics*, *134*(4), 509–528. doi:10.100710551-014-2382-6

Farcane, N., Deliu, D., & Bureană, E. (2019). A corporate case study: The application of Rokeach's value system to Corporate Social Responsibility (CSR). *Sustainability*, *11*(23), 6612. doi:10.3390u11236612

Farmaki, A., & Farmakis, P. (2018). A stakeholder approach to CSR in hotels. *Annals of Tourism Research*, *68*, 58–60. doi:10.1016/j.annals.2017.11.009

Feng. (2006). Recent Research On The History Of The Chamber Of Commerce. *Journal of Huazhong Normal University (Humanities and Social Sciences), 5.*

Feng. (2006). The Limits of Enterprise Cooperative Network-Chamber of Commerce as an Example. *China Industrial Economy, 1.*

Fitriati, A., & Mulyani, S. (2015). Factors that affect accounting information system success and its implication on accounting information quality. *Asian Journal of Information Technology*, *14*(5), 154–161.

Florou, A., & Pope, P. (2012). Mandatory IFRS adoption and institutional investment decisions. *The Accounting Review*, *87*(6), 1993–2025. doi:10.2308/accr-50225

Forget, J. (2005). *Gestion budgétaire: Prévoir et contrôler les activités de l'entreprise*. Éditions d'Organisation.

Fox, J. (2000). Common Sense in Shanghai: The General Chamber of Commerce and Political Legitimacy in Republican China. *History Workshop Journal*, *50*(1), 22–44. doi:10.1093/hwj/2000.50.22

Freeman, R. E., Harrison, J. S., Wicks, A. C., Parmar, B. L., & De Colle, S. (2010). *Stakeholder theory: The state of the art*. Cambridge University Press. doi:10.1017/CBO9780511815768

Friedman, L. M. (1947). The first chamber of commerce in the United States. *Bulletin of the Business Historical Society*, *21*(5), 137–143. doi:10.2307/3111178

Fromhold-Eisebith, M. (2015). Sectoral resilience: Conceptualizing industry-specific spatial patterns of interactive crisis adjustment. *European Planning Studies*, *23*(9), 1675–1694. doi:10.1080/09654313.2015.1047329

Fu, R., Kraft, A., & Zhang, H. (2012). Financial reporting frequency, information asymmetry, and the cost of equity. *Journal of Accounting and Economics*, *54*(2–3), 132–149. doi:10.1016/j.jacceco.2012.07.003

Furlow, N. E. (2010). Greenwashing in the new millennium. *The Journal of Applied Business and Economics*, *10*(6), 22.

Gajos, E., & Prandecki, K. (2016). National Accounting Matrix with Environmental Accounts (NAMEA)-an Overview of Environmentally Extended Input-Output Analysis. *Acta Scientiarum Polonorum. Oeconomia*, *15*(4).

García, A. M., Álamo, F. R., & García-Barba, F. (2011). Antecedentes de la resistencia al cambio: Factores individuales y contextuales. *Cuadernos de Economía y Dirección de la Empresa*, *14*(4), 231–246. doi:10.1016/j.cede.2011.02.007

Gaumnitz, B. R., & Lere, J. C. (2002). Contents of codes of ethics of professional business organizations in the United States. *Journal of Business Ethics*, *35*(1), 35–49. doi:10.1023/A:1012718103007

Gervais, M. (1994). *Budget Management: Plan and control the company's activities* [Contrôle de gestion par le système budgétaire] (3rd ed.). Librairie Vuibert.

Ghobakhloo, M., Zulkifli, N. B., & Azizi, F. A. (2010). The interactive model of user information technology acceptance and satisfaction in small and medium-sized enterprises. *European Journal of Economics. Finance and Administrative Sciences*, *19*(1), 7–27.

Ghosh, A., & Olsen, L. (2008). Environmental uncertainty and managers' use of discretionary accruals. *Accounting, Organizations and Society*, *34*(2), 188–205. doi:10.1016/j.aos.2008.07.001

Giurgiu, A. M., Manciu, I., & Lese, I. (2016). Technological Development–A Tool for Social and Economic Impact of the Chamber of Commerce and Industry of Mures County. *Procedia Technology*, *22*, 1092–1099. doi:10.1016/j.protcy.2016.01.154

Gladwin, T. N., Kennelly, J. J., & Krause, T. S. (1995). Shifting paradigms for sustainable development: Implications for management theory and research. *Academy of Management Review, 20*(4), 874–907. doi:10.5465/amr.1995.9512280024

Global Reporting Initiative - GRI. (2017). *Linking the GRI Standards and the European Directive on non-financial and diversity disclosure document.* Author.

Grande, E., Estebanez, R., & Colomina, C. (2011). The impact of accounting information system (AIS) on performance measures: Empirical evidence in Spanish SMEs. *International Journal of Digital Accounting Research, 11*, 25–43.

Güney, Ü. (1998). İnternet, Intranet, Extranet. *Byte Türkiye, 116.*

Guney, A. (2014). Role of technology in accounting and e-Accounting. *Procedia: Social and Behavioral Sciences, 152*, 852–855. doi:10.1016/j.sbspro.2014.09.333

Gupta, K. (2007). *Auditing and Assurance Standard, basic principles governing an audit.* Academic Press.

Hajira, Z., & Azizi, Z. O. (2011). Effective factors on alignment of accounting information systems in manufacturing companies: Evidence from Iran. *Information Management and Business Review, 3*(3), 158–170. doi:10.22610/imbr.v3i3.929

Hall, D. R. (1969). *Cooperative lobbying: The power of pressure.* University of Arizona Press.

Hanson, S., Stein, J., Sunderman, A., & Zwick, E. (2020). (forthcoming). Business Credit Programs in the Pandemic Era. *Brookings Papers on Economic Activity.*

Harju, E. (2021). Näin meitä huijataan Valmistajan vastuullisuuspuheet voivat olla vain tyhjää sanahelinää. Tässä jutussa asiantuntijat neuvovat, mistä tunnistat viherpesun. *Iltalehti.*

Hartnell, C. A., Ou, A. Y., & Kinicki, A. (2011). Organizational culture and organizational effectiveness: A meta-analytic investigation of the competing values framework's theoretical suppositions. *The Journal of Applied Psychology, 96*(4), 677–694. doi:10.1037/a0021987 PMID:21244127

Hasan, M., & Dridi, J. (2011). The effects of the global crisis on Islamic and conventional banks: A comparative study. *Journal of International Commerce. Economic Policy, 2*(02), 163–200.

Ha, Y. M., & Ahn, H. J. (2014). Factors affecting the performance of Enterprise Resource Planning (ERP) systems in the post-implementation stage. *Behaviour & Information Technology, 33*(10), 1065–1081. doi:10.1080/0144929X.2013.799229

Hecht, J. E. (2000). *Lessons learned from environmental accounting: findings from nine case studies.* IUCN.

He, K., Pan, X., & Tian, G. (2017). Legal liability, government intervention, and auditor behavior: Evidence from structural reform of audit firms in China. *European Accounting Review, 26*(1), 61–95. doi:10.1080/09638180.2015.1100547

Hernandez, A. A. (2020). *Exploring the factors to green IT adoption of SMEs in the Philippines, Start- Ups and SMEs: Concepts, Methodologies, Tools, and Applications.* IGI Global.

Hicks, J. R. (2017). From 'Value and Capital'. In Bond Duration and Immunization (pp. 57-61). Routledge.

Higgins-Desbiolles, F. (2018). Sustainable tourism: Sustaining tourism or something more? *Tourism Management Perspectives, 25*, 157–160. doi:10.1016/j.tmp.2017.11.017

Hilton, C. R. R. (2017). *Hilton Hotels CSR Programs and Initiatives – Research.* https://cr.hilton.com/wp-content/uploads/2018/05/Hilton-Corporate-Responsibility-2017-1.pdf

Hinings, B. (2005). The changing nature of professional organizations. The Oxford handbook of work and organization. doi:10.1093/oxfordhb/9780199299249.003.0021

Hitt, M. A. (1998). Twenty-first-century organizations: Business firms, business schools, and the academy. *Academy of Management Review*, *23*(2), 218–224. doi:10.5465/amr.1998.533223

Hofstede, G. H. (Ed.). (2012). *The game of budget control.* Routledge. doi:10.4324/9780203714874

Holthausen, R. W., & Watts, R. L. (2001). The relevance of the value-relevance literature for financial accounting standard setting. *Journal of Accounting and Economics*, *31*(1-3), 3–75. doi:10.1016/S0165-4101(01)00029-5

Hong, L. (2000). The Singapore Chinese Chamber of Commerce and Industry And the Institutionalization of Chinese Business Networks in Asia. *Historical Recearch, 1.*

Hörisch, J., Schaltegger, S., & Freeman, R. E. (2020). Integrating stakeholder theory and sustainability accounting: A conceptual synthesis. *Journal of Cleaner Production*, *275*, 124097. doi:10.1016/j.jclepro.2020.124097

Horngren, C. T., Datar, S. M., & Foster, G. (2006). *Cost Accounting: A Managerial Emphasis* [Contabilitatea costurilor, o abordare managerială]. 11th ed.). Chisinău, Moldova: ARC.

Horton, J., Serafeim, G., & Serafeim, I. (2013). Does mandatory IFRS adoption improve the information environment? *Contemporary Accounting Research*, *30*(1), 388–423. doi:10.1111/j.1911-3846.2012.01159.x

Horvath & Parteners. (2009). *Controlling* (2nd ed.). Bucuresti, Romania: C.H. Beck.

Hotel Polski Pod Białym Orłem, C. S. R. (2021). *Corporate social responsibility in hotel industry – CORE.* https://core.ac.uk/download/pdf/230306873.pdf

Hou, Q., Jin, Q., Yang, R., Yuan, H., & Zhang, G. (2015). Performance commitments of controlling shareholders and earnings management. *Contemporary Accounting Research*, *32*(3), 1099–1127. doi:10.1111/1911-3846.12111

Houque, M. N. (2012). The effect of IFRS adoption and investor protection on earnings quality around the world. *The International Journal of Accounting*, *47*(3), 333–355. doi:10.1016/j.intacc.2012.07.003

Hussin, H., King, M., & Cragg, P. (2002). IT alignment in small firms. *European Journal of Information Systems*, *11*(2), 108–132. doi:10.1057/palgrave/ejis/3000422

Hyatt Corporate Responsibility. (2021). https://about.hyatt.com/en/hyatt-thrive.html, https://about.hyatt.com/content/dam/HyattStories/thrive/HyattEnvironmentalSustainabilityHighlights20192020.pdf

Iatridis, G. (2010). International Financial Reporting Standards and the quality of financial statement information. *International Review of Financial Analysis*, *19*(3), 193–204. doi:10.1016/j.irfa.2010.02.004

Iatridis, G. (2012). Hedging and earnings management in the light of IFRS implementation: Evidence from the UK stock market. *The British Accounting Review*, *44*(1), 21–35. doi:10.1016/j.bar.2011.12.002

Ibrahim, F., Ali, D. N. H., & Besar, N. S. A. (2020). Accounting information systems (AIS) in SMEs: Towards an integrated framework. *International Journal of Asian Business and Information Management*, *11*(2), 51–67. doi:10.4018/IJABIM.2020040104

Idowu, S. O., Dragu, I. M., Tiron-Tudor, A., & Farcas, T. V. (2016). From CSR and sustainability to integrated reporting. *International Journal of Entrepreneurship and Innovation*, *4*(2).

IFAC. (2002). *E-Business and the Accountant: Risk Management for Accounting Systems in an E-Business Environment.* Available at:https://www.icjce.es/images/pdfs/TECNICA/C01%20-%20IFAC/C.01.082%20-%20ITC%20-%20Other/E-Business_Book.PDF

InterContinental Hotels Group Corporate Responsibility IHG. (2021). https://www.ihg.com/content/us/en/about/corporate-responsibility

International Accounting Standards Board - IASB. (2021). *ED/20215 Proposed targeted amendments to the IFRS Foundation constitution to accommodate an international sustainability standards board to set IFRS sustainability standard.* Author.

International Auditing and Assurance Standards Board – IAASB. (2013). *International standard on assurance engagements – ISAE 3000 Assurance engagements other than audits or reviews of historical financial information.* Author.

International Financial Reporting Standards (IFRS) Foundation. (2020). *Consultation paper on sustainability reporting.* Author.

International Integrated Reporting Council - IIRC. (2021). *International reporting framework.* Author.

International Organization for Standardization. (2010). *ISO 26000 – Guidance of social responsibility.* Author.

International Organization for Standardization. (2015). *ISO 14000 – Environmental management systems - Requirements with guidance for use.* Author.

Ionescu, C. A. (2015). Using Flexible Budgets to manage organizational performance and cost. *Annals of the Academy of Romanian Scientists, 1*(1), 87–96.

Irish Fund - IF. (2020). *Sustainable finance comparing international sustainability reporting frameworks.* Author.

Ismail, N. A., & King, M. (2007). Factors influencing the alignment of accounting information systems in small medium sized Malaysian manufacturing firms. *Journal of Information systems and Small Business, 1*(1), 1-19.

Jackson, S. B., & Liu, X. K. (2010). The allowance for uncollectible accounts, conservatism, and earnings management. *Journal of Accounting Research, 48*(3), 565–601. doi:10.1111/j.1475-679X.2009.00364.x

Jalaludin, D., Sulaiman, M., & Ahmad, N. N. N. (2011). Understanding environmental management accounting (EMA) adoption: A new institutional sociology perspective. *Social Responsibility Journal, 7*(4), 540–557. doi:10.1108/17471111111175128

Jang-Jaccard, J., & Nepal, S. (2014). A survey or emerging threats in cyber security. *Journal of Computer and System Sciences, 80*(5), 973–993. doi:10.1016/j.jcss.2014.02.005

Janvrin, D., Bierstaker, J., & Lowe, D. J. (2008). An examination of audit information technology use and perceived importance. *Accounting Horizons, 22*(1), 1–21. doi:10.2308/acch.2008.22.1.1

Jeanjean, T., & Stolowy, H. (2008). Do accounting standards matter? An exploratory analysis of earnings management before and after IFRS adoption. *Journal of Accounting and Public Policy, 27*(6), 480–490. doi:10.1016/j.jaccpubpol.2008.09.008

Jones, D. A., & Smith, K. J. (2012). Comparing the value relevance, predictive value, and persistence of other comprehensive income and special items. *The Accounting Review, 86*(6), 2047–2073. doi:10.2308/accr-10133

Kanellou, A., & Spathis, C. (2013). Accounting benefits and satisfaction in an ERP environment. *International Journal of Accounting Information Systems, 14*(3), 209–234. doi:10.1016/j.accinf.2012.12.002

Katz, A. (2015). *The Influence Machine: The U.S. Chamber of Commerce and the Corporate Capture of American Life.* Random House Publishing Group.

Kelly, D. (2005). The international chamber of commerce. *New Political Economy, 10*(2), 259–271. doi:10.1080/13563460500144868

Kinderman, D. (2020). The challenges of upward regulatory harmonization: The case of sustainability reporting in the European Union. *Regulation & Governance, 14*(4), 674–697. doi:10.1111/rego.12240

Klein, A. (2002). Audit committee, board of director characteristics and earnings management. *Journal of Accounting and Economics, 33*(3), 375–400. doi:10.1016/S0165-4101(02)00059-9

Kloviene, L., & Gimzauskien, E. (2015). The effect of information technology on accounting system's conformity with business environment: A case study in the banking sector company. *Procedia Economics and Finance, 32*, 1701–1712. doi:10.1016/S2212-5671(15)01476-8

Knoke, D. (2018). *Changing organizations: Business networks in the new political economy*. Routledge. doi:10.4324/9780429501753

Köseoglu, M. A., Hon, A., Kalargyrou, V., & Okumus, F. (2021). Hiring People with Disabilities As a Csr Strategy in the Tourism Industry. *Tourism Analysis, 26*(1), 41–55. doi:10.3727/108354220X15758302602547

Kothari, S. P., Leone, A. J., & Wasley, C. E. (2005). Performance matched discretionary accrual measures. *Journal of Accounting and Economics, 39*(1), 163–197. doi:10.1016/j.jacceco.2004.11.002

Kotler, Ph. T., & Keller, K. L. (2015). *Marketing Management* (15th ed.). Pearson.

Kuszewski, J., & Crowther, Y. (2012). *Canada and the green economy*. Academic Press.

La Notte, A., & Rhodes, C. (2020). The theoretical frameworks behind integrated environmental, ecosystem, and economic accounting systems and their classifications. *Environmental Impact Assessment Review, 80*, 106317. doi:10.1016/j.eiar.2019.106317 PMID:31902970

Lacho, K. J. (2008). Government affairs activities of chambers of commerce. In *Allied Academies International Conference. Academy of Legal, Ethical and Regulatory Issues Proceedings, 12*(1), 11.

Lacho, K. J., & Brockmann, E. N. (2011). Promoting a small business through the services of a chamber of commerce: One chamber's story. *The Entrepreneurial Executive, 16*, 1.

Lacho, K. J., & Brockmann, E. N. (2012). Improving the business skills of the small business owner through the educational services of a chamber of commerce: One chamber's story. In *Allied Academies International Conference. Academy of Entrepreneurship Proceedings, 18*(1), 55.

Laffey, J. F. (1975). Municipal Imperialism in France: The Lyon Chamber of Commerce, 1900-1914. *Proceedings of the American Philosophical Society, 119*(1), 8–23.

Landsman, W. R., Maydew, E. L., & Thornock, J. R. (2012). The information content of annual earnings announcements and mandatory adoption of IFRS. *Journal of Accounting and Economics, 53*(1-2), 34–54. doi:10.1016/j.jacceco.2011.04.002

Lang, M., Raedy, J. S., & Wilson, W. (2006). Earnings management and cross listing: Are reconciled earnings comparable to US earnings? *Journal of Accounting and Economics, 42*(1-2), 255–283. doi:10.1016/j.jacceco.2006.04.005

Laperche, B., Lefebvre, G., & Langlet, D. (2011). Innovation strategies of industrial groups in the global crisis: Rationalization and new paths. *Technological Forecasting and Social Change, 78*(8), 1319–1331. doi:10.1016/j.techfore.2011.03.005

Lee, K. H., & Shin, D. (2010). Consumers' responses to CSR activities: The linkage between increased awareness and purchase intention. *Public Relations Review, 36*(2), 193–195. doi:10.1016/j.pubrev.2009.10.014

Lee, Y. J., & Harrald, J. R. (1999). Critical issue for business area impact analysis in business crisis management: Analytical capability. *Disaster Prevention and Management: an International Journal, 8*(3), 184–189. doi:10.1108/09653569910275382

Lenzen, M., Li, M., Malik, A., Pomponi, F., Sun, Y. Y., Wiedmann, T., ... Gómez-Paredes, J. (2020). Global socio-economic losses and environmental gains from the Coronavirus pandemic. *PLoS One*, *15*(7), e0235654. doi:10.1371/journal.pone.0235654 PMID:32645023

Leuz, C. (2010). Different approaches to corporate reporting regulation: How jurisdictions differ and why. *Accounting and Business Research*, *40*(3), 229–256. doi:10.1080/00014788.2010.9663398

Leuz, C., Nanda, D., & Wysocki, P. D. (2003). Earnings management and investor protection: An international comparison. *Journal of Financial Economics*, *69*(3), 505–527. doi:10.1016/S0304-405X(03)00121-1

Leuz, C., & Wysocki, P. D. (2016). The economics of disclosure and financial reporting regulation: Evidence and suggestions for future research. *Journal of Accounting Research*, *54*(2), 525–622. doi:10.1111/1475-679X.12115

Lewis, C., & Young, S. (2019). Fad or future? Automated analysis of financial text and its implications for corporate reporting. *Accounting and Business Research*, *49*(5), 587–615. doi:10.1080/00014788.2019.1611730

Libbey, J. K. (1985). The American-Russian Chamber of Commerce. *Diplomatic History*, *9*(3), 233–248. doi:10.1111/j.1467-7709.1985.tb00534.x

Li, L., Qi, B., Tian, G., & Zhang, G. (2017). The contagion effect of low-quality audits at the level of individual auditors. *The Accounting Review*, *92*(1), 137–163. doi:10.2308/accr-51407

Lin, S., Riccardi, W., & Wang, C. (2012). Does accounting quality change following a switch from U.S.GAAP to IFRS? Evidence from Germany. *Journal of Accounting and Public Policy*, *31*(6), 641–657. doi:10.1016/j.jaccpubpol.2012.10.006

Li, S. (2010). Does mandatory adoption of international accounting standards in the European Union reduce the cost of equity capital? *The Accounting Review*, *85*(2), 607–636. doi:10.2308/accr.2010.85.2.607

Li, Sh., Xu, L. D., & Zhao, S. (2018). 5G Internet of Things: A survey. *Journal of Industrial Information Integration*, *10*, 1–9. doi:10.1016/j.jii.2018.01.005

Lobo, G. L., & Zhou, J. (2001). Disclosure quality and earning management. *Asia-Pacific Journal of Accounting & Economics*, *8*(1), 1–20. doi:10.1080/16081625.2001.10510584

Lock, I., & Seele, P. (2016). The credibility of CSR reports in Europe. Evidence from a quantitative content analysis in 11 countries. *Journal of Cleaner Production*, *122*, 186–200. doi:10.1016/j.jclepro.2016.02.060

Loi, K. M. (2010). *The Perception of Ethics and Social Responsibility of Malaysian International Chamber of Commerce and Industry Corporate Members in Relation to ISO 26000-Social Responsibility Adoption* (Doctoral dissertation). Universiti Utara Malaysia.

Loughran, T., & McDonald, B. (2020). Textual analysis in finance. *Annual Review of Financial Economics*, *12*(1), 357–375. doi:10.1146/annurev-financial-012820-032249

Louwers, T. J., Ramsay, R. J., Sinason, D. H., & Strawser, J. R. (2007). *Auditing and Assurance Services* (2nd ed.). McGraw-Hill Irwin.

Lukka, K. (2010). The roles and effects of paradigms in accounting research. *Management Accounting Research*, *21*(2), 110–115. doi:10.1016/j.mar.2010.02.002

Lumley, S., & Armstrong, P. (2004). Some of the nineteenth century origins of the sustainability concept. *Environment, Development and Sustainability*, *6*(3), 367–378. doi:10.1023/B:ENVI.0000029901.02470.a7

Luo, J. (2013). Which industries to bail out first in economic recession? Ranking US industrial sectors by the power-of-pull. *Economic Systems Research*, *25*(2), 157–169. doi:10.1080/09535314.2013.775111

MacKenzie, G. (1999). A new world ahead: International challenges for information management. *Informational Managment Journal*, *33*(2), 24–34.

Manente, M., Minghetti, V., & Mingotto, E. (2014). Responsible Tourism. *Responsible Tourism and CSR*, 3–13. doi:10.1007/978-3-319-06308-9_2

Marra, A., Mazzola, P., & Prencipe, A. (2011). Board Monitoring and Earnings Management Pre- and Post-IFRS. *The International Journal of Accounting*, *46*(2), 205–230. doi:10.1016/j.intacc.2011.04.007

Marriott Serve 360 Report. (2020). *Serve 360 Corporate Social Responsibility– Marriott*. https://serve360.marriott.com/wp-content/uploads/2020/12/2020-Serve360-Report.pdf

Maxwell, J. A. (1996). *Qualitative Research Design: An Interactive Approach*. SAGE Publications.

Mayer, R., Scammon, D., & Zick, C. (1993). Poisoning the well: Do environmental claims strain consumer credulity? *Advances in Consumer Research. Association for Consumer Research (U. S.)*, *20*, 698–703.

Meadows, Meadows, Randers, & Behrens. (1974). *The Limits to Growth: A Report for the Club of Rome's Project on the Predicament of Mankind* (2nd ed.). New York: Potomac Associates.

Mechelli, A., & Cimini, R. (2014). Is comprehensive income value relevant and does location matter? A European study. *Accounting in Europe*, *16*(25), 1–35. doi:10.1080/17449480.2014.890777

Meristö, T., & Laitinen, J. (2018). Digital Innovations: Opportunity to Elderly People? *Proceedings of the ISPIM Connects Fukuoka 2018.*

Messier, W. F., Glover, S. M., & Prawitt, D. F. (2008). *Auditing and Assurance Services. A Systematic Approach* (5th ed.). McGraw-Hill Irwin.

Min, M. A. (2003). The Study of Chamber of Commerce History and the Paradigm Change of New Historiography. *Journal of Central China Normal University (Humanities and Social Sciences), 5.*

Minja, U. S. (2011). *Factors Influencing Lab our Turnover In Private Sector Organizations In Tanzania: A Case Study Of Chamber Of Commerce, Industry And Agriculture* (Doctoral dissertation). Open University of Tanzania.

Mitchell, L., & Ramey, W. (2011). Look how green I am! An individual-level explanation for greenwashing. *Journal of Applied Business and Economics*, *12*(6), 40–45.

Moghavvemi, S., Hakimian, F., Feissal, T., & Faziharudean, T. M. (2012). Competitive advantages through IT innovation adoption by SMEs. *Social Technologies*, *2*(1), 24–39.

Montagna, P. D. (1968). Professionalization and bureaucratization in large professional organizations. *American Journal of Sociology*, *74*(2), 138–145. doi:10.1086/224616

Muhrtala, T., & Ogundeji, M. (2013). Computerised accounting information systems and perceived security threats in developing economies: The Nigeria case. *Universal Journal of Accounting and Finance*, *1*(1), 9–18. doi:10.13189/ujaf.2013.010102

Muraleetharan, P. (2011). *Internal Control and Impact of Financial Performance of the organizations special reference public and private organizations in Jaffna district*. University of Jaffna.

Năstase, C., & Kajanus, M. (2009). The impact of the global crisis on SME and entrepreneurship behavior–Romania and Finland cases. *Amfiteatru Economic*, *3*, 752–753.

Nations, U. (2014). *System of Environmental-Economic Accounting 2012*. The World Bank.

Nazir, O., & Islam, J. U. (2019). Influence of CSR-specific activities on work engagement and employees' innovative work behaviour: An empirical investigation. *Current Issues in Tourism, 23*(24), 3054–3072. doi:10.1080/13683500.2019.1678573

Newmark, M. R. (1945). A Short History of The Los Angeles Chamber of Commerce. *The Quarterly: Historical Society of Southern California, 27*(2-3), 56–79. doi:10.2307/41169698

Newton, R. C. (1977). *German Buenos Aires, 1900–1933: Social Change and Cultural Crisis*. University of Texas Press.

Nguyen, T. (2009). Information technology adoption in SMEs: An integrated framework. *International Journal of Entrepreneurial Behaviour & Research, 15*(2), 162–186. doi:10.1108/13552550910944566

Nikolic, G., Vitenberg, V., & Karanovic, B. (2020). Adoption of sustainable accounting practices among croatian SME's. *KnE Social Sciences, 4*(1), 456–480. doi:10.18502/kss.v4i1.6006

Noel, N. M., & Luckett, M. (2014). The benefits, satisfaction, and perceived value of small business membership in a chamber of commerce. *International Journal of Nonprofit and Voluntary Sector Marketing, 19*(1), 27–39. doi:10.1002/nvsm.1485

O'Riordan, M., & Fitzpatrick, F. (2015). The impact of economic recession on infection prevention and control. *The Journal of Hospital Infection, 89*(4), 340–345. doi:10.1016/j.jhin.2014.11.020 PMID:25639208

Obal, M., & Gao, T. (2020). Managing business relationships during a pandemic: Conducting a relationship audit and developing a path forward. *Industrial Marketing Management, 88*, 247–254. doi:10.1016/j.indmarman.2020.05.025

Oduro, S. (2020). Exploring the barriers to SMEs' open innovation adoption in Ghana. *International Journal of Innovation Science, 12*(1), 21–51. doi:10.1108/IJIS-11-2018-0119

Orbis Hotel Group. (2017). *Corporate Social Responsibility ReportCSR Report 2017 4/10/18 / 7910kB - Orbis SA*. https://www.orbis.pl/en/download/filedisplay/csr-report-2017

Organisation for Economic Co-operation and Development - OECD. (2011). *OECD Guidelines for multinational enterprises*. OECD Publishing.

Orgill, M. (2012). *Phenomenography. Encyclopedia of the Sciences of Learning*. Springer.

Orzan, Gh. (2001). *Cyber marketing*. Uranus Publishing House.

Ozkan, N., Singer, Z., & You, H. (2012). Mandatory IFRS adoption and the contractual usefulness of accounting information in executive compensation. *Journal of Accounting Research, 50*(4), 1077–1107. doi:10.1111/j.1475-679X.2012.00453.x

Padachi, K. (2012). Factors affecting the adoption of formal accounting systems by SMEs. *Business and Economics Journal, BEJ-67*, 1–20.

Paralela 45Actiuni CSR. (2021). https://www.paralela45.ro/actiuni-csr/

Parker, L. (2012). Qualitative management accounting research: Assessing deliverables and relevance. *Critical Perspectives on Accounting, 23*(1), 54–70. doi:10.1016/j.cpa.2011.06.002

Parkwater Foundation. (2021). *Corporate Social Responsibility Annual Report 2016-2017*. https://dq7j3ns0e24fe.cloudfront.net/uploads/45ea9ad985a49a523fc55632291befe6-026739600-1500371378.pdf

Paunov, C. (2012). The global crisis and firms' investments in innovation. *Research Policy, 41*(1), 24–35. doi:10.1016/j.respol.2011.07.007

Perrini, F. (2005). Building an European portrait of corporate social responsibility reporting. *European Management Journal, 23*(6), 611–627. doi:10.1016/j.emj.2005.10.008

Peskin, H. M. (1989). A proposed environmental accounts framework. *Environmental Accounting for Sustainable Development*, 65-78.

Pillay, P. (2016). *Barriers to Information and Communication Technology (ICT) Adoption and use Amongst SMEs: A Study of the South African Manufacturing Sector* (Doctoral Dissertation).

Pongpattrachai, D., Cragg, D., & Fisher, R. (2013). IT infusion within the audit process: Spreadsheet use in small audit firms. *International Journal of Accounting Information Systems, 3*(9), 1–21.

Pope, P., & McLeay, S. (2011). The European IFRS experiment: Objectives, research challenges and some early evidence. *Accounting and Business Research, 41*(3), 233–266. doi:10.1080/00014788.2011.575002

Powell, J. L., Chen, S., Pape, U., Chaves-Ávila, R., Pahl, J. B., Petrella, F., ... Savall-Morera, T. (2016). Working under pressure: Economic recession and third sector development in Europe. *The International Journal of Sociology and Social Policy, 36*(7/8), 547–566. doi:10.1108/IJSSP-05-2016-0061

Radisson Hotel Corporate Social Responsibility. (2021). https://www.radissonhotels.com/en-us/social-responsibility/community

Radu, M. (2009). *Standard cost method. Theoretical and practical aspects* [Metoda standard cost. Aspecte teoretice şi practice]. Valahia University Press.

Radu, M., & Giju, G. C. (2015). The flexible budget–basic tool of the management control in the economic entities. *ScientificBulletin: Economic Sciences, 14*(1), 3–10.

Ramanna, K. (2008). The implications of unverifiable fair-value accounting: Evidence from the political economy of goodwill accounting. *Journal of Accounting and Economics, 45*(2-3), 253–281. doi:10.1016/j.jacceco.2007.11.006

Ramus, C. A., & Montiel, I. (2005). When are corporate environmental policies a form of greenwashing? *Business & Society, 44*(4), 377–414. doi:10.1177/0007650305278120

Ratcliffe, T. A., & Landes, C. E. (2009). Understanding of Internal Control and Internal Control Services. American Institute of certified public accountants (AICPA).

Rebmann, T., Wang, J., Swick, Z., Reddick, D., & delRosario, J. L. Jr. (2013). Business continuity and pandemic preparedness: US health care versus non-health care agencies. *American Journal of Infection Control, 41*(4), e27–e33. doi:10.1016/j.ajic.2012.09.010 PMID:23337305

Relhan, A. (2013). E-Accounting practices of SMEs in India. *International Journal of Technical Research, 2*(1), 1–10.

Richard Pearson, J., Romfh, P. C., Habib, J. M., & Frieling, M. J. (1985). The Flexible Budget Process - A Tool for Cost Containment. *American Journal of Clinical Pathology, 84*(2), 202–208. doi:10.1093/ajcp/84.2.202 PMID:4025225

Richardson, A. (2011). Myth, Paradigms and Academic Accounting Research: A Comment on Reading and Understanding Academic Research in Accounting. *Global Perspectives on Accounting Education, 8*, 67–77.

Ridgeway, G. L. (1938). Merchants of Peace. Twenty Years of Business Diplomacy through the International Chamber of Commerce, 1919–1938. *American Journal of Physical Medicine & Rehabilitation, 17*(5), 350.

Ritchie, R. (1912). The modern chamber of commerce. *National Municipal Review, 1*(2), 161–169. doi:10.1002/ncr.4110010201

Rittenberg, L. E., & Schwieger, B. J. (2005). *Auditing. Concepts for a Changing Environment* (5th ed.). Thomson South-Western.

Romney, M. B., & Steinbart, P. J. (2009). *Accounting information system*. Pearson Prentice Hall.

Rose, P., & Hudgins, S. (2008). *Bank Management and financial services* (7th ed.). McGraw-Hill.

Ruder, D. S. (2005). Balancing Investor Protection with Capital Formation Needs After the SEC Chamber of Commerce Case. *Pace Law Review*, *26*, 39.

Ruivo, P., Oliveira, T., & Neto, M. (2012). ERP use and value: Portuguese and Spanish SMEs. *Industrial Management & Data Systems*, *112*(7), 1008–1025. doi:10.1108/02635571211254998

Rusko, R. (2020). Values or Strategy? Comparative Study About the Roles of Values and Strategy in the Web Pages of the Largest Scandinavian Firms. In Sustainability Reporting, Ethics, and Strategic Management Strategies for Modern Organizations (pp. 63-77). IGI Global.

Sakchutchawan, S. (2009). An inquiry into the strict compliance of the international chamber of commerce trade rules in financing process. *Global Journal of International Business Research*, *2*(2), 1.

Salehi, M., & Abdipour, A. (2013). Accounting information system's barriers: Case of an emerging economy. *African Journal of Business Management*, *7*(5), 298–305.

Schaefer, F., Luksch, U., Steinbach, N., Cabeça, J., & Hanauer, J. (2006). *Ecological footprint and biocapacity. In The world's ability to regenerate resources and absorb waste in a limited time period. Eurostat*. Luxemburg.

Schaltegger, S., & Burritt, R. L. (2010). Sustainability accounting for companies: Catchphrase or decision support for business leaders? *Journal of World Business*, *45*(4), 375–384. doi:10.1016/j.jwb.2009.08.002

Schaltegger, S., & Wagner, M. (2006). Integrative management of sustainability performance, measurement and reporting. *International Journal of Accounting, Auditing and Performance Evaluation*, *3*(1), 1–19. doi:10.1504/IJAAPE.2006.010098

Schleicher, T., Tahoun, A., & Walker, M. (2010). IFRS adoption in Europe and investment-cash flow sensitivity: Outsider versus insider economies. *The International Journal of Accounting*, *45*(2), 143–168. doi:10.1016/j.intacc.2010.04.007

Selmer, C. (2014). *Build and defend your budget. Tools, methods and behaviors* [Construire et défendre son budget. Outils, méthodes et comportements] (3rd ed.). Dunod.

Seyal, A., Noah, M., & Rahim, M. (2002). Determinants of academic use of the internet: Structural equation model. *Behaviour & Information Technology*, *21*(1), 71–86. doi:10.1080/01449290210123354

Seyal, A., Rahim, M. N., & Rahim, N. (2000). An empirical investigation of the use of information technology among small and medium business organisations: A Bruneian scenario. *The Electronic Journal on Information Systems in Developing Countries*, *2*(7), 1–17. doi:10.1002/j.1681-4835.2000.tb00014.x

Shafi, M., Liu, J., & Ren, W. (2020). Impact of COVID-19 pandemic on micro, small, and medium-sized Enterprises operating in Pakistan. *Research in Globalization*, *2*, 100018. doi:10.1016/j.resglo.2020.100018

Shane, J. S., Molenaar, K. R., Anderson, S., & Schexnayder, C. (2009). Construction project cost escalation factors. *Journal of Management Engineering*, *25*(4), 221–229. doi:10.1061/(ASCE)0742-597X(2009)25:4(221)

Sikich, G. W. (2008). *Protecting Your Business in a Pandemic: Plans, Tools, and Advice for Maintaining Business Continuity*. Greenwood Publishing Group.

Silva, S., Nuzum, A. K., & Schaltegger, S. (2019). Stakeholder expectations on sustainability performance measurement and assessment. A systematic literature review. *Journal of Cleaner Production, 217*, 204–215. doi:10.1016/j.jclepro.2019.01.203

Simionescu, A., Buse, F., Bud, N., & Purcaru Stamin, I. (2006). *Managerial control* [Control managerial]. Editura Economica.

Simmons, G., Palmer, M., & Truong, Y. (2013). Inscribing value on business model innovations: Insights from industrial projects commercializing disruptive digital innovations. *Industrial Marketing Management, 42*(5), 744–754. doi:10.1016/j.indmarman.2013.05.010

Smith, J. A. (2004). Reflecting on the development of interpretative phenomenological analysis and its contribution to qualitative research in psychology. *Qualitative Research in Psychology, 1*(1), 39–54.

Smith, J. A., Flowers, P., & Larkin, M. (2009). *Interpretative Phenomenological Analysis: Theory, Method and Research*. Sage.

Smith, S. R. (1982). The centenary of the London Chamber of Commerce: Its origins and early policy. *The London Journal, 8*(2), 156–170. doi:10.1179/ldn.1982.8.2.156

Soltani, B. (2014). The anatomy of corporate fraud: A comparative analysis of high profile American and European corporate scandals. *Journal of Business Ethics, 120*(2), 251–274. doi:10.100710551-013-1660-z

Sponem, S. (2004). *Diversity of the budgetary practices of the French companies: proposal of a typology and analysis of the determinants* [Diversité des pratiques budgétaires des entreprises françaises: proposition d'une typologie et analyse des déterminants]. Retrieved from: https://tel.archives-ouvertes.fr/tel-00465697/document

Sprehe, J. T. (2005). The positive benefits of electronic records management in the context of enterprise content management. *Government Information Quarterly, 22*(2), 297–303. doi:10.1016/j.giq.2005.02.003

Standard Auditing Practices No. 6 (SAP 6). (n.d.). Available at: https://pcaobus.org/oversight/standards/ archived-standards/pre-reorganized-auditing-standards-interpretations/details/auditing-standard-no-6_1834

Starwood Hotels and Resorts CSR & Sustainability. (2021). https://www.csrhub.com/CSR_and_sustainability_information/Starwood-Hotels-and-Resorts-Worldwide-Inc

Stiri.ong. (2021). *The Foundation for Civil Society Development*. https://www.stiri.ong/

Strauss, P. L. (2013). Private Standards Organizations and Public Law. *Wm. & Mary Bill Rts. J., 22*, 497.

Sunday, A., Turyahebwa, A., Byamukama, E., & Novembrieta, S. (2013). Financial Performance in the Selected Microfinance Institutions in Uganda. *International Journal of Engineering Research & Technology (Ahmedabad), 2*(2), 1–11.

Sustainability Accounting Standards Board – SASB. (2020). *Promoting clarity and compatibility in the sustainability landscape*. Author.

Sustainable Business Annual ReportN. H. (2021). https://www.nh-hotels.com/corporate/sites/default/files/files-rsc/einf_nhhg_2020_en.pdf

Sustainable Stock Exchanges Initiative – SSEI (2020). *ESG disclosure guidance database*. Author.

Swenson, R. J. (1935). The Chamber of Commerce and the New Deal. *The Annals of the American Academy of Political and Social Science, 179*(1), 136–143. doi:10.1177/000271623517900118

Tajeddini, K. (2015). Exploring the antecedents of effectiveness and efficiency. *International Journal of Hospitality Management, 49*(7), 125–135. doi:10.1016/j.ijhm.2015.06.007

Talwar, M., Talwar, S., Kaur, P., Tripathy, N., & Dhir, A. (2020). Has financial attitude impacted the trading activity of retail investors during the COVID-19 pandemic? *Journal of Retailing and Consumer Services, 58*, 102341. doi:10.1016/j.jretconser.2020.102341

Task Force on Climate-Related Financial Disclosures – TCFD. (2019). *Implementation guide.* Author.

Taticchi, P., Tonelli, F., & Cagnazzo, L. (2010). Performance measurement and management: A literature review and a research agenda. *Measuring Business Excellence, 14*(1), 4–18. doi:10.1108/13683041011027418

Tendeloo, B., & Vanstrelen, A. (2005). Earnings management under German GAAP versus IFRS. *European Accounting Review, 14*(1), 155–180. doi:10.1080/0963818042000338988

The role of CSR in business strategy. (2018). *Strategic Direction, 34*(10), 13–15. doi:10.1108/SD-07-2018-0156

Thong, J. Y., Yap, C. S., & Raman, K. S. (1997). Environments for information systems implementation in small business. *Journal of Organizational Computing and Electronic Commerce, 7*(4), 253–278. doi:10.120715327744joce0704_1

Thong, T. Y., Ding, D. K., & Lim, C. Y. (2008). Firm diversification and earning management: Evidence from seasoned equity offerings. *Review of Quantitative Finance and Accounting, 30*(1), 69–92. doi:10.100711156-007-0043-x

Tijani, O. M., & Mohammed, A. K. (2013). Computer-based accounting systems in small and medium enterprises: Empirical evidence from a randomized trial in Nigeria. *Universal Journal of Management, 1*(1), 13–21. doi:10.13189/ujm.2013.010103

Tong, Y. K., & Arvey, R. D. (2015). Managing complexity via the Competing Values Framework. *Journal of Management Development, 34*(6), 653–673. doi:10.1108/JMD-04-2014-0029

Tordoir, P. (2012). *The professional knowledge economy: The management and integration of professional services in business organizations.* Springer Science & Business Media.

Tsagas, G., & Villiers, C. (2020). Why "Less is More" in non-financial reporting initiatives: Concrete steps towards supporting sustainability, *Accounting, Economics, and Law Convivium, 10*(2).

Tudini, A., & Vetrella, G. (2004). Italian NAMEA: 1990–2000 air emission accounts. ISTAT final report.

Turner, L., Weickgenannt, A. B., & Copeland, M. K. (2020). *Accounting Information Systems: Controls and Processes.* John Wiley & Sons.

Ullmann, A. A. (1976). The corporate environmental accounting system: A management tool for fighting environmental degradation. *Accounting, Organizations and Society, 1*(1), 71–79. doi:10.1016/0361-3682(76)90008-8

United Nations Statistical Office. (1975). Towards a system of social and demographic statistics. New York: United Nations.

United Nations. (2014). *The ten principles of the UN Global Compact.* Author.

United Nations. (2015). *The 2030 Agenda for sustainable development.* Author.

UNWTO World Tourism Organization. (2020). *World Tourism Barometer and Statistical Annex, August/September 2020, UNWTO World Tourism Barometer.* https://www.e-unwto.org/doi/abs/10.18111/wtobarometereng.2020.18.1.5

Valor, C. (2005). Corporate social responsibility and corporate citizenship: Towards corporate accountability. *Business and Society Review, 110*(2), 191–212. doi:10.1111/j.0045-3609.2005.00011.x

Van Dieren, W. (1995). Defensive Expenditures. In *Taking Nature into Account* (pp. 175–186). Springer. doi:10.1007/978-1-4612-4246-8_12

Vardon, M., Castaneda, J. P., Nagy, M., & Schenau, S. (2018). How the System of Environmental-Economic Accounting can improve environmental information systems and data quality for decision making. *Environmental Science & Policy*, *89*, 83–92. doi:10.1016/j.envsci.2018.07.007

Veltri, S. (2020). *The mandatory non-financial disclosure in the European Union. In Mandatory nonfinancial risk-related disclosure*. Springer. doi:10.1007/978-3-030-47921-3

Ven, K., & Verelst, J. (2009). The importance of external support in the adoption of open-source server software. International Federation for Information Processing (IFIP). doi:10.1007/978-3-642-02032-2_12

Verbeke, A. (2020). Will the COVID-19 pandemic really change the governance of global value chains? *British Journal of Management*, *31*(3), 444–446. doi:10.1111/1467-8551.12422

Vladu, A. B., Amat, O., & Cuzdriorean, D. D. (2016). Truthfulness in accounting: How to discriminate accounting manipulators from non-manipulators. *Journal of Business Ethics*, *140*(4), 633–648. doi:10.100710551-016-3048-3

Wadesango, O. V. (2015). The importance of record keeping to the growth of Small and Medium Scale Enterprises (SMEs) in Zimbabwe. *Corporate Ownership and Control*, *12*(4), 44–755. doi:10.22495/cocv12i4c7p5

Wagner, C. Z. (2018). Evolving norms of corporate social responsibility: Lessons learned from the European Union Directive on non-financial reporting. *Transactions: Tennessee Journal of Business Law*, *19*, 619.

Walcott, H. F. (1994). *Transforming Qualitative Data: Description, Analysis and Interpretation*. SAGE Publications.

Wallace, J. E. (1995). Organizational and professional commitment in professional and nonprofessional organizations. *Administrative Science Quarterly*, *40*(2), 228–255. doi:10.2307/2393637

Wang, D. H., & Huynh, Q. L. (2012). *Effects of Environmental Uncertainty on Computerized Accounting System Adoption and Firm Performance*. Feng Chia University.

Wanjau, K., Macharia, N. R., & Ayodo, E. M. (2012). Factors affecting adoption of electronic commerce among small medium enterprises in Kenya: Survey of tour and travel firms in Nairobi. *International Journal of Business. Human Technology*, *2*(4), 76–91.

Watts, R., & Zimmerman, J. (1978). Towards a Positive Theory of the Determination of Accounting Standards. *The Accounting Review*, *53*(1), 112–134.

WCED (The World Commission on Environment and Development). (1987). *Our Common Future*. Oxford University Press.

Werking, R. H. (1978). Bureaucrats, Businessmen, and Foreign Trade: The Origins of the United States Chamber of Commerce. *Business History Review*, *52*(3), 321–341. doi:10.2307/3113734

Whittington, O. R., & Pany, K. (2008). *Principles of Auditing & Other Assurance Services* (16th ed.). McGraw-Hill Irwin.

Wiesböck, F., & Hess, T. (2020). Digital innovations. *Electronic Markets*, *30*(1), 75–86. doi:10.100712525-019-00364-9

Wilk, K. (1940). International organization and the international chamber of commerce. *Political Science Quarterly*, *55*(2), 231–248. doi:10.2307/2143913

Willard, C. D. (1899). *A History of the Chamber of Commerce of Los Angeles, California: From Its Foundation, September, 1888, to the Year 1900*. Kingsley-Barnes & Neuner.

Wizz Air Holdings CSR & Sustainability. (2020). https://wizzair.com/en-gb/information-and-services/about-us/sustainability

World Economic Forum. (2020). *Measuring stakeholder capitalism: top global companies take action on universal ESG reporting*. Author.

Xiaobei, L., & Shengli, D. (2011). Research on flexible budget of marketing expenditure. In *Proceedings of the 8th International Conference on Innovationand Management* (pp. 1309–1313). Retrieved from http://www4.pucsp.br/icim/ingles/downloads/papers_2011/part_7/part_7_proc_50.pdf

Xiong, Y. (2006). Earning management and its measurement; a theoretical perspective. *The Journal of American Academy of Business, Cambridge*, *9*(1), 214–219.

Yadav, N., & Sagar, M. (2013). Performance measurement and management frameworks. *Business Process Management Journal*, *19*(6), 947–971. doi:10.1108/BPMJ-01-2013-0003

Yin, R. K. (1981). The case study as a serious research strategy. *Science Communication*, *3*(1), 97–114.

Yleisradio. (2021). https://yle.fi/uutiset/18-77418

Zainol, F. A., Wan Daud, W. N., Abdullah, Z., & Yaacob, M. R. (2014). Social entrepreneurship via corporate waqf: A case of Islamic chamber of commerce (ICC) in Malaysia. *Global Journal of Commerce & Management Perspective*, *3*(5), 50–53.

Zakaria, W., Rahman, S., & Elsayed, M. (2011). An analysis of task performance outcomes through e-Accounting in Malaysia. *Journal of Public Administration and Governance*, *1*(2), 124–139. doi:10.5296/jpag.v1i2.946

Zamfir, M. (2017). *Management control through the budget system* [Controlul de gestiune prin sistemul de bugete]. ProUniversitaria.

Zeghal, D., Chtourou, S., & Fourati, M. Y. (2012). The effect of mandatory adoption of IFRS on earning quality: Evidence from the European Union. *Journal of International Accounting Research*, *11*(2), 1–25. doi:10.2308/jiar-10221

Zéghal, D., Chtourou, S., & Mnif, S. Y. (2011). An analysis of the effect of mandatory adoption of IAS/IFRS on earnings Management. *Journal of International Accounting, Auditing & Taxation*, *20*(2), 61–72. doi:10.1016/j.intaccaudtax.2011.06.001

Zelezny, L. C., Chua, P. P., & Aldrich, C. (2000). New ways of thinking about environmentalism: Elaborating on gender differences in environmentalism. *The Journal of Social Issues*, *56*(3), 443–457. doi:10.1111/0022-4537.00177

Zemtsov, S., & Tsareva, Y. (2020). Development trends of small and medium-sized enterprises amid pandemic-induced crisis. *IEP*, (9), 16–26.

Zender, J. F. (2011). *Evaluating Financial Performance*. University of Colorado. Retrieved from http://leedsfaculty.colorado.edu/zender/CEDIR/Session3-notes.ppt

Zhu, K., Dong, S., Xu, S. X., & Kraemer, K. L. (2006). Innovation diffusion in global contexts: Determinants of post-adoption digital transformation of European Companies. *European Journal of Information Systems*, *15*(6), 601–616. doi:10.1057/palgrave.ejis.3000650

About the Contributors

Ionica Oncioiu holds a Ph.D. in economy and accounting. Her research interests include the development of SMEs innovation, Project Management, Accounting Information Systems, Asset Management and E-Commerce Marketing. She has had more than 10 years of experience in this area and has published 10 textbooks and more than 70 papers in scholarly peer reviewed international journals.

* * *

Rodica Blidisel graduated at the West University of Timisoara and has a PhD in accounting. Her teaching portfolio includes Financial Accounting, Tax Consultancy, Public Sector Accounting and International Public Sector Accounting Standards. Rodica is an Associate Professor at the Faculty of Economics and Business Administration - West University of Timisoara, member of the Body of Expert and Licensed Accountants of Romania (CECCAR). She has postdoctoral studies in Economics and different courses in education practice. Besides her teaching and research activities, she is still involved in the implementation of several EU projects supporting education. Her current research areas are public sector accounting, international taxation and accounting education.

Oana Bogdan is a Post-Doctoral Researcher and teaching collaborator at West University of Timişoara, Faculty of Economics and Business Administration. Main research focuses on Financial Accounting, Corporate Governance and Corporate Social Responsibility. Author of two books and more than 20 papers published in international journals.

Alexandra Bugnariu is a PhD student at the Doctoral School of Accounting under the coordination of Associate Professor dr. Topor Ioan Dan, graduate of Faculty of Finance and Banking and has the master's degree in Taxes and Financial Management, within "1 Decembrie 1918" University of Alba Iulia. Currently, economist and manager of the internal control system with over five years of experience in a multinational company.

Ovidiu Constantin Bunget is Head of Accounting and Audit Department, West University of Timisoara President, The Body of Licensed Accountants and Expert Accountants in Romania, Timis Branch

Valentin Burca has a PhD in accounting, West University of Timisoara. Post Doctorate in accounting, West University of Timisoara. Research interests include, but are not limited to financial reporting & analysis, corporate reporting (incl. sustainability reporting, integrated reporting), earnings management, internal audit, managerial accounting & performance management. More than 25 papers in scholarly peer reviewed international journals. Author of one book.

Traian Ovidiu Calotă holds a Ph.D. in accounting and had more than 15 years of experience in this area.

Sorinel Căpuşneanu is a PhD. Professor at Titu Maiorescu University of Bucharest. His research focus is the area of Management Accounting, Management Performance, Management Information Systems, Audit and Controlling, and Business Ethics. He is the author of the following books: Elements of Cost Management, Economica Publishing House (2008) and Management Accounting. Performance Assessment Tool, University Publishing House (2013) and co-author of Deontology and Accounting Expertise. Judicial Accounting and Tax Expertise (2019) published by Lambert Academic Publishing and Management Accounting Standards for Sustainable Business Practices (2019) published by IGI-Global. He has participated in numerous national and international conferences and has made a remarkable contribution to managerial accounting by publishing several articles.

Gary Cokins is an internationally recognized expert, speaker, and author in enterprise and corporate performance management improvement methods and business analytics. He is the founder of Analytics-Based Performance Management, an advisory firm located in Cary, North Carolina at www.garycokins.com . Gary received a BS degree in Industrial Engineering/Operations Research from Cornell University in 1971. He received his MBA from Northwestern University's Kellogg School of Management in 1974. Gary began his career as a strategic planner with FMC's Link-Belt Division and then served as Financial Controller and Operations Manager. In 1981 Gary began his management consulting career first with Deloitte consulting, and then in 1988 with KPMG consulting. In 1992 Gary headed the National Cost Management Consulting Services for Electronic Data Systems (EDS) now part of HP. From 1997 until 2013 Gary was a Principal Consultant with SAS, a leading provider of analytics software. His two most recent books are Performance Management: Integrating Strategy Execution, Methodologies, Risk, and Analytics, and Predictive Business Analytics. His books are published by John Wiley & Sons.

Mihaela Denisa Coman obtained the PhD. in Economics, Domain: Accounting within Valahia University of Targoviste, Romania. Her research activities include: Accounting, Managerial accounting, Green economy, Statistics, Environmental economy, Environment impact, Economic Performance, Econometrics, Socio-economic and marketing analysis, Feasibility studies. Her scientific activity includes 18 scientific papers in international journals Indexed ISI and proceeding ISI, more than 25 scientific papers in national and international journals and conferences, 1 book as author and 1 book-chapter as co-author. She has been involved in 3 research projects during the years at national level. Currently, she is Scientific Researcher within the Multidisciplinary Scientific and Technologic Research Institute (ICSTM) from Valahia University of Targoviste. Her experience associated to the project's theme refers to socio-economic and marketing analysis, environmental economy.

Delia Deliu is a Post-Doctoral Researcher (within the Accounting and Audit Department, at West University of Timişoara, Faculty of Economics and Business Administration), with a 11 years' experience of academic teaching (Auditing, Financial Controls, Applied Accounting, IFRS, Internal Audit). Experienced Chartered Certified Auditor and Chartered Certified Accountant with a 17 years' background in

Assurance & Advisory Business Services. Current research encompasses the challenges and perspectives of the financial audit – corporate governance relationship in a sensitive socio-economic context, as well as considering sustainability, digitalisation and urbanisation. Main research projects focus on: - corporate governance, CSR and sustainability in times of crisis; - financial auditor's responsibilities and liabilities in a sensitive socio-economic context; - control and coordination practices within audit teams in the presence of technical, institutional, sociological and cognitive constraints; - quality of (non-)financial reporting and external auditing; - the impact of Blockchain on the accounting and auditing profession; - impact of technology integration in education; - quality of education; (with over 30 articles published in highly ranked peer-reviewed academic journals and conference proceedings). In 2020 she received the "Nicolae Stoica" Award for Economic Sciences, awarded by UCLA (University of California, Los Angeles) and the American Romanian Academy of Arts & Sciences. In 2019 she was awarded the Special Prize of the Chamber of Financial Auditors of Romania for her research: "Stakes and Challenges Regarding the Financial Auditor's Activity in the Blockchain Era". In 2018 she gained the "Bologna Professor of the Year" distinction from the National Alliance of Student Organizations in Romania.

Mihaela Mirela Dogaru holds a PhD in Management from Titu Maiorescu University of Romania, Bucharest. Specialist in, management, entrepreneurship. Strong experience in managing relationships with suppliers, customer relations. Managerial studies have focused on the development of models based on teamwork, organizational culture based on this theory.

Luminita Nicoleta Gudanescu Nicolau was born in Giurgiu City, Romania in 1974. She received BS in finance from the Economic Studies Academy Bucharest in 1997, PHD in economics from National Institute for Economic Reseach-Romanian Academy in 2007, postdoctoral studies focused on Management of European Funds/Human Resources Management from Romanian Academy-Institute for World Economy in 2016 and MS in Economic European Governance in 2018. Experienced University Professor with a demonstrated history of working in the education, management and industry. Skilled in Development of Projects, European Funds financing, Management, HR development and Entrepreneurship. From 1997- 2001 and 2007-2020 – university assistant, lecturer and professor at Ecologic University, Nicolae Titulescu University and Hyperion University, 1997-2020 associate researcher at Romanian Academy, Institute of National Economy.From 2001-2007 – Investments Department Manager and Project Manager at Romtelecom – Telecom Industry. She is the author of more than 50 proiects - research projects, investment projects for industry, European and national funds financed projects, in period 2007-2020 – Project Manager for 6 European Financed Projects from education and human resources field, expert in more than 10 similar projects, trainer and management consultant in many other projects. She is also the author/coauthor of 11 books, 22 articles published in ISI and IDB journals and more than 20 scientific works published in national and international conferences volumes, and ISI proceedings. Also was member in different scientific committees of International Conferences and from 2000 is member of General Association of Romanian Economists, from 2008 ATINER member (Athens Institute of Education and Research).

Constantin Aurelian Ionescu was born in Targoviste, Romania in 1989. He received the B.S. in Accounting and Management Information Systems, in 2011 and M.S. degrees in Accounting, in 2013 and the Ph.D. degree in Economics, domain: Accounting from the Valahia University of Targoviste, Romania, in 2016. From 2009 to present, he is manager of an economic entity. From 2015 to present, he is an Associate Member of the Center for Research and Scientific Studies in Accounting and Finance, ICSTM-Valahia University of Targoviste. From 2017 to present, he is a Lecturer at the Faculty of Economic Sciences, Hyperion University of Bucharest, Romania. In period 2018 to present – expert (trainer and management consultant) for several European Financed Projects from the education and human resources field. His research interests include financial accounting, managerial accounting, accounting, and fiscal management, environmental accounting, and audit. He has published his works in various journals, has participated at numerous conferences, and is a member of the editorial board of Annals of Romanian Scientists, New Series on economy, law, and sociology.

Himmet Karadal is a Professor of Management & Organization since 2014. He conducts academic studies in the fields of entrepreneurship, organizational behavior, management, and strategy. He teaches and conducts consultancy at undergraduate, graduate, and Ph.D. degrees.

Andreea Marin-Pantelescu is a graduate of the Bucharest University of Economic Studies, The Faculty of Commerce, the specialization Tourism-Services (2002) and of the postgraduate program in International Tourism (2003). In February 2007, she becomes a teacher in the Bucharest University of Economic Studies, The Faculty of Commerce, The Department of Tourism-Services. She obtains her PhD in Economics in the year 2008 with a thesis in services, and in 2010 a Master's Degree in the domain Economics and International Business. As a Lecturer in the Department of Tourism and Geography, the Faculty of Business and Tourism, the Bucharest University of Economic Studies, she teaches subjects like the technique of tourism operations, the technique of hotels operations, development strategies for the tertiary sector, services economy, business ethics, etc. She writes articles published in scientific journals and her research interests are in the field of services, tourism and booking systems (Amadeus and Travelport). Currently, she is focused on the services economy course and conducts research in the domain of creative services and business ethics.

Fahri Özsungur graduated from Ataturk University Faculty of Law, Çağ University Department of Private Law- Master of Laws- LL.M., Hacettepe University Department of Family and Consumer Sciences PhD., and Aksaray University Department of Business Ph.D. He serves as a Higher Degrees by Research (HDR) Examiner /Ph.D. Examiner for the University of New England. He is a Eurostars Technical Expert (EUREKA Secretariat). He is the head of the Department of Social Work and Counseling of Mersin University Vocational School of Social Sciences. He is affiliated with Adana Science and Technology University, Rotary International, Osmaniye Korkut Ata University, Çağ University, WEGATE- European Gateway for Women's Entrepreneurship, and Canadian Institute for International Law Expertise (CIFILE). He has 4 books, 12 book chapters, 21 Encyclopedia Chapters, and more than 80 (4 SSCI/SCI/SCI-Expanded,10 ESCI, 8 ISI) published articles and 20 international conference papers. He is the editor of 24 Journals (1 SSCI/SCI/SCI-Expanded), and the reviewer of 309 Journals (10 SSCI/SCI/SCI-Expanded,30 ESCI).

Liliana Paschia was born in Ludesti, Dambovita, Romania in 1968. She received the B.S. in Accounting and Management Information Systems, in 2002, and M.S. degrees in Financial Accounting audit, in 2006 from the Hyperion University of Bucharest, Romania and the Ph.D. degree Economics, domain: Accounting from the "December 1, 1918" University of Alba Iulia, Romania, in 2016. She is a member of the Body of Expert Accountants and Certified Accountants in Romania, specialist in finance, accounting, accounting expertise, audit / Expert Accountant - book no. 28626/2007 and holds since 2012, the diploma of Fiscal Expert, issued by the Ministry of Labor and Social Protection/Ministry of Education and Research. From 2003 until now he is Chief Accountant at Hyperion University, ensuring the organization and management of the Financial - Accounting department, at the same time she fulfilled the position of Financial Manager in over ten European projects of POSDRU type. From 2016 until now, she is Lecturer at the Faculty of Economics of Hyperion University of Bucharest, Department of Economics, participating in lectures and seminars in the disciplines of Financial Accounting and Management Accounting, designing and writing course materials for students in the forms of education IF and ID, in the coordination of the diploma works and in the coordination of the specialized practice of the students of the Accounting and Management Informatics study programs. She is the author of 3 books, over 20 scientific articles published.

Manoela Popescu holds a PhD in Economics from the Academy of Economic Studies in Bucharest, as well as a researcher at Ngo Apollo Resources in Romania. Specialist in marketing, communication, negotiation, management, diagnostic analysis, and organizational culture. Researcher and author of studies, research and books in the fields of: communication, negotiation, marketing, management, organizational culture, CSR, economics and business management. Strong background in project management, customer relations, beneficiary relationship management. Organizational culture studies have also focused on the "melting pot" theory and on the development of organizational culture models based on this theory.

Rauno Rusko is University lecturer at the University of Lapland. His research activities focus on cooperation, coopetition, strategic management, supply chain management and entrepreneurship mainly in the branches of information communication technology, forest industry and tourism. His articles appeared in the European Management Journal, Forest Policy and Economics, International Journal of Business Environment, Industrial Marketing Management, International Journal of Innovation in the Digital Economy and International Journal of Tourism Research among others.

Mansi Shah is an Assistant Professor in Amity University Jharkhand. She possesses an experience of one year in corporate and three years in academia. She has done her Masters in Finance and is also pursuing PhD in Finance. She has published few quality research papers and book chapters in journals and conferences.

Sorina-Geanina Stanescu, VUT scientific researcher, Ph.D. in Accounting (2012) and is working in this university by 2011, with results as: 15 ISI articles, more than 20 articles BDI, member in research projects with national/international funding, numerous scientific works presented in conferences. Expertise and interest topics: environmental accounting, management, economic statistics, circular economy, economic analysis. (brainmap ID: U-1900-061G-9920).

Melinda Timea Fülöp is a Lecturer at the Faculty of Economics and Business Administration in the Babeş-Bolyai University, Cluj-Napoca, Romania. She holds a PhD in Audit and her teaching and research fields are audit profession and ethics, the tripartite function of audit in the context of corporate governance and financial accounting and auditing.

Dan Ioan Topor is a PhD. lecturer at the 1 Decembrie 1918 University of Alba-Iulia, Faculty of Economic Sciences. His research focus is the area of Management Accounting, Management Performance and Management Information Systems, Audit and Controlling, and Business Ethics. He is the author of the following books: New dimensions of cost-related cost information for winemaking (2014) and Basics of Accounting (2016). He has published numerous articles on Managerial Accounting and Management Control and has participated in numerous national and international conferences.

Mariana Zamfir was born in Targoviste, Romania in 1975. She received the B.S. in Accounting and Management Information Systems, in 1997, and M.S. degree in Accounting from the Valahia University of Targoviste, in 2001; she received the Certificate of Postgraduate Skills: Management Control, issued by Conservatoire National des Arts et Metiers Paris and Bucharest University of Economic Studies, in 2001, and the Ph.D. in accounting from Bucharest University of Economic Studies, Romania, in 2009. From 1997 to 1999, she was a economist of an economic entity. From 1999 to 2001, she was a Junior Teaching Assistant, from 2001 to 2004 she was a University Assistant, from 2004 to 2014 she was a University Lecturer with the Faculty of Economic Sciences, Valahia University of Targoviste, Romania. From 1014 to present, she is Associate Professor with Department of Accounting and Finance to Valahia University of Targoviste. Also, she was the member of POSDRU projects. She is a member of the Center for Research and Scientific Studies in Accounting and Finance, ICSTM-Valahia University of Targoviste. His research interests include financial accounting, managerial accounting, controlling. She has published his works in various books, journals, and has participated at numerous conferences.

Index

A

accounting information 35-41, 43-51, 178, 208-216, 218, 241-243, 246
Accounting Policies' 208
activity-based costing 173-174, 184
Airline Companies 103, 121, 126

B

balanced scorecard 16, 171, 173, 178-179, 238-239
brand 88, 92, 102, 243
budget 42, 81, 128-135, 139-143, 146-152, 154-155, 163, 183, 186, 214, 219-224, 227, 234-237, 242
budget control 140, 155, 219, 222-223
budgeting 67-68, 128-130, 132-139, 173, 178, 182, 219-220, 222-223, 228, 236, 240
business development 71-72, 74, 76, 79, 83-86, 211

C

CDP 4-10, 117
CDSB 4-10, 32, 34
Chamber of Commerce 193, 200-207
Chamber of Industry 193, 207
chambers of commerce 189-194, 200, 202-203, 207
chambers of industry 191
Club of Rome 89, 100, 102
control 36, 41-42, 44-46, 50-51, 55, 77-78, 85, 90-91, 104, 119, 123, 128-135, 140-141, 152, 154-155, 168, 171, 175, 178, 185-186, 198, 200-201, 205, 209-210, 219-224, 227-228, 233-237, 239-242
corporate social responsibility 1-2, 5-6, 29, 31, 33-34, 77, 88-90, 99-105, 114, 117-119, 123, 125-126
Corporate Social Responsibility (CSR) 1-2, 5, 29, 33, 88, 90, 101, 103, 119
corporate value 90
cost accounting 54, 155, 173-174, 176, 179-180, 241
costs 5, 12, 22, 31, 36-37, 39, 43, 45, 53, 55, 57-59, 70, 72, 80-81, 90, 120-121, 128-129, 132-133, 135-137, 139, 141-142, 144-152, 154, 165-166, 174, 176-177, 179, 181-184, 186, 209, 212, 219-220, 223-226, 228, 233-237, 243
Costs System 219
CSR 1-6, 9-12, 14-35, 77, 88-90, 94, 97, 99-108, 110-112, 114-115, 117-126, 144-145
customer profitability 173, 176-177, 183

D

development decisions 71-72, 211
deviations 128, 130-132, 134-135, 144-147, 149, 152-154, 222-223, 241
digital age 52, 71-74, 76, 78-80, 82-86, 156-157, 159, 161
digitization 31, 72-74, 82-83, 85, 156-158, 160-162, 165, 169-170
drivers 91, 97, 100, 176, 183-184

E

e-accounting 35-39, 41-46, 48, 50-52
Ecocentrism 90, 100, 102
economic organizations 35
efficient management 233, 243
employment 8, 65-66, 73, 104, 115, 117, 157-158, 160, 167, 181, 189-190, 194, 196-200, 207
Employment-Related Change 207
encryption 40, 44, 52
environmental assets 53, 55, 61, 63-65, 67
environmental costs 53, 55, 90
environmental, social, and governance (ESG) goals 1, 5
environmentalism 88-91, 97-102
Espoused Theory 98, 102
expenditure 55, 63, 65, 128, 131-132, 134-136, 138-141, 146, 148, 151-152, 155, 219-220, 223-227, 235, 237

F

financial information 2, 7, 16, 33, 42, 78, 165, 233
Firewall 44, 52
flexible budget 128, 130, 132-135, 139, 152, 155, 237

G

Global Code of Ethics for Tourism 103, 126
Global Crises 156
global crisis 190-191, 202-205, 207
Global Market 72, 189
green accounting 53-56, 59, 67-68
Greenfashing 102
greenhouse effect 60, 88-89
greenwashing 88-95, 97-102
GRI 4-10, 18, 20, 33
gross domestic product 55, 57, 69, 105

H

Hotel Strategies 126
hotels 103, 105-118, 122, 124-127, 212

I

ICT 35-37, 47, 50, 80, 158-161, 163, 165-166, 169
IIRC 4-10, 18, 33
impact 1-6, 8-10, 16, 18-19, 21-22, 24, 28-29, 31-32, 35-37, 39, 41-42, 45-46, 48, 50-52, 55-57, 59, 67-68, 71, 74, 79-82, 103, 107-109, 111, 115, 118, 120, 123-124, 131, 152, 154, 157-158, 161, 166, 177, 179-180, 182, 186, 199-200, 202-205, 208-215, 229

K

key performance indicators 173, 178, 182

L

Lean accounting 184
level of activity 128, 131, 133-135, 148, 151, 222

M

management accounting 47, 49, 54, 56, 128, 154, 173-176, 178-179, 181-182, 184, 186-188, 216-220, 228, 243-245
managerial accounting 35, 43, 129, 173, 219, 224-225, 227, 233-237, 243
manufacturing sector 50, 191, 194-196, 198, 200-201
marketing 6, 10, 22, 85, 88, 90, 93-94, 97-99, 119-120, 155, 157, 166, 170-171, 173, 176-179, 192-193, 198, 201-202, 205-206, 221, 225, 235, 243

N

National Accounts Matrix Including Environmental Accounts 59, 69

O

Occupational Groups (Professional Committees) 193, 207
Organizational Models 156

P

performance 5, 7-8, 36, 41-43, 48, 50-52, 54-55, 69, 76-77, 82-85, 90-91, 110-111, 116, 125, 128-131, 134-135, 152, 154-155, 165, 169, 171-173, 175-176, 178-180, 182, 185-186, 190, 201, 209-211, 213-214, 216-217, 219, 221, 223-224, 230, 232, 234-235, 238-239, 242, 244-245
Professional Committees 189-190, 193, 207

Q

Qualified Employee Deficit 198, 207

R

rolling financial forecasts 173, 183

S

SASB 4-10, 16, 18, 20, 28, 32, 34
sectoral market share 189-190, 195-196, 200, 207
sectoral problems 189-191, 193-194, 207
service sector 195-196, 198, 200
static budget 128, 134, 141, 149, 151
strategy map 173, 178, 182, 187, 239
sustainability 1-7, 9-10, 12, 14-15, 28-29, 31-34, 52-53, 55-56, 58, 67-69, 88, 90, 99-103, 108-109, 113, 116-117, 120-123, 125-126, 190, 192, 201
sustainability reporting 1-2, 4-7, 9, 14, 28, 32-34, 101
sustainable national income 53-54, 59, 70
System of Environmental and Economic Accounts 59-60, 70
System of Environmental-Economic Accounting 62-64, 69

System of National Accounts 59-60, 70

T

TCFD 4-8, 10, 28, 30, 34
technologies 18, 25, 36, 38-39, 43, 45, 49, 56, 71-76, 78-79, 82-86, 107, 130, 156, 158-159, 163, 165-168, 179, 243
Theory-in-Use 98, 102
tourism 102-107, 112, 115-116, 120-127, 202, 208-215
tourism industry 103-106, 115-116, 123-125, 127
travel agencies 103, 119-120, 124, 127, 214

www.ingramcontent.com/pod-product-compliance
Lightning Source LLC
LaVergne TN
LVHW062154300926
849161LV00010B/2658